GENDER IN H

C000156964

Series editors:
Pam Sharpe, Patricia Skinner and Penny Summerfield

The expansion of research into the history of women and gender since the 1970s has changed the face of history. Using the insights of feminist theory and of historians of women, gender historians have explored the configuration in the past of gender identities and relations between the sexes. They have also investigated the history of sexuality and family relations, and analysed ideas and ideals of masculinity and femininity. Yet gender history has not abandoned the original, inspirational project of women's history: to recover and reveal the lived experience of women in the past and the present.

The series Gender in History provides a forum for these developments. Its historical coverage extends from the medieval to the modern periods, and its geographical scope encompasses not only Europe and North America but all corners of the globe. The series aims to investigate the social and cultural constructions of gender in historical sources, as well as the gendering of historical discourse itself. It embraces both detailed case studies of specific regions or periods, and broader treatments of major themes. Gender in History titles are designed to meet the needs of both scholars and students working in this dynamic area of historical research.

Noblewomen, aristocracy and power in the twelfth-century Anglo-Norman realm

Seal of Alice, Countess of Northampton (1140–60, Egerton Ch.431).
Reproduced by permission of the British Library

NOBLEWOMEN, ARISTOCRACY AND POWER
IN THE TWELFTH-CENTURY ANGLO-NORMAN REALM

—— Susan M. Johns ——

Manchester University Press
Manchester and New York

distributed exclusively in the USA by Palgrave

Published by Manchester University Press
Oxford Road, Manchester M13 9NR, UK
and Room 400, 175 Fifth Avenue, New York, NY 10010, USA
www.manchesteruniversitypress.co.uk

Distributed exclusively in the USA by
Palgrave, 175 Fifth Avenue, New York NY 10010, USA

Distributed exclusively in Canada by
UBC Press, University of British Columbia, 2029 West Mall,
Vancouver, BC, Canada V6T 1Z2

British Library Cataloguing-in-Publication Data
A catalogue record for this book is available from the British Library

Library of Congress Cataloging-in-Publication Data
A catalog record for this book is available from the Library of Congress

ISBN 13: 978 0 7190 6305 3

First published by Manchester University Press 2003

First digital paperback edition published 2007

Printed by Lightning Source

For Tim Thornton

Contents

Tables and figures

Preface

This book began life as a Ph.D. thesis, supervised by Professor David Bates during his time at Cardiff. I had been won over to medieval history, in spite of the excitements of more modern history so ably taught by such as Professor Dai Smith and Professor Harry Hearder, through the willingness of Professor Bates to incorporate a modern approach to the study of medieval history. In particular, the challenge offered by the history of noblewomen in the twelfth century was one that was hard to turn down. The debates surrounding women's history, and the new approaches to the history of the high Middle Ages in the British Isles which Professor Bates and others were developing offered tempting prospects – as too did the frequent affirmations from many to whom I spoke that my particular subject was impossible as material for a Ph.D. One who did not, and who was fortuitously the external examiner for medieval history at the time, Professor Janet Nelson, was particularly supportive (and has remained so over the whole course of the project). Also, Professor David Crouch was kind enough to allow me access to his Comital Acta project.

I was especially fortunate to get a job teaching at the University of Huddersfield when I was only two and a half years into my research, an appointment to replace Professor Pauline Stafford during her British Academy Research Readership. This period of research leave produced *Queen Emma and Queen Edith*, and for me it allowed a very fruitful collaboration with one of the most important scholars of medieval women anywhere in the world. Working there also brought into sharp focus the need for historians to be aware of the need for their work to excite and stimulate the next generation of scholars.

Shortly before leaving Cardiff for Huddersfield, I was able to take up a research fellowship at the Central European University, owing to the kindness of Professor Bak. This allowed further reflection, especially on the way that scholarship on medieval women and power was developing across Europe.

I have, therefore, been fortunate in being inspired and supported in this project by a particularly distinguished group of scholars. It could not have been written without their direct and indirect contributions; I am only too conscious, on the other hand, that its shortcomings remain my own. Trish Skinner has been a very supportive series editor.

Chapter 7 is based on a paper entitled 'Iconography and Sigillography: Noblewomen, Seals and Power in Twelfth-century England', first given at a postgraduate seminar in Cardiff, 1992, at the University of Huddersfield, October 1994, the University of Glasgow, January, 1995, at the Late Medieval Political Culture Seminar, York, at the invitation of Professor Mark Ormrod, in September 1995; and finally at a conference on the subject of medieval material culture at the invitation of Professor Peter Coss in April 1999. My thanks to those whose comments have been so helpful, especially Pauline Stafford, David Bates, Mark Ormrod, David Crouch and Paul Harvey. My thanks go especially to the Royal Historical Society, whose generous financial help facilitated, in part, the production of the catalogue of seals, Appendix 1.

This book would not have been possible without the support of my family: Carys, Lucy and Gwyn have provided their own context to the completion of the final product. Finally, I owe my husband Tim Thornton an immeasurable debt of gratitude for his help and support, and it is to him that the book is dedicated.

Abbreviations

Ancient Charters   *Ancient Charters, Royal and Private, Prior to A.D. 1200*, ed. J. H. Round
(Pipe Roll Society, old ser., 10, 1888).

ANS   *Anglo-Norman Studies*, ed. R. Allen Brown *et al.* (Woodbridge, 1978–).

ASC   *Anglo-Saxon Chronicle.*

Bibl. Nat.   Paris, Bibliothèque Nationale

Book of Seals   *Sir Christopher Hatton's Book of Seals: To which is appended a Select
List of the Works of Frank Merry Stenton*, ed. L. C. Loyd and D. M. Stenton
(Northamptonshire Record Society, 15, 1950).

CDF   *Calendar of Documents preserved in France, 918–1206*, ed. J. H. Round (London:
HMSO, 1899).

Chester Charters   *The Charters of the Anglo-Norman Earls of Chester, c. 1071–1237*, ed.
G. Barraclough (Record Society of Lancashire and Cheshire, 126, 1988).

Clerkenwell Cartulary   *Cartulary of St. Mary Clerkenwell*, ed. W. O. Hassall (Camden
Society, 3rd ser., 71, 1949).

CP   Gibbs, V., and others (eds), *The Complete Peerage of England, Scotland, Ireland,
Great Britain, and the United Kingdom* (rev. edn, 13 vols in 14, London: St Catherine
Press, 1910–59).

Ctl.   Cartulary

Danelaw Charters   *Documents Illustrative of the Social and Economic History of the Danelaw*,
ed. F. M. Stenton (London: Oxford University Press for the British Academy, 1920).

DBC   Documents seen in transcription at the Comital Acta project, University College,
Scarborough, courtesy of Professor David Crouch.

Early Medieval Miscellany   *A Medieval Miscellany for Doris Mary Stenton*, ed. P. M. Barnes
and C. F. Slade (Pipe Roll Society, new ser., 36, 1962 for 1960).

EYC   *Early Yorkshire Charters*, vols I–III, ed. W. Farrer (Edinburgh: Ballantyne Hanson,
1914–16); *Index* (to vols I–III), ed. C. T. Clay and E. M. Clay (Wakefield, 1942);
vols IV–XII, ed. C. T. Clay (Yorkshire Archaeological Society, Record Series, Extra
Series, 1935–65).

Gloucester Charters   *Earldom of Gloucester Charters: The Charters and Scribes of the Earls
and Countesses of Gloucester to A.D. 1217*, ed. R. B. Patterson (Oxford: Clarendon
Press, 1973).

HKF   W. Farrer, *Honors and Knights' Fees* (3 vols, Manchester: Manchester University
Press, 1923–59).

JCAS   *Journal of the Chester Archaeological Society.*

JMH   *Journal of Medieval History.*

Mon. Ang.   Sir William Dugdale, *Monasticon Anglicanum*, ed. J. Caley, H. Ellis and
B. Bandinel (6 vols in 8, London: Longman . . . , Lackington . . . , and Joseph Harding,
1817–30).

Mowbray Charters   *Charters of the Honour of Mowbray, 1107–1191*, ed. D. Greenway
(London: Oxford University Press, for the British Academy, 1972).

Northants. Charters   *Facsimiles of Early Charters from Northamptonshire Collections*, ed.
F. M. Stenton (Northamptonshire Record Society, 4, 1930).

OV *Historia Ecclesiastica: The Ecclesiastical History of Orderic Vitalis*, ed. M. Chibnall (6 vols, Oxford: Clarendon Press, 1969–80).

Oxford Charters *Facsimiles of Early Charters in Oxford Muniment Rooms*, ed. H. E. Salter (Oxford: Oxford University Press, 1929).

P.R. [*regnal year*] Pipe rolls published by the Pipe Roll Society, London.

PRS Pipe Roll Society.

RRAN *Regesta Regum Anglo-Normannorum*, ed. H. W. C. Davis, C. Johnson, H. A. Cronne and R. H. C. Davis (4 vols, Oxford: Clarendon Press, 1913–69).

RD *Rotuli de dominabus et pueris et puellis de XII Comitatibus [1185]*, ed. J. H. Round (Pipe Roll Society, 35, 1913).

RS Rolls Series

Sarum Charters *Charters and Documents illustrating the History of the Cathedral, City and Diocese of Salisbury*, ed. W. Rich Jones and W. Dunn McCray (RS, 97, London, 1891).

Seals BM W. de G. Birch, *Catalogue of Seals in the Department of Manuscripts in the British Museum* (6 vols, London: Trustees of the British Museum, 1887–1900).

Seals PRO R. H. Ellis, *Catalogue of Seals in the Public Record Office: Personal Seals* (2 vols, London: HMSO, 1978, 1981).

Stafford, 'Emma' P. Stafford, 'Emma: the powers of the queen in the eleventh century', in A. Duggan (ed.), *Queens and Queenship in Medieval Europe: Proceedings of a Conference held at King's College London, April 1995* (Woodbridge and Rochester NY: Boydell, 1997), pp. 3–26.

Stafford, *Emma and Edith* P. Stafford, *Queen Emma and Queen Edith: Queenship and Women's Power in Eleventh-century England* (Oxford: Blackwell, 1997).

TRHS *Transactions of the Royal Historical Society*.

VCH *The Victoria History of the Counties of England*.

1

Introduction

THIS BOOK EXAMINES the place of noblewomen in twelfth-
century English and, to a lesser extent, Norman society. An initial
justification for such a study is that the place of noblewomen
in twelfth-century English society has not hitherto been systematically
addressed as a subject in its own right. This is in contrast to Anglo-
Saxon and late medieval women, on whom there is considerable
historiographical debate. Some of the roles of women in twelfth-century
English society have of course been studied, particularly women's
tenure of dower, *maritagium*, and female inheritance. However, much
that has been written about twelfth-century women has been done
to the dictates of an oscillating male-centred historiography about the
creation of institutions, or otherwise of male lordship or 'feudalism'.
The dominant historiographical discourse which considers dynamics of
power in twelfth-century society is that of the study of the multi-faceted
construct that is conventionally called lordship. This book will analyse
the roles of noblewomen within lordship and in so doing will clarify
important aspects of noblewomen's power. The analytical framework
upon which the book is constructed draws on recent theoretical developments in the history of women and power and utilises traditional
scholarly approaches to the study of the twelfth century. In so doing it
re-defines the nature of twelfth-century lordship.

The debate on the roles of medieval women has moved a long way
from seeing them as victims of male dominance, and the ideology of
separate spheres has been superseded by recent theoretical insights which
consider the importance of gender and the impact of the female life
cycle on the roles and power of women. Indeed, modern writers on the
history of women, such as Judith Bennett, Maryanne Kowaleski and
Joel Rosenthal, have raised important questions about the importance
of gender as a category of analysis to explain the complexity of women's

societal subordination.[1] A gender-based analysis considers that the differences in the social identities of men and women, the way that men and women exerted power and influence in society through complex power structures such as the family and lordship, were crucially affected by societal expectation of men's and women's roles based on ideas about the physical, mental and psychological differences between men and women.[2] The inculcation of such expectations was manifested through ideologies which were internalised differently by men and women.[3] These approaches are applicable to twelfth-century society because of the multiplicity of references to female–male interaction, collaboration and difference within contemporary documents.

The paradigms offered by Pauline Stafford and Janet Nelson illustrate ways that a more complex explanation of twelfth-century women's power can be achieved. Stafford and Nelson have done much to clarify the importance of the interactions of the female life cycle and gender in constructions of female power. Stafford convincingly dismissed models of society which seek improvements or decline in women's position or place in society since this undermines important questions concerning the complexities of status measurement. Stafford further argued that the powers of the eleventh-century queens Emma and Edith had multiple bases, through land tenure and in 'marriage and maternity'.[4] Stafford is interested in explaining queenly power in terms of the impact of the female life cycle and the specific political and cultural contexts of late eleventh-century England. In particular Stafford and Nelson are clear on the antipathy of male clerical writers to the portrayal of powerful women, a phenomenon not unique to eleventh-century England.[5]

Constructions of male power and influence as lords in their own right rested on enfeoffment of their lands or inheritance, or knighting. Both were the keys to public function, as well as office holding. For women marriage as entrée into public life served the same purpose, but crucially women's role in relation to public power was differently defined. The multiplicity of meanings of noblewomen's social power is better accommodated within a wider framework which can explain the significance of, for example, women's informal unstructured power to influence events, not as the logical outcome of a system in which women were subordinate to men, but as a result of the conflicting and complex series of ways in which any individual was closed or excluded from power. Thus powerful women as wives and widows may have class interests or political interests, which they defend, but they are also subject to categories of gender which interacted with their other identities. The importance of multiple identities in twelfth-century culture has recently been investigated by Ian Short, who argues that the Anglo-Norman English sought to maintain a sense of cultural distinctiveness, and in so doing they perpetuated a sense of social exclusiveness.[6] This model of self-definition thus unconsciously draws on elements of closure theory to explain increasing twelfth-century aristocratic elitism.[7]

Lordship is one way that such elitism was expressed. Lordship remains at the heart of many interpretations of the twelfth century and its nature has been vigorously debated since the publication of Stenton's *First Century of English Feudalism.*[8] Stenton used charter evidence to depict a seigneurial world in which the unity of the honour, and thus honorial society, was expressed through the *honor* court, guardian of feudal custom.[9] Stenton was interested in lordship as a male role,[10] and his concern with the definition of the internal workings of the *honor* as male-dominated led him, like Maitland before him, to ignore women and to assume that they had no public role.[11] Although the evidential base from which Stenton drew his conclusion, charters, is narrow and necessarily throws the spotlight on the *honor*, it is the lack of a sophisticated paradigm with which to explore nuances of the evidence that is the key problem.[12]

Such a paradigm can utilise some of the approaches to the study of lordship taken by Paul Hyams, Paul Dalton, David Crouch and John Hudson; the ways in which women could exert power can thereby more easily be explained.[13] These recent revisions have clarified the meaning of lordship, land tenure and the importance of the bonds of lordship and hierarchy, and show the complexities and contradictions of twelfth-century lordship, but have yet to incorporate an analysis of noblewomen's power within lordship. For example, Paul Dalton argued that when Agnes de Arches in the reign of Stephen granted land to the nuns of Nunkeeling without the involvement of her lord this shows the weakness of seigneurial lordship and poses a challenge to Stenton's model of society;[14] he declined, however, to draw any conclusions about its implications for the confidence and power of a noblewoman to act independently in the context of religious benefaction.

If, as ideas about property emerged, the key relationship in society was between tenant and land, 'not tenant and lord',[15] this has particular resonance in the context of female land tenure, because the nature of the lands held by women, in particular dower and *maritagium*, affected their powers of alienation, inheritance and, crucially, their place, power and identity in society. It also affected their inheritance patterns.[16] If, in addition, modern hierarchical patterns of thinking obscure the complexities of twelfth-century hierarchies,[17] this is instructive when we consider women, since twelfth-century clerics were themselves aware of the importance of gender, marital status and class when they discussed women. Further, it can be argued (in opposition to Stenton's view of personal relationships as the glue which held society together) that during the twelfth century warranty, an important function of lordship, became institutionalised;[18] but this has a particular relevance for the study of women, since women gave and desired warranty contracts in their charters.

Approaching the subject from a different angle, it can be observed that historians have long been interested in the importance of married women's property and the complexities of dower, since Florence Buckstaff's seminal article of 1893 tracing married women's property and George Haskins's study of dower.[19] This interest has necessitated at least a minimal consideration of the implications of gender. Haskins, who saw lordship and military service as the key to understanding society, believed that the principle of dower was in opposition to 'feudalism', since women were 'useless for performing suit at court'. More recently, however, Joseph Biancalana traced the developments of writs of dower to clarify the way that common law developed and stressed that dower was necessary to the structuring of land and marriage markets.[20] Janet Senderowitz Loengard analysed dower to argue that its allocation was open to many variables, militated against the consolidation of family lands and could cause litigation, confusion, and in practice could alienate lands away from the patrimony for long periods. More significantly, dower brought women into the courts, actively pursuing or defending claims. For Loengard dower was 'the medieval woman's insurance policy' which turned 'accepted convention on its head'.[21] Loengard is influenced by feminist scholarship, which stresses female action and power, whilst as a legal historian Biancalana is more interested in the legal implications of dower. Both approaches, their roots in the quest for an understanding of patterns of land tenure which stretches back to the inception of British medieval studies,[22] imply that an understanding of the gendered nature of lordship will have implications for our understanding of land tenure in general.

Sir James Holt's analysis of twelfth-century social structures saw noblewomen as pawns of men, used to seal political alliances through marriage, their key role being to transmit land and titles to their husbands. Holt's view is important for the way it located the interactions between the key structures of family and lordship which defined twelfth-century women's roles. His study of *maritagium*, dower and inheritance, heritability of title, and the development of the custom of parceny in the 1130s and 1140s set women's roles into the context of the interactions between family and royal lordship.[23] Jane Martindale similarly argued that female succession and thus women's role in transmitting lands and inheritance were established as acceptable in the first decade of the twelfth century, but emphasised that women's inheritance was often a source of instability.[24] Crouch sees women's land tenure as a threat to family hegemony and resources, and views women's role essentially in a similar way to Holt and Martindale – that is, to ensure the transmission of blood line and land.[25] Inheritance by women has been discussed by Eleanor Searle in terms of women's role in legitimising the Norman Conquest through marriage.[26] John Gillingham and RaGena DeAragon have shown the political and strategic nature of marriage in the twelfth century.[27] S. F. C. Milsom analysed female inheritance in the twelfth and thirteenth centuries.[28] Like Holt, his analysis is set into a context of the importance of family and 'feudal' interests in female land tenure with an emphasis on women's role in the transmission of lands, but Milsom's interest was in the development of the legal framework and definitions of women's land tenure and female inheritance patterns. Milsom stressed the difference in nature between customs of male and female inheritance.[29] This latter insight is crucial for understanding the gendered constructions of women's power through land tenure within twelfth-century society. Milsom's analysis of the checks and balances within inheritance structures, to counter the potential instabilities caused by female inheritance, defines women's land tenure as the locus of these conflictive, mutable 'feudal' and family interests.

Scott L. Waugh also saw fluidity as a key determinant of women's land tenure, finding, for example that there was no mechanism for enforcing the allocation of marriage portions to women, allowing lords 'wide discretion'.[30] Fundamentally, Waugh found that women's inheritance became more structured, owing to royal bureaucratic procedures, rather than, for example, the impetus of families who wanted to see daughters well endowed and therefore more marriageable. Judith Green analysed women's land tenure in the context of royal interference in the affairs of noble families. She also stressed the fluidity of the rules about female succession and emphasised the political nature of women's inheritance around 1100. This re-evaluation of the evidence relating to female inheritance shows how it became significant in the specific political circumstances of the reign of Henry I. However, she argues that women were fundamentally 'counters used in political bargains' conducted by male strategists, and thus essentially follows traditional interpretations of the place of women in contemporary society.[31] Pauline

Stafford, on the other hand, questions such a framework and, for example, argues that royal women could be thrust into prominence during periods when male kin were insecure through political instability. In such a context women could effect their own policies and initiatives.[32]

Holt, Milsom, Green *et al.* emphasise the potential instabilities caused by female land tenure, and the potential political and social conflicts and tensions caused by female succession systems when they developed in twelfth-century England. This is a formidable body of scholarship which has clarified important aspects of female land tenure and shown noblewomen as an element in the exercise of lordship. The importance of this and, by extension, the possibility of women's power as active participants therein is not clarified directly, because the authors are interested in discussing succession systems and rules of inheritance, or feudalism and lordship, not in discussing women's power. Yet much can be learned about women's power from these interpretations. For example, inadvertently, like so many of the scholars just discussed, Milsom has begun to analyse gender systems. Modern scholars, without necessarily consciously seeking to do so, have placed women at the centre of debates about twelfth-century power structures. For example, if we accept Milsom's contention that male and female customs of inheritance were different in nature, then it can further be argued that identity, intimately associated with land tenure, was gendered. Such identities, as wives, widows and daughters, defined the participation of twelfth-century noblewomen in land transactions. Such categories of land tenure did not apply to men in the same way because their access to resources was structured around different gendered identities.[33]

In a wider context this book is intended as a contribution to the debate over the role and meaning of female power in the context of the interaction of gender and lordship in twelfth-century society. It is deliberately wide-ranging, since – arguably – it is possible to analyse the dialogue between text, gender and society only if different types of evidence are taken fully into account. The charters analysed include selective surveys of original charters held in the Public Record Office and the British Library. Monastic cartularies such as the cartulary of Stixwould have been considered. These charters, and collections of charters, are used in Chapters 4–8 to re-examine women's power as expressed through lordship, and ultimately to reconsider the nature of lordship itself. In conjunction with this, the book sets out to bring together a *corpus* of previously unanalysed seals to consider their text and image, and sealing practice itself, as an indicator of women's power. Twelfth-century writers discussed in Chapters 2 and 3 include Orderic

Vitalis, William of Malmesbury and William of Newburgh, and the analysis considers the way that women appear in these texts, but also the extent to which women could influence their creation, and thus considers the limitations of those texts as a guide to women's power. The 1185 *Rotuli de Dominabus*, a complex and under-utilised source, is analysed in Chapter 9 to consider the way that royal authority and the law shaped the experience of noblewomen, but also to provide a cautionary account of the degree to which such sources present an external view of the societies in which noblewomen exercised power. Saints' lives provide the opportunity to assess the way that the power of noblewomen interacted with, and to an extent drew upon, the authority of the church – recognising too that these *vitae* were created by a more or less misogynist male clergy who yet had to respond to the reality of the close involvement of their subjects' interaction with the power of women. When text, gender and society are considered together, a surprisingly rich view of twelfth-century noblewomen begins to emerge.

Notes

1 D. Baker (ed.), *Medieval Women* (Studies in Church History, Subsidia I, Oxford, 1978); M. Erler and M. Kowaleski (eds), *Women and Power in the Middle Ages* (Athens GA and London: University of Georgia Press, 1988), contains useful articles by J. Bennett, B. Hanawalt and J. Tibbetts Schulenburg; J. T. Rosenthal (ed.), *Medieval Women and the Sources of Medieval History* (Athens GA: University of Georgia Press, 1990); see also S. Shahar, *The Fourth Estate: A History of Women in the Middle Ages* (London: Methuen, 1983; repr. London: Routledge, 1991); S. Mosher Stuard (ed.), *Women in Medieval Society* (Pennsylvannia: University of Pennsylvania Press, 1976), is still useful if outdated in its analytical framework.

2 I here agree with Joan Hoff, 'Gender as a postmodern category of paralysis', *Women's History Review*, 3: 2 (1994), 80–99. This article neatly summarises the developments of the debates over the use of gender in historical analysis. J. Wallach Scott, *Gender and the Politics of History* (New York: Columbia University Press, 1988) epitomises the use of post-structuralist theory deplored by Hoff. For specific medievalists' approach to the debate racking American scholars see S. Mosher Stuard, 'The chase after theory: considering medieval women', *Gender and History*, 4 (1992), 135–46, and also *Speculum*, 68: 2 (1993), in which all the articles implicitly engage in the debates over the validity of post-structuralist and post-feminist approaches to the study of history.

3 C. Walker Bynum, *Holy Feast and Holy Fast: The Religious Significance of Food to Medieval Women* (Berkeley CA and London: University of California Press, 1987); eadem, *Fragmentation and Redemption: Essays on Gender and the Human Body in Medieval Religion* (New York: Zone, 1991).

4 P. Stafford, 'Women and the Norman Conquest', *TRHS*, 6th ser, 4 (1994), 221–49; Stafford, 'Emma', pp. 12–13.

5 J. L. Nelson, 'Women at the court of Charlemagne: a case of monstrous regiment?' in
   J. Carmi Parsons (ed.), *Medieval Queenship* (Stroud: Sutton, 1994), pp. 43–61; *eadem*,
   'Gender and genre in women historians of the early Middle Ages', *L'Historiographie
   médiévale en Europe* (Paris, 1991), pp. 150–63; *eadem*, 'Women and the word in the
   earlier Middle Ages', in W. J. Sheils and D. Wood (eds), *Women in the Church*
   (Studies in Church History, 27, Oxford, 1990), pp. 53–8. Stafford, 'Women and the
   Norman Conquest'; *eadem*, 'Women in Domesday', in Keith Bate and others (eds),
   Medieval Women in Southern England (Reading Medieval Studies, 15, 1989), pp. 75–
   94; Stafford, 'Emma', pp. 12, 22–3.

6 I. Short, '*Tam Angli quam Franci:* self-definition in Anglo-Norman England', *ANS*,
   18 (1996 for 1995), 154–5.

7 For an application of Weberian closure theory to the medieval period see S. Rigby,
   English Society in the Later Middle Ages: Class, Status and Gender (Basingstoke:
   Macmillan, 1995). See also N. Abercrombie, S. Hill and B. S. Turner, *The Dominant
   Ideology Thesis* (London: Allen & Unwin, 1980); M. Weber, *Economy and Society: An
   Outline of Interpretive Sociology*, ed. Guenther Roth and Claus Wittich (3 vols, New
   York: Bedminster Press, 1968).

8 F. M. Stenton, *The First Century of English Feudalism, 1066–1166* (Oxford: Clarendon
   Press, 1932; 2nd edn, Oxford: Clarendon Press, 1961).

9 *Ibid.*, p. 55.

10 See his analysis of the joint action of Hugh de Gournay and Milisent his wife: *ibid.*
   (1st edn), pp. 107–8.

11 F. Pollock and F. W. Maitland, *History of English Law before the Time of Edward I*
   (Cambridge, 1895, 2nd edn, 1898, repr. London: Cambridge University Press, 1968),
   1. 485; further, 'As regards private rights women [meaning widows] were on the
   same level as men . . . but public functions they have none. In the camp, at the
   council board, on the bench, in the jury box there is no place for them'. See J. G. H.
   Hudson, *Land, Law and Lordship in Anglo-Norman England* (Oxford: Clarendon
   Press, 1994), pp. 7–9, for a discussion of Pollock and Maitland.

12 D. Crouch, 'From Stenton to McFarlane: models of societies of the twelfth and
   thirteenth centuries', *TRHS*, 6th ser., 5 (1995), 184.

13 P. Hyams, 'Warranty and good lordship in twelfth-century England', *Law and History Review*, 5 (1987), 437–503.

14 P. Dalton, *Conquest, Anarchy and Lordship: Yorkshire, 1066–1154* (Cambridge: Cambridge University Press, 1994), p. 269. Agnes de Arches was the foundress of
   Nunkeeling in 1152: *VCH Yorkshire*, 3. 119; *EYC*, 3. no. 1331.

15 J. Hudson, 'Anglo-Norman land law and the origins of property', in G. S. Garnett
   and J. G. H. Hudson (eds), *Law and Government in Medieval England and Normandy: Essays in Honour of Sir James Holt* (Cambridge: Cambridge University Press,
   1994), p. 199; Hudson, *Land, Law and Lordship*, p. 279.

16 J. A. Green, 'Aristocratic women in early twelfth-century England', in C. Warren
   Hollister (ed.), *Anglo-Norman Political Culture and the Twelfth-century Renaissance*
   (Woodbridge: Boydell, 1997), pp. 60, 72.

17 Crouch, 'Stenton to McFarlane', p. 200.

18 Hyams, 'Warranty and good lordship'.

19 F. G. Buckstaff, 'Married women's property in Anglo-Saxon and Anglo-Norman law
   and the origin of common-law dower', *Annals of the American Academy of Political*

and Social Science, 4 (1894), 233–64; G. L. Haskins, 'The development of common law dower', *Harvard Law Review*, 62 (1948), 42–55.

20 J. L. Biancalana, 'The writs of dower and chapter 49 of Westminster I', *Cambridge Law Journal*, 49 (1990), 91–116; *idem*, 'Widows at common law: the development of common law dower', *Irish Jurist*, 23 (1988), 255–329.

21 J. Senderowitz Loengard, '"Of the gift of her husband": English dower and its consequences in the year 1200', in J. Kirshner and S. F. Wemple (eds), *Women of the Medieval World: Essays in Honor of John H. Mundy* (Oxford: Blackwell, 1985), 215–55; *eadem*, '*Rationabilis dos*: Magna Carta and the widow's "fair share" in the earlier thirteenth century', in S. Sheridan Walker (ed.), *Wife and Widow in Medieval England* (Ann Arbor MI: University of Michigan Press, 1993), pp. 59–80, esp. p. 60; *eadem*, 'Legal history and the medieval Englishwoman: a fragmented view', *Law and History Review*, 4 (1986), 161, reprinted with postscript as '"Legal history and the medieval Englishwoman" revisited: some new directions', in J. T. Rosenthal (ed.), *Medieval Women and the Sources of Medieval History* (Athens GA: University of Georgia Press, 1990), pp. 210–36.

22 Crouch, 'Stenton to McFarlane', p. 180.

23 J. C. Holt, 'Feudal society and the family in early medieval England' IV, 'The heiress and the alien', *TRHS*, 5th ser., 35 (1985), 1–28.

24 J. Martindale, 'Succession and politics in the romance-speaking world, *c.* 1000–1140', in M. Jones and M. Vale (eds), *England and her Neighbours, 1066–1453: Essays in Honour of Pierre Chaplais* (London and Ronceverte: Hambledon Press, 1989), p. 32.

25 D. Crouch, 'The local influence of the earls of Warwick, 1088–1242: a study in decline and resourcefulness', *Midland History*, 21 (1996), 9–10.

26 E. Searle, 'Women and the legitimisation of succession at the Norman Conquest', *ANS*, 3 (1981 for 1980), 159–70.

27 R. C. DeAragon, 'In pursuit of aristocratic women: a key to success in Norman England', *Albion*, 14 (1982), 258–67; *eadem*, 'Dowager countesses, 1069–1230', *ANS*, 17 (1995 for 1994), 87–100; J. Gillingham, 'Love, marriage and politics in the twelfth century', *Forum for Modern Language Studies*, 25: 4 (1989), 292–303.

28 S. F. C. Milsom, 'Inheritance by women in the twelfth and thirteenth centuries', in M. S. Arnold, T. A. Green, S. A. Scully and S. D. White (eds), *On the Laws and Customs of England: Essays in Honor of Samuel E. Thorne* (Chapel Hill NC: University of North Carolina Press, 1981), pp. 60–89.

29 *Ibid.*, p. 62; see also his comments on the difference between control of the marriage of male and female heirs by lords in 'The origin of prerogative wardship', in Garnett and Hudson (eds), *Law and Government*, pp. 239–40.

30 S. L. Waugh, 'Women's inheritance and the growth of bureaucratic monarchy in twelfth- and thirteenth-century England', *Nottingham Medieval Studies*, 34 (1990), 88; 'Marriage, class and royal lordship in England under Henry III', *Viator*, 16 (1985), 181–207; *The Lordship of England: Royal Wardships and Marriages in English Society and Politics, 1217–1327* (Princeton NJ: Princeton University Press, 1988).

31 Green, 'Aristocratic women', p. 78; J. A. Green, *The Aristocracy of Norman England* (Cambridge: Cambridge University Press, 1997), pp. 361–90, at p. 365: Green, with an approach similar to that of Holt and Stenton, accepts a minimalist view of women's roles. For the role of dowry and inheritance patterns see K. H. Thompson, 'Dowry

and inheritance patterns: some examples from the descendants of King Henry I of England', *Medieval Proposopography*, 19 (1996), 45–61.

32 P. Stafford, *Queens, Concubines and Dowagers: The King's Wife in the early Middle Ages* (London: Batsford, 1983), p. 115.

33 The meanings of such male-gendered identities as husband and lord are too vast even to be attempted here; as Stafford has pointed out, the meaning of 'lord' alone would take a book on its own: *Emma and Edith*, p. 58.

PART I

Literary sources

2

Power and portrayal

LTHOUGH THE TWELFTH century is often presented as a
'Golden Age' of English historical writing, few historians have
discussed the portrayal of twelfth-century women. An important exception, Marjorie Chibnall's study of women in Orderic Vitalis,
is valuable for the way it explores Orderic's presentation of noblewomen according to their marital status, class and wealth.[1] Essentially, Chibnall agreed with Eileen Power that the image of women in
literature was complex and reflected the place of women in society
generally.[2] Power had warned of the need for careful treatment of
the sources when she argued that women's theoretical position and
their power in reality were contradictory.[3] Lois Huneycutt has begun to
uncover the increased attention paid to gender difference in the twelfth
century, as well as stressing the paradoxical contrasts between the
misogynistic language used to portray women and the practical realities of the complex societal expectations and responsibilities placed
upon them.[4] Pauline Stafford eschews a simple bi-polar 'image and reality' paradigm to place the emphasis on complex interactions of the
political context of textual production, increasing attentions paid to
critiques of wealth, power and gender definition in the twelfth century, and the origination of a new language to effect this.[5] The roots of
this new attention to the language which articulated queenly power,
innovated in the writings of William of Malmesbury, lie in literature
commissioned by royal female patrons in the specific political climate
of late eleventh-century England. A key to Stafford's approach is the
importance of the female life cycle in defining women's power and its
interactions with social, familial and political connections and contexts.
Public authority wielded by powerful women is discussed in masculine
terms, since, as Duby and Stafford argue, power has the capacity to re-
or degender.[6] This is explicable if we accept that male reaction to female

power shows that it is historically often defined as illegitimate, unusual or unnatural.[7]

The following discussion draws on these key themes. It acknowledges the difficulties of analysing images of noblewomen in contradictory sources at a time when the historical discourse was evolving, owing to broader societal cultural shifts.[8] Likewise the complex portrayals of noblewomen and the way that such images present particular views of noblewomen are set into an appreciation of the broader issues of authorial bias and political, social and cultural contexts. This analysis is above all concerned with the difficulty of measuring the power of noblewomen, given the complexities of the sources.[9]

Noblewomen appear in twelfth-century texts as both active subjects and passive objects, in complex ways, pursuing political ambition, as religious, pious wives, mothers and daughters. Such views of women depend very much on genre, date of composition and context of entry of a female character into the narrative. It is important to recognise that medieval writers wrote within convention. When Étienne de Fougères wrote his *Le Livre des Manières* in 1160–70, he described good and bad women, and used the countess of Hereford as his model of female courtly, aristocratic and 'good behaviour'.[10] In the early twelfth century, Baudri de Bourgeuil wrote of the beauty of his subjects within a convention which dated from the poetry of Maximillian; therefore he wrote of eyes that shine like stars or teeth like ivory.[11]

Orderis Vitalis's view of women's power in the context of their political and warlike activity, like his view of men, is ambiguous, and by no means monolithic.[12] For example, Orderic described women actively engaged in the military campaigns of their husbands. Isabel of Conches rode out to war 'armed as a knight among the knights, and she showed no less courage among the knights in hauberks than did the maid Camilla'.[13] His story focuses on the disagreements between Helewise, the wife of William, count of Evreux, and Isabel of Conches, wife of Ralph of Tosny, who caused their husbands to take up arms against each other. Although the female warrior may well be no more than a 'well-worn literary motif',[14] it is striking that Orderic ascribes different personal qualities to each woman. Isabel is praised as a generous, daring and gay character who was well loved. Her opponent Helewise is by contrast 'clever and persuasive, cruel and grasping'. He later commented on Isabel's retirement to a nunnery, where she 'worthily reformed her life' and repented of her 'mortal sin of luxury'.[15] On the presence of women at the battle of Ascalon, he states that women remained off the battlefield with the noncombatants and that they are 'unwarlike by nature'.[16] The emotional weakness of women is made gender-specific in Orderic's discussion of the expedition and aftermath of the defeat and capture of Mark Bohemond when campaigning against the Turks. He states that Tancred, the commander in chief, 'did not give way like a woman to vain tears and laments' but mustered an army and governed the lands.[17] This assertion that women's emotional weakness affects their judgement is a recurring theme in twelfth-century chroniclers.

Powerful women who pursued their own political objectives in contexts that Orderic disapproved of, like their male counterparts, usually meet an ignominious end. The image of a powerful widow such as Adelais, the widow of Roger I count of Sicily, could be mutable. Orderic portrays her in a relatively sympathetic light when she ruled with counsellors for her son. However, he turns her into a murderous poisoner who, after marrying for a third time, is repudiated by her husband and dies 'an object of general contempt' and 'stained with many crimes'. Orderic approves a context for legitimate action which is thus as a widow in the stead of a legitimate heir.[18] Aubrée, the wife of Ralph of Ivry, had built an 'almost impregnable castle'.[19] Yet this achievement is tempered with the tale that she was killed by her own husband for attempting to expel him from it.[20]

Orderic's portrayal of such powerful women is complex. Mabel of Bellême is depicted as a cruel woman who deserved to meet a miserable end, murdered in her bed by a vassal whom she had deprived of his lands. Chibnall believes that the detail of a murder of a warrior in a bath lies within the epic tradition.[21] Thus she implies that the story is a fabrication. The historicity of the detail is not as important here as the significance of the way in which Mabel's death is described. Orderic depicts Mabel using conventions of the epic genre; such a portrayal adds a certain dignity to her reputation whilst paradoxically seeking to destroy it, and thus he inverts the *topos*. In recompense for this Orderic records her obituary, as it was inscribed upon her tomb, but he states this was 'more through the partiality of friends than any just deserts of hers'. The obituary states that she gave good counsel, provided patronage and largesse, protected her patrimony, was intelligent, energetic in action and possessed *honestas* – honour, dignity.[22] Orderic's sharp comment, however, is reflective of the nature of contemporary politics in early twelfth-century Normandy as much as of his distrust of women. The Bellême family were the hereditary enemies of the Giroie family, who were the founders of Orderic's monastery of St Evroul.[23] Orderic's portrayal of Mabel of Bellême is therefore reflective of both contemporary clerical distrust of women in power and the nature of contemporary politics in Normandy.

Orderic's attention to human frailty leads him to praise both men and women or condemn them for lapses in behaviour. Orderic records women's obituaries on several occasions, for example, Countess Sibyl, who allegedly died from poisoning, is praised for her birth, beauty, wealth, chastity, largesse and prudence. Women are usually praised for their beauty, fertility and religiosity: traits which Orderic admired in women.[24] Other clerics in the twelfth century likewise wrote obituaries for women, including Baudri of Bourgeuil and Robert Partes, a monk, of Reading, who in the mid-twelfth century wrote nine obituaries for his mother which he sent to his twin brother.[25]

Orderic voices most approval for women who act within the context of religious patronage, and who are often depicted as acting with their sons and husbands to ensure the security of their gifts to his monastery. In this respect women are portrayed as having a beneficial influence. Avice, the daughter of Herbrand, who married Walter of Heugleville, is praised for her 'advice and wise counsel', her care for 'widows, waifs and the sick', as well as her beauty. She was 'most fair of face', 'well spoken and full of wisdom'; he praised her prudence and her 'golden tongue'.[26] She acted as a civilising influence on her husband and 'restrained him from his earlier folly'. Indeed, Orderic copied her epitaph, which was composed for her by 'Vitalis the Englishman'. Her praiseworthy traits are her nobility, fair face, wisdom, modesty, sound morality, her fertility (she had twelve children 'most of whom died prematurely in infancy'), her generosity to the church, and her constancy and chastity. Stephen Jaeger believes that women played a civilising role in society, and that romance literature created chivalric values, values adapted from a social code of courtliness.[27] Orderic thus apparently articulated the civilising influence of women upon their husbands prior to the emergence of romance literature. Indeed, this beneficial role of a wife in directing the morality of her husband is clear in Orderic's tale of a Breton whose wife persuaded him to give up a life of crime by obeying her wise counsels'.[28]

Orderic's portrayal of women, laced with his perception of the appropriate behaviour of women at different stages of their life cycle, confirms the validity of Stafford's general approach.[29] Thus a good wife encourages her husband in religious patronage, will offer advice and be obedient to her husband's wishes. A wife will give good counsel. Orderic's ambiguous view of women's influence extends to his view of sexual power. He describes how Adela, the wife of William duke of Poitou, used the marital bed to persuade her husband to go on crusade: 'between conjugal caresses' she urged him to go for the sake of Christendom, and to protect his honour. Orderic calls her *mulier sagax et animosa*.[30] The importance of the female life cycle underpins Orderic's portrayal of Windesmoth, the wife of Peter lord of Maule. She is praised for her modesty, chastity, piety, fecundity and her respect for her stepmother. He approves of the fact that she was young and newly married, since she was 'unformed' and thus more open to her husband's influence. Once widowed, she lived as a virtuous and 'happy matron', and remained chaste and unmarried for fifteen years, 'dutifully supported by her son in her husband's chamber up to old age!'[31] This theme of the obedient compliant wife and chaste widow is evident in the portrayal of Windesmoth's daughter-in-law. Her son Ansold, when on his deathbed, urged his wife, Odeline, to live chastely in widowhood, and to continue to guide their children morally until adulthood, and he implored her to release him from the marital bond so that he could become a monk. She 'wept copiously' and obediently consented to his wishes, since 'she had never been in the habit of opposing his will'.[32] Orderic praises the obedience of women to their husband and sons, and approves of chastity in widowhood. The articulation of such values confirms the importance of the female life cycle and gender roles upon the portrayal of the power of wives and widows.

The vulnerability of women, and their dependence on their husband or kin, are a recurring theme in Orderic's history of the great Norman families. It also confirms that wives had important roles to play in lordship. For example, Radegund, the wife of Robert of Giroie, deputised for her husband whilst he was on campaign, but she lost control of the household knights when news of his death reached her.[33] This example is suggestive of the vulnerability of wives to the vagaries of their husband's political fortunes, but also their supportive and martial roles. Such vulnerability is reflected in the exile of Agnes, daughter of Robert de Grandmesnil, after her husband, Robert of Giroie, had disregarded King Henry's will and attacked Enguerrand l'Oison.[34] The difficult position of noblewomen because of contemporary political volatilities and the importance of familial connections is evident in the example of Matilda de L'Aigle. Orderic states that she shared her husband's bed 'fearfully, for three months only, amid the clash of arms' and 'for many years led an unhappy life in great distress' after the imprisonment of her husband. Her second marriage was no greater success: she was repudiated by her second husband, Nigel d'Aubigny, after the death of her brother.[35] The impact that war and political misfortune could have on family members is often depicted. Orderic's story of the resolution of a dispute between Henry I and Eustace of Breteuil, a powerful Norman lord who had control of the strategic castle of Ivry, shows how women used kin networks to their advantage.[36] Eustace was married to Juliana, an illegitimate daughter of Henry by a concubine. The marriage was of course a political alliance, but Orderic illuminates the difficulties this could cause women. Henry had control of Eustace's castle at Ivry, and agreed to return the castle at a later date. In order to show faith between Henry I and Eustace hostages were exchanged, but on malicious advice Eustace put out the eyes of the boy that he received. As a result Henry I handed over his two granddaughters to the father of the blinded boy, who then had them blinded and the tips of their noses cut off.[37] This drove Eustace and Juliana to rebel. Juliana was sent to her husband's castle of Breteuil 'with the knights necessary to defend the fortress', whilst Eustace fortified his castles of Lire, Glos, Pont-Saint-Pierre and Pacy. Juliana's defence of the town of Breteuil was undone by the betrayal of the burgesses of the town. Henry besieged Juliana in the castle and, Orderic states, 'However, as Solomon says there is nothing so bad as a bad woman' – because she plotted to kill her father with a crossbow bolt, having requested a meeting with him. Her bolt missed and she was forced to surrender the castle to her father, who refused to let her leave with dignity. 'By the king's command she was forced to leap down from the walls' into the icy moat 'shamefully with bare buttocks'; Orderic calls her an 'unlucky amazon'. Her defeat and loss of the castle were not enough in Orderic's narrative. The historicity of the tale is less important than the fact that Orderic uses voyeuristic detail to portray her in a demeaning and humiliating way. Juliana was in a difficult political situation where conflicting family ties made her position as wife and daughter of protagonists difficult: her loyalty to her husband is, however, predominant. The allegation of her intention to commit patricide is indicative of Orderic's awareness of her pain, rage and anger at the mutilation of her children.[38]

The image of women supporting their husbands runs through many contemporary sources. Three key narrative sources, Orderic Vitalis, William of Newburgh and William of Malmesbury, confirm that powerful women played important roles in the decisive political campaigns of 1141. Orderic Vitalis states that Matilda countess of Chester and Hawise countess of Lincoln acted as decoys in a ruse by which earl Ranulf managed to capture Lincoln castle.[39] They were 'laughing and talking with the wife of the knight who ought to have been defending the castle' when Ranulf went as though to escort his wife home. Ranulf overpowered the king's guards and seized the castle. This event was a turning point in the civil war and the catalyst of the further events which led to uneasy peace negotiations between the empress and King

Stephen. William of Malmesbury in his *Historia Novella* likewise illustrates the role of wives in supporting their husbands in 1141. He shows that after the battle of Lincoln, which resulted in the capture of Earl Robert of Gloucester and King Stephen, Earl Robert knew he that he could rely on his wife, the countess Mabel, to support his political strategy. When cajoled and then threatened by Stephen's supporters to abandon the empress, he remained steadfast in his opposition, able to do so since he knew that his wife would send Stephen to Ireland should anything happen to him.[40] William of Malmesbury also shows Mabel's concern at the capture and imprisonment of her husband. He states that she was willing to accept a proposal detailing the exchange of the earl for less than his true ransom value, driven as she was by 'a wife's affection too eager for his release'. Malmesbury then adds that Robert earl of Gloucester 'with deeper judgement refused [the offer]'. Malmesbury is careful to stress Mabel's reliance on her husband's decisions even when he was imprisoned. Mabel's political judgement is thus portrayed as affected by her emotions and weaker than that of her husband. Countess Mabel was an important linchpin in continuing the political strategy of the Angevin cause whilst Earl Robert was imprisoned, having a central role in securing the release of Earl Robert. John of Worcester portrays both the countess Mabel and Stephen's queen Matilda as proactively involved in the negotiating process. Both the queen and Mabel are portrayed as supporting their husbands, negotiating with each other through messengers. It is striking that there is no disparaging comment, only recognition of their actions as peacemakers, and indeed power brokers, involved in careful diplomacy.[41]

Later in the twelfth century Petronella countess of Leicester was also involved in the military campaigns of her husband.[42] The main subject of Jordan Fantosme's *Chronique de la Guerre entre les Anglois et les Ecossois* is the war between the Scots and the English in 1173–74, and the rebellion of the earl of Leicester. Fantosme wrote to entertain in a classical tradition, to give moral instruction and to show that human folly was subject to divine law.[43] This purpose only partially accounts for a story about the martial exploits of Petronella countess of Leicester. Fantosme also wrote for an aristocratic audience who would be able to identify with the story, its content and moral code. Fantosme describes the deliberations of the earl's council of war prior to the battle of Fornham on 16 October 1173, at which the earl and the countess were both captured. To the earl's plea 'Ah God! . . . Who will advise me to make a start of this business?' Petronella replies, 'I will, my lord.' Petronella gives her husband counsel, a classic literary *topos*. Fantosme portrays how a powerful countess would argue her case through the use of classic literary conventions. Petronella urges her husband on and incites the council of Flemings, French and Picards with the words 'The English are great boasters, but poor fighters; they are better at quaffing great tankards and guzzling'. Ian Short considers this gibe as a humorous literary effect, since such anti-English sentiments were 'common currency' in twelfth-century literature.[44] Petronella was herself the daughter of a Continental magnate – would such gibes be nothing more than a joke in this context? Is the literary joke a double bluff? Petronella stresses the marriage connection between her husband and the earl of Gloucester, and maintains that their connection as brothers-in-law meant that the earl of Gloucester would not fight.[45] Jordan states that the earl had his wife dressed in armour and gave her a shield and lance. Jordan, with a knowing aside, tells the audience that the earl has made an error in arming his wife that will cost him dear: 'his lunacy will have a hard life'. During the battle Petronella fled the scene of battle, fell into a ditch and, having nearly drowned, lost her rings. In despair at the tide of battle turning against her and her husband, she was dissuaded from suicide by the actions of a knight who rescued her from a ditch and told her, 'My lady, come away from this place and abandon your design! War is all a question of losing and winning.'[46]

The portrayal of Petronella in a dramatic scene and her reported speech given at the council are illuminating. Her advice is poor, since the battle that she urges, however persuasively, leads to the defeat of her and her husband. The inclusion of the detail that she lost her rings in the fosse adds to her humiliation and mirrors her loss of dignity. The portrayal of Petronella is couched within specific literary *topoi* of the counsel she gave and her martial exploits which end in defeat. Fantosme articulates a traditional distrust of women giving counsel, their involvement in military affairs and of their power to effect change. He thus portrays Petronella in an unsympathetic way.

Other sources, however, give a different view of Petronella. Charters, for example, show that she was influential in similar ways to other powerful women in the twelfth century. She was a patron of religious houses in both England and Normandy with her husband. She witnessed his charters. Further she granted her own charters to St Evroult and St Mary's, Lire, held her own court and had her own seal.[47] Four of the major narrative sources for the events of Henry II's reign which describe the events of 1173–74 relate the events of the earl of Leicester's rebellion and note that Petronella was captured with her husband following the battle of Fornham.[48] Of these, three note the capture of

Earl Robert and Petronella without comment. William of Newburgh, however, states, *Captusque est comes cum conjuge, virilis animae femina*, and gives the further details that Petronella was on campaign with Earl Robert and landed with him at Wareham at the start of the rebellion.[49] His comment that Petronella was a woman with a 'man's spirit' describes her in male-gendered terms, evoking Duby and Stafford's contention that the exercise of power could de- or re-gender individuals.[50] Newburgh's view is expressive of the contradictions within sources which show how political women's image was coloured by clerical misogyny. This contrasts with Jordan Fantosme's portrayal, which, despite the depiction of the ultimate humiliation and defeat of Petronella, nevertheless shows her eloquent counsel which enables her to influence action and consequence. Matthew Paris, discussing these events in his thirteenth-century *Historia Anglorum*, states that Petronella threw her ring into the flowing stream indignantly, since she was unwilling to let her enemies have her ring, which was set with a precious gem. This is a more positive portrayal. Petronella, despite defeat, threw her rings away with indignation, suggesting that she somehow kept her poise and deprived her enemies of their spoils.[51] This story also appears in his earlier but lengthier *Chronica Majora*,[52] but the phrase *prae indignatione* is a later addition to his text which adds spice to the story. The discrepancy between the image of Petronella in literary sources and the impression of an important lay religious benefactor evidenced by charters confirms that Stafford's general approach to the study of royal women is applicable to an analysis of noblewomen, namely that the portrayal of royal women was mutable and dependant on a variety of interlocking factors, including political context, genre of text, clerical misogyny, as well as the vagaries of the female life cycle.[53] Certainly, although the image of Petronella is intriguing in literary sources, such sources alone do little justice to the ways that Petronella exerted power and influence; for that story we must turn to her charters, which illustrate her role in secular lordship.[54]

Just as Orderic Vitalis and Jordan Fantosme portrayed women's participation in the military campaigns of their husbands, so too the effect that war or rebellion could have on the political position of noble and aristocratic wives and widows is evident in other sources such as MS D of the *Anglo-Saxon Chronicle* and in sources dependent upon it, such as John of Worcester. For example, Queen Edith was sent to Chester by her brothers Earls Edwin and Morcar in 1066, although, as Stafford has argued, Edith's actions in 1066 are a mystery. Indeed, the image of Edith in the *Anglo-Saxon Chronicle* needs some refinement, since Edith survived her loss of status and lived in retirement on considerable resources.[55] Some women of the nobility may have taken a more direct role in the organisation of resistance to the Normans. Indeed, the countess Gytha may have been central to the English resistance and important in the refusal of the Godwin family to accept the defeat at Hastings as final. She was the focus of resistance at Exeter, and fled only after she was besieged.[56] When she fled from England in 1067, on her way to Saint-Omer, she left via the Isle of Flatholm 'and the wives of many good men accompanied her'.[57] She was thus given a tragically noble role and had the potential to became a symbol of English resistance to the Norman invaders.[58] In the revolt of the three earls of 1075, the wife of Ralph earl of Norfolk and Suffolk held her husband's castle at Norwich whilst he fled for Brittany when he realised his cause was lost. She held out in the besieged castle for some time, and left only once she had made terms with William the Conqueror. She was allowed to leave England: her husband was later imprisoned.[59] Given that such events were often organised by women, the arrangement of the details of the wedding feast may well have been the responsibility of his wife and as such it is likely that she knew about the conspiracy that was hatched.[60] A recurrent theme in twelfth-century chronicles is the way that noblewomen's fortunes were directly linked with those of their male kin: when Baldwin de Redvers refused to accept King Stephen, he and his wife and children were disinherited and exiled.[61]

However, it was not only aristocratic or royal women who could seize the opportunity to exert power and influence. Nichola de la Haye was one such woman from below the ranks of the titled aristocracy who was more than capable of directing and managing her own affairs. Nichola was the daughter and co-heiress of Richard de la Haye, the hereditary constable of Lincoln castle and sheriff of Lincolnshire, and passed the office of constable to each of her husbands.[62] In 1191 after her husband, Gerard de Camville, quarrelled with William Longchamp, the Chancellor and Justiciar of England, she was besieged at Lincoln Castle. Richard of Devizes tells us that her husband was with Count John, and once besieged 'Nicholaa, whose heart was not that of a woman, defended the castle manfully'.[63] She enjoyed a cordial relationship with John, and stoutly defended Lincoln when it was besieged by rebels under Louis of France. Having survived two sieges, the aged Nichola determinedly resisted attempts by the husband of her granddaughter, William, the son of the earl of Salisbury, to eject her from it.[64] Nichola's actions received different interpretations in different sources. Devizes gave her qualities associated with male action, whilst Wendover praised her tenacity in holding the castle in 1217. Indeed, Nichola's defence of

Lincoln in 1217 was a significant factor in turning the tide of events in favour of King John. According to a later tradition recorded at the local shire court, after the death of Gerard de Camville in 1215 Nichola left the castle and went to meet John with its keys in her hand to argue that she was too old to defend it. John replied to his 'beloved Nichola' that she should keep the castle until he ordered otherwise.[65] The *Histoire de la Guillame le Maréchal*, written about 1226, shows that Nichola's defence of Lincoln facilitated the penetration of Lincoln by Peter des Roches bishop of Winchester before the final battle which ended the siege. He entered the castle by a secret entrance and met Nichola, a 'noble lady to whom the castle belonged and was defending it as best she could'. She was apparently delighted to see the bishop, who reassured her that the siege would soon be over.[66] It is interesting that the author of the *Histoire* accepted Nichola's role without comment: she was 'noble' and defended as 'best she could'. It is also apparent that Nichola's actions as a *wife* received a different interpretation from those as an elderly widow; the female life cycle affected how she was portrayed. On the other hand, the same actions might receive different interpretations because of their immediate political significance: Devizes was hostile because her actions in 1191 placed her in opposition to Richard I, and in his case gender stereotyping served as a tool with which to attack her.

Just as we saw in the portrayal of Mabel of Bellême by Orderic Vitalis, the portrayal of women could have a propagandist political edge. For example, John of Worcester eulogises Queen Margaret, praising her in the familiar stereotypical way, lauding her piety, charity and generosity.[67] By contrast the death of William's queen, Matilda, is only tersely noted. The Worcester Chronicle, which drew on the *Anglo Saxon Chronicle* and other sources such as Bede, for its view of events prior to 1121,[68] was completed *c.* 1140. Like MS D of the *Anglo-Saxon Chronicle* it is laced with a pro-English bias,[69] and the view of Margaret is related to the image of her then current in northern England in the context of the succession dispute.[70] Thus her inscription as a tool of propaganda explains the fulsome praise of Queen Margaret. It is possible that Matilda countess of Boulogne attempted to get both of her blood lines sanctified in support of the political ambitions of her husband. It has traditionally been argued that her daughter Matilda, as queen of England, united the bloodlines of the old English royal house with that of the Normans. She also carried Scottish royal blood in her veins. The *Vita* of Queen Margaret commissioned by her daughter had a political intent as much as a stereotypical format. Duby finds a similar political propagandist context to explain the production of the *Vita* of Ida countess of Boulogne, which praised Ida for her fertility and was commissioned by her granddaughter, Matilda, who was also a granddaughter of Queen Margaret. Duby alleges that the monks of Vasconviliers wrote the *Vita* when the count of Boulogne felt he had a claim to the English throne.[71] Whether or not this is a realistic appreciation of contemporary political circumstances, it is significant that both Duby and Stafford acknowledge that the portrayal of powerful women could be propagandist. Stafford's contention that twelfth-century writers found a new language in which to articulate queenly political power[72] is a paradigm applicable to the ways that Orderic Vitalis, William of Newburgh and John of Worcester portrayed political women who were not queens, since the wives of powerful political men were portrayed as able political agents. Significantly, however, where women enter the political narrative roles are presented in a gendered way. Thus the countess Mabel had weaker political judgement than her husband; the countesses of Chester and Lincoln, whilst involved the military campaign of their husbands, were laughing and gossiping whilst Earl Ranulf took the castle. Richard of Devizes, writing at the end of the twelfth century, could describe powerful women only in gendered terms; Nichola de la Haye defended her husband's castle 'manfully'; Hawise countess of Aumâle was a 'woman who was almost a man, lacking nothing except the virile organs'.[73] The qualities Devizes admires in a woman are those of Queen Eleanor, who was beautiful and virtuous, powerful yet gentle, humble yet keen-witted, qualities 'which are rarely to be found in a woman'.[74]

As Stafford has shown, misogyny leads writers to articulate the political power of royal women by recourse to categories of gender, and the image of wives and widows could differ owing to the impact of the female life cycle.[75] Such an analytical framework is applicable to the study of twelfth-century women of the nobility, and the complexity of the image of noblewomen confirms that an image and reality paradigm is inadequate as a conceptual tool to decode women's power. Thus, for example, that Countess Mabel was portrayed as weaker in spirit than her husband Earl Robert of Gloucester, but nevertheless able to assume the reins of power when appropriate, confirms the importance of the female life cycle and thus marital status to women's power. As the discussion of Orderic Vitalis shows, the portrayal of powerful twelfth-century women was complex and is reflective of more than authorial political and cultural biases. Noblewomen were praised in stereotypical ways and their given attributes reveal the way that contemporary authors viewed noblewomen: their beauty, fertility, religious benefaction and fulfilment of dutiful family roles as wives, widows and daughters. The role of countesses such as Mabel of Gloucester or Petronella of Leicester received different interpretations in different sources, and this is suggestive of the complex ways that contemporary writers viewed women. The portrayal of Petronella had a hard political contemporary edge to it. As such noblewomen fared no better or worse than their male counterparts in that historical writing in any period is a political act. Yet women such as these faced a further category of analysis: that of their gender. Although noblewomen were expected to take action, and did, in appropriate contexts their roles were subject to hostile scrutiny based on ideas about gender roles. Nevertheless the ways individual women such as Countess Mabel of Gloucester, or Nichola de la Haye, are portrayed have much to tell us about the language of power and gender, as well as the way that they seized opportunities to affect political events and, in short, acted as powerful individuals at the heart of the power structures of the aristocratic and noble élite of the twelfth century.

Notes

1 M. Chibnall, 'Women in Orderic Vitalis', *Haskins Society Journal*, 2 (1990), 105–21.

2 It must be admitted, however, that a minority of writers continued to portray women in the most limited terms, in essence as simple pawns in the politics of aristocratic marriage (e.g. the Hexham historians: 'The chronicle of John, prior of Hexham, from A.D. 1130 to A.D. 1154' and 'The acts of King Stephen, and the battle of the Standard, by Richard, prior of Hexham, from A.D. 1135 to A.D. 1139', in *The Church Historians of England*, ed. Joseph Stevenson (5 vols, London: Seeley, 1853–58), IV (i) (1856), pp. 1–32, 33–58 respectively).

3 E. Power, 'The position of women', in C. G. Crump and E. F. Jacob (eds), *The Legacy of the Middle Ages* (Oxford: Clarendon Press, 1926), pp. 410–33; cf. E. Power, *Medieval Women*, ed. M. Postan (Cambridge: Cambridge University Press, 1975).

4 L. Huneycutt, 'Female succession and the language of power in the writings of twelfth-century churchmen', in Parsons (ed.), *Medieval Queenship*, pp. 189–201. Cf. J. Weiss, 'The power and weakness of women in Anglo-Norman romance', in C. M. Meale (ed.), *Women and Literature in Britain, 1150–1500* (Cambridge: Cambridge University Press, 1993), pp. 7–23, who asserts an outdated belief in decline in the social and economic position of women in England following the Norman Conquest, epitomised by D. M. Stenton's *The English Woman in History* (London: Allen & Unwin, 1957), and dismissed by Stafford ('Women and the Norman Conquest', pp. 221–49).

5 P. Stafford, 'The portrayal of royal women in England, mid-tenth to mid-twelfth centuries', in Parsons (ed.), *Medieval Queenship*, pp. 143–67, esp. pp. 157–61.

6 Stafford, 'Emma', p. 14; Duby, 'Women and power', p. 78.

7 S. Dixon, 'Conclusion – the enduring theme: domineering dowagers and scheming concubines', in B. Garlick and others (eds), *Stereotypes of Women in Power: Historical Perspectives and Revisionist Views* (New York and London: Greenwood Press,

1992), pp. 210–11. Such categorisations of women and power had tenacious roots, as Janet Nelson has convincingly shown in her study of ninth-century Francia: 'Women at the court of Charlemagne', pp. 49–50.

8 Huneycutt, 'Female succession', p. 191.

9 It is necessarily selective in its choice of sources because the exemplification of central themes is its goal, rather than a detailed analysis of the image of women in all twelfth-century literary sources. One necessary omission, therefore, is the satirical work of Walter Map. The genre in which he worked, unlike those of the other authors treated here, tended to limit him to presentations of the most extreme gendered stereotypes of women, without the need to accommodate their involvement in lordship and politics. For example, we have extreme cases of sexual incontinence by nuns, the abject submission of a loyal wife, and the use of sexual insults in a stereotyped attack on a nobleman's wife: Walter Map, *De Nugis Curialium: Courtiers' Trifles*, ed. M. R. James, revised by C. N. L. Brooke and R. A. B. Mynors (Oxford: Clarendon Press, 1983), pp. 419, 444, 447–8. Thus the discussion is limited by reference to the major narrative sources, including Orderic Vitalis, William of Malmesbury and William of Newburgh, to discuss specific themes or case studies.

10 Étienne de Fougères, *Le Livre des Manières*, ed. R. A. Lodge, Textes Littéraires Français (Geneva: Droz, 1979), verses 302–8, 100–1. The countess of Hereford could either be Cecily countess of Hereford, the daughter of Sibyl de Neufmarché and Roger earl of Hereford (married three times, to Roger earl of Hereford (d. 1155), William de Poitou (d. 1162) and Walter de Mayenne (d. 1190/91): *CP*, 6, pp. 455–7); or possibly Margaret de Bohun, the daughter and eventual co-heiress of Miles earl of Hereford, who married Humphrey de Bohun (*ibid.*, pp. 457–8 and note e).

11 J. Verdun, 'Les sources de l'histoire de la femme en Occident au X–XIII siècles', *Cahiers de Civilisation Médiévale*, XX (1977), 219–50. For a more detailed treatment of Baudri of Bourgeuil see Chapter 3 below.

12 Chibnall argued that Orderic described how women exerted power despite their theoretical subordination: 'Women in Orderic Vitalis', pp. 108–9, 116. Huneycutt, however, began to consider gender issues and demonstrated that women were more likely to fall prey to extremes of virtue and evil and that female wickedness was 'often used as an explanatory device': 'Female succession', pp. 192–3.

13 OV, 4. 212–14.

14 Nelson, 'Gender and genre', p. 150.

15 OV, 3. 128–9.

16 OV, 5. 178.

17 OV, 5. 354–5.

18 OV, 6. 366–7; OV, 6. 428–33. She is accused of poisoning her son-in-law. Poisoning is an allegation levelled at women in Orderic. See OV, 4. 181, where he alleges that the wife of Robert Guiscard attempted to poison her stepson.

19 OV, 4. 290–1.

20 Charter evidence corroborates Orderic's example of a powerful woman who had control of a castle. In 1075 Queen Matilda was present when Countess Adeliza (of Burgundy), who had bought the castle of Le Homme from her brother, granted it to the abbey of La Trinité, Caen: *Regesta Regum Anglo-Normannorum: The Acta of*

William I, 1066–1087, ed. D. Bates (Oxford and New York: Clarendon Press, 1998), no. 58.

21 OV, 3. 137, n. 2.

22 OV, 3. 136–9.

23 K. H. Thompson, 'Orderic Vitalis and Robert of Bellême', *JMH*, 20 (1994), 133–41.

24 OV, 6. 38–9. See also the obituary of Avice, daughter of Herbrand, discussed in the following paragraph. This is a recurring theme; see, for example, Margaret, the wife of Geoffrey of Mortain, OV, 2. 446–7.

25 W. H. Cornog, 'The poems of Robert Partes', *Speculum*, 12 (1937), 215–50. The obituaries occur at pp. 240–3, from BL, MS Egerton 2951. For Baudri, see below, pp. 33–4. For epitaphs, see E. M. C. van Houts, 'Latin Poetry and the Anglo-Norman court 1066–1135: The *carmen de Hastingae proelio*', *JMH*, 15 (1989), 40–3, 45–6.

26 OV, 3. 256–9. Her husband was buried 'at the feet of his wife'; for his obituary see OV, 3. 258–9.

27 C. S. Jaeger, *The Origins of Courtliness: Civilizing Trends and the Formation of Courtly Ideals, 939–1210* (Philadelphia: University of Pennsylvania Press, 1985), p. 209.

28 OV, 3. 342–3.

29 Stafford, 'Portrayal of royal women', pp. 144–5.

30 OV, 5. 324–5.

31 OV, 3. 180–1. A bad wife is one who is 'foolish and nagging', who gives bad counsel – as in the example of Emma, the wife of Richard of La Ferté-Frênel, who encouraged her husband to rebel: OV, 4. 218–19. A bad wife can be conveniently blamed for poor policies.

32 OV, 3. 194–7.

33 OV, 4. 292–5.

34 OV, 3. 134–5.

35 OV, 4. 282–4.

36 OV, 6. 210–15.

37 Orderic states, 'So innocent childhood alas! suffered for the sins of the fathers': OV, 4. 212–13. Facial disfigurement was the punishment in the later Middle Ages for adultery or prostitution.

38 OV, 6. 212–13: Orderic states that both parents' feelings were 'roused by the suffering and maiming of their offspring . . . [and they were] in great distress'.

39 OV, 6. 538–41.

40 William of Malmesbury, *Historia Novella*, ed. K. R. Potter (London and New York: Nelson, 1955), pp. 67–8.

41 *The Chronicle of John of Worcester*, ed. R. R. Darlington and P. McGurk (3 vols, Oxford: Clarendon Press, 1995–), 3. 302–5. Charter evidence shows that Mabel was important in the administrative affairs on the honour of Gloucester beyond crisis intervention in 1141 and was, significantly, responsible for the administration of Gloucester lands in Normandy for her son later in the twelfth century: pp. 94–5 below.

42 A. Gransden, *Historical Writing in England c. 550 to c. 1307* (London: Routledge, 1974), p. 237; M. D. Legge, *Anglo-Norman Literature and its Background* (Oxford: Clarendon Press, 1963), p. 75, gives the date of composition as 1174–75 and 1170–75 respectively.

43 *Jordan Fantosme's Chronicle*, ed. R. C. Johnstone (Oxford: Clarendon Press, 1981), p. xvi.; Legge, *Anglo-Norman Literature*, p. 75; Gransden, *Historical Writing*, p. 236.

44 Short, *'Tam Angli quam Franci'*, p. 153.

45 *Fantosme's Chronicle*, pp. 72, 73, lines 974–83.

46 *Ibid.*, pp. 78–9, lines 1064–71.

47 For example, she gave lands to St Évroul: Cartulary St Evroult, BN, MS Latin 11055, ff. 33v–35r (thirteenth-century); PRO, 31/8/140B, pt 1 (Cartulaire de la Basse-Normandie) 300, copy of *c.* 1835 by Léchaude d'Anisy; *CDF*, 228; *VCH Leicester*, 2. 23 (DBC); she confirmed lands to Nuneaton Priory, which her daughter Hawise entered, *Danelaw Charters*, no. 322, and gave a charter respecting lands in the church of Netheravon, *Sarum Charters*, no. 62. For her role as a witness and grantor to St Mary's Evreux, Fontaine, St Mary's de Sainte Barbe and St André-en-Gouffern see *CDF*, nos 306, 139, 199, 211. For her seal, see a description in *Danelaw Charters*, no. 322, and *Book of Seals*, no. 5, Appendix One, no. 73.

48 Roger of Howden, *Chronica Rogeri de Hoveden*, ed. W. Stubbs (4 vols, RS, 51, 1868–71), pp. 2. 55; *Gesta Regis Henrici Secundi Benedicti Abbatis: The Chronicle of the Reigns of Henry II, and Richard I, AD. 1169–1192, Known commonly under the Name of Benedict of Peterborough*, ed. W. Stubbs (2 vols, RS, 49, 1867), 1. 62; William of Newburgh, 'Historia Rerum Anglicarum', ed. R. Howlett, in *Chronicles of the Reigns of Stephen, Henry II and Richard I* (4 vols, RS, 82, 1884), 1. 179; Gervase of Canterbury, *The Historical Works of Gervase of Canterbury: The Chronicles of the Reigns of Stephen, Henry II., and Richard I., by Gervase, the Monk of Canterbury*, ed. W. Stubbs (2 vols, RS, 73, 1879–80), 1. 246.

49 William of Newburgh, *Historia Rerum Anglicarum*, p. 246.

50 Stafford, 'Emma', p. 14; Duby, 'Women and power', p. 78.

51 Matthew Paris, *Historia Anglorum*, ed. F. Madden (3 vols, RS, 44, 1866–69), 1. 381: *Comitissa vero superba nimis, annulem habens in digito cum gemma pretioissima, in amnen prope fluentum prae indignatione projecit, nolens hostibus de sua captione tantum habere proventum.*

52 Matthew Paris, *Chronica Majora*, ed. H. R. Luard (7 vols, RS, 57, 1872–83) 2. 290.

53 Stafford, 'Portrayal of royal women', pp. 146–9.

54 The charters are discussed below, pp. 69–70.

55 *Chronicle of John of Worcester*, 2. 604–5; Stafford, *Emma and Edith*, pp. 274–5.

56 M. T. Flanagan, *Irish Society, Anglo-Norman Settlers, Angevin Kingship: Interactions in Ireland in the late Twelfth Century* (Oxford: Clarendon Press, 1989), p. 59.

57 *ASC*, MS D 1067.

58 Stafford, *Emma and Edith*, p. 277.

59 *ASC*, MS D 1076 [1075].

60 For prominent examples of women sponsoring marriages and their celebration see Adela of Blois's 'generous provision' for a marriage which 'was celebrated magnificently': OV, 3. 182. See also *The Letters of John of Salisbury*, ed. W. J. Millor, H. E. Butler and C. N. L. Brooke (2 vols, vol. 1: London: Nelson, 1955; vol. 2: Oxford: Clarendon Press, 1979), p. 2, no. 144, where in a letter of John of Salisbury of January 1165, he states that the wife of Robert count of Dreux sent a present of 300 ells of cloth to Henry II in the hope that he would arrange favourable marriages for her children.

61 *Chronicle of John of Worcester*, pp. 218–19.

62 *HKF*, 3. 56; for further discussion of Nichola, see pp. 160–1.

63 *Girardus erat cum comite, et uxor eius Nicolaa, nichil femineum cogitans, castellum uirilter custodiebat*: Richard of Devizes, *The Chronicle of Richard of Devizes of the Time of King Richard the First*, ed. J. T. Appleby (London and New York: Nelson, 1963), pp. 30–1.

64 C. Hill, *Medieval Lincoln* (Cambridge: Cambridge University Press, 1948), p. 199.

65 *Rotuli Hundredorum temp. Hen. III. & Edw. I. in Turr' Lond. et in Curia Receptae Scaccarii Westm. asservati*, ed. W. Illingworth (2 vols, London: Record Commission, 1812–18), 1. 309.

66 *Histoire de la Guillaime le Maréchal*, ed. and trans. P. Meyer, in *English Historical Documents*, III, *1189–1327*, ed. H. Rothwell (London: Eyre & Spottiswoode, 1975), pp. 88–9.

67 *Chronicle of John of Worcester*, pp. 66–7; for Margaret see p. 31. Her seal, Appendix 1, no. 20.

68 Gransden, *Historical Writing*, p. 146.

69 *Ibid.*, p. 147. For the image of Queen Margaret see L. Huneycutt, 'The idea of a perfect princess: the *Life of Saint Margaret* in the reign of Matilda II (1100–18)', *ANS*, 12 (1990 for 1989), 81–97. Her meaning as a saint: R. Folz, *Les Saintes reines de Moyen Âge en Occident (VIe–XIIIe siècles)* (Brussels: Société des Bollandistes, 1992), p. 94, who notes that her husband King Malcolm is portrayed as a crude warrior. See OV, 4. 270–5, where she is praised for her piety and her preparations for death.

70 Stafford, 'Portrayal of royal women', p. 154.

71 G. Duby, 'The matron and the mis-married woman: perceptions of marriage in northern France *circa* 1100', in T. H. Aston, P. R. Coss, C. Dyer and J. Thirsk (eds), *Social Relations and Ideas: Essays in Honour of R. H. Hilton* (Cambridge: Cambridge University Press, 1983), pp. 95–9.

72 Stafford, 'Portrayal of royal women', p. 161.

73 *Richard of Devizes*, pp. 10, 31. This was a private view written for a friend.

74 *Ibid.*, p. 25.

75 Stafford, 'Portrayal of royal women', p. 148.

3

Patronage and power

TWELFTH-CENTURY NOBLEWOMEN exerted power and influence through cultural patronage, and scholars have begun to
clarify ways that noblewomen were important. Janet Nelson has
stressed that, although women were excluded from the formal religious
and political authority most often associated with literacy, they still participated in the culture of literacy.[1] June McCash has similarly argued
that noblewomen overcame socio-cultural obstacles to participate in
cultural patronage in the various literary, religious, artistic and poetic
fields.[2] Elisabeth van Houts confirmed the importance of female patrons
of historiography, and their role as repositories of family history and
in the instruction of their sons, and more importantly their central
role in the creation of social memory.[3] Susan Groag Bell traced a tradition whereby medieval noblewomen were important as cultural ambassadors and in the literary education of their daughters.[4] The importance
of female patronage in providing distinctive, innovative forms of literature is an important element in Lois Huneycutt's reassessment of the
cultural patronage of Queen Matilda, wife of Henry I.[5] Huneycutt and
McCash argue that relations between noblewomen and churchmen were
one way that women could enact strategies to achieve their own objectives. Pauline Stafford emphasised the political context of late eleventh
and early twelfth-century royal female patronage to argue that female
patrons could manipulate the images portrayed, including the image of
their male kin.[6]

Thus the recent historiography on medieval women and literacy
stresses ways in which women participated in literary culture as a way
of pursuing their own strategies. In the context of the twelfth-century
evidence, the following discussion of women's participation in spiritual
relationships with churchmen argues that this was an important route
for male–female interaction, and that this stimulated the production of

devotional literature written for specific women. Thus such relationships between churchmen and noblewomen were a route for indirect female influence in the context of the production of specific texts. The role of twelfth-century secular noblewomen in procuring, commissioning and selecting literature is further developed in an examination of their role as patrons of books and literature.

Women and literature: letters, prayers and poems

Women participated in personal relationships with churchmen. For example, Eva Crispin (d. 1099), who retired to the abbey of Le Bec, treated the brother of Gilbert Crispin as her spiritual son. A relationship such as this probably involved spiritual guidance and counselling as well as practical advice and support. Margaret, Queen of Scotland, adopted Lanfranc as her 'spiritual father' c. 1070–89,[7] and Lanfranc wrote to her to express his joy at accepting the role. Queen Margaret had requested Lanfranc to send her some monks; in his letter he states that he was sending three, who were, in effect, on loan. The monks, he states, are 'really indispensable' in his church, and this statement, no doubt, served to flatter the queen, since he had sent her men of ability. Further, if she was willing, he wanted them returned at a later date. They were clearly to give her practical support and advice concerning her establishment of Holy Trinity, Dunfermline.[8] Thus a spiritual relationship could take a very practical form. The patronage of the church was intrinsic to aristocratic culture, and royal women were often involved in patronage of not only the fabric of the buildings through grants of land and emoluments but also interior furnishings, books and relics.[9] For example, Countess Judith of Flanders presented a fine crucifix to Durham and sacred relics and objects of art to the abbey of Weingarten, including a relic of the holy blood that she had inherited from her father.[10] Queen Matilda, the wife of the Conqueror, gave a richly decorated chasuble to the monks of Saint-Évroul, and Adeline, the wife of Roger of Beaumont, gave them an 'alb richly ornamented with orphrey'.[11] Queen Matilda, the wife of Henry I, established an Augustinian house of canons, patronised other religious institutions and made personal gifts of bronze candlesticks to Hildebart of Lavardin and Cluny.[12] She provided Chartres with two bells and Westminster Abbey with liturgical garments.[13]

Queen Matilda received a letter and prayer composed for her by Bishop Herbert Losinga of Norwich in 1118.[14] The prayer to St John is a lyrical plea for healing and health, for the saint to act as an intercessor for the forgiveness of sins and for Matilda to be given to the protection of the Virgin Mary. Given that Matilda died in May 1118, it is possible that the prayer was composed for her in the context of illness. The choice for the direction of this prayer is interesting, since St John was a virgin, and this is stressed within the prayer. The virgin John was a suitable intercessor with the supreme Virgin – the Virgin Mary. Herbert, when composing the prayer, would have carefully selected appropriate imagery befitting a queen. The fruit of Queen Matilda's artistic and literary connections, the letters and literature which survive, served to 'create an aura of legitimacy and prestige' in her position as queen.[15] Spiritual counsel could be an important part of the relationship between leading churchmen and important political women such as the queen, or powerful countesses. The relationship between important noblewomen and clerics thus stimulated the production of letters and spiritual texts. A critical re-evaluation of these texts could begin to trace the developing discourse of twelfth-century female spirituality in the particular context of prescriptive spirituality for the recipient in her public role as queen. The cultivation of a spiritual relationship could yield political dividends and it could thus be used to influence political events of significance.[16] Thus spiritual relationships were an expression of aristocratic social cohesiveness and a route whereby women could exert power.

An impressive illustration of these themes is provided by Adela of Blois, the daughter of William the Conqueror, and Matilda, who married Stephen count of Blois (d. 1102). Adela was a keen patron of the arts. As Elisabeth van Houts pointed out, she was a patron of the poet Godfrey of Rheims, who, in 1080–5, wrote to Adela praising her as a *regia virgo*, a royal virgin.[17] Godfrey wrote that it was God's will that William had been successful at Hastings, since Adela was then born the daughter of a king instead of a duke.[18] Hugh of Fleury dedicated his *Historia Ecclesiastica* to her. He praised her for her literacy, generosity and intelligence.[19] Adela had also received the *Flowers of Psalms* and seven prayers selected by Anselm at her request. He also sent some prayers that he had composed for her. These were a decisive break with previous traditions in personal prayer, and marked a significant step in the development of the Anselmian revolution in the composition of texts for personal devotion. He also included advice on how to meditate.[20]

The relationship between Adela and Anselm was of both a political and a spiritual, personal nature. Eadmer reveals that it was Adela who played a pivotal role in resolving a dispute between her brother Henry and Anselm in 1105 at the height of the conflict between them. Eadmer informs us that she sent to Anselm to tell him that she was ill and he diverted to minister to her. She was appalled to hear that her brother was about to be excommunicated and arranged a meeting between Anselm and Henry at which they resolved their differences for good.[21] Her illness was probably a pretext to divert Anselm to her court, where she could influence him.[22] Adela was a peacemaker in the dispute between her brother and the exiled archbishop of Canterbury, and arguably she acted to care for her brother's soul in a familial context. However, the resolution of the dispute is also of political significance, and here Adela's actions assume a wider context, since she used her informal influence, which was strengthened through a spiritual relationship, to resolve a political dispute. There is a further dimension to the fact that Anselm diverted to see Adela on hearing that she was ill. Evidently his role as a spiritual adviser involved an obligation for the care of her soul to attend her in the case of serious illness to prepare Adela for death.

This network of spiritual guidance and social intercourse was normal and part of the culture of aristocratic and noble women – indeed, the women of the Conqueror's family were particularly prominent as patrons.[23] Adela attracted the attention of important clergy who were keen to foster relations with her. For example, Baudri abbot of Bourgueil (1079–1130) wrote a poem of 1,367 lines for Adela which describes the furnishings and rich decorations of her hall and bedchamber.[24] It used to be thought that the rich visual imagery and the detail in his descriptions were suggestive of a personal relationship between Adela and Baudri, and that he might have visited her palace.[25] However, Shirley Ann Brown and Michael Herren have cast doubt on this assumption in their comparison of the Bayeux Tapestry itself with the descriptions of the tapestry which Baudri purports to have seen hanging in Adela's chamber, which historians have assumed was the Bayeux Tapestry.[26] Whether or not Baudri visited Adela, the poem is significant, since it illustrates what an important abbot thought was a suitably flattering description to offer an important woman, as well as providing clues about the material culture of an aristocratic secular woman. It also illustrates the range of cultural influences in northern France, and significantly Baudri emphasised the role of Adela in the design and creation of tapestries.[27] Firstly, he described a role which women of Adela's status undertook, that is, to oversee and direct the women who made cloth and designed tapestry, and, secondly, he flattered her artistic skills.

Baudri's relationship with Adela was not unique: he wrote poetry and obituaries for other women, although none of such length and detail as those to Adela.[28] He wrote to Adela's sister, Cecilia, a nun at Holy Trinity, Caen, as well as to a certain Agnes, a Lady Emma and

Beatrice.[29] He also wrote to Constance, his spiritual daughter, who had received her education at the convent of Le Ronceray in Angers, and who replied to his poetry.[30] He composed poetry for Muriel, who was likewise at Le Ronceray and from whom he received poetry in return.[31]

Anselm was therefore not alone in the way that he fostered relationships with powerful women. Eadmer reveals that on one journey Anselm was delayed and entertained by Countess Ida of Boulogne, when he 'conferred' with her.[32] According to Sally Vaughn, Ida was his 'closest and most intimate confidante, student, spiritual daughter and political ally', with whom he corresponded until his death.[33] Powerful women were worth cultivating: Matilda countess of Tuscany provided him with an escort whilst he was passing through her lands on his way from Rome in 1104. Anselm afterwards sent her a complete copy of his *Prayers* and *Meditations* which was made and illustrated for her at Canterbury: a step which again confirmed the shift from private meditation to public consumption of his devotional literature. Wilmart argues that the letters and prayers date from *c.* 1104, and that Anselm praised Matilda for her prudence; he informed her that her people had taken him on a short safe route, and he praised her for her religious patronage and urged her to take the veil when the moment of death arrived. This is good evidence of the importance of the involvement of a secular noble woman in cross-cultural exchanges, and shows Matilda's importance in her cultural, religious and political activities. It is also worthy of note that Anselm urged her to take the veil only at the moment of death, not before.[34]

Other churchmen dispensed spiritual advice to women throughout the twelfth century, for example through the medium of hagiography. The study of *Vitae* has been an area of increased scholarly interest, and the meaning of saints and saints' cults has likewise received considerable attention, as has women's mysticism and spirituality.[35] Despite the hagiographic convention and the Christian didactic purpose of saints' lives, they are valuable sources which can be used to study aspects of noblewomen and power in twelfth-century society, although such a project has its own methodological difficulties. Indeed, Jocelyn Wogan-Browne discussed three female-authored twelfth-century *Vitae* and showed the specific problems inherent in recovering women's experience from hagiographic sources.[36] The twelfth-century *Vita* of Christina of Markyate has been studied for its value as a source for twelfth-century female religious.[37] Thomas Head, however, analysed the *Life* in terms of the socio-cultural contexts of twelfth-century developing notions of marriage. He stressed the power of Christina to seize control over her own life to become 'a primary actor in the drama of her own salvation'.[38] Her difficult adolescence where she was in fear of marriage is a *topos* typical in *Vitae* of female saints.[39] Yet the female life cycle can be seen as paramount in defining Christina's options, since Christina became secure in her vocation only once her childbearing years were over.[40] Other *Vitae* confirm that social and spiritual relationships were important forms of male–female interaction and collaboration. The *Life of St Hugh of Lincoln* by Adam of Eynsham was written as part of the campaign for Hugh's canonisation.[41] It depicts a courtly political bishop attending to the spiritual needs of his flock, including, for example, 'devout matrons' and the bereaved Queen Berengaria following the death of Richard I, and adjudicating in cases of adultery.[42] More interestingly, women's voices can be detected as witnesses to his sanctity. A significant number of those who testified to miracle cures were women; of twenty-nine individuals who are listed as having been cured of some affliction by miracles eighteen were women.[43] In this respect this 2 : 1 pattern of imbalance in women : men miracle cures is a phenomenon that applies to other twelfth-century saints.[44] Women's testimony and role as sources of information on the saint are therefore one way in which they could influence the shape and content of the text. Georges Whalen has shown that in Goscelin's *Life* of Edith statements of women's theological equality in Christ were employed where women were the majority of witnesses to allay fears about the validity of female witnesses. No such statements were required for male witnesses.[45] Women were prominent as witnesses, and thus in the creation of social memory, in John of Ford's *Life* of Wulfric of Haslebury, a parish priest turned anchorite in rural Somerset who died in 1154. These witnesses included women from the nobility, five local anchoresses and village women.[46] The *Life* also depicts social interaction between the anchorite and women, as well as spiritual advice and relationships.[47]

The dispensation of spiritual advice could be achieved through social/spiritual interaction, and also through letters. Peter of Blois wrote to the archdeacon of Picardy that his niece Alice should not be forced to become a nun, but in a later letter to her he congratulated her on her choice of vocation.[48] In the mid-twelfth century Amice countess of Leicester received a letter from Gilbert Foliot. Writing c. 1163–68, he apologises for being unable to visit her, owing to his duties and obligations, and states that he ought to have written to her before.[49] Gilbert Foliot was also in correspondence with her husband Earl Robert (II) of Leicester (d. 1168) in the same period, which suggests that the extant letters were sent together but were intended for each individual separately.[50] These socially exclusive circles of friendship, cultivated through spiritual relationships, reinforced aristocratic and noble social and political cohesion.[51] Noblewomen, as part of the landed élite, actively participated in such relationships.

Women as patrons: the high nobility

Noblewomen exerted power and influence through patronage. They were involved in the production and patronage of the written word not in only a personal/spiritual context, through personal letters and charters, but also through other forms of literature such as poetry, histories and literature. They were patrons for political, religious, personal and familial, educational and cultural reasons.[52] This tradition of female involvement with literacy, books and book production can be seen in the Carolingian period, and continued into the late Middle Ages.[53] In this context it is high-status women who are most visible, and this may well reflect the cost of books and also their access to resources.[54] A striking example of a rich patron of book production is Countess Judith of Flanders, who acquired at least two illuminated gospels from Winchester, and whose library contained at least two other manuscripts possibly of Flemish origin. Her daughter-in-law, Countess Matilda of Tuscany, received a copy of Judith's book as a wedding gift in 1086, and she may have presented it to her favourite abbey.[55] Judith and Matilda had royal connections, and this tradition of royal women's patronage of books continued into the twelfth century. In twelfth-century England and Normandy it is significant that women had a role in the patronage of innovative forms of literature which affected the development of secular literature. Royal women or women of high status were in the vanguard of patronising these new forms of literature.

As discussed earlier, Adela of Blois was a patron of poets, and writers were able to articulate a positive image of lay women as readers. Hugh of Fleury in the dedication of his *Ecclesiastica Historia* praised Adela's generosity, intelligence and literary skills, and stated that women were often capable of acquiring such capabilities. He illustrates this theme with a biblical passage where women seated at the feet of Christ understood His teaching better than Pharisees and Saducees.[56] Adela's sister-in-law, Queen Matilda, commissioned the *Life* of her mother, Queen Margaret of Scotland.[57] Queen Margaret's granddaughter, Matilda countess of Boulogne, commissioned the *Vita* of her maternal grandmother, Ida countess of Boulogne.[58] Queen Matilda also requested that the poem 'The Voyage of St Brendan' should be translated into French.[59] It is possible that Anselm was involved here, since it appears that a certain Brendan left the abbey of Bec with Gilbert Crispin in the service of Anselm. He may well have been introduced to Anglo-Norman courtly circles c. 1085. 'The Voyage of St Brendan' is a description of the life of St Brendan. Although it is not a hagiographic piece it was immensely popular, and over 120 versions survive.[60] It is the earliest surviving example of a poem in octosyllabic form, and prefigured romance literature.[61] It is a Celtic version of the classical odyssey poem, a well worn literary theme, and thus possibly particularly popular at the Anglo-Norman court, given eleventh-century Norman expansion into England, Wales and Sicily as well as the recent preaching and popular response to the first Crusade.[62] Thus Queen Matilda patronised a poet who was not only experimental and at the vanguard of creativity with fictional forms but who could provide the court with a cosmopolitan and exciting travel story. It was possibly part of her duty to provide courtly entertainment.[63] Her cultural patronage was extensive and included the acquisition of genealogies.[64] It was Matilda who asked William of Malmesbury to write *The Deeds of the Kings of England*.[65] Henry I's second wife, Adeliza of Louvain, likewise had an appetite for new literary styles. She was a patron of Philippe de Thaon, who dedicated a bestiary to her, the oldest surviving example in the French language.[66] She commissioned a life of Henry I which is unfortunately now lost. The tradition of royal women's patronage continued under Eleanor of Aquitaine and her daughter by the French king Louis VII, Marie countess of Champagne, for whom Chrétien de Troyes wrote *Lancelot* and *Chevalier de la Charette* between 1177 and 1181.[67] She also features holding court in Andreas Capellanus's *De Amore*, composed in 1183–86.[68]

Women as patrons: the lesser nobility

There is evidence that secular women of the lesser nobility patronised writers and poets, actively fostered the production of books and were themselves literate. In the mid-twelfth century Constance, the wife of Ralph fitz Gilbert (of an old Lincolnshire family), was a patron of the poet Gaimar, who wrote his *L'Estoire des Engleis* in 1135–50. He tells us that Constance bought 'for one silver mark burnt and weighed', and frequently read 'in her chamber', a copy of the now lost *Life of Henry I*, which had been commissioned by Henry's second wife, Adeliza of Louvain, after his death in 1135.[69] Gaimar evidently thought that the *Life of Henry I*, a panegyric, was dull and suggested that the author, David, should include some material about feasts, 'love and gallantry, of woodland sports and jokes'.[70] This is interesting, since it illustrates that Constance read and reread material which Gaimar considered devoid of the positive virtues of courtly life. It also perhaps indicates a certain professional rivalry: Gaimar made an implied threat that David ought to 'amend his book' or 'I will go for him'.[71] Legge, however, points out that Gaimar had included such material in his *Estoire*, and indeed goes so far as to suggest that the inclusion of such material was directly related to the fact that he wrote for a female patron and thus described household furnishings and included details such as the wooing of Æthelfryth by King Edgar.[72] Other twelfth-century writers likewise included fables and stories.[73] Yet Gaimar wrote of Æethlfryth when her reputation within England was in decline. He portrayed Æthelfryth as a romantic heroine who seduced King Edgar, and as such he 'dehistoricised' his subject.[74] He portrayed her in romance style and thus utilised a stereotypical view of Æthelfryth's sexual power as the cause of the downfall of King Edgar. Within this misogynistic framework she is accorded the power to choose, act and effect events. Gaimar wrote for a female lay patron whose tastes accorded with the contemporary fashion. It is hard to assess whether Gaimar shaped his material to suit the taste of a female reader and it is difficult to assess whether Constance had an influence on the content of Gaimar's *Estoire*. Gaimar wrote to entertain and in the romance genre, and although some of his figures are without doubt fabrications, he wrote using images and words to which his audience could relate. Indeed, John Gillingham goes so far as to suggest that Gaimar articulates an alternative and secular set of values to puritanical monastic authors.[75] Elisabeth van Houts finds the issue of female patronage to be important and considers that female influence affected the tone and content of contemporary writers such as Henry of Huntingdon.[76]

Constance acquired a copy of Geoffrey of Monmouth's *Historia Regum Britanniae* and commissioned Gaimar to translate it for her into Anglo-Norman from the Latin. Gaimar states that Constance 'sent to Helmsley' for a copy of the *Historia Regum*. Walter Espec had a copy at his castle in Helmsley in 1153, and had asked Robert of Gloucester for a copy, and subsequently lent it to Ralph fitz Gilbert. Constance borrowed it 'Of her lord, whom she loved much'.[77] The impetus for the process of translating the *Historia Regum* thus came from Constance, and it was she who sent for the copy to borrow. It is clear that her husband borrowed the book on her behalf but that the key initiative was hers. Both Legge and Gransden ascribe the enterprise to her husband, yet clearly it was Constance's. The important conclusion that is offered by this evidence points to the active involvement of noblewomen in patronage of the written word, but also illustrates that a noblewoman such as Constance had her own policy and could take her own initiatives in selecting which text to acquire. It is clear therefore that she could exercise her own choice and enact a strategy, in short utilise her power as a lay patron.

The dedications of many historical works reveal that women were important patrons of historiography, and some women, usually abbesses, composed history.[78] Secular women who commissioned historical works did so as part of their role in the preservation of *memoria*, the commemoration of the dead.[79] As such they also participated in the creation of social memory, as part of the broader process by which 1066 was remembered.[80] Constance too can be considered to have had a taste for history. Her choice, Geoffrey of Monmouth, was very much in vogue in the Angevin world, and thus she was innovative in her choice of literary acquisition. With King Henry II on the throne it can have done her and her family no harm to have a poet such as Gaimar adding to her reputation as a member of a family of taste and discernment, the implicit message behind his statement that she was particularly fond of the *Life* of Henry II's grandfather. The alleged lack of fanciful material and anecdotes in the *Life* therefore reflects on Constance as courtly, serious, interested in history, and cultured. As a noblewoman in twelfth-century Lincolnshire she had an interest in literature, was perhaps literate herself, and exercised her cultural patronage with political astuteness. Yet her role may well have gone beyond that of active patron but passive consumer of the written word. Gaimar states that before he could finish the translation of the *Historia Regum* he had 'procured many copies' of English books and books on Latin and French grammar. He goes on to say that

> If his lady had not helped him,
> Never by any day could he have finished it.[81]

It is unlikely that this is merely idle flattery of his patron's learning. His statement goes beyond the literary *topos* of most writers, in which they usually avowed protestations of humility in their prologues, since most writers were only too happy to declare their industriousness if not their skill.[82] Thus Gaimar may well be revealing the active hand of his patron in the translation process. Other noblewomen may also have been literate. Although clerics often bemoaned the general level of literacy in secular society, it is clear from a letter of Adam of Perseigne to the countess of Chartres that she had learned Latin.[83] Some secular women of the nobility at least could read in a language other than the vernacular. This is important, since it shows that not all secular noble-women were excluded from a knowledge of Latin, the language of much law and learning in the twelfth century.

Geoffrey of Monmouth was among the most fashionable contemporary writers to endure in popularity beyond the twelfth century. Over 200 copies of his works survive, over two-thirds from the Continent, and they were translated into Welsh, Old English and Anglo-Norman. He was used as an authentic and reliable source by historians in France, Normandy, including Robert of Torigny, and England. Only one of his contemporaries writing in England in the mid-twelfth century, William of Newburgh, was critical. Ambiguity best characterises the attitude to Geoffrey of Gerald of Wales, who both relied upon and doubted Geoffrey's truthfulness.[84] Geoffrey's *Historia Regum*, whilst fictitious and of dubious methodology, is nevertheless peppered with positive images of women in power. Gransden states that Geoffrey was a 'romance writer' who was 'masquerading as a historian' and whose writings 'reflect contemporary ideas and institutions'. Geoffrey praises women rulers, shows the calamity of disputed succession and illustrates succession by inheritance.[85] Julia Crick suggests that Geoffrey was 'not inventing freely, but picking the spoils of the post-Conquest degeneration of the Celtic Epic'.[86] This contrasts with Peter Noble's view that neither writers nor audience in England were interested in Celtic material.[87] Noble also states that the idealisation of women likewise held no interest for English writers and audiences. Crick suggests that the success of Geoffrey of Monmouth's *History* lay in the fact that, as a fictional form, it entertained and amused society. It also had a functional role in expounding the values that Geoffrey admired.[88] The depiction of women within those values is central to the unfolding of the central narrative. Geoffrey's positive message that women can and did rule successfully may in part account for his popularity with a female readership such as Constance. Geoffrey was in tune with society's values – hence his popularity. The relationship between author and patron is complex but undoubtedly authors such as Geoffrey wrote to please their patron. The reception and circulation of the *Historia* suggest that he was different, and the *Historia*'s popularity is testimony to the appeal of its many images, including the portrayal of women. The political context is striking. Geoffrey's positive images of female rulership were constructed at precisely the time when such images were required by the Angevin cause. Geoffrey wrote in 1136–37, when the empress, who did not land until 1139, had yet to begin pressing her claim. The women who rule in the *Historia Regum* do so in specific contexts and under certain conditions, but are portrayed as powerful nonetheless.

Geoffrey's view of women is varied and gives an insight into the ideal roles of women in society. Powerful women usually act in a specific familial context. For example, Geoffrey creates a fictional female ruler, Marcia, and ascribes to her the creation of (Offa's) Mercian law code.[89] She is the mother of the heir to the kingdom, who was under age. She ruled as a powerful widow in the stead of a minor and after her death her son took over. Thus she is situated within a family context, ruling for her son. Women in contemporary society were at the most powerful stage of the female life cycle as widows, so Geoffrey here draws on a cultural norm to reinforce his message because Marcia's situation as a widow was one with which secular society could identify.[90]

Happy marriages feature in Geoffrey, for example the daughter of Claudius was happily married and he ordered the town of Gloucester to celebrate the fact.[91] In choosing Gloucester as the location of this happy marriage Geoffrey no doubt flattered his patron. Geoffrey shows how women could be schooled in the skills necessary to govern a kingdom in the example of Helen, who was instructed by her father in the liberal arts so that she could govern the kingdom.[92] This again may well have struck a resonant note in the Gloucester household, given the political context of the association of the empress with her father, Henry I. Even so, Helen, although trained to rule, is also endowed with outstanding beauty, and fulfils her function by marrying and producing a male heir to the kingdom.

Yet Geoffrey's women could in fact be cruel and as vicious as any male character. He recites the tale of Gwendolen and Estrildis. Locrinus, one of the three sons of Brutus, the mythical founder of Britain, after defeating one of his brothers in war, reserved for himself the spoils of war, which included Estrildis, a native princess. Geoffrey provides a lyrical description of her beauty, a standard *topos* to praise women in all literary forms of the period, and states that Locrinus wanted to marry her. This caused concern to his followers, since he was already promised to Gwendolen, the daughter of a powerful follower. He married his betrothed, Gwendolen, but loved Estrildis, so he kept her as his mistress for seven years. Both women became pregnant by him, the legitimate wife doing her duty and producing a male heir, Estrildis, the mistress giving birth to a daughter called Habren. Locrinus then deserted Gwendolen for Estrildis. Gwendolen took to arms against her husband and joined with him in battle, in which Locrinus was killed. Gwendolen then had her rivals Estrildis and her daughter drowned in a river, which was named after Habren – and became known as the river Severn.[93] Geoffrey may have included this local detail to please his patron in situating the story so close to the Gloucester heartland and the information may have been given to Geoffrey by oral sources. After the death of her husband Gwendolen ruled for fifteen years until her son came of age and then *sceptro regni insiginivit illum contenta regione Cornubie dum reliquum vite duceret*.[94] Gwendolen is most powerful as a widow and rules successfully for her son until he is of age to assume power for himself.

Geoffrey of Monmouth also provides the earliest version of the story of King Lear.[95] The most striking aspects of the development of this story are the values and familial context in which the daughters of Lear act. The role of the daughters in maintaining family social relations is one important aspect which contemporary society may well have endorsed, particularly the emphasis on the proper maintenance of the dignity of the father by his daughters at their court, which was expressed through the maintenance of paid retainers. When Lear has only one retainer left, owing to the refusal of his elder daughters to pay for more, he decides to fall on the mercy of his youngest daughter. She refuses to receive him at her court until he is properly dressed and with a suitable retinue and sends him away with the means to procure appropriate equipment, retainers and clothing. Clearly his impoverishment would reflect poorly on her dignity at her court.[96]

It is hard to measure the reception of positive images of women, but, given her acquisition of a copy of Geoffrey's *Historia*, it is likely that they appealed to noblewomen such as Constance. She may have been a relation of Alice de Condet,[97] the patron of Sanson de Nantuil, who translated the Proverbs of Solomon into French verse for 'a distinguished and beautiful lady' in the mid-twelfth-century. He inscribed the name of his patron in his prologue. Again, it is striking that a lay noblewoman patronised new forms of literature: the *Proverbs* was the first moral textbook in the French language. The book was produced for educational use at home, possibly under the guidance or tutelage of his mother.[98] This shows that the choice of subject matter could be at the discretion of the mother and is indicative of the possible choices that noblewomen could make in deciding the content of instructive texts for their children.[99] Kindred networks such as this acted as vehicles for women's cultural patronage, and matrilineal patronage is now generally accepted as important.[100]

It is also noteworthy that Alice ensured that her son was taught in French. It is possible that books of hours were the most popular choice for lay women in twelfth-century Europe, and indeed women may have directly influenced the images that were portrayed in them.[101] Aristocratic and noble women continued to procure books and manuscripts throughout the twelfth and thirteenth centuries. Matthew Paris wrote a book of verse for the countess of Winchester c. 1240. He wrote a *Life of St. Edward* for Eleanor of Provence, the wife of Henry III; for Isabel countess of Arundel he arranged a loan of a copy of the *Life of St Thomas* (c. 1250) which was destined for the countess of Cornwall.[102]

Noblewomen's cultural patronage of literary forms was one legitimate avenue for the exercise of power. Thus women's acquisition of books, historiography, genealogies, prayers, poems and saints' lives was an important channel of political, religious and social influence. Their relations with churchmen produced personal devotional literature. These relationships demonstrate how spiritual advice was only one sphere of male–female interaction. It was possible for women, through their oral testimony, to exert influence in shaping the reputation and literary form of the saint's life. Female patronage of literature may well have affected the popularity of texts such as Geoffrey of Monmouth, and noblewomen were in the vanguard of patronising new literary forms. Further it is possible that some noblewomen were not merely passive commissioners of such work; the examples of Alice de Condet and Constance fitz Gilbert show that some twelfth-century women of the nobility were able to read and participate in the production of literature. As such they were able to exert lasting cultural influence as well as influence in contemporary society.

Notes

1 J. L. Nelson, 'Gender and genre in women historians of the early Middle Ages', *L'Historiographie médiévale en Europe* (Paris, 1991), p. 150.

2 J. McCash, 'The cultural patronage of medieval women: an overview', in J. H. McCash (ed.), *The Cultural Patronage of Medieval Women* (Athens GA: University of Georgia Press, 1996), pp. 1–49.

3 E. M. C. van Houts, *Local and Regional Chronicles* (Typologie des Sources du Moyen Âge Occidental, fasc. 74, Turnhout, Belgium, 1995), pp. 40–2; *eadem, Memory and Gender in Medieval Europe, 900–1200* (Basingstoke: Macmillan, 1999), pp. 137–45. Van Houts's stress on male–female collaboration confirms my view that gender was decisive in shaping both the form and content of our sources, and male–female interactions were normal and an accepted part of social relations among male clergy and secular noblewomen. Such relationships represented more than one-way male-to-female spiritual guidance, but were a route for, among others things, the exertion of female cultural and political influence.

4 S. Groag Bell, 'Medieval women book owners: arbiters of lay piety and ambassadors of culture', *Signs: Journal of Women in Culture and Society*, 7: 4 (1982), 742–68, repr.

M. Erler and M. Kowaleski (eds), *Women and Power in the Middle Ages* (Athens GA and London: University of Georgia Press, 1988), pp. 149–87, esp. p. 179.

5 L. Huneycutt, ' "Proclaiming her dignity abroad": the literary and artistic network of Matilda of Scotland, queen of England 1100–18', in McCash (ed.), *Cultural Patronage of Medieval Women*, pp. 155–74.

6 P. Stafford, 'The portrayal of royal women in England, mid-tenth to mid-twelfth centuries', in Parsons (ed.), *Medieval Queenship*, pp. 143–67, at p. 167.

7 *The Letters of Lanfranc, Archbishop of Canterbury*, ed. H. Clover and M. Gibson (Oxford: Clarendon Press, 1979), pp. 160–3 (no. 50). For Eva Crispin see *ibid.*, pp. 100–3 (no. 20).

8 *Ibid.*, p. 161 (no. 3).

9 L. Huneycutt, 'Images of queenship in the high Middle Ages', *Haskins Society Journal*, 1 (1989), 68–9, discusses the patronage of Matilda II, wife of Henry I, and Margaret of Scotland. For examples of the rich gifts of books made by Countess Judith of Flanders see M. Harrsen, 'The countess Judith of Flanders and the library of Weingarten Abbey', *Papers of the Bibliographic Society of America*, 24 pts, 1/2 (1930), 1–13. For women and books in the Middle Ages generally see Bell, 'Medieval women book owners'.

10 Judith married Tostig earl of Northumbria in 1051 and subsequently Duke Welf IV of Bavaria; she died in 1079: Harrsen, 'Countess Judith of Flanders', pp. 2–8.

11 OV, 3. 240–1.

12 Huneycutt, 'Images of queenship', p. 68.

13 Huneycutt, ' "Proclaiming her dignity abroad" ', p. 160.

14 Herbert de Losinga bishop of Norwich, *The Life, Letters, and Sermons of Bishop Herbert de Losinga (b. circ. A.D. 1050, d. 1119): The Letters (as Translated by the Editors) Being Incorporated with the Life, and the Sermons being now first Edited from a MS. in the Possession of the University of Cambridge, and Accompanied with an English Translation and Notes*, ed. E. Meyrick Goulburn and H. Symonds (2 vols, Oxford and London: James Parker & Co., 1878), I, letters no. 25, pp. 298–303, and no. 28, pp. 303–13.

15 Huneycutt, ' "Proclaiming her dignity abroad" ', p. 162.

16 McCash, 'Cultural patronage', pp. 17–18; Huneycutt, ' "Proclaiming her dignity abroad" ', p. 161.

17 E. M. C. van Houts, 'Latin poetry and the Anglo-Norman court, 1066–1135: the *Carmen de Hastingae Proelio*', *JMH*, 15 (1989), 39–62, at pp. 47–8.

18 R. R. Bolgar, *The Classical Heritage and its Beneficiaries* (Cambridge: Cambridge University Press, 1954), pp. 185–6. For the debate on the recipient of this letter see K. LoPrete, 'The Anglo-Norman card of Adela of Blois', *Albion*, 22 (1990), 571, n. 7.

19 Hugh of Fleury positively sings her praises: *Ex Historia Ecclesiastica editio prima libris IIII. digesta*, ed. G. Waitz (Monumenta Germaniae Historica . . . Scriptorum, 9, 1851), p. 345, lines 20–4; for a note on Hugh see A. Gransden, *Historical Writing in England c. 550 to c. 1307* (London: Routledge, 1974), p. 188, n. 8. R. W. Southern, *Saint Anselm and his Biographer: A Study of Monastic Life and Thought, 1059–c. 1130* (Cambridge: Cambridge University Press, 1963).

20 R. W. Southern, *Saint Anselm: A Portrait in a Landscape* (Cambridge: Cambridge University Press, 1990), pp. 92–3, 104.

21 Eadmer, *Historia Novorum in Anglia*, ed. M. Rule (RS, 81, 1884), pp. 164–5; see LoPrete, 'Anglo-Norman card of Adela of Blois', p. 581, who sees this as Anselm's initiative; Southern, *Saint Anselm: A Portrait in a Landscape*, p. 300, however, emphasises Adela's role in effecting the meeting at Laigle between Henry and Anselm which resolved the dispute.

22 Eadmer, *Historia Novorum*, pp. 27–9; see S. N. Vaughn, *The Abbey of Bec and the Anglo-Norman State, 1034–1136* (Woodbridge: Boydell, 1981).

23 Van Houts, 'Latin poetry and the Anglo-Norman court', pp. 45–53.

24 *Les Oeuvres poétiques de Baudri de Bourgeuil (1046–1130)*, ed. P. Abrahams (Paris: Champion, 1926), pp. 196–231. Gransden, *Historical Writing*, pp. 103–4 and n. 108; P. Lauer, 'Le poème de Baudri de Bourgeuil adressé à Adèle, fille de Guillaume le Conquérant et la date de la tapisserie de Bayeux', in *Mélanges d'Histoire offerts à M. Charles Bémont par ses amis et ses élèves à l'occasion de la vingt-cinquième année de son enseignement à l'École pratique des hautes études* (Paris: Alcan, 1913), pp. 43–58.

25 *Les Oeuvres poétiques de Baudri de Bourgeuil*, pp. 103–4.

26 S. A. Brown and M. W. Herren, 'The *Adelae comitissae* of Baudri of Bourgeuil and the Bayeux Tapestry', *ANS*, 16 (1994 for 1993), 55–73.

27 *Les Oeuvres poétiques de Baudri de Bourgeuil*, p. 200, line 104.

28 For his obituaries, *Les Oeuvres poétiques de Baudri de Bourgeuil*, no. 118 (for Elpse, a countess; three lines), no. 127 (for Osanna, countess; ten lines); no. 74 (for Benedicta, a recluse; six lines).

29 *Ibid.*, no. 198 (to Cecilia), no. 200 (to Agnes), nos 201, 215 (to Emma), nos 202–3 (to Beatrice).

30 *Ibid.*, nos 204, 238; for her reply see no. 239.

31 *Ibid.*, no. 199. For personal poetry by women see P. Dronke, *Women Writers of the Middle Ages: A Critical Study of Texts from Perpetua (203) to Marguerite Porete (1310)* (Cambridge: Cambridge University Press, 1984), who points out that none survives from northern France or England, pp. 84–106, esp. p. 97. This conflicts with Tatlock, who thought that the above Muriel was in fact a nun at Wilton in Wiltshire, based on an early twelfth-century entry in Herman of Laon's *De Miraculis* to the effect that some monks on a fund-raising trip to England were shown the grave of Muriel *versificatrix*: J. S. P. Tatlock, 'Muriel: the earliest English poetess', *Publications of the Modern Language Association of America*, 48 (1933), 317–21.

32 Eadmer, *Historia Novorum*, pp. 29–30.

33 S. Vaughn, 'Anselm in Italy, 1097–1100', *ANS*, 16 (1994 for 1993), 245–70, at pp. 251–2.

34 Wilmart, *Auteurs spirituels et textes dévots du moyen âge latin: études d'histoire littéraire* (Paris: Bloud & Gay, 1932). Southern, *Saint Anselm: A Portrait in a Landscape*, pp. 111–12, 163, n. 30. This contact, although not with an Anglo-Norman woman, illustrates Anselm's perceptions.

35 D. Weinstein and R. M. Bell, *Saints and Society: The Two Worlds of Western Christendom, 1000–1700* (Chicago and London: University of Chicago Press, 1982), sets the study of saints in a broad European framework. On pilgrims and pilgrimage see R. C. Finucane, *Miracles and Pilgrims: Popular Beliefs in Medieval England* (London: Dent, 1977); E. A. Petroff, *Body and Soul: Essays on Medieval Women and Mysticism* (New York and Oxford: Oxford University Press, 1994); on the role of gender and the body in defining in medieval religion see C. Walker Bynum, *Holy Feast and Holy*

Fast: The Religious Significance of Food to Medieval Women (Berkeley CA and London: University of California Press, 1987); *eadem, Fragmentation and Redemption: Essays on Gender and the Human Body in Medieval Religion* (New York: Zone, 1991). F. Beer, *Women and Mystical Experience in the Middle Ages* (Woodbridge: Boydell, 1992), studies three medieval mystics: Hildegard of Bingen, Julian of Norwich and Mechtild of Magdeburg; V. M. Lagario, 'The medieval Continental women mystics: an introduction', in P. E. Szarmach (ed.), *An Introduction to the Medieval Mystics of Europe: Fourteen Original Essays* (New York: State University of New York Press, 1984), pp. 161–89, seeks a wider canvas. For twelfth-century England see S. K. Elkins, *Holy Women of Twelfth-century England* (Chapel Hill NC and London: University of North Carolina Press, 1988); for anchoresses see A. K. Warren, 'The nun as anchoress: England, 1100–1500', in J. A. Nichols and L. Thomas Shank (eds), *Distant Echoes: Medieval Religious Women*, I, *Distant Echoes* (Kalamazoo MI: Cistercian Publications, 1984), pp. 197–212. For the functions of a twelfth-century saint see H. Mayr-Harting, 'Functions of a twelfth-century shrine: the miracles of St Frideswide', in H. Mayr-Harting and R. I. Moore (eds), *Studies in Medieval History presented to R. H. C. Davis* (London and Ronceverte: Hambledon, 1985), pp. 193–206.

36 J. Wogan-Browne, ' "Clerc u lai, muïne u dame": women and Anglo-Norman hagiography in the twelfth and thirteenth centuries', in C. M. Meale (ed.), *Women and Literature in Britain, 1150–1500* (Cambridge: Cambridge University Press, 1993), pp. 61–85. Cf., with particular reference to the *Ancrene Wisse*, Bella Millett, 'Women in no man's land: English recluses and the development of vernacular literature in the twelfth and thirteenth centuries', in Meale (ed.), *Women and Literature in Britain*, pp. 87–103; Bella Millett and Jocelyn Wogan-Browne, *Medieval English Prose for Women: Selections from the Katherine Group and* Ancrene Wisse (Oxford: Clarendon Press, 1990).

37 Holdsworth, 'Christina of Markyate', in D. Baker (ed.), *Medieval Women*, Studies in Church History, Subsidia I (Oxford, 1978), pp. 185–204. *The Life of Christina of Markyate: A Twelfth-century Recluse*, ed. and trans. C. H. Talbot (Oxford: Clarendon Press, 1959).

38 T. Head, 'The marriages of Christina of Markyate', *Viator*, 21 (1990), 101.

39 Weinstein and Bell, *Saints and Society*, p. 48.

40 Head, 'Marriages of Christina of Markyate', p. 89, n. 51.

41 Gransden, *Historical Writing*, p. 313.

42 Adam of Eynsham, *Magna Vita Sancti Hugonis: The Life of St Hugh of Lincoln*, ed. D. L. Douie and D. H. Farmer (2 vols, 1961; corrected repr., Oxford: Clarendon Press, 1985), 1. 31–2; 2. 48; 136. See, for an exploration of the role of courtly bishops as 'political instruments', Jaeger, *Origins of Courtliness*, pp. 15, 255. Jaeger's main contention is that romance literature created the chivalric values of the feudal nobility. One significant problem which is not resolved in his treatment of the subject is that of the composition of the court.

43 Hugh Farmer, 'The canonization of St Hugh of Lincoln', *Architectural and Archaeological Society of the County of Lincoln Report and Papers*, new ser., 6: 2 (1956), 86–117, brought together papal letters and sworn testimonies made during the canonisation campaign. The role of women as sworn witnesses would be a fruitful line of enquiry for further research into the incidence of specific illnesses and, for

example, deformities among men and women. For example, in this sample, of the eighteen women, six, or one-third, were cured of paralysis, whereas only one man suffered paralysis; five women were cured of madness, compared with three men – i.e. over 50 per cent of the men were mad, compared with 36 per cent of the women. Likewise there are illnesses which seem to apply only to men or to women, e.g. two men suffered from acute ulcerated tonsillitis (quinsy), which no women suffered, whilst four women suffered from 'dropsy' (inflammation of the body due to fluid retention). Other conditions cured include one case of pleurisy, one of female infertility, two cases of blindness (one male, one female), one boy brought back from the dead, one boy cured of dumbness and one woman cured of a hunch back. This offers a fascinating insight into conceptions of illness, and equally a social map could be drawn to discover which type of person suffered which affliction, since the social status of significant individuals is made clear, e.g. a nobleman cured of madness is listed as a *nobilis*. Equally the social status of sworn witnesses to the alleged cures could be studied to see whose testimony was considered important.

44 Mayr-Harting, 'Functions of a twelfth-century shrine', p. 197.

45 G. Whalen, 'Patronage engendered: how Goscelin allayed the concerns of nuns' discriminatory publics', in L. Smith and J. H. M. Taylor (eds), *Women, The Book and the Godly: Selected Proceedings of the St Hilda's Conference, 1993* (Woodbridge: Brewer, 1995), pp. 128–9. See also van Houts, *Memory and Gender*, p. 51.

46 *Wulfric of Haselbury, by John, Abbot of Ford*, ed. M. Bell (Somerset Record Society, 47, 1933), pp. 38–9. A translation, unfortunately heavily abridged, can be found in *The Cistercian World: Monastic Writings of the Twelfth Century*, ed. P. Matarasso (London: Penguin, 1993), pp. 235–72; a new translation is in preparation by Keith Day for Cistercian Publications.

47 Visits from an important lady: *Wulfric*, chapter 41; gifts of parchment and food from women: *ibid.*, chapters 27, 43, 104.

48 *Petri Blesensis Bathoniensis Archidiaconi Opera Omnia*, ed. J. A. Giles (4 vols, Oxford: I. H. Parker, 1846–47), repr. J. P. Migne, *Patrologiae cursus completus, Patrologia Latina*, 207 (1904), Epistle nos 54, 55; he congratulated her for accepting Christ as her spouse.

49 *The Letters and Charters of Gilbert Foliot, Abbot of Gloucester (1139–48), Bishop of Hereford (1148–63), and London (1163–87)*, ed. A. Morey and C. N. L. Brooke (London: Cambridge University Press, 1967), no. 195, pp. 266–7.

50 *Ibid.*, no. 194, pp. 265–6.

51 J. Haseldine, 'Understanding the language of *amicitia*: the friendship circle of Peter of Celle (*c.* 1115–83), *JMH*, 20 (1994), 260, stresses the importance of such relationships, but does not address the role of women. For a general survey see C. P. McGuire, *Friendship and the Community: The Monastic Experience, 350–1250* (Cistercian Studies, 95, Kalamazoo MI, 1988).

52 McCash, 'Cultural patronage', pp. 20–5; Bell, 'Medieval women book owners', pp. 163–5, 175.

53 Nelson, 'Gender and genre', pp. 150–1.

54 Bell, 'Medieval women book owners', p. 154.

55 Harrsen, 'Countess Judith of Flanders', p. 9.

56 He continues: *Sexus enim femineus non privatur rerum profundarum intelligentia, rerum ut sequenti lectione lucide declaribimus, solet aliquando feminis inesse magna*

mentis industriae et morum probatissimorum elegantia. Hugh of Fleury, *Historia Ecclesiastica*, pp. 345, lines 20–4, 350, lines 12–16.

57 For a discussion of the political significance of this *Life of St Margaret of Scotland* see Huneycutt, 'Images of queenship', pp. 61–72; Stafford, 'Portrayal of royal women', p. 162.

58 Duby, 'Matron and the mis-married woman', pp. 95–6.

59 Van Houts, 'Latin poetry and the Anglo-Norman court', p. 51.

60 *The Anglo-Norman Voyage of St Brendan*, ed. I. Short and B. Merrilees (Manchester: Manchester University Press, 1979) is the most recent translation with parallel texts. The editors state that it is unclear whether Matilda or her successor Adeliza of Louvain commissioned the work but are content to cite a date of 1106–21 for composition, see *ibid.*, pp. 4–5.

61 Legge, *Anglo-Norman Literature*, pp. 9–14.

62 Which refutes Peter Noble's assertion that romance writers were not interested in Celtic material: P. S. Noble, 'Romance in England and Normandy in the twelfth century', in D. Bates and A. Curry (eds), *England and Normandy in the Middle Ages* (London and Rio Grande OH: Hambledon Press, 1994), pp. 69–79.

63 McCash, 'Cultural patronage', p. 23.

64 Nelson, 'Gender and genre', p. 152.

65 Huneycutt, ' "Proclaiming her dignity abroad" ', pp. 157, 164.

66 Legge, *Anglo-Norman Literature*, pp. 22–6.

67 R. Lejeune, 'La femme dans les littératures françaises et occitanes du XIe au XIIIe siècle', *Cahiers de la Civilisation Médiévale*, 20 (1977), 207, lists the prominent women who patronised romance writers in southern France.

68 Andreas Capellanus, *On Love*, ed. P. G. Walsh (London: Duckworth, 1982), p. 3.

69 Adeliza married Henry in 1121 and died in 1151. Gransden, *Historical Writing*, p. 211; Legge, *Anglo-Norman Literature*, p. 28; Weiss, 'Power and weakness of women', pp. 7–23; van Houts, *Memory and Gender*, p. 132.

70 I cite Gaimar, *Lestorie des Engles solum la Translacion Maistre Geffrei Gaimar*, ed. S. Thomas Duffy and C. Trice Martin (2 vols, RS, 91, 1888–89), 2. 205, lines 6510–19. A more recent edition of the text is available in Gaimar, *L'Estoire des Engleis*, ed. A. Bell (Anglo-Norman Text Society, 14–16, 1960). For comments see Gransden, *Historical Writing*, p. 211.

71 Gaimar, *Lestorie des Engles*, p. 205, lines 6522, 6524.

72 Legge, *Anglo-Norman Literature*, p. 36.

73 Gransden, *Historical Writing*, p. 210.

74 Stafford, 'Portrayal of royal women', p. 156.

75 J. Gillingham, 'Kingship, chivalry and love: political and cultural values in the earliest history written in French: Geoffrey Gaimar's *Estoire des Engleis*', in C. Warren Hollister (ed.), *Anglo-Norman Political Culture and the Twelfth-century Renaissance: Proceedings of the Borchard Conference on Anglo-Norman History, 1995* (Woodbridge: Boydell, 1997), p. 57.

76 Van Houts, *Memory and Gender*, p. 132.

77 Gaimar, *Lestorie des Engleis*, p. 203, lines 6446–57. Walter Espec's copy of the *Historia Regum* at Helmsley in 1153: Legge, *Anglo-Norman Literature*, p. 28; Gransden, *Historical Writing*, p. 209.

78 Van Houts, *Local and Regional Chronicles*, pp. 31, 40.

79 Nelson, 'Gender and genre', pp. 151–2.

80 Van Houts, *Memory and Gender*, p. 142.

81 Gaimar, *Lestorie des Engleis*, 2. 203, lines 6444–5.

82 Gransden, 'Prologues in the historiography of twelfth-century England', in D. Williams (ed.), *England in the Twelfth Century: Proceedings of the 1988 Harlaxton Symposium* (Woodbridge: Boydell, 1990), pp. 55–81, reprinted in A. Gransden, *Legends, Traditions and History in Medieval England* (London: Hambledon Press, 1992), pp. 138–9.

83 J. Westfall Thompson, *The Literacy of the Laity in the Middle Ages* (Berkeley CA, 1939, repr. New York: Franklin, 1960), p. 145.

84 Gransden, *Historical Writing*, pp. 206, 246, 262–4.

85 *Ibid.*, pp. 203–6.

86 J. C. Crick, *The Historia Regum Britannie of Geoffrey of Monmouth, IV, Dissemination and Reception in the later Middle Ages* (Cambridge: Brewer, 1991), pp. 223–4.

87 Noble, 'Romance in England and Normandy', p. 76.

88 Crick, *Historia Regum*, p. 224.

89 I cite *Historia Regum Britannie of Geoffrey of Monmouth, I: Bern, Bürgerbibliothek MS. 568*, ed. N. Wright (Cambridge: Brewer, 1985), chapters 45, 31; a convenient translation is available as Geoffrey of Monmouth, *The History of the Kings of Britain*, trans. L. Thorpe (Harmondsworth: Penguin, 1966).

90 Stafford, 'Portrayal of royal women', pp. 145–6.

91 *Historia Regum* I, chapters 69, 44.

92 *Ibid.* I, chapters 78, 51.

93 *Ibid.* I, chapters 25, 15–17.

94 *Ibid.* I, chapters 25, 17.

95 Gransden, *Historical Writing*, p. 203.

96 *Historia Regum* I, chapters 31, 19–22.

97 Legge, *Anglo-Norman Literature*, p. 38. Alice de Condet may be Alice, the sister of Ranulf II earl of Chester, who was married to Richard fitz Gilbert (d. 1136), who remarried Robert de Condet (d. 1140); for the de Condet family see *The Registrum Antiquissimum of the Cathedral Church of Lincoln: Volume 1*, ed. C. W. Foster (Lincoln Record Society, 27, 1931), pp. 277–95.

98 Legge, *Anglo-Norman Literature*, p. 41; available only in an early thirteenth-century manuscript.

99 For a wider discussion of women using texts as instructive texts see Bell, 'Medieval women book owners', pp. 160–5. Janet Nelson states this contrasts with the all-male world of the twelfth-century schools: 'Women and the word in the earlier Middle Ages', in W. J. Sheils and D. Wood (eds), *Women in the Church* (Studies in Church History, 27, Oxford, 1990), pp. 53–78, at pp. 76–7. Yet it may be argued that the schools were for secular clergy – Alice taught her son at home, which was a lay environment, which could reflect different roles of women to educate their children to meet the different needs of society.

100 McCash, 'Cultural patronage', p. 14.

101 Bell, 'Medieval women book owners', pp. 160–5.

102 Gransden, *Historical Writing*, pp. 358–9.

PART II

Noblewomen and power:
the charter evidence

4

Countesses

C HARTERS SHOW that women of comital rank routinely fulfilled administrative roles at various stages in the female life cycle. The focus here is on charter evidence relating to those aristocratic women who were explicitly accorded the title *comitissa*, or else were married to men of comital rank, or were born into such families. Comparison with other high-ranking women is included where appropriate, in order to illustrate the central argument that women's power was constructed through the family in their role as wife or widow, and was thus tied to the female life cycle. Such power, like that of men, was rooted in land tenure.

The definition of categories of women is fraught with problems, yet arguably countesses were a distinct status group.[1] Andreas Capellanus, writing in the late twelfth century, recognised social gradations based on rank and distinguished countesses as a group which he placed amongst the high nobility.[2] Charters relating to the *honor* of Chester demonstrate the formal public power, spheres of influence, land holdings, economic interests, and the religious and cultural roles of the countesses. It will be considered whether they were unusual in the range of roles and functions that they fulfilled. These formal public roles can be explored through an examination of their activity as witnesses, signers, consentors, alienors and co-alienors, which can be related to the gendered functions of wife, mother, heiress or conversely widow or mother of the heir. Each category could define the role of each countess, or more than one could affect her position within the family. The close examination of charters also raises some fundamental problems of the nature of the source material itself, but examples of other powerful countesses who acted in similar roles to those of the countesses of Chester do show useful patterns in the way that women of comital rank exerted power throughout the female life cycle.

The Chester evidence

The earls of Chester were among the greatest nobles of the Norman and Angevin realms, the high political élite of twelfth-century society. Their power was rooted in extensive land holdings in Cheshire and beyond, which by 1086 consisted of land scattered throughout twenty of thirty-four English counties.[3] Two of the most famous, or, more correctly, infamous, earls were Ranulf II (1129–53), whose change of allegiance during Stephen's reign has been often cited as a typical example of the troublesome baronage that bedevilled both Stephen and Matilda, and Ranulf III (1181–1232).[4] The wives, mothers and widows of these powerful figures are the subject of this section.

In the late eleventh century, Earl Hugh I of Avranches married Ermentrude, the daughter of Hugh count of Clermont. Their son and heir Richard succeeded to the earldom of Chester at the age of six on his father's death in 1101. He married Matilda (I), a daughter of Stephen count of Blois, but they were both drowned in the wreck of the *White Ship* on 25 November 1120. Ranulf I 'le Meschin', Richard's first cousin, succeeded to the earldom and he married Lucy, the widow of both Ivo Taillebois and Roger fitz Gerold. Their son Ranulf II 'de Gernons' was earl from 1129 to 1153. He married Matilda, daughter of Robert earl of Gloucester. She outlived Ranulf and his heir, dying in 1189. Their son Hugh II married Bertrada, daughter of Simon count of Evreux, who also outlived her husband and died in 1227. Ranulf III 'de Blundeville', earl from 1181, married twice, first in 1189 Constance, daughter and heir of Conan earl of Richmond and duke of Brittany, widow of Geoffrey Plantagenet, Henry II's third son. They were divorced in 1199. Secondly, he married Clemencia, the widow of Alan de Dinan, a daughter of William de Fougères, which lay to the south of the Chester lands in Normandy, on the borders of Brittany, Maine and Normandy. She survived her husband, dying in 1237.[5] These marriage alliances were diverse. What they have in common is that the women who were married to the earls were of high aristocratic status, Constance of Brittany's marriage marking the twelfth-century apogee in the Chester marriage strategy. More interestingly, and reflective of the disparity of age between men and women at the time of their marriage in the twelfth century, most of the women who married the earls then managed to survive their husbands – and it is during these periods of relative independence that they are most visible.

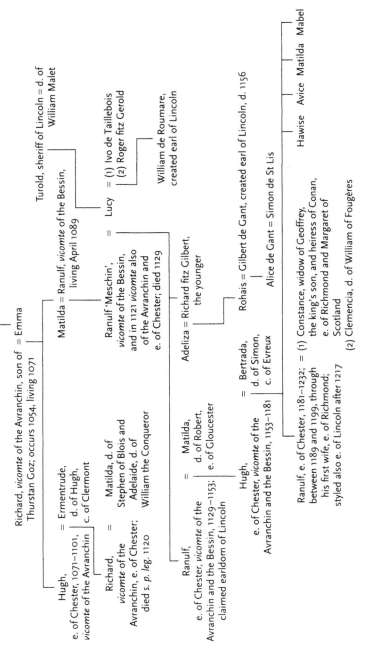

FIGURE 1 The earls of Chester in the eleventh and twelfth centuries

ERMENTRUDE

The earliest evidence relates to the countess Ermentrude. Orderic Vitalis condemned Earl Hugh as a 'slave to gluttony . . . given over to carnal lusts'.[6] Ermentrude's character is not commented upon: it was her pedigree and role as mother of the heir which was important. The charter evidence, however, shows that the role of the countess as wife to the earl was to support his policies, and as mother of the heir to the earldom her role was to support her son. As wife Ermentrude played a consultative role. Of the five extant charters of Earl Hugh, Ermentrude appears in three. A letter to Rainald abbot of Abingdon states that Hugh agreed to grant the land in question only after consulting his wife and barons.[7] Ermentrude clearly participated in the decision-making process of the *honor*; her advice is sought along with the *consilium* of Hugh's barons.[8]

Ermentrude also played a crucial role in the foundation of St Werburgh's Abbey, Chester. The so-called 'Great Charter' of Ranulf II, dated to the early 1150s, reveals that it was Ermentrude who, at the order of her husband, placed the gift of Weston upon Trent on the altar at the public founding ceremony.[9] The importance of such public ceremonies was to secure the grant in memory before the use of written records became routine, yet their precise mechanisms are often obscured in charters where routine formulas were used to convey routine ceremony.[10] The precision of the detail concerning Earl Hugh ordering Ermentrude to place the gift on the altar is unusual, but there are other examples of husband and wife conjointly placing gifts on altars. For example, Jordan Paynel and Gertrude, his wife, c. 1125–35 and Robert de Percy and Agnes, his wife, in 1160–65 symbolically transferred livery of seisin by placing gifts on the altar of the beneficiary.[11] The 'Great Charter' was probably drawn up by the monks of Chester in the period of Hugh II's minority (1153–62), and, although questions have been raised about its diplomatic, the details concerning the role of Ermentrude probably reflect a reliable oral tradition.[12] This was an important occasion; Archbishop Anselm had been involved in the negotiations prior to foundation and witnessed the charter.[13] It was Ermentrude who symbolically enacted the transfer of property on this important public religious occasion.

If the foundation of St Werburgh's was an expression of the cohesiveness of the honorial community created by Earl Hugh in the aftermath of the Conquest, and a focal point for personal loyalty to Earl Hugh,[14] the role of Ermentrude as wife of Earl Hugh is also as a focus of loyalty – her role in the foundation ceremony is doubly important and symbolic. Firstly, she symbolically enacts the transfer of land – the land is passing to the church through the actions of the wife of the earl. Ermentrude was the vessel through which the land became the inheritance of the church and passed into its control, thus she symbolically and practically conveyed a new phase in the ownership of the land. Secondly, she made the gift at the order of her husband, emphasising his power and authority as head of the family, as superior lord, and this emphasises his control over the ceremony. This also indelibly associated her with his authority. Hence there is another dimension to the foundation of the abbey – it could be argued that in fact the foundation is a joint act which demanded the loyalty of Earl Hugh's followers to both him and his wife, who then as countess enacted the donation. Therefore the foundation is a focal point of loyalty to the family acting together in lordship. The familial nature of this endowment was further stressed when both Hugh and Ermentrude gave their bodies for burial to St Werburgh's.[15] If the document was created during Hugh II's minority, the period which saw his mother, Matilda, assume a more powerful role as guardian of the heir and when she co-granted charters with him,[16] then quite possibly the monks of Chester recorded Ermentrude's role with care, since Countess Matilda was the key to ensuring the charter was accepted. As such the monks were emphasising the role of a previous countess to ingratiate themselves with the current dowager countess. Thus recording the role of a previous countess as subservient to, but crucially involved with, their religious patronage of her husband may well have functioned as a model of behaviour appropriate for the wife of an earl. This model of Ermentrude sustained a positive image of female activity on behalf of the monastery which served the purposes of the monks who wished to secure their gift. This was in sharp contrast to the memory of her daughter-in-law Matilda, whom Richard married in 1115. According to later tradition Matilda poisoned Richard's mind against the abbey; he was indeed not a generous benefactor to the abbey and he left the abbacy open for three years prior to his death by drowning in 1120.[17] This is important corroborative evidence of women's counsel. More significantly, it also indicates that monks would expect women to influence the monastic benefaction of their marital family.

Ermentrude's role assumed a new prominence in the affairs of the *honor* when as widow she had an important role to play as guardian of the heir. She conjointly granted a confirmation charter with her son Richard on the day of Pentecost 13 May 1106 in favour of Abingdon.[18] The Abingdon Chronicle states that this charter was issued after Ermentrude and Richard *cum melioribus suorum baronum* were received at the abbey.[19] Abbot Faritius and Ermentrude petitioned Richard to issue the charter, which was then attested with Ermentrude's seal.[20] The chronicler accords Ermentrude a key role in this confirmation. Firstly she and Abbot Faritius acted together to ensure that Richard issued a confirmation charter. Her seal was used to authenticate the charter. Both of these are important, since her role is more than one of support, as Barraclough maintained – it is as mother of the unbelted earl (*nondem militare baltheo cinctus*). This is a rare early reference to a non-royal female seal, the earliest of which dates from *c.* 1136–38.[21] It is also a rare insight into the basis of the power of the mother of the earl. Her seal was important since her son is not yet knighted, and the implication is that this is the reason why he has no seal.

The negotiations behind the eventual confirmation charter are evidenced in the Abingdon Chronicle in a way that the charter alone does not reveal, and thus neatly illustrate one problem of charter evidence, that often the long series of negotiations which they validated and settle are lost. In the text of the charter, which survives only as a cartulary copy, the language used is non-gender-specific. The joint verbs of actions convey a sense of joint comital authority. The ordering of names in the opening clause gives Richard's name first: *Ricardus Cestrensis comes et Ermentrudis comitissa, mater eius* gave greeting to Nigel d'Oilly and Roger fitz Ralph and all the barons of Oxfordshire. The major verbs of action use the plural in simple donation verbs like *concedimus*, and the barons are clearly *nostri baroni*. No sense of female dependence is conveyed, only joint authority. The formal negotiation evidenced in the preamble in the Abingdon Chronicle is left out of the text of the cartulary copy of the charter, possibly because the charter records the basis on which legal claims could later be built. Ermentrude continued to maintain a powerful interest in Abingdon as her status changed from wife to widow – in the context of religious patronage at least, she maintained a continuity in her public role. As mother of the heir Ermentrude clearly had wardship of his body if not his lands, and the sources emphasise that she played an intercessionary role as well as acting with joint authority, since Richard was still a minor. The author of the Abingdon Chronicle felt that the security of the gift was important and included a sealing clause to emphasise her authòrity. If she did acquire a seal she did so when widowed, and this reflects her greater involvement in business. There is no evidence to show whether Ermentrude remarried, and likewise owing to lack of sources it is difficult to know how long she survived Hugh.

An instructive comparison with the case of Ermentrude is that of another high-status noblewoman, Adeliza, the wife of Gilbert fitz Richard (d. 1114 × 1117), who acted with her children to confirm the gift of an undertenant to the church of St Mary's and St Botolph's, Thorney, *c.* 1136–38.[22] This charter shows that Adeliza as mother acted with her sons and daughter: Gilbert, Walter, Baldwin and Rohais were included in the address clause and witnessed the charter. This charter has long been recognised for the genealogical information it reveals, but it is also important in that it shows that Adeliza and her sons and daughters acted conjointly in lordship to confirm an undertenant's grant. Most important of all it shows that Adeliza was using a seal at the relatively early date of 1136–38. There is other evidence of Adeliza's involvement in religious patronage: the cartulary of Thorney records that she gave to Thorney one hide in Raunds (Northamptonshire) at the concession of her son and heir Hervey.[23] The copyist gives the opening address clause as Adeliz a *mater*, with *comitis* added in a later hand. By this concession she was entered into the abbey's confraternity list; in another grant to Thorney she gave 5s worth of rents.[24] This charter was placed upon the altar in token of its security *et scripto sigillato super altare posuit confirmauit*. Adeliza also patronised Castle Acre: in a thirteenth-century cartulary copy of her original grant, given at the concession of her son Earl Gilbert, she is called *quondam uxor* of Gilbert fitz Richard.[25] Mother and son were linked as benefactors of Castle Acre in a conjoint gift where Gilbert fitz Richard and Adeliza gave the tithes of various mills. The cartulary copy of Adeliza's surviving charter is an almost exact rendition of the original wording, suggesting that the second thirteenth-century copy of her *acta* giving her rents at Raunds may also be a reliable copy. This is important because it shows that the status of Adeliza as patron was defined at different times by different address clauses which stress her relationship to her male kin, by different abbeys. She is defined as mother in the majority of her charters, which suggests that this was the empowering role in her life cycle. It also shows that these clauses were variable and flexible, reflective of the changing social position of a widow, since the most important consideration of an abbey was the accurate identification of individual patrons. For noblewomen this could be identification through the marital family, which illustrates the importance of patrimonial kindred structures through marriage in the process of the accurate identification of individuals. When Adeliza co-granted and sealed documents it was her authority that gave the grant validity and security, symbolised by the authentication of her seal.

LUCY

Adeliza's contemporary, the countess Lucy of Chester, was a considerable heiress to land in Lincolnshire.[26] She was married three times and had four children by her various marriages. She outlived all her husbands. Her position as heiress made her an attractive marriage partner. It was as a widow that Lucy was most independent of family control. The 1130 Pipe Roll shows that she fined with the king, paying 500 marks for the privilege of not marrying within five years; she also fined £266 13s 4d for her father's lands and paid all but £100 of this sum. She also paid 100 marks for doing 'right' in her court, indicating that she had control of her court and exercised the rights of lordship when administering her lands.[27]

Lucy managed to further the interests of her favourite religious foundation, Spalding Priory in Lincolnshire, throughout all three marriages. Ivo Taillebois, her first husband, founded Spalding in 1085. During her third marriage, to Earl Ranulf I, she acted as co-alienor in 1123–29, granting to Spalding the churches of Belchford, Scamblesby and Minting, which may have been her inheritance.[28] Lucy as heiress may have maintained some intrinsic interest in their alienation – her consent or involvement in the act was necessary, but the gift probably also reflects her initiative. It was confirmed by Henry I at the request of both Ranulf and Lucy, so here Lucy acted as intercessor in the royal court with her husband. The continuity of her interest is striking. As widow Lucy augmented these gifts to Spalding when in 1135 she granted the manor of Spalding to the monks in free alms as she herself had held it in the time of Ivo Taillebois, Roger fitz Gerold and Earl Ranulf. The precise wording of the charter indicates that Lucy had held the manor herself during all three marriages and that she retained some administrative control, which explains her role as co-alienor when married to Ranulf.[29] The Spalding cartulary shows that Lucy augmented this gift, possibly on the same occasion.[30] In all these charters Lucy is described as *comitissa*. In the charter co-granted with Ranulf she was *Lucia comitissa uxor mea*, and in her widowhood she retained the use of the title. It is significant that public status derived from marriage to an earl was thus retained by his widow.

As the founder of the convent of Stixwould in 1135 Lucy is one of the few aristocratic women of the late eleventh and twelfth centuries to achieve the role of independent lay founder. Her gift was made independent of royal support, thereby differing from earlier foundations made by other powerful widows.[31] A fragment of her foundation charter is still extant.[32] More details of the foundation are provided by a letter to two sons, the half-brothers Ranulf of Chester and William of Roumare, which shows that she granted all her land in Stixwould, Honington and Bassingthorpe.[33] This letter, in which Lucy asks her sons to uphold her gift, superbly illustrates the difficulties associated with the maintenance of a gift after the death of a benefactor and especially the particular problems of female monastic communities.[34] The language in this letter is interesting. Lucy addresses her sons as *karissimis filiis suis*. The writ/letter changes half-way through from standard writ form to an epistolary and an almost emotional appeal. Lucy as mother begs her sons to honour her gift: she stresses that the maintenance of the gift would benefit them all when they were before God. Lucy was able to further her own aims more effectively during her widowhood, exercising greater control of her lands. Like any magnate Lucy attempted to ensure the security of her gift after her death. Thus there is a continuity in her role in religious patronage. As a wife she had used her influence at both the royal court and that of the honour to act as intercessor for Spalding Priory, then as a widow she founded her own religious institution. In the context of religious patronage Lucy shared her husband's comital authority, building on, but not simply restricted to, the interest she had brought to the marriage as an heiress. Husband and wife collaborated in religious patronage through their comital authority. She used this to further her own aims and used her greater powers as widow to reinforce her previous patronage.

MATILDA

Public activity during both marriage and widowhood is also evident within the charter evidence relating to the next countess, Matilda, who was a granddaughter of Henry I by his illegitimate son, Earl Robert of Gloucester, and Mabel, daughter and heir of Robert fitz Haimo. She was thus a niece of the empress Matilda. She was involved in Earl Ranulf II's campaigns of 1141 – acting as the decoy in a ruse by which he seized Lincoln Castle.[35] During her marriage to Ranulf, Matilda witnessed his charters, granted her own, and was a recipient of lands from her father. In 1141–47 she granted a bovate of land in Woolsthorpe (Lincolnshire) to Belvoir Priory, granting the service of Joscelin and his wife. The charter opens with a clause which closely follows that of her husband's practice in which Matilda greets the 'constable, sheriffs, barons, castellans, justices, bailiffs, officials and all men both French and English'. The grant was confirmed by her husband during the same period, probably on the same occasion, as both have the same witness list.[36] Since the grant concerns land that Ranulf had only recently gained during the period after his capture of Lincoln Castle in 1141, the unusual circumstances of the 1140s may well explain this charter. Matilda was granting land acquired thanks to Ranulf's seizure of Lincoln Castle, in which she had played a central role. Matilda's grant of the land to a religious beneficiary may reflect that she had been given some interest in the land by Ranulf, possibly as dower. However, according to Glanvill, a woman had no legal right to claim dower in her husband's acquisition 'if nothing was said about acquisitions when the dower was originally assigned'. Further, Glanvill states, 'It should be known that a woman cannot alienate any of her dower during the life of her husband.' He is silent on the subject of a woman alienating a portion of her husband's acquisitions irrespective of the status of the land in question.[37] It has been pointed out that Glanvill was concerned with the rights of heirs, and that he considered acquisitions more freely alienable 'inside or outside the family'.[38] Matilda's grant suggests that there was more flexibility in the arrangements that families made, irrespective of formal custom.

Out of eight charters which Matilda witnesses, four concern grants made by her husband in favour of ecclesiastical foundations.[39] The other four are *acta* granted by her son during her dowager period, some of which confirm his mother's grants.[40] Matilda participated in, and was associated with, the *honor's* public affairs in a supportive capacity for her husband and son. Matilda also granted land to one of her servants, which indicates her ability to make independent gifts as a wife, although the grant was confirmed by her husband.[41] Matilda also granted a charter in favour of the church of Repton, a grant confirmed by her husband.[42] Ranulf's confirmations resemble those of a lord confirming a vassal's grant to a tenant, which may well therefore have been normal honorial practice. Matilda also conjointly granted with her son a confirmation of a gift made by her husband in favour of Bordesley Abbey in 1153, which was probably granted shortly before Ranulf's death the same year.[43]

Politics impacted upon Matilda's land holding. She received lands in *maritagium* from her father, so resolving a politically sensitive situation. The lands in question near Chipping Campden in Gloucestershire had been part of the Chester land holdings since 1086. Possibly the manor had fallen to Matilda's father, the earl of Gloucester, during the civil wars following the landing of the empress Matilda in 1139.[44] Chipping Campden was a valuable manor, strategically important to both Robert of Gloucester and Ranulf of Chester: the gift to Matilda as part of her *maritagium* was thus used by her father as a way of returning the lands to the control of her husband as part of the traditional *honor* of Chester. Ranulf's charter confirming the gift of Earl Robert to Matilda may also have been the earl's public acceptance of his wife's *maritagium* to resolve a political and familial dispute.

Matilda was a widow for thirty-six years, a considerable period. According to the *Rotuli de Dominabus*, she was more than fifty years old in 1185, yet she must have have been nearer sixty than fifty, since it is possible that she may have been no more than a child when married, and was thus widowed at perhaps only twenty-eight to thirty. In 1185 she had dower in the manor of Waddington worth £22.[45] Matilda is most visible during Hugh's minority, which lasted from 1153 to 1162, which implies that she had a definite public role when acting as representative of the heir. In 1159 the farm of the *honor* was fixed at £294, of which Matilda and her son Earl Hugh were allowed £30, which was subsequently increased to £40.[46] This allowance was part of her dower and implies that, in having wardship of the body of Earl Hugh, for tax purposes they were assessed as one unit. Out of six charters issued by Hugh as a minor, Matilda witnessed four and was a co-alienor with Hugh in two.[47] One of them attempted to repair injuries to the church for which Ranulf II had died excommunicate. Here Matilda was acting to care for her husband's soul. The second is part of Henry II's attempt to normalise relations at the start of his reign.[48] The charter was issued at London in 1155 and Earl Hugh, aged six, was evidently at the great meeting of the important magnates held by Henry II, along with his mother. Matilda functioned in some capacity as his representative, which engendered the right to attend the royal court. It must be noted, however, that the Chester lands were administered by the king's officials, during Hugh's minority, although Matilda had received her dower, since the charter states she is restoring lands from it to Walter of Verdun.[49] Matilda witnessed four charters during her marriage and four as dowager countess. Her own charters reveal the same patterns of participation as wife and widow: she issued six in total, three during marriage and three as a widow. Matilda's earliest charter dates from *c*. 1141–47, whilst Ranulf was still alive.[50] One possibly dates to *c*. 1153, may have been granted when Ranulf was on his deathbed, and confirms Ranulf's grant.[51] The other dates from 1150–4 but may possibly be a charter from her widowhood.[52] Thus possibly two of these charters were granted at a period close to the change in Matilda's status and position that occurred when Ranulf died. This underlines the fact that her power was greatest when she was a widow. The context of the change in power and uncertainties of the new political situation both with the *honor* and the kingdom as a whole is also significant.

As dowager countess Matilda continued to fulfil a religious role as benefactor: during her dowager period she issued three *acta*, all in favour of ecclesiastical foundations. She founded a priory at Repton shortly after Earl Ranulf's death.[53] She stipulated that the convent at Calke should be moved to Repton and that Calke should be subject to Repton. Matilda acquired a seal in the period 1164–72 to authenticate another charter to Repton.[54] In 1172 she endowed Repton with lands in Great Baddow, Essex, that she had received as *maritagium*.[55] As widow she asked for and received permission from her son (who attained his majority in 1162) to augment her previous patronage of Repton in 1164–72.[56] Even as a powerful widow, as a landholder she had to seek permission of her 'lord' to alienate lands that she held by right of *maritagium*. In 1178–81 Matilda was present at the making of a charter in favour of St Werburgh's, along with her daughter-in-law Bertrada and her grandson, the future Ranulf III.[57] Here Matilda was present in her role as dowager countess in the context of a public ceremony of reaffirmation of family support for St Werburgh's. This confirmed the possessions and rights of the abbey, but also confirmed the change in status that occurred to all the family members, both the dowager countesses and the future earl: he was now the future authority in the earldom, and his participation in the confirmation of the previous ancestor's grants was important. It is in the context of religious patronage that Matilda's own policies can be seen: each countess as widow thus fulfilled a socially acceptable public function, which was predicated upon powers to alienate land and marital status.

As with Ermentrude and Lucy, differences in Matilda's role and function occur in matters of degree. This must be related to a change in function from wife to mother of the heir, roles sometimes evidenced within the charters by the titles accorded each countess. In all her charters Lucy is referred to as countess of Chester; thus, despite her position as heiress, she kept the title acquired through her third marriage. Matilda likewise in all charters is entitled *comitissa*, yet when she was present at the making of a charter in favour of St Werburgh's, discussed above, her position in the family was more closely identified, as was that of her daughter-in-law Bertrada. Both are defined by their relation to Earl Hugh. Matilda is *mater comitis*, Bertrada is *B. comitissa sponsa eius*. They precede the heir Ranulf (III) in the list of those named who gave their consent. In her son's charters Bertrada is listed as *comitissa mater mea*. When Bertrada made her convention with Troarn she was Bertrada *relicta comitis Cestrensis*. As a witness her status was defined always as countess, and sometimes in relation to either her husband or her son. Bertrada's example shows that there was little difference in her witnessing activity despite her progression through the female life cycle.

BERTRADA

Bertrada, wife of Hugh of Chester, was, like Matilda, a widow for a considerable period. She was born in 1156, married to Hugh at the age of thirteen in 1169, and widowed at twenty-five in 1181. In 1185 she was recorded as having been allocated dower of the earl of Chester's demesne by Henry II. Both *maritagium* and dower were overseas.[58] She lived until 1227 and died at the age of seventy-one. Thus she was a widow a total of forty-six years. Bertrada, like Matilda and Lucy before her, participated in the affairs of the *honor* during both marriage and widowhood. Yet her role during marriage is less visible in the charter evidence: she appears in only four charters. In 1169 she acted as both witness and petitioner in a grant by her husband to one of her servants of a boat for fishing on the river Dee.[59] She witnessed the important grant of the church of Prestbury to St Werburgh's in the period 1178–81. This was a grand family restatement of public support for this institution, and which was made in the presence of Matilda, Earl Hugh's mother, Bertrada and Ranulf, Hugh's son.[60] Thus all prominent members of the comital family were present. In 1169–73 she witnessed a charter of routine nature when Earl Hugh granted lands to Godfrey, his homager.[61] She was also a witness to a charter of 1178–80 which made a marriage agreement for her husband's illegitimate daughter Amicia. The role of a wife such as Bertrada was to support her husband's policies, and it is possible that she may have had some role in arranging this marriage.[62]

During her forty-six-year period as dowager countess Bertrada issued three charters in her own right. One was in favour of the abbey of Troarn, in Normandy, in which the appearance of her own chamberlain, the son of her husband's chamberlain, indicates that as widow Bertrada maintained her own household.[63] The other grant *c.* 1200–10 to Ralph Carbonel probably concerns lands which she held in dower.[64] There is evidence of another charter issued by Bertrada which has not survived in a confirmation charter of her son in the period 1194–1203 in which Bertrada exchanged lands with the canons of Repton.[65] She also witnessed seven grants by her son.[66]

In the period 1181–89 the coexistence of two dowager countesses, Matilda and Bertrada, who both had claims on the Chester lands through legally held rights to dower of a third, posed a potential threat to the Chester patrimony. The right to dower land did not necessarily entail easy entry to it; indeed, it is hard to discover whether any countess actually received her third.[67] Thus one possible method of avoiding the dispersal of patrimonial lands, as in the case of Bertrada, was to delay the widow's entry to them. Indeed, the lands in Lincolnshire which were used as dower lands were brought to the *honor* of Chester by Lucy, and parts of them, for example Waddington, were granted successively to each countess when widowed.[68] The mould was broken in the marriage between Ranulf III and Constance of Brittany.

CONSTANCE[69]

Constance of Brittany (d. 1201) appears to have had no role within the *honor* of Chester during her tumultuous marriage to Ranulf, which lasted from February 1187–88 until *c.* 1198. The marriage was negotiated at the same time that Ranulf was knighted by Henry II.[70] It was exceptional in that Constance's position as heiress to Brittany made her more than a rich prize for an aspiring prince, if it is accepted that this is how Ranulf viewed himself.[71] Constance was the widow of Geoffrey Plantagenet (d. 1186), mother of Arthur, the heir to Brittany, who was a direct threat to King John. Her marriage to Ranulf and the antagonisms between them symbolised Breton resistance to Plantagenet influence in Brittany: it became a microcosm of wider political antagonisms and rivalries.[72] In 1195–96 Constance was captured by Ranulf and imprisoned by him at the castle of St James sur Beuvron whilst on her way to conclude a treaty with Richard I.[73] Her main interest was her inheritance of Brittany: she played no role within the *honor* of Chester and she pursued her own policies and strategies concerning her inheritance. She supported the claims of her son to the duchy and, as mother, she pursued the dream of her son gaining the Angevin Continental inheritance.[74] Constance was therefore in pursuit of her own political ambition, which she wanted to see realised through her son. It seems that the marriage slowly deteriorated.

Constance and Ranulf were, however, able to put aside their personal antagonisms in the period 1190–95, when they both wrote to Richard bishop of London, asking him to help the canons of Fougères get possession of land in Cheshunt (Hertfordshire). Ranulf's letter was written in support of that of his wife, a rare intervention in the affairs of Brittany.[75] The land in question was of the gift of both Earl Conan, Constance's father, and Constance herself. It was land of her inheritance, which explains both her interest and the fact that she attached her seal to her letter. She was also defined through her father's name and retained the title countess of Brittany and duchess of Richmond even when married to Ranulf. As heiress she maintained an interest in her patrimony. She took those interests with her when she married Guy de Thouars, her third husband, in 1199. It was Constance who possibly started proceedings to repudiate her marriage to Ranulf on the grounds of consanguinity.[76] There is evidence to show that she alienated lands of her inheritance in Richmond shortly before her death in 1201.[77]

CLEMENCIA

Clemencia, the widow of Alan of Dinan, quickly replaced Constance as countess of Chester in September/October 1199. In 1201–4 Ranulf granted a charter in favour of Savigny with her consent.[78] He augmented this gift in 1220–26, again with her consent, since the lands in question were part of her *maritagium*.[79] Married for thirty years, she remained unmarried after the death of Ranulf in 1232 until she died in 1252. She confirmed Ranulf's gifts to Savigny as widow, since the abbey was her favourite foundation.[80] Clemencia had her own seal and counterseal as widow, and this, combined with specific language in her charters, reflects her greater powers of deposition as widow, with the use of phrases such as *in ligia potestate mea* in two of her charters in the period 1233–35 and *tempore viduatatis mee* in her later charter, datable to 1239–52. Such phrases reflect the greater legal definition of a widow's rights which occurred during the thirteenth century.[81] In one charter she revoked a grant made by Ranulf from her marriage portion to Dieulacres, and instead gave the lands to Savigny, despite having apparently freely given her assent at the time of Ranulf's gift.[82] If there are any conclusions to be drawn from a comparison of the role of Clemencia with those of the earlier countesses, it would seem that the countess, as wife, is less visible in charter evidence. Clemencia, as wife, appears in charters giving her consent, and may have received religious benefits, but she played no role in witnessing her husband's charters, unlike the earlier twelfth-century countesses. It was as a widow that she granted her own charters, again reflecting the greater autonomy of the widow's powers of alienation.

The charter evidence has shown how in the twelfth century the countesses of Chester performed various functions at both the *honor* and royal courts, and shows that there was continuity in an active public role from marriage to widowhood, a role which seems to have been normal and accepted. Through the twelfth century there was usually a change in level of activity rather than in function as the countesses moved through the stages of the female life cycle. They were supportive of their husbands during marriage, and then were representative and supportive of their sons during widowhood. Their religious role was sometimes, but not always, associated with their role as representatives of their husbands and sons. Yet it also reflects their right to alienate property themselves which they held through inheritance or dower. Thus it could be said that they enacted their own policies and strategies, and the potential for such action was magnified as a widow.

It is striking that Matilda and her daughter-in-law Bertrada remained unmarried for thirty-six and forty-six years respectively. It has been calculated that 43 per cent of dowager countesses married only once; the remaining 57 per cent married for a second time, with a small proportion of these marrying for a third.[83] Thus the countesses were somewhat unusual. Neither Bertrada nor Matilda was an heiress, unlike the thrice-married Countess Lucy, which may in part explain their prolonged dowager period. Given the length of the dowager period of Matilda and Bertrada, it is notable that, as with Ermentrude and Lucy, they fulfilled similar roles as wife and widow, that is they acted as alienors, witnesses and so on.

The visibility of the involvement of the countesses of Chester in the affairs of the *honor* may have declined through the twelfth century. A statistical breakdown illustrates this apparent decline. The figures show involvement as either witness or (co-) alienor, since both represent proactive behaviour, authority, recognition and influence. No distinction is made between types of grant, or beneficiary. The earliest record sources show that Ermentrude was involved in three out of her husband's five charters – i.e. a participation rate of 60 per cent. Lucy was involved in 11 per cent of her husband's charters, Matilda in 16.3 per cent – as a widow her participation rate in the affairs of the *honor* was 7.8 per cent. The production of her own charters was the same. Bertrada's participation rate as wife was 19.5 per cent. As dowager countess she witnessed six charters of her son, Ranulf III, before her death in 1227. During this period Ranulf issued 220 charters, making her participation rate 3.5 per cent. Statistical analyses, however, only give part of the overall explanation. Such visible activity may not in fact be indicative of their power and authority, because of a major drawback to charter evidence: conclusions have to be based on incomplete documentation which changed in nature, form, content and style. The apparent decline in participation is not, for example, reflected in Bertrada's power as an alienor – expressed in comparative statistical terms this shows an increase of 200 per cent for Bertrada, 300 per cent for Lucy and no change for Matilda. Both Matilda and Bertrada were routinely issuing charters as dowager countess. They both acquired seals, which is indicative that other charters probably existed which have not survived. Charters show continuities in the roles of the countesses across the various stages in the life cycle, whether as wives or as widows. In addition, in spite of the dramatic increase in the number of surviving charters, and therefore probably of their production, the participation of the countesses remains significant.

Comparisons and contrasts

Powerful countesses who were active as wives are not unusual. Hawise countess of Gloucester (1150–97) was associated with her husband in the affairs of the *honor* of Gloucester throughout her marriage and as a widow after his death in 1183. She witnessed over 75 per cent of Earl William's *acta*, which compares with 23 per cent for the countesses of Chester.[84] She issued her own charters alienating land from her marriage portion during her marriage, implying that as wife she had some control over what were essentially her lands, and her husband witnessed the charter.[85] As a widow she issued five charters in favour of Durford Abbey, Sussex. She granted land of her *maritagium* at Pimperne to Fontevrault, and also to St Mary's, Nuneaton, along with her body for burial, thus giving her body to the religious institution founded by her father, Robert earl of Leicester, *c.* 1155.[86] She authenticated some of her charters with her seal.[87] She also issued a charter of liberties for Petersfield, Hampshire, in 1183–89.[88] Hawise was active in the administration of the Gloucester lands as wife, yet it was as widow that she was able to enact her own policies and strategies – in her patronage of her father's monastery, for example, rather than those of her marital family, she expressed a cultural choice and familial preference through the conduit of religious patronage.

Likewise, Petronella countess of Leicester (d. 1 April 1212) co-granted charters with her husband and as widow (after his death in 1190) granted and acquired a seal.[89] Her husband Earl Robert gave land to St Mary's Evreux in 1189–90 for the souls of his parents, Petronella and his children.[90] There is also evidence to show that, like Matilda, the countess of Chester in 1141, she was involved in the military campaigns of her husband. In 1173–74 she was captured with him at the battle of Fornham when he rebelled against Henry II.[91] Yet it was as a widow that she granted the majority of her charters, all of which were in favour of religious houses in Normandy, France and England.[92] She held her own court, where her vassals made agreements which she witnessed.[93]

Hawise countess of Gloucester and Petronella countess of Leicester are two examples of women who, like the countesses of Chester, were most powerful as widows. Charters reveal how powerful women utilised their economic resources. As might be expected they conform to patterns of behaviour reflective of their rank. In medieval society widows were the most independently economically enfranchised of women of the nobility. Such power was magnified greatly if a widow who was also an heiress could exert influence in her second marriage by retaining some control or influence over her inheritance. Dowager countesses-heiresses had the potential to be among the most powerful independent women in society. They can be considered a sub-set of widows who were a distinct status group who enacted their own policies and stratagems, and had economic power rooted in land tenure and rank. This can be illustrated by the examples of Matilda and Agnes de Percy, the heiresses of Earl William of Warwick, Margaret de Bohun, the daughter and heiress of the earl of Hereford, and Hawise, countess of Aumâle, the daughter and heir of William le Gros.

Matilda de Percy countess of Warwick was the co-heiress of William de Percy (II), who died in 1175.[94] She married, as his second wife, William (III) earl of Warwick, who died in 1184. In 1185 she fined for 700 marks for her inheritance, dower and for not being compelled to remarry.[95] As a widow she granted twenty charters. Her sister and co-heiress Agnes de Percy was married to Jocelin de Louvain (d. 1180), the brother of the queen. The greater powers of the widow are clearly shown in the charter evidence relating to both these powerful women. Both women were associated with their husband's *acta* as consentors, but both women had their own seals, and most of their charters date from after the death of their respective husbands. Matilda's favourite foundation was Fountains Abbey: over half her charters were issued to this institution. Matilda fulfilled all the roles of a great lay landholder, confirming vassals' gifts and making depositions to favoured individuals, thereby dispensing secular patronage. Of particular interest is her charter in favour of Juliana, her chamberlain, since this shows Matilda had at least one female household retainer.[96]

As a wife Matilda's advice and concession had been sought by her husband when making depositions to Sawley Abbey which concerned her patrimonial lands and familial foundation.[97] This implies that she had some right to be consulted and involved in the alienation of lands from her inheritance. Sawley Abbey had been founded by her father, William de Percy, in 1147 and was in a state of decline. On 25 March 1189 Matilda took action. At the advice of various clerics, including Julian abbot of Igny and William abbot of Mortemer, William Vavasour, *aliorum proborum hominum et fidelium meorum et totius curie mee*, she re-endowed the monastery.[98] The witness list included, among others, William Vavasour, Richard Vavasour and Nigel de Plumpton, significant individuals. The grant was made for the soul of her husband, King Henry, William de Percy, her father, Alice of Tonbridge, her mother, Alan de Percy, her brother, and Agnes de Percy, her sister. The relationship between the two sisters was amicable: they confirmed each other's gifts, acting together to ensure the security of their donations, and Matilda may have persuaded her sister to augment her refoundation of Sawley Abbey when Agnes confirmed her sister's grant of the church of Tadcaster and gave an additional gift of 140 sheep.[99] They granted land to family members; Agnes de Percy gave pasture for over 600 sheep to her nephew which he then granted to Sawley Abbey.[100] In 1182 Agnes arranged for the future marriage of her illegitimate nephew, William, son of Alan de Percy. This concord dating from 1182 agreed in the king's court gave specified lands to William which were to return to Agnes if she found him an heiress worth between £10 and £12.[101] Agnes received a share of over £100 of silver which her husband received on his departure on crusade. She had clearly been involved in this money-raising exercise, supporting her husband's plan to go on crusade. The manor in question had been granted to Jocelin on his marriage to Agnes, so the transaction was depriving Agnes of revenue.[102]

Margaret de Bohun is an example of a woman of this rank who controlled her affairs and retained independence as a widow, exercised the powers of a lay magnate and was important in familial affairs. Margaret was the daughter of Miles earl of Hereford and his eventual heir. She married Humphrey de Bohun, a steward of Henry II, who died in 1177. Margaret held her own court to manage the routine administration of her lands.[103] As a great lay landholder Margaret enfeoffed military followers, confirmed undertenants' charters and granted over twenty charters in favour of St Mary's Priory, Llanthony Secunda, having acquired a seal to authenticate documents.[104] In 1167 she began her patronage of Llanthony with a ceremonial occasion presenting her grant on the altar of the church.[105] At the petition of her undertenant, William of Stokes, Margaret confirmed his grant by placing a book upon the altar of St Mary's, here acting as lord securing a vassal's grant by symbolic action and cultural patron in the context of religious patronage.[106]

Widows sometimes used their role in religious patronage to designate their place of burial in charters, which in effect functioned as wills. Hawise countess of Gloucester willed that her body should be buried at Durford Abbey, her favourite foundation.[107] Alice de St Quintin willed her body to be buried at Nun Appleton Priory, Yorkshire, a priory of Cistercian nuns that she had founded.[108] Matilda de Percy and Petronella countess of Leicester similarly chose their burial place.[109] Husbands and wives could act together to designate their burial place.[110] The designation of an individual's final resting place could prove contentious, and indeed widows did not necessarily enjoy harmonious relations with the religious houses of their husbands and sons. Rohais de Beauchamp was in dispute with the monks of Walden in a squabble over the body of her son, Geoffrey de Mandeville (d. 1166). On his death whilst on campaign against the Welsh the monks attempted to make off with his body without informing the countess. A clerk 'escaped' and warned her. She hurriedly assembled some armed men, and attempted to waylay the cortège, but was foiled in the attempt. Once his body was secured and laid before the altar at Walden the abbot sent to Rohais to invite her to her son's funeral. In retaliation Rohais arranged for all their hangings, furniture and belongings to be stripped from his private chapel to be hung in her own foundation at Chicksand.[111] As with other countesses already discussed, it was as a widow that Rohais granted the majority of her charters and held her own court, although she did grant lands to Colne Priory *c.* 1150.[112]

Widowhood was the most powerful stage in the life cycle of twelfth-century noblewomen. Increasingly in the late twelfth century, widows who made agreements were careful to stress the legitimacy of their position to do so. This was expressed in a gender-specific phrase in the text of charters which begins to occur in the late twelfth and early thirteenth centuries, becoming more routine as the thirteenth century progressed. The phrase conveyed legitimacy or power through the use of the Latin *potestas*, often accompanied by the words *in legia potestate* and *in viduitate*. The process of identification begins in the address clauses, with the name of the widow granting the charter more frequently followed by the phrase *quondam uxor*, with the name of deceased husband(s), and then the *legia potestate* clause. This closer attention to the definition of noblewomen's status in charters is evidence of changes in documentary forms as a result of the proliferation of documents in the twelfth century. It was also a statement of female identity in a document intended for public consumption. With more individuals granting charters the need to record precisely who was who grew. The development of such clauses occurs after the impact of the Angevin reforms and hence perhaps reflects a greater legal concision in the techniques for recording property conveyances.

For example, if the greater title to land was due to inheritance rights, the opening clause of a charter granted by a woman might contain a *filia* phrase. This is not status-specific: women of all ranks are described as 'daughter of' in their charter opening address clauses. It may be termed a filial description and was applicable to men also. Inheritance rights then give greater status and self-defining gender parity, since in this respect noblewomen's charters are similar to those issued by males, who as heirs will define themselves as 'son of'. Matilda of Wallingford gave lands *de hereditate mea* so that her right to alienate land was clear.[113] When in the lifetime of her husband Brian fitz Count she granted a charter it was done with him *assentiente pariter ac laudante*.[114] The inclusion of this clause shows that the scribe was careful to stress the legitimacy of his patron's position. The *in legia potestate* clause is to be found only in the charters of widows. It is thus a gender-specific tool of definition in that it clarifies the legal position of the woman through a declaration of her marital status. In 1202–3 Isabel de Warenne granted a virgate of land to a certain Richard, son of Robert de Combe. She did so as *ego Isabella comitissa War[ennie] post obitum domini et viri mei Hamelin comitis Warennie* and sealed the charter.[115] Another good example is in a charter by Hawise countess of Aumâle (d. 1214) which illustrates that the linguistic construction of charters was capable of development to reflect wider legal changes occurring in the twelfth century, often considered to be the age of the definition of the individual. This careful phrasing of charters is illustrated in this charter quit-claiming various important rights to Fulco de Orili, including all her wards *et estagis castellorum*. Hawise greets all to whom the charter may come, and then carefully explains, *Noveritis me in libera viduitate mea et in legia*, and goes on to explain that the gift is made *et gratuita voluntate mea et postquam feci finem meum cum domino J(ohanne) rege Angl'*.[116] This is a reference to the fine that Hawise made with John of £5,000 to remain single after the death of her third husband, Baldwin de Bethune, in 1212.[117] The document carefully emphasised her greater powers of deposition as a widow.[118]

Charters have shown how aristocratic women such as the countesses were active within the *honor* as wives and as widows. Such countesses were significant individuals who wielded power and authority. Their marital status, and thus the female life cycle, underpinned their power, which was rooted in social status and familial connections as well as political circumstance. Throughout the twelfth century the wives and widows of powerful earls participated within the affairs of the *honor* and the family, as well as wider 'public' society. These roles were magnified when women entered the stage of the life cycle which gave them most access to land in their own right – widowhood. However, marriage defined the moment when a woman of the nobility could become a more active member of society wider than her natal family. A countess, as wife, could assume participation in public affairs to a much greater extent than as merely the unmarried daughter of a noble family. Wives are more visible in the sources as active participants than daughters, who, although they may be seen to give their consent to familial grants and may witness, rarely grant land away as unmarried single women. Maidenhood was not an empowering role in the context of land transfers. It would be possible through a close study of charters to discover whether minors granted charters with guardians who were not relatives. The roles and spheres of activity of the countesses of Chester are typical of their rank. It is clear that one role of a wife of a powerful earl was to support her husband's policies, and this was visibly represented in the public role of witnessing. The participation of the wives and widows of powerful nobles in the transfers of familial lands was not unusual in the twelfth century. Hence powerful countesses are a feature of twelfth-century society, not exceptions within it.

The countesses of Chester were thus not unique in the twelfth century in their public roles as wives or widows. Their public roles were explicitly linked with their position as wife, mother and widow. They attended the royal court. They accessed the rights of lordship, since they derived authority from their position as the wife or mother of the earl. Further, charters show how noblewomen exerted power and influence when utilising the aristocratic prerogative of bestowing patronage. In so doing they melded the interests and influence of their rank with symbolic, practical and cultural roles in the public domain. Further, they utilised a sphere of influence sanctioned by the church and society: the use of wealth for the purpose of religious patronage. This behaviour was traditional, individual, familial and optional. Given the church's claim to afford widows special protection, the cultivation of church support by a powerful widow would not only make sense spiritually but may also have served to create links with churchmen should the widow require their support in the future. More than this, however, the evidence has shown that a countess, as a wife, could participate in the alienation of family land as a witness, a consentor or a grantor. The charter evidence from Chester demonstrates a certain continuity of involvement by the countesses in the public affairs of the *honor* throughout the twelfth century. They appear in their husbands' and sons' *acta* as co-alienors, consentors and witnesses. They granted their own *acta*, acted as guardians over minors, alienated their dower lands as widows, and as dowagers continued to have some involvement in familial acts of donation to religious houses. The charter evidence shows continuities in their roles despite variable participation rates. These roles, of course, had long been a function of high-ranking women. Charter evidence suggests that countesses were most prominent in the sphere of religious patronage, but this is indicative of the limitations of the nature of the evidence, since relegous institutions were more assiduous in the retention and preservation of their charters. There is no doubt that the power and influence each countess could exert were variable. Lordship was an essential element which could empower individuals in the twelfth century; and countesses who as widows acted as lords were thus at the most influential stage in their lives. The power that countesses exercised was fundamentally rooted in the gendered familial role of wife or widow, and this was intimately linked with the female life cycle.

The way that women's power in lordship was constructed through gendered roles as wives and widows in twelfth-century England explains the participation of noblewomen in the functions of lordship. This was a gendered construct, because noblewomen's rights and roles in lordship were circumscribed by the authority of their male kin. As wives their husband was their 'lord'. As widows noblewomen could achieve greater authority which was based on the rights of lordship acquired through land tenure. The female life cycle was the fundamental defining criterion which affected this. Noblewomen during the key stages of the female life cycle as married women and as wives participated in, and accessed rights of, lordship. They did so when they made formal agreements which have survived as charters attached to which are their seals, the visible signs and symbols of lordship which themselves mediated gendered ideas about female roles. More than this, however, all this was underpinned and mediated through the institutions of lordship and the family. The two are inseparable. The family acted as a unit of lordship. There is thus no doubt that the significance of the countesses' roles in the political, economic and social structures of the *honor* was directly related to the impact of the female life cycle within a gendered construct of lordship.

Notes

1 P. Stafford, 'Women and the Norman Conquest', *TRHS*, 6th ser., 4 (1994), 221–49, at pp. 228–30.

2 Andreas Capellanus, *On Love*, ed. P. G. Walsh (London: Duckworth, 1982), pp. 16–18, 44–7. Status distinctions were also recognised in contemporary literature written for women: 'A letter on Virginity', in Bella Millett and Jocelyn Wogan-Browne,

Medieval English Prose for Women: Selections from the Katherine Group and Ancrene
Wisse (Oxford: Clarendon Press, 1990), p. 7; these distinctions interlocked with
spiritual gradations based on virginity, marriage and widowhood (*ibid.*, p. 21).

3 C. P. Lewis, 'The formation of the honor of Chester, 1066–1100', *JCAS*, 71 (1991),
37, 41.

4 J. H. Round, 'King Stephen and the earl of Chester', *EHR*, 10 (1895), 87–91;
P. Dalton, 'Aiming at the impossible: Ranulf II, earl of Chester and Lincolnshire in
the reign of King Stephen', *JCAS*, 71 (1991), 109–34 (esp. p. 109 n. 2); *idem*, '*In neutro
latere*: the armed neutrality of Ranulf II, earl of Chester in King Stephen's reign',
ANS, 14 (1992 for 1991), 39–59. For Ranulf III see J. W. Alexander, *Ranulf of Chester:
A Relic of the Conquest* (Athens GA: University of Georgia Press, 1983).

5 *CP*, 3. 164–9: a strategic marriage alliance for the earls of Chester and for King John.

6 OV, 2. 260–2.

7 *Chester Charters*, no. 2.

8 *Mando tibi, quod de terra, quam erga mei petiisti, locutus sum cum uxore mea et cum
baronibus, et inveni in meo consilio quod concedam eam Deo.* She also gained spiritual
benefits, since Earl Hugh stipulated that he should be treated as a brother of the
house, and that he, his wife and his parents should be entered into the abbey's book
of commemorations.

9 *Chester Charters*, no. 28.

10 M. Clanchy, *From Memory to Written Record: England, 1066–1307* (2nd edn, Oxford:
Blackwell, 1993), p. 156; J. G. H. Hudson, *Land, Law and Lordship in Anglo-Norman
England* (Oxford: Clarendon Press, 1994), p. 163.

11 *EYC*. 2, no. 805 (1125–35); see also *ibid.*, no. 749.

12 *Chester Charters*, no. 28 and nn. 45–7, *VCH Chester*, 3. 133–4. It may have been a
precautionary measure to safeguard the abbey's rights and possessions.

13 *VCH Chester*, 3. 133.

14 Lewis, 'Formation of the honor of Chester', p. 55.

15 *VCH Chester*, 3. 133.

16 See below, pp. 61–4, for a full discussion of the role of Countess Matilda.

17 *VCH Chester*, 3. 134.

18 *Chester Charters*, no. 6.

19 *Chronicon Monasterii de Abingdon*, ed. J. Stevenson (2 vols, London: Longman, RS 2,
1858), 2. 68–9.

20 *Quod descriptum sigillo quidem matris signari constitit; nondum militare baltheo cinctus,
materno sigillo littere quolibet ab eo directe includebantur. Hac de re quod eo annotatur
comitissae potius quam comitis sigillo signatur.*

21 See pp. 126ff.

22 *Northants. Charters*, no. 18.

23 Cambr. Univ. Libr., Add. MS 3021, ff. 206–206r (thirteenth-century) (DBC).

24 Cambr. Univ. Libr., Add. MS 3021, ff. 206–206r, 324v (fourteenth-century) (DBC).

25 Ctl. Castle Acre, BL, MS Harley 2110, f. 81v. (DBC).

26 *HKF*, 2. 154–5. For her disputed parentage see *CP*, 7. 743–6; K. S. B. Keats-Rohan,
'Antecessor noster: the parentage of the countess Lucy made plain', *Prosopon*, news-
letter of the Unit for Prosopographical Research, 2 (1995), 1–2, states that Lucy was
the daughter of Thorold, sheriff of Lincolnshire.

27 *Magnum Rotulum Scaccarii vel magnum rotulum pipae, de anno tricesmo primo regni Henrici Primi*, ed. J. Hunter ([London]: Record Commission, 1833), p. 110.

28 *Chester Charters*, no. 14.

29 *Ibid.*, no. 16.

30 BL, MS Add. 35,296 (Spalding Register), f. 388v; *Chester Charters*, no. 17.

31 S. Thompson, *Women Religious: The Founding of English Nunneries after the Norman Conquest* (Oxford: Clarendon Press, 1991), pp. 165–7.

32 *Chester Charters*, no. 18.

33 *Ibid.*, no. 19.

34 Thompson, *Women Religious*, p. 216.

35 OV, 6. 538–41 (see above, p. 18).

36 *Chester Charters*, no. 53.

37 *Tractatus de legibus et consuetudinibus regni Anglie qui Glanvilla vocatur*, ed. G. D. G. Hall (London: Nelson, 1965, repr. 1993), pp. 58–60.

38 S. Reynolds, *Fiefs and Vassals: The Medieval Evidence Reinterpreted* (Oxford: Oxford University Press, 1994), pp. 380–1.

39 *Chester Charters*, nos 41, 53, 84, 99. This represents about 6 per cent of the *acta* which can be dated to the period after 1135 which are not writs and are not spurious: although this may seem a relatively low figure, it should be seen in the light of diplomatic practice, in which relatively few men and women witnessed, for example, writ charters.

40 *Ibid.*, nos 121, 127, 129, 146.

41 *Ibid.*, no. 42.

42 *Ibid.*, no. 105.

43 *Ibid.*, no. 102.

44 *Ibid.*, no. 59.

45 RD, p. 15. The marriage had taken place *c.* 1141; her father was born *c.* 1090.

46 *P.R. 6 Hen. II*, p. 7; HKF, 2. 7–8.

47 *Chester Charters*, nos 127–9, 146.

48 *Ibid.*, no. 124.

49 *Ibid.*, no. 141.

50 *Ibid.*, no. 53.

51 *Ibid.*, no. 105.

52 *Ibid.*, no. 102.

53 *Ibid.*, no. 119 (1154–60).

54 *Ibid.*, no. 122.

55 HKF, 2. 46, *Chester Charters*, no. 173.

56 *Chester Charters*, no. 123.

57 *Ibid.*, no. 133.

58 RD, pp. 15–16.

59 *Chester Charters*, no. 185.

60 *Ibid.*, no. 133.

61 *Ibid.*, no. 184.

62 *Ibid.*, no. 193.

63 *Ibid.*, no. 251.

64 *Ibid.*, no. 331.

65 *Ibid.*, no. 272.

66 *Ibid.*, nos 206, 223–4, 227, 267, 271, 334.

67 Under the developing notion of common law dower widows came to be entitled to a third of her husband's lands that he had held at the time of his death: see J. Biancalana, 'Widows at common law: the development of common law dower', *Irish Jurist*, 23 (1988), 255–329, at p. 299. For a brief discussion of the problem of dowager countesses generally see R. C. DeAragon, 'Dowager countesses, 1069–1230', *ANS*, 17 (1995 for 1994), 87–100, at p. 93.

68 *HKF*, 2. 174, 199–200.

69 *The Charters of Duchess Constance of Brittany and her Family, 1171–1221*, ed. Judith Everard and Michael Jones (Woodbridge: Boydell, 1999).

70 *Annales Cestriensis: or, Chronicle of the Abbey of S. Werburg, at Chester*, ed. R. C. Christie (Record Society of Lancashire and Cheshire, 14, 1887 for 1886), p. 40.

71 A. T. Thacker, 'Introduction: the earls and their earldom', *JCAS*, 71 (1991), 15–21.

72 Y. Hillion, 'La Bretagne et la rivalité Capétiens–Plantagenets. Un exemple: la duchesse Constance (1186–1202)', *Annales de Bretagne et des pays de l'ouest*, 92 (1985), 111–44.

73 M. Jones, 'La vie familiale de la duchesse Constance: le témoignage des chartes', in G. Le Menn with J. Y. Le Moing (eds), *Bretagne et pays celtiques: langues, histoire, civilisation. Mélanges offerts à la mémoire de Léon Flemscot, 1923–1987* (Saint-Brieuc-Rennes: SKOL, 1992), p. 353.

74 Hillion, 'La Bretagne', p. 126.

75 Ranulf's charter: *Chester Charters*, no. 243; Constance's: BL, Cotton Ch. xi, 45 (*EYC*, 4. no. 83).

76 *EYC*, 4. 93; Jones, 'La vie familiale de la duchess Constance', p. 354.

77 *EYC*, 4. 85, granting rents worth £10 to Villeneuve (Nantes), the abbey which she founded in March 1200.

78 *Chester Charters*, no. 334.

79 *Ibid.*, no. 335.

80 *Ibid.*, no. 442.

81 Senderowitz Loengard, '*Rationabilis dos*: Magna Carta and the widow's "fair share" in the earlier thirteenth century', in S. Sheridan Walker (ed.), *Wife and Widow in Medieval England* (Ann Arbor MI: University of Michigan Press, 1993), pp. 59–80, at pp. 33–58.

82 *Chester Charters*, no. 443; for Ranulf's grant see *ibid.*, no. 388 (*assensu et voluntate spontanea Clemencie*).

83 DeAragon, 'Dowager countesses', p. 89.

84 *Gloucester Charters*; see below, Chapter 5 n. 1.

85 *Gloucester Charters*, no. 39.

86 *Ibid.*, no. 78, 67; *VCH Warwicks.*, 2. 66–7.

87 *Gloucester Charters*, nos 67, 78, 160.

88 *Ibid.*, no. 160.

89 BL, Add. Ch. 47552, *Danelaw Charters*, no. 322.

90 A charter of Earl Robert was issued for his soul, his parents, his children and Petronella: *CDF*, no. 306. She witnessed his charter to Fountains, *ibid.*, no. 417; in 1168–90. Earl Robert confirmed her gift to St Mary's (in Lisieux) for the souls of her parents: *ibid.*, no. 571; in 1198–1204 her son, Earl Robert, confirmed the joint gift of

Earl Robert and Petronella to the abbey of Saint-André-en-Gouffern (diocese of Sées): *ibid.*, no. 607.

91 See above, pp. 19–20, for a discussion of the way that this episode is portrayed in the chronicles of the reign.

92 Ctl. Saint-Evroult, Bibl. Nat., MS Latin 11055, ff. 35v–35v (thirteenth-century; a general confirmation charter); PRO, 31/8/140B, pt 1 (Cartulaire de la Basse-Normandie), 300 (copy of *c.* 1835 by Léchaude d'Anisy); Bibl. Nat., Collection du Vexin, xiii, f. 45v (eighteenth-century copy du cartulaire de l'abbaye de Lire) for the anniversary of her son; Ctl. Salisbury, Wiltshire Record Office, D1/1/2 (lib. Evid. B), f. 109v (thirtenth-century) (DBC); *Sarum Charters*, p. 53; *Records of the Borough of Leicester: Being a Series of Extracts from the Archives of the Corporation of Leicester, 1509–1603*, ed. Mary Bateson, Helen Stocks, G. A. Chinnery and A. N. Newman (7 vols, London: C. J. Clay, under the authority of the Corporation of Leicester, 1899–1974), 1. 10–11, no. 13; Northants. Record Office, MS Finch Hatton 170 (Hatton Book of Seals), f. 2, no. 5 (seventeenth-century facsimile *ex armario cartarum prenobilii domine Katerine ducisse Bucks decimo Iulit anno 1641*) (description of seal as above); PRO, C 56/16, m. 18 (Confraternity Roll, 3 Henry VII); two grants in Reg. Leicester, Bodl. Libr, MS Laud misc. 625, f. 5v (fifteenth-century digest of charter in lost cartulary), and *ibid.*, f. 7v (fifteenth-century) (DBC).

93 Cartulary of Woodford of Bretingby, BL, MS. Cott. Claudius A xiii, f. 239v. (fifteenth-century), *ibid.*, f. 242v.; Ctl. Lyre, eighteenth-century transcript by Dom Lenoir Coll. M. De Mathan, Château de Semilly Manche (microfilm AD Eure, I MI2 472, no. 48) (DBC).

94 *EYC*, 11. 5.

95 *P.R. 31 Hen. II*, p. 76; she continued to account for this amount when in 1202 she still owed £159 11s 4d.

96 *EYC*, 11. no. 63, nos 38–46, 50–67. For Juliana the chamberlain (no. 63) see below, p. 159.

97 *Ibid.*, no. 49.

98 *Ibid.*, no. 50.

99 *Ibid.*, no. 77.

100 *Ibid.*, no. 80.

101 *Ibid.*, no. 74.

102 *Ibid.*, no. 68.

103 The cartulary of Llanthony, PRO, C 115/k1/6681 (sect. 20, no. 250), f. 79 (fourteenth-century), records that an undertenant's donation to Llanthony was made *coram domina mea Margaret de Bohun*. The same cartulary contains another, similar agreement which lists Margaret as first witness: *ibid.* (sect. 20, no. 251) (DBC).

104 'Charters of the earldom of Hereford, 1095–1201', ed. D. Walker, in *Camden Miscellany*, XXII (Camden Society, 4th ser., 1, 1964), pp. 1–75, lists thirty-three *acta*, nos 90–123; in favour of Llanthony Secunda are nos 90–7, 99–102, 104–9, 112–16.

105 *Ibid.*, no. 90.

106 *Ibid.*, no. 116: *ego ad petitionem ejusdem Willemi eandem elemosinam presenti carta mea confirmavi et super altare sancte Marie **per textum posui pro me** . . .* (1165–*c.* 1197; my emphasis).

107 *Gloucester Charters*, no. 67.

108 *EYC*, 1. nos 541, 543 and notes.

109 *EYC*, 11. no. 45; B: Reg. Leicester, Bodl. Libr., MS Laud misc. 625, f. 7v. (fifteenth-century) (DBC).

110 *EYC*, 2. no. 847.

111 *VCH Bedfordshire*, 1. 390–1. Her first husband, Geoffrey de Mandeville (I), died in 1144; she subsequently married Payn de Beauchamp, who died in 1156: *CP*, 5, 114–17, note g, states that the Walden Chronicle 'C' version is the source of the allegations of the dispute over her son's corpse. This may be an unfounded rumour in an unreliable source, since this version states that he died in 1167 and may be related to disapproval of her foundation of Chicksand Priory, a rival for patronage.

112 *Cartularium Prioratus de Colne*, ed. John L. Fisher (Essex Archaeological Society, Occasional Publications, I, 1946), no. 55; *ibid.*, no. 54 (*c.* 1170). Other benefactions were to Thorney Abbey (Ctl. Thorney, pt. 2, Cambr. Univ. Libr., MS Add. 3021, f. 295; *ibid.*, f. 297, fourteenth-century; two grants); and, with her second husband, Payn de Beauchamp, in favour of Chicksand (BL, MS Lansdowne 203 (seventeenth-century copy of Elias Astrude), f. 16; Ctl. Newnham, BL, MS Harley 3656, f. 24v. (fifteenth-century; three grants). Her *curia*: Ctl. Missenden, BL, MS Harley 3688, f. 165v. (fourteenth-century) (DBC).

113 King's College Library, Cambridge, OGB/23 (Old Deed 17); another example, *ibid.*, OGB/24 (Old Deed 18) (DBC).

114 Windsor D and C Muniments, xi, G. 1 (DBC).

115 BL, Add. Ch. 24634, pd *EYC*, 8. no. 86 and plate 20.

116 Humberside County RO, DDCC/135/1 (Chichester-Constable Deeds); seventeenth-century transcript of the same: *ibid.*, DDCC/135/51 (2) (DBC).

117 *P. R. John 14*, p. 37.

118 She also granted, for her service, forty bovates of land in Preston to Agnes de Preston *nutrici mee qui me lacte suo nutriuit pro seruitio suo*: Humberside County RO, DDCC/76/1 (Chichester-Constable Deeds) (DBC). This shows the personal attachment of Hawise to her wet nurse (for which see Shahar, *Fourth Estate*, p. 140), her obligation to reward her and the potential to do so through a grant of land.

5

Witnessing

H AWISE COUNTESS of Gloucester (d. 1197) attested 75 per cent of the charters of her husband, Earl William.[1] Her title is *comitissa*, sometimes elaborated as *comitissa Glouc(estrie)*. On one charter she is *Haw(is)ia uxore mea*. She is the first witness in all but four *acta*.[2] The charter witness lists place Hawise at the apex of the internal hierarchy of the Gloucester power structure on her husband's charters. Hawise was also involved in transactions where she was the recipient of countergifts. One is a charter confirming the grant by a tenant to Holywell Priory, London, in which Earl William received seven marks and Hawise two bezants.[3] The other charter records the enfeoffment of Richard de Lucy, a justiciar of Henry II, on Gloucester lands. Both Hawise and Earl William received a gold ring in return for recognition.[4] Not only was Countess Hawise a regular witness to the *acta* of her husband, Earl William, in 1185 she witnessed a charter of Margaret, the widow of Henry II's eldest son, Henry the Younger.[5]

How can we account for such a high level of visible public activity by a twelfth-century countess? David Postles, whilst noting Hawise's prominence, suggests that she was associated with her husband's *acta* to prevent her from claiming dower in the future.[6] However, although as Maitland noticed on the evidence of one charter women 'sometimes' witnessed documents, there are no examples of women's testimony being brought forward in the courts of the twelfth century.[7] Postles, like Pollock and Maitland before him, tends to view female witnessing from a legal perspective, and whilst the legal nature of charters is well accepted, this legalistic interpretation is problematical. It seems to imply that Hawise witnessed because her claims to dower were a threat to the Gloucester patrimony, and that therefore her witnessing reflected consent to a grant. Indeed, Postles elsewhere argues that, where family members were involved, witnessing may have necessarily implied consent or, at the very least, acceptance of a transaction, since it is possible that witnessing, in some cases, took the place of the consent of relatives, the *laudatio parentum*.[8] The importance of witnessing as a measure of consent to a transaction is particularly difficult to verify, since the references to consent in charters are inconsistent.[9] If Postles's view about wives and dower was applied to all *acta*, one would expect that all major transactions by men would have involved their wives, which is clearly not the case.

Reading socio-cultural contexts from a legal perspective is more difficult, however. It is generally assumed that the process of attesting and witnessing documents was a method of ensuring the security of a transaction, because attestors and witnesses could be called upon to verify the transaction recorded in the charter in the event of a legal dispute at a future date.[10] Precisely because charters were legal records the views of Timothy Reuter provide a useful context here. Reuter points out that, although they may appear to be legal records, they are more often 'fragmentary (and often contextless) narratives . . . frozen records in the course of a narrative'.[11] They are disjointed as a series of narratives because they were made in different contexts and to meet different needs Further, cartulary copies were subject to tampering, sometimes malicious, sometimes explanatory in the light of changes in vocabulary. Thus complexities within texts were subject to smoothing out in the light of local knowledge.

The variety of documents that Hawise witnessed suggests that there may have been more to her participation as a witness than a legalistic device predicated on her potential claims to land. For example, she was sole witness to a charter in favour of Queen Eleanor which gave her the ivory dice that Elias the clerk owed. Such a small gift speaks of personal relationships rather than Hawise as threat to the integrity of the Gloucester patrimony. When Hawise witnessed a chirograph between Hamo de Valognes and Durand, son of Robert of Torigni, she was witnessing a complicated settlement of inheritance in her husband's court.[12] By contrast she also witnessed a charter of her husband to Walter the harper granting some land for a full dish of beans rendered annually at the earl's exchequer in Bristol.[13] The agreements that Hawise witnessed thus concerned both important tenants and household servants.

One of the key problems when studying witness lists is how to evaluate their significance as indicators of the personal, social and political power of twelfth-century noblewomen. Several issues affect the interpretation of charter evidence. The use of documentary records became more routine, as did the formulas which were used to express commonplace happenings, and phrases were developed to express what may in fact not have occurred.[14] Thus charters may have been statements of pretension rather than expressions of real power and authority, and therefore propaganda.[15] Thus witness lists may have also been pretensions to power rather than evidence of gatherings of individuals at specific occasions. The date of composition within a wider chronology of change in the twelfth century is also significant, since the Angevin legal reforms may have had an impact upon the way that charters were drawn up. The significance of witnessing and the procedures for recording an act changed during the twelfth century, and charter formulas reflect those changes.[16] Everything indicates considerable variation in the construction of witness lists.

The historiography of witnessing turns on two axes within broader debates about the nature of charter evidence. Empiricists such as Thomas Keefe, Donald Fleming, C. R. Cheney and Janet Burton tend to see witness lists as the product of political influence.[17] Other historians such as Emily Tabuteau have considered the social status of witnesses, whilst John Hudson suggests that a broad cross-section of trustworthy people, including some of high rank, was important and that witness lists show that honorial courts were often attended by non-tenants.[18] Diana Greenway suggests that witness lists commonly included a core group of family members who were supplemented by tenants.[19] David Postles argues that by the twelfth century witness clauses generally suggest the presence of a witness at a ceremony and the importance of that presence.[20]

On the other hand Dominique Barthélemy's reassessment of charter evidence has set witnessing into debates about the importance of documentary provenance against a background of production and custom.[21] He believes that monastic charters and cartularies reveal the social context in which they were produced. Barthélemy attacks Duby's view of a cataclysmic transformation in French society c. 1000 and argues that the change in the nature of charters between c. 1050 and 1150 ('la mutation documentaire') did not necessarily reflect wider social changes, but might reveal practices which earlier styles of document had hidden. Barthélemy, Olivier Guyotjeannin and Susan Reynolds believe that charters are problematic because they emanate from an ecclesiastical élite which had a different ideology from that of secular society.[22] Barthélemy attacks methodologies which statistically analyse specific phrases within charters, because charters should be studied within the complex cultural and political processes which affected how they were produced. Jan Hendrik Prell argues against a crisis in documentary forms and that the legal status of witnesses declined in importance so that their function changed from a juridical corroborative role: they became 'témoins instrumentaires'.[23]

The key problem with this debate, although it is subtle and sophisticated, is that it is ultimately a sterile postmodern argument about male power and action which fiercely contests the difficulties of reading social realities from constructed narratives. It does little to address the difficulties of measuring the power of women, for example as witnesses. The debate about 'la mutuation documentaire' has shown the significance of documentary provenance, but nevertheless charters offer the historian superb opportunities to study the dynamics of power, and facilitate a reading of female power which challenges assumptions about the interactions of gender and lordship on women's power. Despite the relatively barren nature of postmodernist debates about documents, they nevertheless, in varying degrees, see witnessing as important. Thus, in terms of understanding female witnessing, an empirical view would see female witnessing as important because presence as a witness indicates that individuals were key political players. Alternatively, a postmodern perspective would suggest that witnessing represents the importance of women in a mythologised narrative which is reflective of the views of those party to and who created the document.

There are two useful approaches which are suggestive of new ways that women's power as witnesses could be examined. Bates's analysis of the *acta* of William I in terms of the context of production indicates that the historian needs to be particularly aware of the interaction of 'public' and 'private' forms of power.[24] Bates argues that frequency of attestation was important, but, crucially, changes in diplomatic practice affected the process of the creation of witness lists.[25] Thus documentary provenance is important. Hence, for example, the witness lists of confirmation charters of the late eleventh century are problematical, since they may not be an accurate reflection of gatherings of individuals when agreements were made, but, rather, they indicate that the beneficiary felt it was important that such names were recorded on such documents.[26] The significance of witnesses of royal writs on the other hand is placed in the political context of the royal court to cast light on ways that a new élite supplied documentary authority.[27] Bates argues that the personal power of William I's wife Matilda is evidenced in the number and frequency of her attestations. Her special place in consenting to, and confirming, the grants of her husband elevated her above the powerful aristocracy.[28] Thus this way of viewing charters as products of socio-cultural conditioning and immediate political context acknowledges the importance of documentary provenance whilst accepting that both were important as legal devices and reflective of social realities. Thus female witnessing may be considered to have had real significance.

Pauline Stafford also considers that witnessing had social and political significance. She has shown that in the eleventh century witnessing was part of the role of a queen.[29] Stafford suggests that the exercise of office, which could degender or regender, was at the heart of queenly power.[30] Further, witnesses of eleventh-century *acta* were all office holders, and such groupings reflected the perception of the Anglo-Saxon kingdom as a series of office holders.[31] Queenly witnessing was thus an expression of queenly power, rooted in office. The paradigms offered by Bates and Stafford can be applied to explain the witnessing of Hawise countess of Gloucester. If twelfth-century witnessing was thus a form of public 'office', or power, which had the capacity to re- or even degender, it facilitated the participation of women. The basis of Hawise's power was of course her marital status: as the wife of the earl of Gloucester, Hawise's social status at the pinnacle of aristocratic society was assured. This explains the frequency of her attestations and her place above her husband's noble followers usually as head of the secular witnesses to his charters. A model of female witnessing existed in the royal household, where queenly witnessing was well established, and perhaps Earl William, who was styled *consul* in his *acta*, a title which associated him with high office and prestige, saw also that his wife as the wife of a *consul* could also play an important role as a witness similar to that of the queen for the king. Hawise as the wife of the earl was possibly therefore involved regularly, since the Gloucester secretariat had imitated royal practice under Earl Robert (d. 1147) and then Earl William. Thus Hawise's position as a witness was underpinned by a recognition of her office as countess.

However, high-status witnessing by females was more than a part of their role as office holders. Janet Nelson argues that women had a role to play in social memory: 'the *memoria*, the commemoration of the dead . . . the ancestors, of the dynasty of the *gens*'.[32] The confirmation of a sense of community that is represented by group witnessing was part of the purpose of witnessing: charters preserved *memoria* as well as the legal implications of the transaction recorded.[33] This places women's power in religious benefaction in its cultural context, but if the analysis is extended to apply to female witnessing it provides one paradigm which explains why women witnessed documents. This of course raises important questions about the purpose of the original gifts and the need to record *memoria*,[34] and who was who in relation to them, and also the importance of those witnesses as time passed and as their significance diminished, which in part may explain the truncation of cartulary witness lists.

The issue of documentary provenance can partly be resolved where there are extant charters written by the same scribe in favour of numerous beneficiaries. Professional writers were employed in the Gloucester household. Countess Hawise in her widowhood maintained at least one clerk in hers.[35] The existence of a secretariat suggests a developed administrative framework which Hawise controlled. The secretariat framed documents from her perspective, not from that of the beneficiaries.

These themes – the importance of documentary provenance, the preservation of social memory, the socio-cultural significance of witnessing and the complex contexts of female participation – are superbly illustrated in a charter dated 18 March 1101/02. By this charter William, son of Baderon, gave to St Florent and St Mary Monmouth land near the mill at Goodrich Castle.[36] His wife, Hawise, and their daughters, Iveta and Advenia, confirmed the gift. On the day the gift was made William, his wife and daughters 'and almost all their barons and their wives' received the benefits of fellowship, 'and all who were present, male and female, small and great, young and old, confirm and testify to the grant'. There follows a list of named witnesses, all of whom all are male. Thus although many women were present, received spiritual benefits and witnessed the charter, only male witnesses were listed by name, key office holders and their sons or members of Abbot William of St Florent's entourage. It is striking that, when this grant was augmented by William, son of Baderon, by a later charter, *Domina Hadewis*, Iveta and Advenia placed their crosses on the charter. Thus they participated in the ceremony of transfer of seisin.[37] The charter of 18 March was drawn up the scribe of the abbot, the beneficiary; this may reflect anxiety about the nature and security of the gift. It was also a product of the socio-cultural conditioning which underpinned the way that the ceremony was constructed, recorded and witnessed. It also illustrates the complexities of measuring witness lists as a guide to participation, since although we know that numbers of women were present, their names were not recorded. This is in turn suggestive that the role of witnessing was generally gendered male. The transfer of seisin by symbolic action of the knife on the altar served to assist the memory of those witnesses present, both male and female.

As the twelfth century progressed there was a marked growth in female attestations: whilst at the start of the period high-status women such as Countess Hawise witnessed documents, by the end of the century, groups of women of freeholder status witnessed charters. This may be related to the increasing awareness of procedures and jurisdiction typical of documents of this period and therefore of a trend to record more precisely those individuals involved in a grant.[38]

The twelfth-century development of co-parceny, that is, the division of inheritance among female heirs,[39] may also have created tenurial relationships which brought women into business in the courts.

There is sparse evidence of non-royal noblewomen witnessing prior to 1100.[40] There are limited examples from 1100 until the 1130s.[41] Thereafter the incidence of noblewomen witnessing documents increased in the 1130s.[42] The period 1140–60 is also notable as a period when female witnessing increased.[43] After 1160 there are examples of groups of women and also lower-status women witnessing documents, which will be discussed below. The most common context for female participation as a witness is that of a wife either with or for her husband. Of all the examples cited above almost all the female witnesses were wives of the grantors or co-witnessed with their husbands.[44]

Rates of female participation in witnessing are particularly hard to evaluate. Out of 391 private deeds relating to Waltham Abbey only four were witnessed by women. All were wives of grantors, even if two of them were also queens.[45] Out of 178 twelfth-century charters relating to Eynsham Abbey, eight were witnessed by women. Of these witnesses six were wives of the grantors, one witnessed her brother's charter, and Alice de Langetot as a witness has no obvious connection with kin.[46] It is noteworthy that the main context of female witnessing was as wives of the main grantors. If we set female witnessing into a broader analysis of their appearances in charter evidence, a fuller picture of the significance of female witnessing is apparent. For example, single or married women issued 10 per cent of the charters in favour of Waltham Abbey and with their husbands conjointly made agreements with the abbey, consented to gifts and received spiritual benefits in grants made by male kin.[47] Similarly women were involved with Eynsham Abbey in a variety of ways. In addition to the female participation as witnesses, thirty-five charters show that women participated in transactions, as co-alienors, alienors in their own right, as recipients of countergifts or gave concessions to grants.[48] Thus the total female participation in the Eynsham charters is 24 per cent, a significant figure: witnessing as sole guide to the power of noblewomen is problematic and needs to be set into the socio-cultural and political contexts. Further, these two examples show the variable nature of rates of female participation as witnesses.

This variability of rates of female participation can be seen in the cases of individual women. In the early twelfth century Matilda de L'Aigle, the wife of Nigel d'Aubigny, witnessed three of his charters during her marriage to him (1107–18), 50 per cent of the sample.[49] She witnesses as *coniuge mea*, and is third witness after Thomas archbishop of York and Ranulf Flambard bishop of Durham in two, and second witness after Archbishop Thomas in the third. All three charters were in favour of religious houses: Bec, St Peter's Hospital, York, and St Cuthbert's, Durham. It is possible that all three charters were ratified on the same occasion, because the witness lists are similar.[50] In one notification charter to Aubrey de Vere that Nigel had given Bec £20 worth of land in Essex there is evidence that he had made the gift *supradicta benigno concessu uxoris mee*.[51] Matilda countess of Chester attested 6 per cent of the charters of her husband, Earl Ranulf, usually as first witness. The beneficiaries were the religious houses of Basingwerk, Lenton, and the nuns of St Mary's Chester in the period 1135–53.[52] In a charter of Earl Ranulf *c.* 1150 Hugh, son of Oliver, quitclaimed a number of crofts *coram me et comitissa et plurimus baronum meorum*. Yet in this charter Matilda is placed third in the witness list, after John and Roger the chaplains.[53] Thus the charter specifically states that Matilda was present when the quitclaim was made and the phrasing implies that her place at the ceremony was beside her husband, before the barons. Given this, her position as third witness is surprising, and may be a scribal oddity. Other high-status women witnessed their husband's charters, for example Margaret duchess of Brittany witnessed six of her husband's charters in the period *c.* 1160–71.[54] Lescelina, the wife of Geoffrey de Mandeville (I), witnessed his foundation of Hurley Priory in 1085–86.[55] Rohais countess of Essex witnessed a charter by her first husband, Geoffrey de Mandeville earl of Essex, to Holy Trinity Aldgate in 1140–44.[56]

There are rare examples that demonstrate that grants were made on the advice of a wife who then also witnessed the charter. On the advice of Margaret, his wife, William de Chesney gave William 'Walensis' half a hide of land *c.* 1165–72, and Margeret witnessed the charter.[57] When Mabel, the wife of Ralph, son of Nicholas, witnessed her husband's charter her name was last on the witness list and the scribe added a clause specifically stating that the grant had been made at the advice of Mabel and with her concession.[58] *Circa* 1160–73 Bertrada countess of Chester used her personal influence to secure a grant to her servant and witnessed her husband's charter.[59] However, the striking feature of these examples is that the beneficiaries were secular individuals, whereas the majority of twelfth-century charter evidence relates to religious insititutions.

There is important evidence to suggest that when husbands and wives acted as joint witnesses they did so as conjoint lords. For example, Maurice of Windsor and Edith, his wife, were conjoint *signa* to a document dated 25 May 1130. This agreement, made at the episcopal court, details their joint benefaction of Wix Priory.[60] Edith's title next to her *signa* is *domine*, whereas her husband's name reads only as *Mauricii*, and Bishop Herbert of Norwich, who confirmed the grant, is *Eboradi episcopi*. It is possible that the lands were Edith's inheritance.[61] Husbands and wives who made conjoint benefactions were *jointly* liable to warrant a gift and did so conjointly in lordship, since ensuring the security of a tenant's property conveyance was one of the functions of lordship.[62] Lordly witnessing of a tenant's agreement was one way of ensuring that the superior lord(s) knew of a tenant's conveyance; it implied lordly consent and therefore bound the lord to uphold the agreement.

The following examples of noblewomen who conjointly witnessed charters with their husbands illustrate conjoint action of husband and wife in their capacity as superior lords for their tenants in their seigneurial court. Hudson has argued that lordly witnessing of a vassal's charter is an indication that lords dealt with business between vassals and their tenants.[63] As discussed earlier, Hawise countess of Gloucester and her husband Earl William both witnessed a charter made in their court which ratified a complicated settlement of inheritance.[64] In the late twelfth century Isobel countess of Pembroke witnessed with her husband, William Marshall, a grant of dower by Matthew de Luci to his wife, Dionisia.[65] *Circa* 1100–14 William count of Evreux and his wife, Hawise, made various grants to the abbey of Troarn. They acted as principal witnesses of their own endowment charter, witnessing second and third respectively after King Henry I.[66] Such an interplay of forces shaping documentary form places the emphasis on wider contexts – whereas Hudson, on the basis of one example of familial witnessing by the earl of Shrewsbury, his sons and the countess Adeliza in the late eleventh century, explains Earl Roger's witnessing only in the context of his power as the 'dominant lord of the area'.[67] This model needs modification in order to take account of the participation of the countess and her sons. It is arguable that the family acts as a unit of lordship. Indeed, the above examples suggest that Bates is essentially right to stress the importance of kinship and lordship as the dominant influences upon the making of diplomas.[68] This approach also confirms that the stress placed by Hyams on the family when lords acted to give warranty is a paradigm that can be applied to witnessing.[69]

Certainly the importance of kin connections is apparent when Matilda de Lucy, the wife of Walter fitz Robert, the son of Matilda de Saint Liz, witnessed second after her husband for her mother-in-law in the mid- to late twelfth century. The charter granted land of her mother-in-law's dower.[70] In the late twelfth century two women alongside their husbands as part of a family group witnessed a charter which granted land to their mother-in-law.[71] In 1148–55 Roger earl of Hereford gave various lands to St Mary Monmouth; Baderon of Monmouth, and his wife, Rohais, witnessed his charter.[72] A key context for female involvement in witnessing was as wives for and with their husbands in the context of tenurial lordship.

Noblewomen as widows witnessed charters with and for their sons; for example, in 1144–59 Matilda, the mother of Henry de Lacy, witnessed an agreement of Lacy tenants made by the Chevrecurt family with her son.[73] As a widow Ada de Warenne countess of Northumberland witnessed seven charters of her son, King William the Lion of Scotland, in the period 1152–71.[74] As well as witnessing the charters of husbands and sons some women witnessed charters granted by their mothers, and the involvement of a daughter could be related to her claims to the land in question as heiress. When in 1135–45 Cecily de Rumilly made a gift to the canons of St Mary and St Cuthbert in Embsay her grant was witnessed by Amice de Rumilly *filia mea seniore*.[75] Amice, or Avice, subsequently augmented and confirmed her mother's gift in 1138–50.[76] She thus witnessed her mother's charters as her eldest co-heir. When in 1147–c. 1152 Amice notified the bishop of Lincoln and archdeacon of Leicester of her grant to the canons of Drax, her son-in-law, Robert de Gant, and daughter from her second marriage, Alice Paynel, consented to the gift and witnessed the charter. It is intriguing that the sister of Robert de Gant also witnessed.[77] Another example of a female heir co-witnessing with her husband her mother's grant of land is that of Michael Capra and his wife Roesia in 1156–62, when they witnessed a charter made by Jordan de Bricset and his wife, Muriel. Here the daughter witnessed her parents' grant to the religious institution that they had founded and was the heiress to the lands alienated.[78]

There are examples where a daughter, possibly unmarried, witnessed as part of a sibling family group: Rohais, Gilbert, Walter and Baldwin, the sons and daughters of Alice, the wife of Gilbert fitz Richard de Clare, witnessed a charter granted by Alice 1136–38.[79] When c. 1123 Walter de Gloucester gave his nephew Little Hereford in fee, he compensated his daughter-in-law Sibyl through an exchange of one manor for another, since the land was of her dower. The witness list has fourteen male witnesses as well as Margeret, *filia ipsi' Mil'*.[80] Given that Sibyl had married Miles of Gloucester in 1121, Margaret must have been only one or two years old.[81] Her witnessing can hardly reflect consent, since she was so young, and more probably reflects her position as potential heir to the lands conveyed; her inclusion must have had more to do with notions of family participation in alienation rather than consent.

The ranking of witnesses is an indication of the interaction of gender and status. In 1144–50, when Alice de St Quintin with her son Robert made a grant to the nuns of Appleton, her daughter Agnes witnessed the charter and is second to last after ten male witnesses.[82] Agnes also witnessed her mother and stepfather's charter confirmation and augmentation of Alice's grant *c*. 1163, when she was again placed second to last, following seven male witnesses.[83] As last witness she subsequently witnessed a confirmation of this grant made by her brother in 1163–70.[84] As part of a family group Agnes witnessed a confirmation charter *c*. 1150–70 made by her stepfather, with the assent and consent of his wife, Alice de St Quintin, concerning lands which were of her dower. There were six female witnesses to this charter, whose names follow the list of male witnesses: they were Alice de St Quintin, as *domina* Alice de St Quintin, and Agnes, Denise and Sibilla, her daughters, as well as Agnes and Alice *neptibus ejus*.[85] The lands alienated were Alice's dower from her first marriage, and it is possible that her daughters retained some interest in them. Agnes de St Quintin's support for her mother's foundation of a nunnery entailed witnessing the original foundation charter as part of a kindred group of six women: such group witnessing is unusual. Their names appear last on the list and where groups of women witness that is the norm.

There are few examples of charter witness lists containing more than one or two female names. There are fifteen examples of groups of women witnessing which all date from the mid to late twelfth century, the earliest dating from 1150–70, the latest *c*. 1198. Although the absolute number of this sample is small, each example is nevertheless significant, because the inclusion of women as witnesses was relatively uncommon in general in twelfth-century witness lists and such witness lists are not necessarily accurate records of all those present when agreements were ratified. Six women witnessed a charter of *c*. 1170–80 by William Lenveise and Denise, his wife. The witness group included the sister of Denise, the lady Eularia, and the wives of three of the male witnesses, as well as the daughters of the donors.[86] Thus all six women had kin connections with the alienors. The importance of kindred connections of female witnesses is demonstrable in a charter of 1166–76 by Asceria, the widow of Asketil de Habton. Asceria gave a carucate of her dowry to Rievaulx Abbey. This charter confirmed her husband's previous grant and was witnessed by six women. The women's names are placed at the end of the list of male witnesses and include that of the wife of Ranulf de Glanville, the sheriff of York, as *Bertha vicecomitissa*, Matilda, her daughter, and four other women whose familial and marital status is made explicit.[87] In a grant to Kirkstead in the mid to late twelfth century by Agnes, daughter of Hugh de Pincun, seven male witnesses attested, after whom four women, including Lady Amicia, mother of 'Haket', and her daughter, Emmelina, as well as Margeret and Emmelina, the daughters of the grantor, also witnessed.[88] The women's names are last on the list, following male witnesses, suggesting that women were perceived at the bottom of the hierarchy of witnesses.[89] Social status mattered as well as gender.

In an unusual charter dating from the late twelfth century Alexandria, the daughter of Ralph Bernard, her sisters, Matilda, Hawise, Agnes and Beatrix, and her husband, William, gave lands to Stixwould. Of the sixty-three witnesses twenty were women, one of whom, Ragenild, wife of Ailmer, witnessed twice – in the general witness list and in the list for Agnes at the end of the charter. The named individuals were attesting on behalf of each sister, since the list is divided into three. Those witnessing for Beatrix and Agnes are listed sequentially. Beatrix made her gift at Heuton, and Agnes, her sister, also made her gift on a different occasion attested with a separate witness list. A general feature of all these female witnesses is that most of the women are listed after their male kin, and wives witness as daughters and mothers of male attestors.[90] In 1172 Alexandria, as a widow, and after the death of her son, again granted a charter in favour of Stixwould, which lists nine female witnesses and thirty men.[91] When Alexandria's son had previously granted a confirmation charter at about the same date as his mother's grant there was only one female witness.[92] Such group female attestations show the importance of kin connections, the definition that marital status gave to women, and the role of witnesses as guardians of the social memory of the occasion.

There is less evidence of groups of women witnessing independently in contexts divorced from family connections and tenurial obligations. It is striking that in the following examples groups of noblewomen witness for other noblewomen. Seven noblewomen who witnessed a charter by Hawise countess of Aumâle in 1181 were possibly her ladies-in-waiting.[93] When in 1212–14 she confirmed to Garendon Abbey various gifts three women, Alice *de Fontibus*, Richeuda and Clementia, *puellis meis*, witnessed her charter. Their names are last on the list of *testes*, following three male office holders, two abbots and a sheriff, and three other men.[94] It is possible that these 'girls' held important office or performed defined functions within her household. There are other examples of high-status women witnessing charters for other women: for example, in 1185 Marie countess of Champagne and Hawise countess of Gloucester witnessed a charter of Queen Margaret, the widow of Henry the Younger (d. 1183), made for the benefit of his soul.[95] Alice duchess of Burgundy, Matilda countess of Tournai and Matilda abbess of Fontevrault witnessed a charter of Eleanor of Aquitaine in favour of Alice prioress of Fontevrault *c.* 1200.[96] There are also examples of lower-status women witnessing for other women, and it is unclear whether these witnesses had a kindred connection with the female grantor. When *c.* 1170–98 Matilda, the daughter of Roger of Huditoft, gave lands to Revesby held by Alice, sister of Hugo *Habba*, the lady Margaret and Elena, the wife of Roger the cleric, both witnessed last after six male witnesses. A further grant by Matilda *tempore viduitatis mee* was witnessed by ten male witnesses and lastly by Christina, wife of Henry de Claxby, and Eda, wife of Richard, *clerici de Mar'*.[97] In 1160–70, when three women witnessed a charter granted by Emma de *Selveleia*, their names are listed sequentially following those of their husbands, who also witnessed.[98] Only one, Athelina, is named: the other two simply witness as *uxor eius* [of their husband, named] and they are at the bottom of the witness list, following fourteen male witnesses, who are listed in descending social status. It is unclear whether these female witnesses had any relationship with Emma, the grantor. A grant by Margaret, the wife of Roger de Bray, in the early thirteenth century was witnessed by two women, one who witnessed as the wife of a male witness, and one who is listed as *Petronille vidua et fuit uxor Rob' le gag'*.[99] The use of *vidua* to define a woman's status in a witness list is unusual. In the late twelfth century three sisters and co-heiresses, Dianisia, Seiva and Agnes, sold to a certain William the Weaver lands worth 19*s*. The charter, agreed in the lord's court, listed six female witnesses, as well as twenty-one named men and *multis aliis*.[100]

The formulaic closing protocol *et multis aliis* on many charters is indicative of more than diplomatic practice, and the way that male names are listed in descending hierarchical order of social rank and personal importance due to office holding is well established. The way that women's names fit into this schema is indicative of the mutable interactions of rank and gender which influenced female identities. When high-ranking women such as queens and countesses witness, whether as wife or widow, their name is usually at the head of a witness list. Like-wise, the importance of the female life cycle in the way that it gave women social definition can be seen in the way that women's names are recorded on charters, as can the importance of a gendered hierarchy as an organising principle on witness lists. When Isabella countess of Warenne witnessed a vassal's charter made in her court, she was fulfill-ing one of the functions of lordship. However, she did so during the period of her first widowhood, 1159–65, before her second marriage.[101] She is listed as first witness as *Ipsa Isabel comitissa*. The names of the countesses of Gloucester and Chester appeared at the head of witness lists. Their social status overrode the disability of gender conventions in the specific context of female witnessing. By contrast, in the last quarter of the twelfth century lower-status female group witnesses are listed at the end of the lists of *testes* after named male witnesses.[102] For example, in 1180–4 Hamo, son of Meinfelin, granted land to Aldith, the wife of the king's forester.[103] The charter was witnessed by eleven male witnesses and two women, Cecilia, *sponsa Alani*, and Margaret, *sponsa Mauricii*.[104] Aldith's daughters-in-law, who witnessed as part of a family group, appeared after their husbands and last on the list.

The impact of the female life cycle upon the participation of women as witnesses can be assessed where a series of extant charters relate to the same woman across her life cycle. Mabel countess of Gloucester, mother-in-law of Hawise, attested four charters for her husband, Earl Robert, as first witness. Her participation rate in his *acta* as a witness was over 30 per cent.[105] In her husband's foundation charter of Margam Abbey her consent was specifically mentioned, since the lands were of her inheritance.[106] Of those *acta* that she witnessed two were in favour of Montacute Priory (Somerset) and date from 1132 and *c.* 1135 respec-tively. In a charter of 1140–47 in favour of St Peter's Abbey, Gloucester, she is entitled *Mabilia comitissa*.[107] In a charter of Earl Robert's, in favour of Tewkesbury Abbey, which may have been issued as early as 1121–22 but possibly as late as 1147, she is listed as *Mabilia coniuge mea*.[108] At a critical period in the 1140s Earl Robert of Gloucester and Miles earl of Hereford made a treaty whereby Miles surrendered his son to Earl Robert as surety of his support for the earl and the Angevin cause. Countess Mabel was made responsible for ensuring that Earl Robert adhered to the agreement, so much so that if he did not keep to it she was respon-sible for bringing him back to it.[109] The clause details Countess Mabel's affadavit to 'use her power' to ensure the agreement was fulfilled and is paralleled by a similar clause to ensure that Earl Miles abided by the agreement. However, the affidavit was made by Earl Miles's son

Roger. This careful delegation of responsibility defines Mabel as *comitissa* responsible for ensuring her lord (*suum dominum*) complied, Roger for *patrem suum*. No doubt the scribes who composed the charter did so with great care, and thus the way that the role of the individuals concerned was described was important. Mabel was defined in terms of lordship, Roger by his family status. This treaty shows Mabel's role at the epicentre of the Gloucester administration at a critical period in the Angevin cause. It is possible that Mabel acted as regent for Earl Robert whilst he was abroad helping Count Geoffrey of Anjou.[110]

There is evidence to suggest that as a widow Mabel retained some authority as dowager countess. In 1147–48 conjointly with her son she restored lands to Jocelin bishop of Salisbury, a 'significant policy decision' in a charter which stressed her name first.[111] In 1147–57 she co-granted with her son a charter in favour of St Gwynollyw's church (Newport, Monmouthshire).[112] There is charter evidence to suggest that Mabel acted in some official capacity for her son in Normandy. In 1147–57 Earl William granted protection to Savigny Abbey. The writ-charter is addressed specifically to Mabel, his mother, his *bailli* and his Norman men, and commanded her to maintain Savigny's rights in proper lordship by the use of his power. It is thus evidence that Mabel was in control of, and responsible for, the Norman territories of the earldom of Gloucester.[113] Mabel's role, her power and authority changed as she moved through the female life cycle from wife of the earl to dowager countess. Thus the witnessing activity of both countesses of Gloucester should be seen in their social and political contexts and her importance as the wife of the earl of Gloucester. It was as the countess, or 'my wife', that Mabel as countess of Gloucester headed witness lists which include key office holders, the dapifer and constable, within the Gloucester administration. The impact of the female life cycle is apparent as other evidence from the *acta* relating to the Gloucester lands show that Mabel's role as a widow was important administratively for her son. Thus as an index of Mabel's personal power witnessing presents only a partial and fragmentary view, since she did not witness her son's *acta* but nevertheless had an important role to play in supporting his policies.

Gundreda de Gournay witnessed eight of her son Roger de Mowbray's charters, usually as first witness, in 1138–54.[114] All the charters she witnessed were in favour of religious houses. In four cartulary copies she is listed as Roger's mother.[115] In two charters which survive in the original she is listed as *domina Gundreda matre mea* and *domina Gund(reda)*.[116] In a charter where she witnessed first, in front of her daughter-in-law, she was *Gundreda matre mea* and Roger's wife, Alice de Gant, was Alice *uxore mea*.[117] In another charter where she witnessed as part of a family group, Gundreda as *matre mea* was first witness, followed by Nigel, his son, and Alice, *uxore mea*, witnessed third, before four named male witnesses *et al.* Two forged original charters include Gundreda as a witness, one lists her as *Gundrea mater mea* before his sons Nigel and Robert, the other places her second to last as *Gundrea matre mea* before *Aelizia uxore mea*.[118] Gundreda conjointly granted three charters with her son Roger de Mowbray early in his majority in *c.* 1138–40[119] but she witnessed only one charter of her son, which confirmed a conjoint grant.[120] When Roger augmented this gift and confirmed it in 1140, Gundreda witnessed the grant.[121] Setting Gundreda's role into context as a witness is further complicated when we consider Roger's later augmentation and confirmation of this gift in the same year.[122] Gundreda did not witness further grants by Roger to Byland in the period to 1154.[123] However, she did maintain an interest in the abbey. In 1147 the monks of Byland were in conflict with various local landholders. They appealed to Roger de Mowbray as their superior lord, who arranged for legal proceedings in the king's court. Gundreda acted as Roger's informant and adviser, since she sent a letter containing information to Normandy with Abbot Roger, who ensured its safe delivery to Roger. In response, Roger de Mowbray wrote a letter to 'Gundreda his mother and his steward and his bailiffs of York that they were to protect and defend Abbot Roger'.[124] Gundreda's interests in religious houses were not confined to Byland Abbey: she granted land to other ecclesiastical beneficiaries, including Garendon Abbey, Newburgh Abbey, Rievaulx Abbey, St Leonard's Hospital, York, and St Michael's Hospital, Whitby.[125] Gundreda de Gournay's role as a witness for her son, when set into the context of her interests, is one facet of her role as a widow; as with Mabel countess of Gloucester, witnessing is one gauge of her personal power. The basis of her authority was her position as mother, her relationship with her son, the current lord. She may have had an important role as the protector of Byland's rights, and may perhaps have been acting as a Roger's representative when he was absent from Yorkshire defending his castle of Bayeux in 1147. This suggests that Gundreda may have had some official role, responsible for Roger's lands in Yorkshire during his absence in France.

All the above evidence shows that women participated as witnesses in land transfers as wives, widows and as part of family groups. Rates of female participation are hard to assess, since survival rates of documents are haphazard and there was variation in diplomatic practice, and thus there may well be instances where women's property is the subject of a charter but where the woman does not witness. This of course reflects on women's role as witnesses, but, as the discussion of Gundreda de Gournay and Mabel countess of Gloucester has shown, witnessing is just one gauge of an individual's power. Female witnessing is reflective of the fluctuations in women's power through the impact of the female life cycle, as Stafford suggested. Bates and Barthélemy are right to suggest that charters should be studied in the socio-cultural contexts which produced them. As Bates noted, attestations are a problematic guide to power, politics or the significance of individuals, and developments in documentary forms must also be taken into account.[126] Despite this, certain lessons can be drawn from the evidence, and it is clear that the evidence supports a maximalist view that, although it may not be directly apparent, family participation was important.[127]

By the end of the twelfth century witnessing had spread through society so that women of all ranks of landholder participated as witnesses. Social rank, as expressed through title, took precedence over limitations of gender to define their place on witness lists, since high-status women and wives of grantors usually appear at the head of witness lists. Where women witness, their position is clarified through a definition of their marital status or family connections with male kin. When women acted as a joint witness with their husband as confirmers of a vassal's charter they did so as wives who acted conjointly with their husband in performing a function of lordship. All this reflects on the role of the witness as a male-gendered function, because male witnesses predominate in twelfth-century charters. Thus noblewomen witnessed mostly for their husbands and male kin, and although they could witness in other contexts – for female kin, or for other women – they did so only rarely. This is in contrast to male witnesses, who witnessed as office holders, as family members or as interested parties with tenurial connections with the land conveyed. This is gender-specific because women's participation was founded on their marital status, and the life cycle was predominant in the definition it gave to their participation. It could be argued that gender precluded participation in witnessing more than rank and social status, since it has been shown here that women's participation in witnessing was relatively restricted whatever their social rank. Bates, on a more limited range of documents than has been surveyed here, contended that lordship, family and custom shaped documents and that witnessing must be therefore understood in a context which takes account of the interplay of 'private and public' forms of power.[128] As Professor Vincent noted, not only does such a methodology convincingly undermine Warren Hollister's analysis of witness lists but, more important, it also confirms that several interactive factors, including opportunity, chance and personal relations, contributed to the appearance of individuals as witnesses.[129] In terms of understanding female witnessing this insight is crucial. We can go further, however, and argue that although female witnessing is a limited guide to the power of any individual, witnessing nevertheless reflects the ways that gender, lordship, the female life cycle, familial, social and tenurial connections impacted upon the power of twelfth-century noblewomen and thus served to define their roles.

Notes

1 As first witness, *Gloucester Charters*, nos 5, 7, 35–7, 44, 47, 49, 51–2, 65, 69, 71, 77, 88–9, 99, 102–3, 106, 118 (forgery), 120, 124–36, 168, 180, 182–3, 186–9; second witness in nos 116, 191; third in no. 111. Of the 111 *acta* listed, forty-one were excluded because they present no witness list, were issued prior to the marriage of William and Hawise or else are forgeries; excluded charters include nos 5, 11–30, 36, 85, 86, 96, 118, 171–2, 178–9. For Hawise's seal see Appendix 1, no. 54.

2 In a chirograph of 1155–60 made at the earl's court at Torigny-sur-Vire she is second after Earl William (*Gloucester Charters*, no. 186); in a charter in favour of Llanthony Priory (Monmouthshire) in 1150–65 she is listed as third witness after her parents Robert earl of Leicester and Amice the countess (*Gloucester Charters*, no. 111); she is second witness after bishops in charters in favour of ecclesiastical beneficiaries (*Gloucester Charters*, nos 116, 191). She is third witness in no. 100, after the abbot and prior of St Augustine's, Bristol.

3 *Gloucester Charters*, no. 113.

4 *Ibid.*, no. 115.

5 *CDF*, no. 41, a charter by which Margaret, daughter of Philip, king of France, made provision for monks of Clairvaux to pray for her husband's soul. In 1185 Margaret's dowry, the Vexin, was transferred to her sister Alice, who was betrothed to Richard. It is intriguing that Hawise associated with Margaret in their widowhoods – had they become friends during their husbands' rebellions? See W. L. Warren, *Henry II* (London: Eyre Methuen, 1977), pp. 598–603, 609–11.

6 D. A. Postles, 'Choosing a witness in twelfth-century England', *Irish Jurist*, 23 (1988), 336.

7 F. Pollock and F. W. Maitland, *A History of English Law before the Time of Edward I* (Cambridge, 1895, 2nd edn 1898, repr. London: Cambridge University Press, 1968), 1. 484–5.

8 Postles, 'Choosing a witness', p. 335.

9 J. Hudson, 'Anglo-Norman land law and the origins of property', in G. S. Garnett and J. G. H. Hudson (eds), *Law and Government in Medieval England and Normandy: Essays in Honour of Sir James Holt* (Cambridge: Cambridge University Press, 1994), pp. 198–222, at p. 210.

10   J. G. H. Hudson, *Land, Law and Lordship in Anglo-Norman England* (Oxford: Clarendon Press, 1994), pp. 158–9; S. D. White, *Custom, Kinship and Gifts to Saints: The* Laudatio Parentum *in Western France, 1050–1150* (Chapel Hill NC: University of North Carolina Press, 1988), p. 3; E. Z. Tabuteau, *Transfers of Property in Eleventh-century Norman Law* (Chapel Hill NC: University of North Carolina Press, 1988), pp. 142–69; M. Clanchy, *From Memory to Written Record: England, 1066–1307* (London: Edward Arnold, 1979; 2nd edn Oxford: Blackwell, 1993), pp. 254–5.

11   T. Reuter, 'Property transactions and social relations between rulers, bishops and nobles in early eleventh-century Saxony: the evidence of the *Vita Meinwerci*', in W. Davies and P. Fouracre (eds), *Property and Power in the Early Middle Ages* (Cambridge: Cambridge University Press, 1995), pp. 169–70.

12   *Gloucester Charters*, no. 186. Cf. witness to quitclaim made by Avice, wife of Philip of Galway to William de la Mare, who had challenged possession: *ibid.*, no. 106.

13   *Ibid.*, no. 188.

14   Postles, 'Choosing a witness', p. 345; Tabuteau, *Transfers of Property*, p. 142; Reuter, 'Property transactions and social relations', p. 170. For a cartulary which does not include original documents see 'Early charters of Sibton Abbey, Suffolk', ed. R. Allen Brown, in Patricia M. Barnes and C. F. Slade (eds), *A Medieval Miscellany for Doris Mary Stenton* (PRS, new ser., 36, 1962 for 1960), pp. 65–76.

15   P. Dalton, *Conquest, Anarchy and Lordship: Yorkshire, 1066–1154* (Cambridge: Cambridge University Press, 1994), p. 259; Hudson, *Land, Law, and Lordship*, p. 159.

16   Clanchy, *Memory to Written Record*, pp. 254–6. Postles, 'Choosing a witness', p. 345, suggests the role of the witness in ensuring the security of a gift declined in the later twelfth century. See Hudson, *Land, Law, and Lordship*, p. 159. For Normandy, Tabuteau, *Transfers of Property*, p. 119.

17   T. K. Keefe, 'Counting those who count: a computer-assisted analysis of charter witness lists and the itinerant court in the first year of the reign of King Richard I', *Journal of the Haskins Society*, 1 (1989), 135–45. T. Webber, 'The scribes and the handwriting of the original charters', *JCAS*, 71 (1991), 139. D. F. Fleming, '*Milites* as attestors to charters in England, 1101–1300', *Albion*, 22 (1990), 185–98; *English Episcopal Acta*, II, *Canterbury, 1162–90*, ed. C. R. Cheney and B. E. A. Jones (London: Oxford University Press, for the British Academy, 1986), p. xxv; *English Episcopal Acta*, V, *York, 1070–1154*, ed. J. E. Burton (Oxford: Oxford University Press, for the British Academy, 1988), p. xxxiii; M. Chibnall, 'The charters of the empress Matilda', in Garnett and Hudson (eds), *Law and Government in Medieval England and Normandy*, pp. 291–3. For royal households see *RRAN*, 'Introduction', to vols 1–3. For intra-familial politics see Jones, 'La vie familiale de la duchesse Constance', and Chapter 4 nn. 66–7 above.

18   Tabuteau states that for Norman churches the length of a witness list was not a particular concern – practice varied from church to church – and that neither rank nor class made an individual suitable to witness: *Transfers of Property*, p. 156; Hudson, *Land, Law, and Lordship*, p. 159; J. Hudson, *The Formation of the English Common Law: Law and Society in England from the Norman Conquest to Magna Carta* (London: Longman, 1996), p. 42.

19   *Mowbray Charters*, p. lvii, where the lord's family were supplemented by members of the household, knights and those who held by socage tenure.

20 Postles, 'Choosing a witness', p. 333. For Normandy see Tabuteau, *Transfers of Property*, p. 153.

21 D. Barthélemy, *La Société dans le comté de Vendôme de l'an mil au XIV siècle* (Paris: Fayard, 1993).

22 O. Guyotjeannin, '*Penuria Scriptorum* : le myth de l'anarchie documentaire dans la France du nord (Xᵉ–première moitié du XIᵉ siècle), *Bibliothèque de l'École des chartes*, 155 (1997), 11–44. For Guyotjeannin the spread in literacy was due to the church's Gregorian reform, and was not about power relations. Reynolds, *Fiefs and Vassals*, p. 64, suggests this is a particular problem in the debate over the origins of property law and English feudalism.

23 J. H. Prell, 'Les souscriptions des chartes des comtes de Poitiers, ducs d'Aquitaine (1030–1137), *Bibliothèque de l'École des chartes*, 155 (1997), 214.

24 D. Bates, 'The prosopographical study of Anglo-Norman royal charters', in K. S. B. Keats-Rohan (ed.), *Family Trees and the Roots of Politics* (Woodbridge: Boydell, 1997), p. 90.

25 Bates, 'Prosopographical study', p. 90. For comments on the twelfth century see *Mowbray Charters*, p. lxix, which likewise discusses the problem of the construction of witness clauses in the context of the authentication of documents by beneficiaries.

26 Bates, 'Prosopographical study', p. 92.

27 *Ibid.*, pp. 100–1.

28 *RRAN: The Acta of William I, 1066–87*, pp. 93–4; Duchess Matilda, wife of William I, witnessed half the ducal diplomas (a role she continued as queen): *Recueil des Actes des ducs de Normandie de 911 à 1066*, ed. M. Fauroux (Mémoires de la Société des antiquaires de Normandie, 36, Caen, 1961), p. 58; for Matilda, the wife of Henry I, see *RRAN*, 2, e.g. nos 524, 534, 538, 544, 547–8, 550, 554, 601, 607, 624, 634, 645; she both witnessed and acted as a *signa*.

29 Stafford, 'Emma', pp. 6–8.

30 *Ibid.*, p. 6.

31 *Ibid.*, p. 14.

32 Nelson, 'Gender and genre', p. 151.

33 Reuter, 'Property transactions and social relations', p. 168. See also M. Innes, 'Memory, orality and literacy in an early medieval society', *Past and Present*, 158 (1998), 5.

34 Reuter, 'Property transactions and social relations', p. 168.

35 *Gloucester Charters*, pp. 25–30.

36 *CDF*, 1. no. 1136.

37 *Ibid.* no. 1138.

38 Stafford, 'Emma', p. 8, shows that Emma was the only secular woman to witness royal charters. In eleventh-century Normandy women witnessed charters very rarely, except for the duchesses: Tabuteau, *Transfers of Property*, pp. 146–7.

39 J. C. Holt, 'Feudal society and the family in early medieval England', IV, 'The heiress and the alien', *TRHS*, 5th ser., 35 (1985), 1–28, esp. pp. 10–19; S. F. C. Milsom, 'Inheritance by women in the twelfth and thirteenth centuries', in M. S. Arnold, T. A. Green, S. A. Scully and S. D. White (eds), *On the Laws and Customs of England: Essays in Honor of Samuel E. Thorne* (Chapel Hill NC: University of North Carolina Press, 1981), pp. 60–89, esp. pp. 65–73.

40 For 1085–6: Lescelina, the wife of Geoffrey de Mandeville, 'The original charters of Herbert and Gervase abbots of Westminster (1121–1157)', ed. P. Chaplais, in *A Medieval Miscellany for Doris Mary Stenton*, ed. Patricia M. Barnes and C. F. Slade (PRS, new ser., 36, 1962 for 1960), pp. 89–110, at appendix A, pp. 105–8; she witnesses as the 'Lady Lesclina my wife'. 1090–96: Emma de Port, *EYC*, 2. no. 855.

41 For 1100–01: Hawise and her daughters Iveta and Advenia, *CDF*, nos 1136, 1138. *Circa* 1100–14: William count of Evreux and his wife, Hawise, *CDF*, no. 478. 1107–19: Matilda de L'Aigle, *Mowbray Charters*, nos 5, 7, 10. For 1123: *Ancient Charters, Royal and Private, Prior to A.D. 1200*, ed. J. H. Round (PRS, old ser., 10, 1888), no. 11 and notes following.

42 For 1130: Edith, wife of Maurice de Windsor, 'Some charters relating to the honour of Bacton', ed. B. Dodwell, in *A Medieval Miscellany for Doris Mary Stenton*, ed. Patricia M. Barnes and C. F. Slade (PRS, new ser., 36, 1962 for 1960), pp. 154–5 and 161–2, no. 6. For 1130: Rohais, the daughter of Alice de Clare, *Northants. Charters*, no. 18. For 1132–47: Mabel countess of Gloucester, *Gloucester Charters*, nos 156–7, 84, 283 (176a). For 1135–50s: Matilda countess of Chester, *Chester Charters*, nos 37, 84, 98–9. For 1138–54: Gundreda de Gournay, *Mowbray Charters*, nos 21, 32, 37, 40, 49 (fabrication), 98–9, 200, 228 (forgery), 289. For 1135–8: Adeliza, wife of Richard fitz Gilbert, *Chester Charters*, no. 39.

43 For 1140–4: Rohais countess of Essex, *The Cartulary of Holy Trinity Aldgate*, ed. G. A. J. Hodgett (London Record Society, 7, 1971), no. 962. For 1144–50: Alice de St Quintin, *EYC*, 1. no. 541. For 1144–56: Matilda, wife of Henry d'Oilli, *EYC*, 2. no. 1239. For 1148–55: Rohais, wife of Baderon, *CDF*, no. 1143. For 1150–65: Hawise countess of Gloucester, see n. 1 above. For 1154–63: Lescelina de Trailli, 'Charters relating to the honour of Bacton', pp. 162–3, no. 8. For 1157: Emma, wife of Roger of Arundel, *Sarum Charters*, no. 31. For 1160–71: Margaret duchess of Brittany, *EYC*, 4. nos 58–9, 64–7. For 1160–72: Bertrada countess of Chester, *Chester Charters*, no. 185. For 1165–72: Margaret de Chesney, *Oxford Charters*, no. 48. For 1169–87: Oliva de Vaus, 'Charters of Sibton Abbey', p. 72, no. 6.

44 Exceptions: Adeliza, the wife of Richard fitz Gilbert, who witnessed for her brother, Earl Ranulf of Chester (see n. 42 above); Iveta and Adevenia, daughters of William, son of Baderon (see n. 43 above); Rohais, the daughter of Alice de Clare (see n. 43 above). Alice de Gant witnessed as a wife and widow (see n. 96 below); Gundreda de Gournay as a widow (see pp. 95–6 and n. 42 above).

45 *The Early Charters of Waltham Abbey 1062–1230*, ed. R. Ransford (Woodbridge: Boydell, 1989), nos 1, 12, 311, 626, and see lxix.

46 *Eynsham Cartulary*, ed. H. E. Salter (2 vols, Oxford Historical Society, 49, 51, 1907–08) 1, charters nos 7–184; of these nos 7–9, 11–12, 15A, 16, 18, 21, 23, 24–5, 34, 40, 44A, 44B, 48–9, 51–4, 58, 61, 67, 78, 90A, 110, 131A, 143, 146, 150, 159A, 173, 176–9, 181–5 were excluded because they were either too early or too late, or have no witness list. Women witness nos 59 (third, wife of grantor), 65 (second after husband), 72 (fourth, sister of male witness), 79 (third after son and a clerk, Alice de Langetot, witnessing for grandson), 101 (first, wife of grantor), 105 (second, wife of grantor), 132 (first, wife of grantor) 133 (first, wife of grantor).

47 *Early Charters of Waltham Abbey*, lxviii.

48 Conjoint husband and wife grants: *Eynsham Cartulary*, 1. nos 64 (with son), 66 (with son), 67, 80, 81, 84, 90, 109, 112, 113, 116, 138, 153, 166, 172. Female grantors: nos 67, 83, 92–3 (same grantor), 109, 111, 124, 126 (mother and son), 130, 139, 145, 167; 142. Other female involvement: 110 (wife involved as petitioner in concord made at the king's court), 148 wife (and sons) received countergift; nos 167, 170: husband and wife received countergifts; no. 147: mother involved in affidavit; no. 179: wife involved in final concord.

49 Of seventeen charters granted by Nigel d'Aubigny, seven must be excluded, since they date possibly to the period after 1118, and four have no witness list or are heavily abbreviated: *Mowbray Charters*, nos 1–3, 6, 12–17.

50 *Mowbray Charters*, nos 5, 7, 10; *EYC*, 2. no. 855 (1090–96), where Emma de Port witnessed for her husband, William de Percy.

51 Given the dating limits of this charter of 1109–24 it could possibly relate to Gundreda de Gournay, Nigel's second wife; for the *acta* of Nigel d'Aubigny: *Mowbray Charters*, nos 1–17, the concession of *uxoris mee*, no. 11. There is no evidence to show that Nigel d'Aubigny's second wife, Gundreda de Gournay, whom he married in 1118, witnessed his documents. There is only fragmentary evidence relating to the period 1118–29 (when Roger de Mowbray died), and no original charters survive: *Mowbray Charters*, nos 11–17.

52 *Chester Charters*, nos 37, 84, 98–9. Of 103 *acta* (nos 15–119) which relate to Earl Ranulf, 37 were excluded because they presented no witness list, were not Earl Ranulf's *acta*, were spurious, were writs or were charters of notification: nos 15, 17–19, 20, 23, 28–33, 48–9, 51, 53–4, 59, 70, 75, 79, 83, 86, 89, 91, 94, 97, 100, 102, 105–6, 110, 112–14, 116. See above, Chapter 4, for a detailed discussion of the *acta* of Matilda and her role as a countess.

53 *Chester Charters*, no. 98.

54 *EYC*, 4, nos 58–9, 64–7.

55 'Original charters of Herbert and Gervase abbots of Westminster', pp. 105–8.

56 *Cartulary of Holy Trinity Aldgate*, no. 962 (1140–44), and for her son, Earl William; *Clerkenwell Cartulary*, no. 46 (before April 1176); and see above, p. 72, for Rohais. Other examples of wives witnessing: *EYC*, 2. no. 1239 (*c.* 1145–56); *Sarum Charters*, no. 31 (21 March 1157), no. 79 (*c.* 1201); *Clerkenwell Cartulary*, nos 21, 22 (1176, *ante* 1178–79); *Oxford Charters*, nos 8, 15, 48, 89; 162–3. 'Charters relating to the honour of Bacton', pp. 162–3, no. 8.

57 *Oxford Charters*, no. 48; her husband acted with her assent and at her petition.

58 *Cujus consilio et concessionem hanc donationem feci* (late twelfth to thirteenth-century): *The Chartulary of St John of Pontefract*, ed. R. Holmes (2 vols, Yorkshire Archaeological Society, Record Series, 25, 30, 1899 for 1898, 1902 for 1901), 2. no. 407.

59 *Chester Charters*, no. 185. In 1145–53 Richard de Curcy, *peticione et concessione Alicie uxoris mee*, gave to Jordan de Furches lands to hold by service of three-quarters of a knight's fee; unfortunately the cartulary copy of this charter has an abbreviated witness list, so it is unclear whether Alice witnessed or not: *EYC*, 4. no. 61. See below, Chapter 6, for discussion of countergifts more generally.

60 'Charters relating to the honour of Bacton', pp. 154–5 and 161–2, no. 6.

61 Possibly dowry: 'Charters relating to the honour of Bacton', pp. 154–5.

62　For the role of lordship in guaranteeing a tenant's right see Hyams, 'Warranty and good lordship', pp. 447–8, which argues that lordship was synonymous with protection over both vassals and their lands.

63　Hudson, *Land, Law, and Lordship*, pp. 140–1.

64　*Gloucester Charters*, no. 186.

65　Original charter: Huntington Library, San Marino CA, Stowe Grenville evidences, STG box 5, no. 18 (DBC). Cf. Matilda countess of Eu, who co-witnessed with her husband, Count Henry, the grant by a tenant, Odard the doctor, of Foucarmont, with his wife, Avicia, and with the concession of his niece Elizabeth and her husband, Eustace de Stoquis, of lands which were of Avicia's *maritagium*: Cartulary of Fourcarmont, Rouen, Bibliothèque Municipale Y13, f. 72r (thirteenth-century) (DBC). Also Alice countess of Eu and Earl Henry, her husband, witnessed charters by Thomas de St Leger and Renger de Northie: *Calendar of Charters and Documents relating to the Abbey of Robertsbridge co. Sussex, Preserved at Penshurst among the Muniments of Lord de Lisle and Dudley*, ed. P. Sidney (London: printed by Spottiswoode & Co., 1873), nos 4–5.

66　*CDF*, no. 478. Alienors witnessing their own charters were in fact an anomaly in eleventh-century Normandy, according to Tabuteau, *Transfers of Property*, p. 159. Their appearance is related to changes in the social significance of witnessing: Postles, 'Choosing a witness', p. 330. Another example of a wife co-witnessing with her husband: 1169–87, Oliva de Vaus, as second witness, 'Charters of Sibton Abbey', p. 72, no. 6.

67　Hudson, *Land, Law and Lordship*, pp. 141–2.

68　Bates, 'Prosopographical study', p. 94.

69　Hyams, 'Warranty and good lordship', pp. 440–1 and n. 8.

70　BL, Harl. Ch. 55. G. 9, dated 1154–89; for the seal of Matilda de Saint Liz see Appendix 1, no. 115.

71　*Luffield Priory Charters*, ed. G. R. Elvey (2 vols, Northamptonshire Record Society, 22, 26, 1968 for 1956–57, 1975 for 1973; jointly published with the Bedfordshire Record Society), 2. no. 757.

72　*CDF*, no. 1143. St Mary's, Monmouth, was a dependency of St Florent, Saumur: see *CDF*, no. 1136.

73　*EYC*, 3. no. 1771. Other examples: Rohais countess of Essex for her son, *Clerkenwell Cartulary*, no. 46; Muriel de Munteni for her daughter and son-in-law, *ibid.*, no. 79.

74　*Regesta Regum Scottorum*, II, *The Acts of William I, King of Scots, 1165–1214*, ed. G. W. S. Barrow (Edinburgh: Edinburgh University Press, 1971), nos 3, 39, 48, 55, 61, 75, 100. Cf. Agnes Basset, who witnessed her son's charter confirming her previous grant of dower to Stixwould: BL, MS Add. 46,701, f. 5v. Alice de Gant, as *domina matre mea*, witnessed a charter for her son, Nigel de Mowbray, and is the only named witness in the truncated cartulary copy (1186–90 or 1150–54): *Mowbray Charters*, no. 189. As *Aliz de Gant* Alice is listed as third witness, after the chaplains, Nicholas and Hugh, in a charter of her mother-in-law, Gundreda de Gournay, in favour of St Leonard's Hospital, York, in 1142–54: *ibid.*, no. 300. Her appearance as a witness to her son's charter and to that of her mother-in-law is no indication of her spheres of interest, nor of her relative power to pursue her own objectives. Alice issued six charters in favour of Fountains Abbey, and one each to Pontefract and

St Peter's, York: *Mowbray Charters*, nos 100–1, 104, 106–7, 131 (Fountains), 229 (Pontefract). Alice de Gant was married twice, firstly to Ilbert de Lacy (d. 1141–42) and subsequently, in 1142–43, to Roger de Mowbray; she predeceased him, dying 1176 × 1181: *Mowbray Charters*, pp. xxvii–xxviii, xxxxii. She acquired a seal in 1144–55: see Appendix 1, no. 48. In 1147 Alice de Albemarle, Gundreda, the mother of Roger de Mowbray, her second husband, and Matilda, the mother of Alice de Gant's first husband, Ilbert de Lacy, all witnessed a charter by Henry de Lacy confirming a grant of a carucate for the soul of Alice's first husband: *EYC*, 3. no. 1495 (1144–55); *Chartulary of St John of Pontefract*, I, 16, which gives the date as 1147. The land in Ingoldmells (Lincolnshire) that she granted to Pontefract was Alice's dower land that had been given to her by her first husband, Ilbert de Lacy: *Mowbray Charters*, no. 229; *EYC*, 3. no. 1494.

75 *EYC*, 3. no. 1861.

76 *Ibid.* no. 1862. Avice married *ante* 1130 William de Curcy, steward of Henry I. Amice was co-heir with her sister Alice to the barony of William Meschin following the death of their brother Ranulf *c.* 1135: *EYC*, 3. no. 1862, notes following.

77 *Ibid.* no. 1864; 6. no. 62.

78 *Clerkenwell Cartulary*, no. 74.

79 *Northants. Charters*, no. 18. For her seal see Appendix 1, no. 32. In 1154–89 both the son and the daughter of Agnes de Pincun witnessed her charter in favour of Kirkstead Abbey, which was in effect her will, and in which Agnes bound her heirs to warrant her gift: BL, Harl. Ch. 50. B. 21 (*Danelaw Charters*, no. 178); for her seal see Appendix 1, no. 101; cf. n. 109 below.

80 *Ancient Charters*, no. 11, and notes.

81 *Ibid.*, no. 6.

82 *EYC*, 1. no. 541.

83 BL, Cott. Ch. xii, 46 (*EYC*, 1. no. 543). The lands were the inheritance of Alice de St Quintin.

84 *EYC*, 1. no. 545.

85 *Ibid.* no. 546.

86 *Cartulary of the Abbey of Old Wardon*, ed. G. H. Fowler (Bedfordshire Historical Society, 13, 1930), no. 299; see also no. 300, which records four female witnesses to a grant by the same donor.

87 *EYC*, 2. no. 780; the other women are Matilda, the daughter of Tochman, Eda, the wife of Brian the Clerk (her daughter; cf. *EYC*, 2. no. 781), Hawise, the daughter of Literi, and Othild, the wife of Godwin Givenout.

88 BL, Harl. Ch. 50. B. 19 (*Danelaw Charters*, no. 177).

89 Three women witnessed sequentially, following their husbands, a charter of 1162–*c.* 1175 by Beatrice, the widow of Walter fitz Ivo, when she confirmed her husband's gift of lands to Rievaulx: *EYC*, 2. no. 1249.

90 BL, Egerton Ch. 428.

91 *Ibid.* Ch. 434.

92 *Ibid.* Ch. 433.

93 Stenton, *English Woman in History*, p. 36.

94 *Book of Seals*, no. 444.

95 *CDF*, no. 41.

96 *CDF*, no. 1108, giving Alice, her 'dear maid', £10 of lands from Poitou. Eleanor did not in fact routinely use female witnesses. See *ibid.*, nos 1061, 1080, 1092–4, 1096–1101. Of these charters only no. 1100 has a woman witnessing, a solitary female alongside eighteen men. For Eleanor's charters see F. G. Richardson, 'The letters and charters of Eleanor of Aquitaine', *EHR*, 74 (1959), 193–213; cf. W. W. Kibler (ed.), *Eleanor of Aquitaine: Patron and Politician* (Austin TX and London: University of Texas Press, 1976).

97 Dorothy M. Owen, 'Some Revesby charters of the soke of Bolingbroke', in *A Medieval Miscellany for Doris Mary Stenton*, ed. Patrica M. Barnes and C. F. Slade (PRS, new ser., 36, 1962 for 1960), pp. 232–4, nos 12, 13; Postles, 'Choosing a witness', pp. 340–2.

98 *Luffield Priory Charters*, 1. no. 107; the lands were Emma's inheritance, see *ibid.*, 267. She witnessed a charter for her son 1170–75, when he confirmed the grant made by his parents: *ibid.*, no. 111.

99 BL, Harl. Ch. 84. I. 22: Bertha *uxor Richard le Fre' Petronilla vidua et fuit uxor Rob. le gag'* witnessed last following eight male witnesses; for Margaret's seal see Appendix 1, no. 82.

100 *Northants. Charters*, no. 42; see also no. 43. For their seals see Appendix 1, nos 136–8. See Chapter 6 for a discussion of women's sealing practice.

101 *EYC*, 8. no. 111.

102 BL, Egerton Ch. 428; BL, Egerton Ch. 434; BL, Harl. Ch. 84. I. 22; *EYC*, 2. no. 780; *Cartulary of Old Wardon*, nos 299, 300.

103 *Luffield Priory Charters*, 2. no. 757.

104 *Ibid.*, nos 758, 759, 761. Two female witnesses following four male: BL, Add. Ch. 20,394 (grant by Matilda de Wateville, mid-twelfth-century; for her seal see Appendix 1, no. 134).

105 The following *acta* listed in the appendix to *Gloucester Charters* were excluded, since they are not reliable for these purposes: nos 192–4, 199–200, 209, 211, 216, 219, 226, 239–40, 242–3, 249–52, 255, 258, 273, 275, 278; see notes to *Gloucester Charters*, appendix 169. Of twelve *acta* granted by Earl Robert (*Gloucester Charters*, nos 6, 68, 70, 82–4, 95, 109–10, 119, 157, 283 (176a)), no. 82 has no witness list; Mabel witnessed nos 156–7 (1132–35), 84 (1140–47) and 283 (176a) (1121/22–47).

106 *Gloucester Charters*, no. 119.

107 *Ibid.*, nos 156–7; no. 84 and notes following, where Patterson suggests that, although the main text of the charter is problematical because there are discrepancies between different versions of the text, the witness list is not doubted.

108 *Ibid.*, no. 283 (176a).

109 *Ibid.*, no. 95.

110 *Ibid.*, 96, no. 95, and notes following.

111 *Ibid.*, no. 171.

112 *Ibid.*, no. 86.

113 *Ibid.*, no. 172, and notes following.

114 *Mowbray Charters*, nos 21, 32, 37, 40, 49 (fabrication), 98–9, 200, 228 (forgery), 289, all as first witness, except no. 37, where she is listed third. Gundreda was the second wife of Nigel d'Aubigny (d. 1129); she died in 1154, having remained unmarried.

115 *Ibid.*, nos 21, 32 (third witness after two male), 37 (in front of his brother), 40.

116 *Ibid.*, nos 98–9.

117 *Ibid.*, no. 200.

118 *Ibid.*, no. 228.

119 *Ibid.*, nos 33 (Byland 1138 × 1140), 170 (Hospitallers, York, *c.* 1138), 288 (Whitby, 1138 × 1140).

120 *Ibid.*, no. 33.

121 *Ibid.*, no. 37.

122 *Ibid.*, no. 35. According to this version of the confirmation charter transcribed into the Byland Chronicle, Gundreda did not witness the agreement with the monks, but the charter contains some suspicious elements. According to a different version, Gundreda witnessed the grant: *ibid.*, no. 37. It is therefore hard to be sure whether Gundreda was an authentic witness or not. The witness list on the original grant with her son may also be open to doubt, although the details of the gift itself are not.

123 *Ibid.*, nos 36–50.

124 *English Lawsuits from William I to Richard I*, ed. R. C. Van Caenegem (2 vols, Selden Society, 106, 107, 1990–91), 1. no. 323.

125 *Mowbray Charters*, nos 47 (Byland, 1147–54), 156 (Garendon, *c.* 1146), 232 (Rievaulx, 1138–43), 235 (Rievaulx, 1144–54); 287 (St Michael's Hospital, Whitby, 1130–38), 300 (St Leonard's Hospital, York, 1142–44).

126 Bates, 'Prosopographical study', p. 90.

127 As Hyams's analysis of charters and Glanville suggests: 'Warranty and good lordship', pp. 470–1. Yet closer attention to legal developments in twelfth-century society, especially after 1170, means that charters are relatively more reliable, although it is dangerous as yet to speculate upon a chronology of change in documentary forms: *ibid.*, pp. 474, 477.

128 Bates, 'Prosopographical study', p. 90.

129 N. Vincent, 'Review of *Family Trees and the Roots of Politics*', *EHR*, 114 (1999), 408.

6

Countergifts and affidation

Countergifts

THE EXCHANGE of material and spiritual countergifts was a method of ensuring the security of the land transfers which charters record. Historians view their significance in differing ways. Emily Tabuteau's pragmatic interpretation argues that contemporary society received both juridical and spiritual benefits through gift exchange and that material countergifts given to relatives of a donor represented a form of compensation for loss of land.[1] According to John Hudson, countergifts re-emphasised the mutuality between parties, that is, between donor(s) and beneficiary, could be symbolic and were usually voluntary.[2] This approach is similar to that of Barbara Rosenwein, who stressed the relationships between donors which were created when gifts were exchanged.[3] Dominique Barthélemy argues that social class was exhibited when precious objects such as gold rings were exchanged.[4] Stephen White also argues that the social context of gift exchange is important because countergifts were tangible expressions of specific social hierarchies and served to define the place of individuals within kin groups.[5] Further White stresses that as land transfers became more like sales by the early thirteenth century, and with the introduction of warranty clauses, the need for *laudatio parentum* declined because an effective method of cutting off family claims had been achieved.[6]

This discourse on the meaning of countergifts rightly debates the juridical implications and their symbolisms within social contexts. Little has specifically been written which directly addresses the problem of interpreting countergifts as a guide to the power of noblewomen, because the above historians are, for example, interested in the meaning of gift exchange ceremonies, or of the consent of relatives, rather than the power of women. White's suggestions that countergifts served to memorialise social status, were an aid to memory and were always exchanged to secure a gift are a useful way to consider the significance of countergifts as a guide to women's power.[7] Thus countergifts may also have had an important role in the creation of social memory, in which women had a role in commemoration of the *gens*.[8] This memorialisation role of the countergift is illustrated in the text of a charter given by Alice de Gant in 1176 whereby she received one gold ring for confirmation of her husband's grant of her dower. The charter's closing protocol states, *Et in testimonium et in rememorationem dederunt michi predicti monachi unum annulum aureum*.[9] Although few historians have addressed the significance of countergifts as a guide to the power of noblewomen, Lady Stenton's suggestion that countergifts to noblewomen represented 'signs of uneasy social conscience' on the part of beneficiaries when their husbands disposed of land they had acquired through marriage at least recognised the possibility that there were differences in the meaning of countergifts given to men and women. For Lady Stenton countergifts were a 'personal gift' which were to deter women's future claims to lands alienated by male kin.[10]

The following discussion, based on a wide survey of twelfth-century charters and cartularies, will consider the importance of material, as distinct from spiritual, countergifts given to secular noblewomen as a guide to their power. The analysis will be put into the context of an appraisal of the importance of gender, lordship and the way that family connections were indicated through countergifts. This will be achieved through a consideration of the importance of the type(s) of countergift that women received, and, where appropriate, this will be put into a comparative framework with those received by men. Thus it is argued that an analysis of countergifts should properly be studied in socio-cultural contexts but with an awareness of the impact of gender and the demands of tenurial lordship. Lordship is important because countergifts symbolised and reinforced hierarchy in lordship and were thus a social barometer of those involved in patronage. Likewise patterns of land tenure related to the female life cycle – dowry, dower and inheritance – are significant because this was increasingly important for the definition it gave to the relationship between lords and tenants, and the powers of husbands and wives or widows to control property. However, the right by which a woman held land is not always made clear in the texts of charters. Crucially, it is also imperative that the meanings and symbolisms of countergifts should be set into a paradigm which acknowledges that changes in diplomatic may have affected documentary forms. Thus as a gauge of social realities this assessment of countergifts is placed in a framework similar to that established in the previous chapter to analyse witnessing.

Although both men and women received an array of items as countergifts in twelfth-century England, male recipients of countergifts tended to receive horses, armour, hunting birds or money.[11] Barthélemy's study of the Vendôme 1050–1150 found, for example, that, out of fifty-five men at Marmoutier, twenty-one received objects relating to equitation. Barthélemy points out that it was not seemly for the nobility to receive farm animals as countergifts and that luxury objects were procured through the acquisition of countergifts.[12] Stephen White pointed out that benefactors of monastic institutions received objects as varied as clothing, jewellery, animals, grain and wine as well as both small and large amounts of money.[13] Both rightly stress the important influence of social status upon the nature of countergifts that were given to patrons. Yet gender also impacted on the sorts of gifts that were exchanged. For example, although in the twelfth century noblewomen did on occasion receive horses, only two examples have hitherto been located, and both recipients were heiresses. In 1160–70 Emma de 'Selveleia' received, with the consent of 'H.', her second husband, two marks and a palfrey when she gave lands worth 15s to Luffield Priory.[14] When c. 1170–5 her son and heir by her first marriage subsequently confirmed the grant, he received 20s and a palfrey.[15] Matilda countess of Warwick received 15s and a palfrey from Henry du Puiset, her nephew by an illegitimate daughter of her father, when she enfeoffed him with lands worth a quarter of a knight's fee c. 1175–94.[16] The sparsity of the evidence relating to the receipt of gifts such as horses as countergifts suggests that objects and accoutrements associated with horses were deemed more appropriate for male recipients. This was possibly related to ideas about lordship as a male role, and also military functions, which of course were generally associated with men.

Where noblewomen received objects of symbolic value, their participation could be linked with their tenurial claims to the land alienated. *Circa* 1149–56 Rohais, the wife of Gilbert de Gant, received a gold ring in return for a confirmation charter concerning her dower lands that had been granted to Kirkstead Abbey by her husband.[17] In 1150–60 William earl of Albermarle granted to his niece Eufemia, wife of Robert de Brus (II), her marriage portion, which she then granted to him for life in return for a gold ring and some money.[18] Eufemia's uncle thus retained control of family land, and perhaps provided her with a wedding ring, since the lands were of her marriage portion, and dowry in the form of a sum of money to take with her to her marriage. *Circa* 1160–70 when

Walter of Ingram sold land to Rievaulx Abbey he received fifteen marks, and his wife, Holdeard, who had consented to the sale, which concerned lands of her dower, received a gold ring.[19] Alice de Gant, as well as spiritual benefits, received a gold ring for her confirmation charter to Fountains Abbey of lands of her dower which had been previously granted by her husband, Roger de Mowbray.[20] In 1194–95 Atheliza Holebagge received one gold brooch from Gilbert de Reding in return for a grant in hereditary right of land worth 2s per year.[21] In 1189–1220 Juliana of Shudy Camps received a gold ring from her younger son, Moses, when she gave him lands for which he had to render £1 of cumin yearly.[22] When he received lands from his elder brother, Moses gave in return a sparrowhawk.[23] Gender, social status and land tenure interacted to define the sorts of gift that noblewomen received.

Both noblemen and noblewomen also received sums of money as countergifts, indeed Tabuteau found that in Normandy this was the most common form of material countergift.[24] In the late twelfth century Reginald de Meiniers and his wife confirmed their grant in frankalmoign of various lands to the abbey of Robertsbridge. The lands came to Reginald by right of his wife, Matilda, and he thus gave her £12 Anjou of rent out of his mill at Meiniers because she quitclaimed all her land in England to her husband. The monks of Robertsbridge paid £120 for the concession.[25] In another example the countergift apparently functioned as payment of relief. Matilda de Avranches in the late twelfth century received one gold mark for making recognition by charter of a vassal entering lands by right of inheritance.[26] When Basilia, daughter of Ailrich, c. 1210–15 quitclaimed lands to Robert, son of Matilda, she finalised the agreement in the court of her lord. For the quitclaim and her *abjuratione* Robert gave her 6s and his wife, Anne, gave Basilia a robe, *peplum*.[27] This example shows that both husband and wife were involved in giving countergifts to seal a specific transaction and that the wife of Robert was involved in the proceedings at court even though the text of the charter itself does not specifically mention to whom the quitclaim was made. That is, the text states that Basilia quitclaimed to Robert, not to Robert and his wife. The countergifts and stipulation of services related to dressmaking were the foundations of an economic agreement agreed between 'lord' and vassal. When Emma, daughter of Wimund Ravenildescroft, gave countergifts to Muriel de Munteni and subsequently to her daughter Lecia, she secured her tenure of lands by a combination of money and goods in payment. When Muriel granted the lands to Emma she received a *peplum*, and her daughter Lecia, on confirming this gift, some sandals. The lands were to be held by a render of 2s annually after Emma's death by her heirs.[28] These agreements of Lecia de Munteni and her mother, Muriel, with Emma Ravenildescroft suggest the variety of countergifts and that a countergift could apparently be a payment.

When husbands and wives were involved in joint actions both could receive countergifts; for example, c. 1167–78/79 Hawise countess of Gloucester and her husband, Earl William, both received gold rings from Richard de Lucy when Earl William enfeoffed Richard.[29] In 1192 Ralph fitz Geoffrey and his wife Matilda received twenty marks for their quitclaim made in the king's court from the monks of Eynsham Abbey.[30] These examples suggest ways that wives were conjointly recognised alongside their husbands when they acted in lordship. The specific place of women within familial social hierarchies and their social status in the wider community were both symbolised and confirmed when different amounts of money or different objects were exchanged. For example, in 1135–40 Robert de Sarz and his wife Ragnahild gave lands to Fountains to be held by a render of half a mark yearly. The grant had been given by the counsel and with the goodwill of Ragnahild.[31] In the same period Thurstan archbishop of York confirmed this to Fountains Abbey and Robert received one mark and Ragnahild received 3s.[32] In the late twelfth century William of Lanvallay received four marks for his acknowledgement of a tenant's right to land, whilst his wife received two talents.[33] When in the same period Stephen Canute of Whittlesford disposed of lands relating to his wife's marriage portion he received 14s and his wife Matilda received 12d.[34]

Since countergifts reveal social hierarchy such as the place of the individual within the kin, or such as those between husbands and wives, it follows that symbolic countergifts will reflect gender differences related to the meaning and power of those roles. *Circa* 1160 Regenerus the Painter gave Hugh de Camville and his wife, Christina, a countergift, Hugh received a *scaccarium* (chessboard or exchequer cloth) and Christina *wimplaria* (wimple/s). Whilst it may be the case that this gift 'transcended normality' it also shows gender divisions.[35] Hugh received a countergift which was of practical use, Christina an item of clothing which was gender-specific, since veils were used to cover the hair of married women. If the *scaccarium* was an accounting cloth, this countergift also reflects the predominance of his economic interest in the joint interest of husband and wife. Husband and wife here acted together to grant land to a painter, indicating patronage of an artist in an aristocratic household in which husband and wife were both involved. There are other examples which suggest that countergifts symbolised an individual's place in the family and in lordship. When in 1123–53 Hugh fitz Richard enfeoffed John of Kington in certain lands in Preston Bagot, Warwickshire, John in return gave him three marks, his son William half a mark and a sword, and Margaret, his wife, half a mark.[36] Margaret, the wife of Hugh fitz Richard, received a payment worth less than that of her husband, but nevertheless her place as wife of the lord was recognised; the gifts of a sword and money received by the son and heir were symbolic of his social status, function and place in the familial and social hierarchy. When Roger earl of Warwick confirmed this gift he received in return a white *brachet*, a hunting bitch.[37] When the widow of Earl Roger, Countess Gundreda, confirmed this the cartulary makes no mention of a countergift.[38] Her son, Earl William, however, received an iron-grey horse and five marks for his confirmation charter.[39]

There are therefore complex interrelated factors which explain the sorts of countergifts given. These include the type of transfer the countergift reinforced as well as such contexts as lordship, gender, social status and family links. *Circa* 1150–80 Ralph de Aincurt, Matilda, his wife, William, his son, and Robert gave to John the clerk and Basilia, the daughter of Ralph, four acres of land in Hanworth (Lincolnshire). In return John gave one mark to Ralph and his sons and Matilda received a 'certain gold ring' and a coverlet of Lincoln green.[40] Henry II *c.* 1175 confirmed a sale of a house in Rouen whereby Bernard Comin and his wife, Hawise, received £140 Anjou and a palfrey.[41] In the late twelfth century Gunnilda, the wife of Robert Sturmi, with the assent of her husband, confirmed his previous grant to the monks of Margam Abbey. For this concession she received four marks, a lambskin for a pellice and twenty sheep.[42] This grant concerned eighty acres of Gunnilda's dower lands, and since it was her dower land that was sold Gunnilda had to quitclaim, or make public recognition of the sale by charter to ensure the finality of the sale: the countergifts were thus in reality the price of the sale. It is difficult to know the precise negotiations which preceded the grant which the charters ratify, but the above examples suggest that wives acted in lordship with their husbands and this was recognised through countergifts, and that the socio-legal contexts affected the type of gift. Thus the nature of the transaction, as well as the land transacted, were equally important: a sale, or exchange of lands for specified 'countergifts' which were in reality payments, would obviously be a way of raising funds for a specific need such as financing a journey to Jerusalem,[43] or for combating poverty in widowhood,[44] or gaining goods or services.[45] It is more difficult to assess whether there was a decline in the symbolic value of countergifts. It is easier to detect that an increasing number of transactions in the twelfth century were sales. When Cecilia, daughter of Sabelina, granted a confirmation charter to Southwark Convent and Priory (Surrey), the countergifts given to her and her sons were given *in gersum*. The payments, however, reflected proprietary interest and status; Cecilia received five marks, her three sons, Geoffrey, Lawrence and John, one gold bezant respectively. This charter was sealed with four seals, and they too reflect hierarchy, since Cecilia's seal is the largest and the seals of her sons are graded in descending size.[46] In the early thirteenth century Margaret de Bray, as Margaret, daughter of *Aluffi de Merch'*, granted a confirmation charter of gifts made to St Mary's *Betelesden*. For her confirmation and quitclaim the monks gave her one mark, Miles her son and heir half a mark and his brothers similarly half a mark. These amounts have the character of monetary payments, which reinforced hierarchy in the differing amounts given but also symbolised her proprietary interest in the property conveyed.[47]

The above examples illustrate that countergifts could symbolise complex meanings and that noblewomen received countergifts in a variety of contexts. The conjugal relationship of husband and wife could be defined in the countergift, as in the de Camville example.[48] Noblewomen also received countergifts from their children, for example, from son to mother, as in the case of Juliana de Shudy Camps.[49] Matilda de Percy received a countergift from her half (illegitimate) nephew.[50] Sisters could participate in transactions with their male kin such as brothers. When, for example, Beatrice de Chevrecourt acted with her brother Ralph, between 1144 and 1155, with the consent of Ralph's sons, to give the town of Barnsley to the Cluniac priory at Pontefract in preparation for his entry into the monastery, the place of each was clearly evaluated in the countergifts that they received. The monks would appoint three monks, one for their mother, one for Beatrice and one for Ralph. Ralph would enter the monastery at his will and receive a small cash allowance and a monk's habit annually. In return for this concession Beatrice received ten marks, and Ralph received three, a monk's tunic and boots yearly. His sons too received gifts: Jordan received a palfrey, and Richard five marks. Their lord, Henry de Lacy, and his mother were present when the grant was agreed.[51] The example of Eufemia, the niece of William earl of Albermarle, suggests that nieces could also be the recipients of countergifts from within the family.[52] The family hierarchy was mapped out in economic terms, which could also have a symbolic aspect; this tends to confirm White's suggestion that kinship positions were demonstrated by countergifts.

Yet countergifts also illustrate networks of hierarchy beyond the family since women received countergifts from tenants/vassals. In this respect they also reinforced the place of women within social hierarchies within the community. When Gunnilda de Sturmi received her sheep and sums of money from Margam Abbey she did so as lord, with claims to the lands, and as wife: both roles empowered her socially and economically.[53] Thus the other hierarchy illustrated in the above examples is that of lordship, patronage and the administration of land. When Matilda de Percy enfeoffed her father's illegitimate son she acted as patron and landholder, operating in a wider family context.[54]

Precisely because ideas about gender underlay the way that women held land, that is, on the basis of the female life cycle, it underpinned ways that they participated in land transfers. Just as witnessing was gendered male, so countergifts when they expressed social status could also symbolise gendered ideas about the place of women in lordship. Where countergifts were of a monetary value in those transactions which had the character of a sale, women's subordinate position was demonstrated by the lesser amount that they received, but also their claim was symbolised and reinforced. Countergifts served to demonstrate the subordinate position of a.wife to her husband in society, but also paradoxically placed her at the centre of agreements whilst enshrining her position as a subsidiary but intrinsic party to them. Female participation could thus be predicated on their tenurial interests and thus women appear in transactions as witnesses or as the recipients of countergifts.

Affidation

The affidation ceremony was, like witnessing and the exchange of countergifts, a method of ensuring the security of an agreement. The ritualised public nature of affidation was briefly discussed by Herbert Fowler, who commented on the oddity of these occasions. He stated that affidation overlapped the beginning of warranty and that, according to Pollock and Maitland, 'it may look like an oath; we may think it implicitly contains all the essentials of an oath; but no relic or book or other thing is sworn upon and no express words of imprecation are used'. Affidation was a personal act which further strengthened the intent of the donee and was part of a ceremony to ensure the security of the gift. Indeed, Fowler noted that the affidation worked to ensure no future claims on the land by the parties or to warrant the land and that an 'affidation in the hand' was an 'ancient and solemn formality . . . by which a man placed his soul or honour in the hand of another should he fail to observe his part'.[55] Evidence of female participation in twelfth-century affidation ceremonies will be discussed as a guide to the power of noblewomen in the context of an analysis which considers the impact of gender, social status and lordship.

Circa 1166–76 Asceria, the widow of Asketil de Habton, made her affidavit in the hand of Bertha de Glanville, the wife of Ranulf de Glanville.[56] The charter recorded the occasion with particular care. The fact that Bertha's husband is listed as first witness suggests his presence at the ceremony, and therefore that she acted in a role which was related to his, but not necessarily in his place. There are six female witnesses listed, and female affidation is clearly often accompanied by female witnessing. The phraseology employed is concise: *Hanc donationem firmiter tenendam et fideliter observandam manu propria affidavi in manu vicecomitisse, videlicet Bert[he] uxoris vicecomitis Rannulfi de Glanvilla.* In addition, however, the use of the *vicecomitissa* title is suggestive that Bertha acted in an official capacity, and a way of expressing this was found. Certainly Bertha's role was rooted in her marital status and this was gendered because her husband's position of sheriff was not predicated on his marital status. The grant concerned lands which had been granted by Bertram de Bulmer to Asketil, son of Gospatric de Brageby, in 1147–66. His widow, Asceria, confirmed the grant to Rievaulx, since the lands in question were part of her dower. She also in the same charter accepted an exchange of lands made by her husband which also concerned lands that were hers by right of dower.

The evidence suggests that when women, whether as wives or widows, made an affidation they could, on occasion, make it in the hand of a woman. Circa 1175 Richard le Moine notified that his wife Alice had quitclaimed half a hide in Wardon which was of her dower. She made her affidation in the hand of Lecia, wife of William de Kirkby.[57] The witnesses were *March'*, presbiter, and Eularia and Lecia, sisters of the same, and Eva, wife of Jordan Inchegale. Alice made her affidation in the hand of her sister, which suggests that this was a public ceremony designed to forestall the claims of kin to the lands granted. A further example confirms the above patterns. Circa 1170–80 William Lenveise and his wife Denise sold and confirmed to Wardon Abbey whatever they held of its fee at Wardon, for the use of the hospices of the poor, by consent of Robert, son of Alfred. For this the abbey gave them three marks from the moneys of the hospice of the poor and 2s to Denise, his wife.[58] William made his affidation in the hand of William de Bedford, Denise in the hand of Lady (*domine*) Eularia. This conjoint grant and sale to the abbey was enacted in the court of the abbot, by the grant of

Robert fitz Alured. There is some slippage within the text between verbs which describe both the actions of William and Denise, for example the opening address uses verbs in the plural: William and Denise *uendidimus et presenti carta confimauimus*. Yet it was William who enacted the symbolic action which transferred seisin: *Et hanc cartam obtuli pro me et pro uxore mea super altare sancte Marie abbacie de Wardon*. There were six female witnesses, the lady Eularia, who received the affidation of Denise, Milisent, the wife of Malclerc, who also witnessed, Agnes, the wife of the clerk, Anschetill, Ralph the Clerk, the husband of Emma, and Emma, along with their daughters Alice and Olympiade. The monks gave them three marks and 2s to Denise. In another charter, granted in the same period, William Lenveise *per grantum et per uolantatem Dionisie uxoris mee* gave a croft and a messuage and a little land at Old Wardon at the rent of 1d for the use of the hospice of the poor; for this the abbey gave them 12s 4d as *gersum* from the moneys of the hospice. Denise's role was recorded separately from that of her husband, and when she participated in the ceremony she again made her affidation *in manu domine Eularie* whereas her husband made his in the hand of William *scriptoris*. The same witnesses attested this charter, according to the cartulary copy.[59] This evidence of female affidation indicates that when women made an affidation they were likely to do so in the hand of a woman. However, c. 1210 Alienora, the daughter of William de *Monte Alto* and Amicia de Swinton, gave land to Fountains she made her affidation *in curia de Richemund*. Thus the location of the ceremony was recorded, but to whom she swore her affidavit is not.[60] The affidation clause is immediately followed by a sealing clause to enhance further the security of the charter.

When Walter Bech and Agnes, his wife, made an agreement to exchange certain lands with Kirkstead Abbey in 1162, and licensed their men to do so, they both promised to warrant the exchange, and they both made an affidation in the hand of Walter abbot of Bardney.[61] This would seem to suggest that husband and wife could conjointly make an affidation. Most interestingly, however, there is an additional witness list to the affidation of Agnes which is exclusively female.[62] Thus although Agnes, acting with her husband, made her affidation in the hand of the abbot the witnesses to the occasion were all women. When in the mid to late twelfth century Beatrice, the widow of Joslan of Ingleby, confirmed her husband's gifts and granted lands of her dower to Kirkstead, she made her affidation in the hands of Edith, the wife of Brian de *Welletun*. Edith also witnessed the charter along with two other women, who are listed after nine male witnesses.[63]

Affidation was made by women in a public arena to disbar future claims and ensure the security of a gift. There is little evidence of women of the high nobility, such as countesses, making or receiving affidations. The highest-ranking woman who was involved in this public ceremony so far uncovered is Bertha de Glanville, *vicecomitissa*, and her role was to receive, not to make, the affidation. This suggests that social status mattered when making affidation, as did gender. Where women made affidations they usually did so in the hands of women, and on these occasions the participation of women in the ceremony was witnessed by women.

The concern of beneficiaries and patrons to ensure the security of their transactions explains the development of certain features of charters, including the inclusion of relatives in consent clauses to disbar future claims, the public ritual acts of placing gifts on altars, affidation, warranty, witnessing and countergifts. Warranty clauses are an indication of the concern to ensure good lordship, and were also a mechanism which neutralised family claims to land transactions.[64] Warranty clauses routinely appear in charters from the late twelfth century. It is possible that as early as 1140 specific clauses within charters appeared which ensured that both sexes were warranted against;[65] however, there is no simple timetable of documentary change in the late twelfth century.[66] Certainly it can be established that in the late twelfth century warranty clauses were developed which contained a phrase whereby the warrantor bound him/herself to uphold claims *contra homines et feminas*.[67] This development of what may be termed double warranty clauses against men and women to disbar claims from either sex shows that women were recognised as posing a threat to the security of gifts in claiming land, and may be related to the development of co-parceny – the division of land among female heirs. It confirms Hudson's view that warranty was primarily a way of securing a grant from an outside challenge.[68]

The exchange of material countergifts, affidation ceremonies and warranty clauses were methods intended to ensure the security of charters. The material countergifts that women received publicly confirmed noblewomen's societal position and place within the kin. They also confirmed the bonds of lordship and thus the relationships of both men and women with patrons and with beneficiaries. Social status mattered when countergifts were exchanged, as did gender in some instances. This is directly related to social status since noblewomen received gold rings or luxury objects, lower status women received sums of money, as did lower status men. Social status and gender also affected the way that affidation ceremonies were enacted. Only lower status women participated to make an affidavit: noblewomen received it. This study thus suggests that White, Tabuteau and Barthélemy are right to see countergifts as reflective of juridical concerns, social status and important for memorialisation of ceremonies.[69] If, however, the complex symbolisms of countergifts combined with the legalistic role of warranty and affidation, as discussed in the previous chapter concerned with female witnessing, were to be set into a reappraisal of the way that documentary forms changed and developed in the late twelfth century,[70] it would be clearer whether and how countergifts changed in symbolic meanings, and how ideas about gender affected this development.[71] The evidence here provides only a fragmentary and partial view of the nature of women's power because charters only imperfectly record the countergifts, warranty and affidation. It is important that the interactions of gender, social status and land tenure upon the power of twelfth-century noblewomen are incorporated into the analysis. If this is done, the involvement of women in the exchange of countergifts, warranty and affidation ceremonies develops the picture already presented in Chapters 4 and 5. Not only can we see charters as a representation and narrative of the power of countesses, or an indication of the involvement of women as witnesses, but also as an indication of the interaction of women of different social status and its importance, with kinship and lordship, in shaping noblewomen's identities.

Notes

1 E. Z. Tabuteau, *Transfers of Property in Eleventh-century Norman Law* (Chapel Hill NC: University of North Carolina Press, 1988), pp. 114–19, 133. Tabuteau emphasises that the receipt of a countergift did not necessarily indicate consent to a transaction, and that charters which mention countergifts were in the minority: *ibid.*, pp. 115, 118.

2 J. G. H. Hudson, *Land, Law and Lordship in Anglo-Norman England* (Oxford: Clarendon Press, 1994), pp. 165–6. For the symbolic meaning of objects attached to charters to secure conveyances see M. Clanchy, *From Memory to Written Record: England, 1066–1307* (London: Edward Arnold, 1979; 2nd edn, Oxford: Blackwell, 1993), pp. 37–43, 254–60. H. B. Teunis similarly argues that countergifts were voluntary, but focuses on religious institutions and sees countergifts as a method by which they attempted to encourage benevolent behaviour from patrons: 'The countergift *in caritate* according to the cartulary of Noyers', *Haskins Society Journal*, 7 (1997 for 1995), 88.

3 B. Rosenwein, *To be the Neighbor of Saint Peter: The Social Meaning of Cluny's Property, 909–1049* (Ithaca NY and London: Cornell University Press, 1989), pp. 136–43.

4 D. Barthélemy, *La Société dans le comté de Vendôme: de l'an mil au XIV siècle* (Paris: Fayard, 1993), p. 690.

5 S. D. White, *Custom, Kinship and Gifts to Saints: The* Laudatio Parentum *in Western France, 1050–1150* (Chapel Hill NC: University of North Carolina Press, 1988), pp. 27, 166.

6 *Ibid.,* p. 203.

7 *Ibid.,* pp. 26–8; Tabuteau similarly argues that countergifts were given as an aid to memory: *Transfers of Property,* p. 118.

8 M. Innes, 'Memory, orality and literacy in an early medieval society', *Past and Present,* 158 (1998), 1–36, at p. 5; J. L. Nelson, 'Gender and genre in women historians of the early Middle Ages', in *L'Historiographie médiévale en Europe* (Paris, 1991), 150–63, at p. 151.

9 *Mowbray Charters,* no. 131.

10 D. M. Stenton, *The English Woman in History* (London: Allen & Unwin, 1957), p. 31.

11 Ranulf (II) of Chester received a roan warhorse from his butler in return for land (1141–3): *Chester Charters,* no. 55. Ranulf (III) received two greyhounds called Lym and Libekar for a concession to his *hostarius* (1194–1202): *ibid.,* no. 271. Roger de Mowbray received a gold ring from his clerk in 1154–70: *Mowbray Charters,* no. 331; and for confirming a charter Roger received a palfrey (1154–79): *ibid.,* no. 333. For 100s Nigel de Mowbray confirmed his father's grant (1160–79): *ibid.,* no. 334. A fine and quitclaim of 1205 made in the king's court resulted in Robert abbot of Eynsham, giving ten marks, a palfrey and and an unmewed goshawk in of a dispute: *Eynsham Cartulary,* 1. no. 183.

12 Barthélemy, *La Société dans le comté de Vendôme,* p. 695.

13 White, *Laudatio Parentum,* p. 27.

14 *Luffield Priory Charters,* 1. no. 107. This grant was a confirmation of a previous conjoint gift made by Emma and her first husband, Eustace: *ibid.,* no. 114 (1140–60). She granted another charter to the monks with her third husband *c.* 1170–75: *ibid.,* no. 106. Emma was heiress to fees in Berkshire, Suffolk and Silverstone, Northamptonshire: *ibid.,* 267.

15 *Ibid.,* no. 111.

16 *EYC,* 11. no. 62.

17 BL, Harl. Ch. 50. F. 32; for her seals see Appendix 1, nos 49A and 49B.

18 *EYC,* 3. no. 1352.

19 *EYC,* 2. no. 710; see also *ibid.,* no. 712, where Walter Ingram gave William, son of Richard, the land of William, the father of Richard's wife. Walter Ingram's wife, Holdeard, received one mark from William, son of Richard, since the land was of her dowry. Thus the dowry was passing between the husbands of two sisters.

20 *Mowbray Charters,* no. 131. Roger's charter: *ibid.,* no. 120.

21 *Cartulary of Holy Trinity Aldgate,* no. 687.

22 *Early Charters of Waltham Abbey,* no. 188. See another grant by Juliana, *ibid.,* no. 189, with a similar countergift to seal the transaction.

23 *Ibid.,* no. 192.

24 Tabuteau, *Transfers of Property,* pp. 21, 27.

25 The lands conveyed were Matilda's marriage portion, given to her by Ingelram de Frescheville: *Calendar of Charters and Documents Relating to Robertsbridge,* no. 11. For King Richard's confirmation of this and other gifts see *ibid.,* no. 47.

26 Devon Record Office, 1262/M T531 (Fortescue Deeds) (DBC).

27 *The Early Records of Medieval Coventry*, ed. P. Coss (British Academy, Records of Social and Economic History, new ser., 11, 1986), no. 29.

28 *Clerkenwell Cartulary*, nos 65, 73 (*c.* 1193–96). For a further discussion of these charters see below, Chapter 8.

29 *Gloucester Charters*, no. 115.

30 *Eynsham Cartulary*, 1. nos 108, 110. For Matilda de Lucy's charter confirming the agreement, probably made at the same time, see *ibid.*, no. 109.

31 *EYC*, 1. no. 65: *cum consilio et bona volunatate uxoris mee.*

32 *Ibid.*, no. 66.

33 Before 1180 or 1185–1215: *Early Charters of Waltham Abbey*, no. 165. Other examples, *Eynsham Cartulary*, nos 170, 172.

34 *Early Charters of Waltham Abbey*, no. 146.

35 *Oxford Charters*, no. 54. Hudson, *Land, Law, and Lordship*, p. 166, following Stenton, considers the gift to be of a chessboard and some veils. There is some doubt in different editions of this charter whether Christina received just one veil or more.

36 *Reading Abbey Cartularies*, ed. B. R. Kemp (2 vols, Camden Society, 4th ser., 31, 33, 1986, 1987), 1. no. 577. For the significance of swords as symbolic objects see Clanchy, *Memory to Written Record*, pp. 38–41. John's wife, as Agnes de Preston, in her widowhood was involved in a dispute with the monks of Reading over part of this land, which was her dower, which was settled by Final Concord in the king's court at Oxford in August 1193. By an assize of mort d'ancestor her three daughters and co-heiresses settled a dispute with the monks: *Reading Abbey Cartularies*, 1. nos 583, 584.

37 *Reading Abbey Cartularies*, 1. no. 578.

38 *Ibid.*, no. 579.

39 *Ibid.*, no. 580. The horse was probably worth 16s; see *ibid.*, no. 652.

40 Leeds Archives, Ingilby Records, no. 249.

41 *CDF*, no. 32.

42 National Library of Wales, Aberystwyth, MS Penrice and Margam 11. *Circa* 1203 Isabella countess of Warenne granted lands to a tenant after the death of her husband, Earl Hamelin, for which she received one mark; she here acted as a superior 'lord' in the context of enfoeffment: BL, Add. Ch. 24,634; for her seal see Appendix 1, no. 132.

43 *EYC*, 11. no. 68; also printed, *Transcripts of Charters relating to the Gilbertine Houses of Sixle, Ormsby, Catley, Bullington and Alvingham*, ed. F. M. Stenton (Lincoln Record Society, 18, 1922), no. 15. Roger de Mowbray raised considerable sums of money after the rebellion of 1174–75: *Mowbray Charters*, nos 120–2, and see xxxi.

44 *EYC*, 2. no. 807, where Agnes de Rotessa, in 1188, made a grant *in magna necessitate mea.*

45 As in the case of Muriel and Lecia de Munteni: see above, p. 103 n. 73.

46 BL, Harl. Ch. 50. B. 33. This seal is discussed in Chapter 7.

47 *Ibid.* Ch. 84. I. 22 (early thirteenth-century); for her seal see Appendix 1, no. 82. Margaret was the wife of Roger de Bray, who with her consent made grants to the monks at Old Wardon (Bedfordshire): *Cartulary of Old Wardon*, no. 97, *c.* 1190–1200.

48 See above, n. 35.

49 *Early Charters of Waltham Abbey*, no. 188.

50 *EYC*, 11. no. 62.

51 *EYC*, 3. no. 1771.

52 *Ibid.*, no. 1352.

53 National Library of Wales, Aberystwyth, MS Penrice and Margam 11. As did Cecilia, daughter of Sabelina, and Margaret, the wife of Roger de Bray; see above, p. 113. See also Lecia and Muriel de Munteni, as discussed above, *Clerkenwell Cartulary*, nos 65, 73.

54 *EYC*, 11. no. 62.

55 Fowler, *Cartulary of Old Wardon*, p. 8, citing Pollock and Maitland, *History of English Law*, 2. 186–90.

56 *EYC*, 2. no. 780.

57 *Cartulary of Old Wardon*, no. 280.

58 *Ibid.*, no. 299.

59 *Ibid.*, no. 300.

60 Vyner deeds, deposited at Leeds Archives, no. 4939; for her seal see Appendix 1, no. 86.

61 BL, Harl. Ch. 45. H. 7; *Danelaw Charters*, no. 172.

62 *Ibid.*; they are Nogga, the wife of Richard, son of Henry, Clementia, the niece of Walter Bech, Sigga, the wife of Osbert, and Lucy, the wife of Robert de *Wispintuna*.

63 BL, Harl. Ch. 49. H. 3; *Danelaw Charters*, no. 214 (*temp.* Henry II); the other women who witness are Eda, the wife of Goseclin de Areci, and Emma de la Kernel. Beatrice received 20s from the monks and a cow for her remission.

64 Hyams, 'Warranty and good lordship', pp. 443–5; White, *Laudatio Parentum*, p. 203; Hudson, *Land, Law and Lordship*, pp. 162–5.

65 *Mowbray Charters*, no. 35 (suspicious).

66 Hyams, 'Warranty and good lordship', p. 474.

67 BL, Harl. Ch. 48. F. 27; BL, Harl. Ch. 83. D.30, *Cartulary of Old Wardon*, nos 25, 110, 248, 305, 308, 319 (late twelfth-century); *Clerkenwell Cartulary*, nos 24 (1190–94), 58 (20 March 1190), 104 (Michaelmas 1196); *EYC*, 2. no. 807 (*c.* 1188). Other late twelfth to early thirteenth-century examples: *Early Charters of Waltham Abbey*, nos 69, 172, 175–6, 178.

68 Hudson, 'Anglo-Norman land law and the origins of property', p. 58; for warranty, *ibid.*, pp. 51–8.

69 See nn. 1, 4 and 5 above.

70 Hyams, 'Warranty and good lordship', pp. 470–1.

71 Bates, 'Prosopographical study', p. 90.

7

Seals

Representation, image and identity

THERE ARE OVER 145 extant secular women's seals from the twelfth and early thirteenth centuries.[1] They present the historian with unique opportunities to study the portrayal of female identity in twelfth-century England. Seals were visual representations of power, and they conveyed notions of authority and legitimacy. They publicly presented a view of both men and women which visibly crystallised ideas about gender, class and lordship. The modern historian of seals owes a considerable debt to antiquarian scholars such as Sir Christopher Hatton, and to Sir Walter de Gray Birch, who did much to catalogue the extensive collections of extant impressions of British medieval seals.[2] Ultimately, however, these approaches are unsatisfactory because they treat seals as interesting artefacts without taking account of the complex socio-cultural processes within which they were created. Equally difficult is the lack of precise contextualised chronologies which determine how seal images became conventionalised and why.[3] Thus although it is now established that, for example, on the seals of male nobility the equestrian figure was the most enduring and dominant form of iconography which symbolised 'feudal lordship',[4] it is difficult to relate this to changes in 'feudal lordship' because such studies float free from the debates about changes in the nature of lordship or society, or any consideration of portrayals and meanings of masculinity.[5] Similarly, for noblewomen, it is known that iconographic devices were used on their seals, such as the fleur-de-lys, or the ambivalent bird of prey image,[6] yet why and how these symbols emerged is obscure.

Fundamentally, there is a static feel to the study of seals. Jean Luc Chassel's important contribution to the study of twelfth-century French seals has, however, placed them in the context of the broader social changes concurrent in the twelfth-century renaissance. He argues that the use of seals grew at the expense of the placing of *signa* upon charters.[7] David Crouch considered the iconography of seals as part of the insignia of the aristocracy and in terms of class distinctions and thus stressed their importance as symbols of the élite.[8] T. A. Heslop, like Chassel, has begun the important task of placing seals into their socio-cultural contexts and has, for example, studied the Virgin Mary's regalia in terms of its production and varied meanings.[9] In particular he warned of the difficulties in analysing the iconography of Romanesque seals of twelfth-century England. His work which has discussed the development of seal iconography has done much to distinguish the way that broader artistic and cultural changes affected seal iconography, use and design. Thus, for example, he related the iconography of croziers to the cultural context of the pastoral roles of bishops, and his work is especially useful for the way it locates biblical imagery as a key influence.[10] He has related seal iconography to the use of seals in the twelfth century by the nobility in the contexts of the wider cultural changes due to the twelfth-century renaissance.[11]

Women's seals have been particularly poorly served. C. H. Hunter Blair briefly considered women's seals, but he was interested in the development of armorial devices and his approach was descriptive rather than analytical.[12] The seals of royal women, such as Matilda, the wife of Henry I, or Empress Matilda, have been studied, but their significance as a guide to queenly power has yet to be assessed.[13] The key exception, the work of Brigitte Bedos-Rezak, is innovative in suggesting ways that gender symbolisms were related to notions of the roles of women.[14] Influenced by Duby, and thus seeing the emergence of patrilineal primogeniture structures as the key social dynamic, Bedos-Rezak locates gender differences in men's and women's seals.[15] She relates the use of seals to the socio-cultural contexts which produced them and shows the ways that symbols, such as the fleur-de-lys and birds of prey displayed on women's seals, were multi-vocal and ambivalent. Locating women's actions firmly within the family, she sees seal iconography as a mechanism for denying the 'female personality' in order to 'reinforce the structure of patrilineage'.[16] Nevertheless, by placing gender as an integral part of her analysis Bedos-Rezak has brought much needed fresh light to the subject.

Hitherto in Britain the way that gender affected symbolisms has been unconsciously accepted by scholars even as they have begun to delineate the importance of gender as an analytical tool (albeit similarly unconsciously!). For example, Harvey and McGuinness stated that the emergence of heraldic devices on men's seals was 'all but spontaneous' but for the seals of women 'it had to be consciously introduced'.[17] Such categories rely on the definition of the seals of men as 'natural' and women's seals as 'other'; the utilisation of such categories is ahistorical, gender-blind and simplistic. This interpretation of differences in men's and women's seals divorces the interpretation of the meaning of seals from differences in the meaning of power to men and women based on the interactions of gender, the impact of the female life cycle upon women's power, their place in lordship and the impact of status upon their identity.

In order to study seals in their full complexity we need a framework which acknowledges the problems of analysing them as symbols of female power. There is a need to be aware of the ambiguities inherent in female power, the impact of the female life cycle upon that power, and thus the conflicting, and possibly competing, multiple identities and contexts of power. The following analysis therefore considers Bedos-Rezak's approach, but also takes account of the wider methodological approaches of Bates, Stafford and Short. Chassel's study of twelfth-century French seals attempted to analyse the spread of seals within a framework which took account of specific political and cultural contexts. Thus he saw the spread of seals from the seigneurie to the castellanry in France in, for example, Berry as a product of the internal rivalries within Berry.[18] Whilst this is instructive it does little to address the spread of female sealing practice or the meaning of seals for an interpretation of the power of twelfth-century noblewomen. The important insights of David Bates and Pauline Stafford, used earlier in connection with the texts of charters, are as useful in considering seals. We must take account of socio-cultural contexts of production, and be sensitive to the ambiguities of female power and the way that that power fluctuated and changed over time, depending on the interactions of contemporary politics and the vagaries of the female life cycle.[19] Ian Short stresses the competing multiple identities of the noble elite of twelfth-century England,[20] and this way of viewing individuals' identities as fluid and dependent on context will be considered here through the way seals vocalised women's identities.

Crucially seals identified women's power in the context of land tenure, lordship, social status and the female life cycle. Further, any individual exerted power in contexts, not as absolutes: thus an individual could be powerful in their locality, such as on the manor, but weak at the royal court; powerful religious benefactors but weak as women in the view of churchmen.

It is worth while considering the beginnings of royal women's sealing to put the discussion of secular noblewomen's seals into context; it is, however, beyond the scope of this book to do justice to the seals of twelfth-century queens. The earliest extant secular woman's seal from post-Conquest England belonged to Queen Matilda, the wife of Henry I, and dates from the period 1108–16.[21] Chronologically the English evidence parallels the French, since the earliest evidence of French female sealing is also a woman of royal status, Bertrada de Montfort, the dowager queen, whose seal dates from 1115.[22] Queen Matilda's seal is appended to a writ addressing Ranulf bishop of Durham and the sheriffs of Northumberland, informing them that she gave a church to St Cuthbert's, Durham. Since the seal is attached to a writ whose diplomatic form is entirely normal, and whose contents are a typical grant of property, it is reasonable to assume that it represents routine and presumably extensive usage. The survival of a second seal of Matilda's, cast from the same die and made in white wax, as well as the existence of a significant number of copies of what would once presumably have been writs in her name similarly sealed, reinforce this conclusion.[23] In contrast to the red wax frequently used for the seals of noblemen, Matilda's seal is of green wax. It depicts the queen standing crowned, wearing a long embroidered robe which falls in folds over her feet. Over this is a seamless mantle which has an embroidered border and is draped over her head. It is fastened at her throat by a brooch, and falls in folds over her arms. In her right hand she holds a sceptre surmounted by a dove, and in her left an orb surmounted by a cross.[24]

The standing female form had Anglo-Saxon roots represented in that unique survival, the seal of St Edith of Wilton, daughter of King Edgar and the half-sister of King Edward the Martyr (975–78) and King Æthelred (978–1016).[25] This seal is, however, stylistically very different from Queen Matilda's which was executed in the modern Romanesque style. It is possible that Matilda, the wife of William the Conqueror, had a seal, since a writ in her name survives.[26] The custom of queenly sealing may have originated earlier in England than in France. Whatever the case, the Anglo-Norman court was at the forefront of innovation as part of the cultural renaissance of northern Europe. It is possible that Henry I's second wife, Adeliza of Louvain, used the same seal matrix.[27] Queen Matilda, the wife of King Stephen, appended a charter in favour of Holy Trinity, London, with her seal in 1147–52. She is depicted standing but crowned, wearing a mantle and gown; she holds a fleur-de-lys in her right hand and a hunting bird in her left.[28] This iconography became a standard depiction on noblewomen's seals during the twelfth century, and further it was in this period during the mid-twelfth century that the practice of sealing documents by aristocratic women spread. The seal of Margaret, the sister of the Scottish king, who married Conan of Brittany, depicts a standing female figure holding an orb surmounted by a cross in her right hand, an image which may well be a direct allusion to the royal house of Scotland.[29] The seal of the empress Matilda is striking. It expresses the authority of the state, and her regalia leave this in no doubt: her seal of 1141–42, critical years in the civil war, depicts her enthroned and holding the sceptre – royal insignia designating royal powers.[30] It has been suggested that the shape and iconography were a statement of her royal authority which conveyed her royal legitimate right to rule.[31]

The earliest extant impression of a non-royal secular noblewoman's seal may be that of Matilda of Wallingford. It is difficult to date the charter precisely, but it may have been written between 1122 and 1147.[32] The surviving seal of Alice, wife of Gilbert fitz Richard de Clare, may be dated more closely to 1136–38.[33] Three more noblewomen may have appended seals to their charters in the 1140s. Firstly, Alice de Gant, daughter of Walter de Gant and wife of Ilbert de Lacy (d. 1141) and Roger de Mowbray, sealed a charter which dates to 1144 – May 1155.[34] Secondly, there are two extant impressions of the seal of Alice countess of Northampton, the wife of Simon de Saint Liz, one in use 1140–60 and the other from c. 1154.[35] Finally, her daughter, Rohais countess of Lincoln, the wife of Gilbert de Gant, had two seals, the earliest of which dates from the period 1149–56.[36] Her second dates from after 1156.[37]

To these surviving noblewomen's seals, which were possibly in use in the 1140s, can be added twelve which may date from the 1150s.[38] Ten more possibly originated in the 1160s,[39] eleven in the 1170s,[40] six in the 1180s[41] and six in the 1190s.[42] Two more can be dated to Richard's reign.[43] Thirty-three impressions can be dated only to the twelfth century,[44] bringing the total for the twelfth century to ninety-two. Four noblewomen's seals can be dated only as being from the reign of John;[45] seven date from c. 1200.[46] Twenty women's seals date from the early thirteenth century to c. 1210, [47] some of which can be dated to specific years, for example the seal of Emma Mustel of 1204, or that of Eufemia de Saquenville of 1206.[48] Nineteen date from c. 1210 – c. 1232,[49] bringing the early thirteenth-century total to fifty-one.

To these surviving specimens can be added numerous references in sealing clauses which although inherently problematic may provide evidence of lost impressions.[50] For example, in 1106 Ermentrude dowager countess of Chester may have appended her seal to a charter in favour of Abingdon conjointly confirmed with her son, Earl Richard, who was a minor.[51]

The spread of the use of seals by women therefore follows the established pattern in the use of seals by secular noblemen, in that the practice originated on the documents of royalty and then spread firstly to male then to female high nobility, and thence, in the last quarter of the twelfth century, down through the social hierarchy until, by the mid-thirteenth century, sealing was common to all ranks of society. Thus the key stage of the development of female sealing practice was the period 1140–60, with a steady growth thereafter. Chassel found that 1140–60 was the period when male French and Norman lay aristocracy began to seal more widely, and c. 1150 is the turning point for female aristocracy in France more generally.[52]

The seals of men are almost always round, a shape perhaps inspired by Roman intaglios and *bullae*.[53] Most non-royal women's seals are pointed oval; of the total, about 13 per cent are round, the earliest example dating from c. 1150 and two from the 1170s.[54] The reason for the adoption of the pointed oval shape is still a matter of conjecture. Sandy Heslop has suggested that such seals originated in Flanders and northern France in the mid-eleventh century.[55] It may have been a matter of convenience: the tall standing figures so prevalent in ecclesiastical and women's seals required the proportions of the pointed oval.[56] It may also have been a question of gender ambiguity: as Swanson has recently argued, gender impacted on clerical status. Perhaps the shape of clerical and women's seals intentionally conveyed such ambiguities.[57] Thus the inspiration for secular noblewomen's seal iconography in shape and in the portrayal of standing figures may have been ecclesiastical seals, such as those of bishops or abbots, which depict standing figures in their official garb.[58] However, artistic convention could be circumscribed: two round seals depicted standing female figures.[59] The size of a seal is also important: the round equestrian seals of important lay magnates were large.[60] The seals of male heirs who were in their mother's wardship were round and smaller than their mother's.[61] As minors they represented potential future full authority. Female heirs who were minors appear never to have used seals. As in France, unmarried women of the high nobility did not seal.[62] It is above all significant that the seals of high-status women such as countesses were always pointed oval.

Seals therefore in different ways signified both gender and status. This was achieved through the shape of the seal and the iconography. The earliest extant impressions of non-royal secular noblewomen's seals, those of Alice, wife of Gilbert fitz Richard de Clare, of 1136–38, and

Matilda of Wallingford, of 1122–47, both depict a standing female figure. The figure on Alice's seal faces to the right, in a long dress with maunches (full sleeves), and holds an indistinct object, possibly a fleur-de-lys, in the right hand.[63] That of Matilda of Wallingford faces to the right, similarly in a long gown, looped over her arm, and holds a flower in the right hand.[64] Eighty-six, or nearly 64 per cent, of noblewomen had seals which depict a full standing female figure.[65] The figure may hold a fleur-de-lys and/or bird of prey. Thirty-one seals, nearly 24 per cent, depict sole images derivative of the fleur-de-lys,[66] eight depict birds only, a few more depict an eagle and a tortoise,[67] two incorporate fish in the design[68] and eight feature armorial or heraldic motifs.[69] There is increasing variety in the imagery deployed in the late twelfth and early thirteenth centuries, for example a seal of 1170–74 depicts a lady who is handed a hawk by her attendant, a late twelfth-century seal shows a figure who holds a child, and in the early thirteenth century a seal depicts a mermaid, another a roman intaglio.[70]

The chronological development of the iconography of secular noblewomen's seals through the twelfth and thirteenth centuries is one of continuity and change, since the standing female figure remained the conventional iconography of the seals of high-status women.[71] This suggests that the origins of the conventions of noblewomen's seals, which Sandy Heslop placed in the thirteenth and fourteenth centuries,[72] lie in the twelfth century. Indeed, Chassel found that the twelfth century was similarly crucial for the development of French seals.[73] Thus the images of standing female forms must from the inception of secular noblewomen's sealing have been a powerful motif which symbolised noble status, confirming Harvey and McGuinness's view that this was the equivalent of the equestrian imagery deployed on men's seals.[74] Yet, although it suggests that the image of status was already subject to convention, it also shows that the image of nobility was gendered, and remained so, since the seals of high-status women continued to display this motif.

Within the stylistic convention of the full-standing female figure in the centre of the seal there are variations in posture and form. The figure of the woman is usually clear, but she may face to the left, the centre or the right. The damp-fold style was a technique which was intended to show the form and movement of the body, using folds of clothing and gathered ridges to emphasise the roundness of the breasts and hips.[75] This was a realistic feature common to women's seals as they developed in France in late twelfth and thirteenth centuries.[76] The standing female forms are depicted wearing a long dress, usually belted at the waist, and sometimes a cloak or mantle, as in the seals of Hawise Blund or Constance of Brittany.[77] Others depict the figure wearing a cap, as with Burgesia, sister of Walter Burre.[78] Conical or flat headdress was a mid-twelfth-century development.[79] The hair is bound or may be covered, but sometimes it is depicted as flowing over the shoulders.[80] The robe or dress often has long maunches, but these became less frequent in the later twelfth century, since they slowly went out of fashion around 1180, as did close-fitting dresses.[81] The field around the standing female figure is usually clear on twelfth-century seals. Later impressions show detail in the field, as in the early thirteenth-century example belonging to Matilda de Auberville.[82] The standing female figure may hold an object in her hand(s): ten depict the figure holding a bird of prey in one hand and a fleur-de-lys or staff in the other.[83] Thirty-four depict the figure holding only a fleur-de-lys, or lily flower, in one hand, the other hand being placed on the body, usually at the waist or the breast.[84] Twelve show the figure holding only a bird of prey.[85] In three examples the empty hands are raised.[86] There is thus variety in the way that standing female figures are depicted, owing to the influence of fashion or the choice of the craftsman who made the seal. The feet are usually visible below the hemline of the dress, which may flare outwards at the feet.

In some impressions the natural imagery depicts the female figure holding a flower, which was a common motif in twelfth-century art, symbolising the labour for April, and hence springtime and love.[87] The adoption of the lily flower or fleur-de-lys upon the seals of noblewomen requires explanation, since the symbol was the most common device employed on English noblewomen's seals from the mid-twelfth century onwards.[88] The symbol is present on one of the earliest surviving English noblewomen's seals, that of Matilda de Wallingford, and upon the seal of Rohais de Gant countess of Lincoln, of 1149–56. [89] After 1170 seals used by noblewomen which depict solely a stylised fleur-de-lys appear.[90] A woman standing holding a fleur-de-lys remained the standard depiction upon high-status women's seals in the thirteenth century and beyond.

The fleur-de-lys is a non-existent heraldic flower: the inverted triangle at its base represents water, and the two crosses represent 'conjunction and spiritual achievement': the flower points to heaven. Further, the fleur-de-lys was regarded as 'an emblem of illumination and as an attribute of the lord'.[91] Women were associated with a moist temperate humour in the Middle Ages, which would explain the association with water. Yet the fleur-de-lys was used as a symbol of royalty in Capetian and Carolingian art and became an emblem of the French kingdom in the thirteenth century.[92] R. A. Koch argues that the fleur-de-lys originated from the biblical flower the white lily, which had a long history of representation in ancient and Near Eastern art. It was invested with profound religious symbolism in Christianity and it became 'the supreme symbol of the Virgin Mary and also of Christ'.[93] In the twelfth century Bernard of Clairvaux expounded on the mystical meaning of the white lily.[94] On the seals of noblewomen it symbolised female virtue and spirituality through the association with the supreme Christian female icon, the Virgin Mary. Thus the fleur-de-lys, when depicted on women's seals, represented motherhood and fertility, and expressed lineage through the ambivalent forms of motherhood and virginity.[95] Its emergence also occurred within the emergence of a wider twelfth-century discourse within medieval grammar: the discourse on family structure and changes in structures concerning marriage and property,[96] a discourse which was thus utilising gendered imagery upon seals.

The symbolism of the bird of prey is equally ambivalent. The bird is the second most common motif deployed on secular noblewomen's seals from the twelfth and early thirteenth centuries. Eighteen seals show a woman holding a hawk, and eight a bird of prey only.[97] Traditionally the bird-of-prey motif has been seen to represent both high social status and secular life. Bedos-Rezak has suggested that the motif was gendered when depicted as an object being held by a standing female figure. She argued that the hawk shifts the emphasis from Mary to Eve and that it represents the beauty, the cruelty and the amorous conversation of women.[98] Her interpretation is based on a reading of John of Salisbury, who states that women are better at breeding falcons because they are more rapacious.[99] However, the hawk in Romanesque art could also represent the evil mind of the sinner, as well as victory over sexual desire.[100] Thus in those seals where the figure holds the bird captive it suggests that the figure is in control of the values associated with the hawk. Above all, it is an active symbol and it represents and illustrates status consciousness in that it symbolises aristocratic status, life style, prestige and exclusivity. The ambiguous meanings associated with birds of prey in general, however, indicate that a complex array of spiritual and worldly meanings were mediated through the noblewoman's seal.

The incorporation of heraldry on both men's and women's seals was a further development in seal iconography in the mid-twelfth century.[101] By the end of the thirteenth century it had become common for the seals of noblewomen to depict the arms of husband and father, which denoted lineage defined through the male kin, made illustrious and enhanced through the female. The earliest example of a heraldic device employed on a woman's seal dates from 1149–56 and was used by Rohais de Clare countess of Lincoln, the wife of Earl Gilbert de Gant.[102] Her seal is of red wax, and conventional in that the depiction is of a standing female figure, but in the field on the right there is a wavy sprig, on the left a quatrefoil depicting the chevrons of the Clare family. This seal is a precocious example and pre-dates the earliest French example of women using heraldic imagery by about thirty years.[103]

The seal of her daughter and heiress Alice, who married Simon de Saint Liz, is striking. The seal is oval and depicts solely the six chevrons of the Clare family.[104] Although Alice acquired a seal when married to Earl Simon, her seal represented her position as heiress. Further, the stress on matrilineal kinship is remarkable, since during the twelfth century generally it was becoming more usual for the patrilineal line to take precedence. Yet seals confirm that it was the nature of the lands that mattered. Her charter confirms a tenant's grant to Stixwould Abbey, and her husband's charter is still extant.[105] Both charters have the same witness list, which suggests that they were both confirmed at the same time. This is important evidence of the contradictions inherent in the power of noblewomen, since although as a married woman Alice's lands were legally under the control of her husband Alice still had some future interest in the lands conveyed. Her position as an heiress was imaged on her seal, and the symbolism made no allusion to gender. This example indicates that the competing multiple identities which defined noble-women were, in the mid-twelfth century, predicated on the intercon-nections of marital status and kin connections as underpinned by land tenure. Thus arms could follow lands through heiresses.[106] Bloch sees the development of heraldry as a symbolic lineal grammar of land and lineage,[107] and this confirms that the key relationship for the definition of individual function and rights was the relationship between tenant and land, not tenant and lord.[108]

The use of heraldic or armorial motifs on men's and women's seals was still uncommon in the late twelfth and early thirteenth centuries, and became general only in the first quarter of the thirteenth century.[109] The armorial seal of c. 1195 of Agatha Trussebut depicts a water bouget that was taken from the shield of her father.[110] Agatha, with her sisters Roese and Hilary, was co-heiress of her father, Robert Trussebut.[111] Her position as heiress was imaged on her seal, and thus her power was imaged in that context. Although armorial seals were usually round,[112] there are two early exceptions belonging to women. The seal of Alice de Rumeli in c. 1209–10 depicts a standing female figure holding a fleur-de-lys, the standard emblems on the seals of high-status women, but also with a large armorial motif on her left breast.[113] The seal of Matilda, daughter of Norman, displayed an armorial motif of a shield upon an oval seal.[114] The armorial seal of Hawise countess of Aumâle, which dates from the early years of King John's reign, is an example of the use of arms on the counterseal of a noble woman. The charter dates from c. 1212–14 and is evidence that countersealing was an early thirteenth-century development for secular noblewomen.[115]

Countersealing, the application of a further distinct impression from a smaller seal to the reverse of the impression of the (great) seal, was important because it added extra authentication to documents. It may have been adopted by women of the high aristocracy as an extra method of differentiation from other ranks of the nobility, with the practice of sealing becoming so prevalent generally. Ailes argues that for male aristocracy this facilitated dual identification: the equestrian image on the obverse of, for example, the seal of Robert earl of Leicester facilitated an association with his function as a 'feudal lord' whilst the counterseal allowed identification 'with all that the family stood for'.[116] This is evident in the legend of the counterseal of Isabella countess of Gloucester and Mortain, dating from c. 1197–1214.[117] Despite changes in her marital status the image of her seal and counterseal remained unchanged.[118] The counterseal bears the legend [+ *EGO SV'AQI*]*LA : CVSTOS D'NE MEE*. Isabella had changed the counterseal in use by her father, although the obverse is the same as her mother's. Armorial devices were not restricted to members of the aristocratic elite, yet the practice of countersealing was. Women of lesser noble rank began to adopt armorial devices in the early thirteenth century; Letia de Edisfield, for example, used an estoile of eight points on either side of the usual standing female form.[119] However, the comparative rarity of female countersealing suggests that the practice was restricted to the high elite; as such it is further evidence of the process of cultural diffusion and aristocratic social exclusivity. Further, countersealing was a later development on women's seals than on those of men.

The standing female form is the most dominant motif, but there is variety in the imagery on women's seals. The seal of Matilda countess of Clare, of which the surviving specimen dates from 1173–76, may be a depiction of an Annunciation or Visitation scene. It shows two women facing each other, wearing cloaks; one figure holds a bird of prey with jesses on a staff. The legend, unfortunately, is defaced.[120] This imagery is so different from that on other contemporary seals that the countess must have commissioned the seal herself. As discussed earlier, the seal of Alice, wife of Gilbert fitz Richard de Clare, in use in the late 1130s, is indicative of innovation in the use of armorial designs on the seals of high-status women. The 'chevron' seal of Alice countess of Northampton utilised an armorial motif at an early date for both male and female sealers. The female sealers of the Clare family had a tradition of innovation. The network of female association and spheres of influence through the matrilineal line is evidenced, since each countess had a distinctive seal, two using armorial designs, and the third innovating in its use of two female figures: all are distinct from contemporary trends. Each countess was therefore making a public statement of individuality, status and lineage, as well as reflecting distinctive tastes in their cultural patronage. It is also notable that they imaged their matrilineal ancestry, rather than their father's lineage.

As the twelfth century progressed and sealing practice became more widespread through the social classes, and thus as women of the lesser nobility used seals, so there is more variety in detail, even humour, with the use of zoomorphic images upon women's seals. For example, the seal of Alice Capra depicts a female figure standing on a goat, a pun on her name.[121] The seal of Cecilia, mother of William de Avranches, depicts an eagle with wings displayed, standing on a tortoise facing to the right.[122] The eagle or the bird of prey as sole device was a popular development in the late twelfth and early thirteenth centuries. Agnes, the daughter of William, the Constable of Chester, may have had a seal which depicted a bird perched on a branch in 1157–66.[123] In the early thirteenth century Hawise, the daughter of Philip de Kime, had a seal which depicted a mermaid.[124] Other women's seals depict a fleur-de-lys device.[125] Ornate geometrical designs, a late twelfth-century development but one which emerged coterminously with the development of heraldry on seals, were also used on women's seals. *Circa* 1190 Pavia, the daughter of Svan Thornet, *c.* 1195–1200 Mabel, the wife of Bertram the chamberlain, Emma Mustel *c.* 1200 and Alice Foliot in the late twelfth century had seals which depicted geometrical knots or ornate designs.[126] Women of the lower nobility used designs based on sheaves of corn or barley.[127]

However, in England more generally the practice of sealing charters had spread throughout the secular landholding classes by the end of the twelfth century. Seals were part of the conscious creation of twelfth-century aristocratic group identity. The practical and symbolic roles of secular noblewomen as lords, wives and widows were thus visually expressed through the representational form of lordship, validation and thus personal authority: the seal. The gendered iconography reflects gendered roles: the imbalance of power relations between men and women is visually constructed and linked with function. Seals are the expression of lordship, and the basis of women's status is represented allegorically, using symbols, and explicitly through text. The growth in the use of seals by secular women illustrates how the process of cultural diffusion itself was gendered, since sealing originated on the seals of male secular aristocracy, and male ecclesiastics. The tall standing female figure originated on the seals of royal women and became the norm on women's seals by the end of the twelfth century. The imbalance of power relations, or gender roles, is at the heart of the iconographic representations. If seals are reflective of aristocratic culture, they are representative of the aristocratic symbolic ordering of the world. The symbolism on high-status noblewomen's seals reflects ambiguity, status, gender, lordship, culture, sexuality through dress codes, and so on, and thus confirm that symbols are multivocal, ambiguous and varied. The representational forms of noblewomen's seals symbolised noblewomen's cultural identities and served to endorse gendered norms of women's role in lordship.

Usage and life style

These themes can be further explored through an analysis of the use of seals by women in the context of the relationship of seals with the form and content of charters. This can be achieved through an analysis of seal legends, especially *filia* designations to indicate female heirs, for example, and also an analysis of the contexts in which women sealed documents, such as conjointly with husbands, or solely as wives or as widows. Certainly, seals themselves provide clues about important identities of women through the legends. Seal legends served to identify the user, and were concise. Bedos-Rezak noted differences in seal legends based on women's social status: married women of the aristocracy were designated by their own name, followed by their husband's; the use of *uxor* was rare in this social group, and aristocratic female heirs were not identified by their conjugal relations but used their own name and a patronymic. Widowed but unmarried women retained their husband's title.[128] This suggests the primacy of social status in the design of women's seal legends and the importance of the female life cycle in the definition it gave to women's identities. Certainly the legends of the seals of countesses usually describe them as *Comitissa*.[129] Although the 1156 armorial seal of Rohais countess of Lincoln bears the legend (SIGI)LLVM ROHS . . . (COMITI)SSE. LINCOLNIE, her previous seal in use 1149–56 used the *uxor* formula.[130] Likewise the legend on the seal of Amice countess of Leicester described her as countess (1150–53),[131] as did the legend of the seal of Hawise countess of Gloucester *c.* 1183–97.[132] The legends of the seals of both Margaret duchess of Brittany[133] and Constance, her daughter,[134] describe them as DUCISSE. Yet in the text of her charter Constance is described as 'daughter of Earl Conan, duchess of Brittany and countess of Richmond'. Unfortunately the legend on the seal is partly defaced, so whether the legend bore the title *comitissa* is unclear: yet as her father's heir her DUCISSA title conveyed greater status. Hawise countess of Aumâle was so designated on the legend of her seal, and the seal may have been in use during her second and third marriages.[135] Aristocratic female heirs tended to be identified through the patronymic – because that name was the most prestigious and identified the connection of the heir with the family lands. It thus structured their power.[136]

Bedos-Rezak has suggested that it is likely that the use of *filia* on the legends of French aristocratic women's seals may designate an heiress.[137] On English noblewomen's seals the term first appears during the latter part of the reign of Henry II. In England the designation was restricted to members of the lesser nobility, and just over a fifth of the known examples exhibit this characteristic.[138] There are examples of seal legends of married women of the lower nobility which deploy the title *uxor*, and the seals of two high-status women, Rohais, as wife of Gilbert de Gant, and Isabella countess of Pembroke and wife of William Marshall, also used the *uxor* designation.[139] As Bedos-Rezak found, other forms of kin connections are rarely referred to in seal legends:[140] only one seal legend describes the owner as *sorori*.[141]

However, seal legends are problematic as sole guide to women's identities. The charter address clause may give one name, but the seal legend may give another, as in the example of Alice 'de Hakethorn'.[142] The *filia* formula is not the only way that heiresses were identified, for example Matilda, the daughter of Pagan *de Hotun* and Alice de Raimes, the wife of Robert Grimabal, of Houghton, Northamptonshire, had two seals. The legend of her earlier seal uses the *filia* designation, her later seal identifies her with the patrilineal toponymic, *de Hohtvne*.[143] Thus her marital status is not referred to in the seal legend: her position as heiress is the key to her identity in the context of land tenure. Matilda, the wife of Reginald de Meiniers, the daughter of Ingleram de Frescheville, had two seals. The legend of her earlier seal, in use during her marriage to Reginald, describes her by her patrilineal association: she is *M . . . FRESSENVILLA*.[144] Her seal may have depicted a figure holding a child in swaddling clothes, a unique reference to maternity on a secular noblewoman's seal. Her later seal, acquired as a widow, identifies her by her husband's name, Matilda de Meiniers, in a confirmation of the earlier gift of her father to the monks of Robertsbridge concerning lands of her *maritagium*.[145] The seal depicts more conventional motifs, the standing figure, fleur-de-lys and staff.

The seal of Margaret de Bray is a good example of the way that women's identities could change according to the female life cycle, and thus shows how seals are a valuable, even if incomplete, record. Margaret was married firstly to Robert the Chamberlain of Dunton, by whom she had two sons and three daughters, who were in the king's gift in 1185.[146] She married as her second husband Roger de Bray (d. *ante* 1205), and was identified as his wife when they were involved in actions against Waltham Abbey.[147] When Margaret granted a document in her own name, possibly after the death of Roger, she is described as *Margerie filia Aluffi' de Merch'*; the seal which is appended to the charter bears a *filia* designation; she quitclaimed lands which may have been of her inheritance. In return the monks gave her one mark, and her two sons half a mark each.[148] A cartulary copy of a later grant to the canons of Waltham Abbey by Margaret introduces it as *Carta Mylonis de Bray. Confirmatio Margarete matris Milonis de Bray de terra*, yet in the address clause she is described as *Margareta de Walton uxor quondam Rogeri de Bray*.[149] Thus the text of the charter and the seal legends signify different identities that impacted on her status as alienor, and thus Margaret's power was based on marriage and maternity.[150]

Where the right to alienate the land in question is stated in the text of the charter it is possible to define the relationship of the alienor to the land in question. Yet this is still complex. For example, reference to dower may also suggest that the sealer is widowed. However, the dower alienated may be that from a first marriage, granted during the second.[151] It is often difficult to date a charter precisely, so there is a difficulty in discerning whether a woman's husband was still alive, and thus the impact of the female life cycle is hard to assess. However, twelfth-century and early thirteenth-century charters may contain a phrase such as 'in my free and lawful state' or the phrase *quondam uxor* which indicates that the grantor was widowed.[152] The relationship between the woman and the land concerned may also be apparent by reference to *maritagium* within the text of the charter.[153]

Although there are very few extant documents where both seals have survived, there is evidence to show that married couples conjointly granted and sealed *acta*. For example, the seals of both Hawise and Helias de Albini are appended to a charter which dates to 1150–c. 1180.

His seal is of a conventional equestrian type, showing a mounted figure and hunting hounds, hers a standing female figure holding a fleur-de-lys.[154] Similarly, early in the reign of John both Richard de Camville and his wife, Eustachia Basset, sealed a charter, his seal an equestrian device, hers a standing female figure holding a fleur-de-lys.[155] Bertram, the chamberlain of Hugh earl of Chester, and his wife, Mabel, gave their daughter *maritagium* when she married William fitz Bernard *c.* 1195–1200, and they may have co-sealed the grant.[156] Milisent de Stafford and her husband, Hervi Bagot, conjointly sealed a charter in the early thirteenth century.[157] Basilia, the wife of Hugh le Moine le Marsh, may have co-sealed with her husband, as did Cecily de Crevequer.[158] Such examples are rare but they reflect possibilities and variety in sealing practice, and there are no extant examples of women of comital status co-sealing documents.[159] A charter of Matilda de Chesney, the wife of Robert *Pincerna*, to Henry II was authenticated with Robert's seal, which suggests that a husband's seal could be used to validate the *acta* of a wife.[160] Women's seals, however, were not used to validate *acta* of their husbands except in the context of conjoint sealing practice.

There is evidence that mothers could co-seal with their son(s). Avicia, the widow of Robert Blund, co-sealed with her son when she granted lands to Southwark.[161] In another charter in favour of Southwark, Cecilia, daughter of Sabelina, co-sealed with her three sons, each of whom attached his own seal via woven threads, and the size of the seals is graded. Cecilia's seal is appended to the far left of the charter, the three other seals graded in descending order according to size from left to right. As principal alienor Cecilia gave warranty against all men and women, which implicitly reinforced her status as 'lord'.[162] These familial links and contractual obligations are therefore central to the construction of the basis of the power and authority of wives who co-alienate and co-seal.

The same context of family links rooted in rights to land as heiresses explains a charter validated by three women in the thirteenth century. In the 1220s three sisters who were co-heiresses to a socage tenure conjointly sealed a charter by which they sold land worth 12s to Roger Cordel. All three seals are circular, depict a fleur-de-lys and have a legend where each sister is described as the daughter of William (their father).[163] Such family group sealing to authenticate and confirm family group action also explains an interesting charter from the late twelfth century in which two sisters, along with their brother and mother, co-sealed a charter by which their brothers sold eighteen acres to a certain Odo Galle.[164] The sale was made by two brothers, John and Alan, the sons of Arnald Galle, with the assent of their mother, Pupelina, and Alice and Geva, their sisters. John sealed the charter, as did Pupelina, Alice and Geva. The women's seals confirm their assent to and corroboration of the sale. A further development in the thirteenth century is women co-sealing with non-familial members. *Circa* 1225 'Agnes daughter and heiress of Maud' authenticated her charter with her own seal and 'the common seal of the city of Chichester'. She emphasised the legality of her position by stating that she gave 'in my widowhood and liege power' and this combined with the seal of the community shows sealing practice could be varied.[165]

Given the difficulty of dating charters precisely, it is difficult to know at which stage in the female life cycle an individual woman acquired a seal. Alice, the widow of Gilbert fitz Richard de Clare, acquired a seal in 1136–38.[166] Matilda countess of Chester acquired a seal in the period 1164–72 as dowager countess.[167] Her daughter-in-law Bertrada likewise sealed charters only as a widow, acquiring her seal in or before *c.* 1200: she had by this time, however, been widowed for nineteen years.[168] The charter is in favour of a tenant on her dower lands, which her position as a dowager countess gave her the right to administer, and thus the text of her seal provides the identification which gave her most authority. Margaret duchess of Brittany sealed documents in 1160–75; it is unclear whether she did so as a wife or as a widow, although it is evident that whilst married she granted charters, since her first husband, Earl Conan of Brittany (d. 1171), confirmed at least one of her *acta* in the period 1160–67.[169] Constance duchess of Brittany was her father's heiress, and this status as duchess took precedence over her two marriages to Geoffrey Plantagenet and Ranulf of Chester. She acquired a seal in 1190–98 which she used to validate her *acta* and the text of the charter makes no mention of her husband, Earl Ranulf.[170] Hawise countess of Gloucester sealed documents as a widow.[171] Isabel countess of Gloucester, the youngest daughter of William earl of Gloucester and Hawise, acquired a seal in 1214 whilst married to her second husband, Geoffrey de Mandeville, and sealed documents in the period 1214–17 as both wife and widow.[172] Her seal legend remained unchanged despite the changes in her marital status, since she used the same seal to validate charters which were granted *in libera viduitate mea*.[173] Petronella countess of Leicester acquired a seal as a widow.[174] It is harder to be sure at what stage of the female life cycle women from lower ranks of society acquired a seal, if the text of the charter does not make it clear and the *uxor* formula is not used. Of ninety-one women who sealed documents where marital status can be determined, forty-three were wives when they acquired a seal, of whom twenty-five were heiresses and two granted lands of dower of her first husband.[175] Forty-six sealed documents only when a widow, of whom seventeen can be established as heiresses.[176] In four of these cases it can be established that a woman sealed as wife and widow.[177] These figures demonstrate that a wife who was an heiress could participate in land transfers as an alienor and could acquire a seal, itself a sign of veracity and authentication, as a symbol of her power to alienate land.

Female non-noble sealers began to seal documents in England in the late twelfth century, and it is interesting that their Norman counterparts likewise adopted this practice ahead of other regions in France. It is possible that the links with England affected female sigillographic practice, since the appearance of non-noble women's seals appears contemporarily in both regions of the Angevin empire.[178] Although Scotland was politically independent of the Angevin empire there was cultural symbiosis, with evidence that women were using seals in the mid-twelfth century, since Isabella, the wife of William Wallace, co-sealed a charter with him *c.* 1160.[179] In the mid-twelfth century Margaret duchess of Brittany, the wife of Conan duke of Brittany (d. 1171) and sister of William the Lion, sealed a grant of land in Forset, Yorkshire.[180]

It is interesting that in areas in the British Isles where royal control was weak or non-existent the practice of sealing documents with personal seals was a much later development. For example, the Isle of Man retained political independence of both the Normans and Angevins, yet the kings of Man were close culturally to the Norman and Angevin court. Whilst the kings of Man sealed documents in the mid-twelfth century, there is little evidence that noblewomen with Manx connections were sealing documents. Yet the ship symbol of the kings of Man was used on the seal of the Scottish Argyll family descended from the sister of Godred II (1154–87). This shows political and cultural influences passed through the female patrilineal line.[181] Although it is evident they were active in land administration as, for example, co-alienors with their husbands, women from the Channel Islands seem not to have sealed their charters in the twelfth and early thirteenth centuries.[182] Isobel countess of Pembroke sealed charters relating to lands given to Margam Abbey, yet there are few extant women's seals relating either to Marcher lordships, except Cheshire, or to other land in Wales.[183]

The use of seals by twelfth-century noblewomen reinforces the argument of earlier chapters, that noblewomen had important roles to play within the construct of lordship in the specific context of land transfers. Similarly female inheritance patterns affected women's sealing practice, since female heirs were particularly prominent as sealers when married. The use of seals by married women who co-sealed with their husbands suggests that wives could be important partners in power within marriage. The use of seals by noblewomen is also suggestive of the complex patterns of land tenure, since this underpinned personal and familial identities. The variety of contexts in which women sealed documents suggests the variety of ways in which women participated in land transfers. The female life cycle was important in the acquisition of seals by noblewomen, since patterns of women's tenure of dower and *maritagium* were intimately related to women's marital status.

In addition, however, the use of seals indicates further important ways in which noblewomen reinforced aristocratic dominance and their role within lordship. Seal legends suggest the nature of social stratification within the landed élite, since, for example, the *filia* designation was rare on the seals of high-status women and is suggestive that this formula was used on the seals of middle-ranking female nobility. Most important, however, in their imagery seals symbolised and simultaneously reinforced contemporary notions of both the cultural meaning and identity of female power and a view of lordship which was deeply gendered.

Notes

1 Throughout the following discussion reference is made to Appendix 1, Catalogue of seals, as Catalogue, *xx*. In all calculations royal women's seals have been excluded. It could be argued that, statistically, the sample of women's seals, 145, is small in the context of medieval British seal survivals. Patterns of survival are difficult to evaluate, indeed one scholar estimates that up to 90 per cent of figurative seals from the twelfth century to the fourteenth have been lost: Bony, 'An introduction to the study of Cistercian seals', p. 201. Seals were, until the late twelfth century, made of more fragile materials than later impressions: J. L. Chassel, 'L'usage du sceau au XIIe siècle', in Françoise Gasparri (ed.), *Le XIIe siècle: mutations et renouveau en France dans le première moitie du XIIe siècle* (Paris: Léopard dior), pp. 79–81, where the problem of forgery is also confronted. The sample is nevertheless significant as evidence of the origins of seal conventions, being created, perhaps, when such conventions had not become hardened. They are also more meaningful as *early* examples. Further, given the difficulties of dating charters precisely, it is hard to assess patterns of use. Also marital status may be unclear from the text of the charter, or the legend of the seal, and this is compounded when the seal has became detached from the charter to which it was once appended. Ultimately, however, treated with care, the sample can tell us much.

2 Evidence of twelfth and thirteenth-century women's seals: *Book of Seals*, nos 5, 88, 92, 104, 107–8, 145, 219, 345, 352, 424–5, 444, 514–15. The seals of Durham Cathedral

have been extensively catalogued by C. H. Hunter Blair, 'Durham seals: catalogue of seals at Durham from a manuscript made by the Reverend Greenwell', *Archaeologia Aeliana*, 3rd ser., vols 7–9 (1911–13), 11–16 (1914–19). *Seals BM*. See also *Seals PRO*. For British medieval seals in general see P. D. A. Harvey and A. McGuinness, *A Guide to British Medieval Seals* (London: British Library and Public Record Office, 1996).

3 The meaning of seal iconography is, of course, debatable. E.g., as Ailes has pointed out in discussion of seals as evidence of the development of heraldry, it is hard to be sure whether depictions of armorial motifs accurately record the use of that motif on individual families' coats of arms: A. Ailes, 'Heraldry in twelfth-century England: the evidence', in D. Williams (ed.), *England in the Twelfth Century: Proceedings of the 1988 Harlaxton Symposium* (Woodbridge: Boydell, 1990), p. 7. Heslop suggests that it is hard to be sure whether seals were designed with specific meanings in mind, but has also argued that motifs may have been adopted to reinforce the self-importance of the seal owner: T. A. Heslop, 'The Virgin Mary's regalia and twelfth-century seals', in A. Borg and A. Martindale (eds), *The Vanishing Past: Studies in Medieval Art, Liturgy and Metrology presented to Christopher Hohler* (Oxford: BAR, 1981), p. 52; *idem*, 'Towards an iconology of croziers', in D. Buckton and T. A. Heslop (eds), *Studies in Medieval Art and Architecture presented to Peter Lasko* (Stroud: Sutton, 1994), pp. 36–7. On the other hand Chassel is definite: seals were designed to convey an individual's notion of functions and power: Chassel, 'L'usage du sceau', p. 86. This issue is difficult to resolve, since the relationship of the individual who owned a seal with the craftsman who made it is unknowable, but where patterns emerge in the evidence and unusual specimens occur, and when the seal is studied in the social, cultural and political contexts of production, indications of the purposefulness of seal design can be discerned.

4 Harvey and McGuinness, *Guide to British Medieval Seals*, p. 50. Ailes, 'Heraldry: the evidence', pp. 8–9, argues that the equestrian seal maintained the image of 'a feudal lord and warrior'.

5 J. L. Nelson argues that there were 'competing and conflicting models of masculinity' in the tenth century: 'Monks, secular men and masculinity, *c.* 900', in D. M. Hadley (ed.), *Masculinity in Medieval Europe* (London and New York: Addison Wesley Longman, 1998), p. 142; whilst M. Bennett argues that men were offered 'flawed models of archetypes': 'Military masculinity in England and northern France, *c.* 1050–*c.* 1225', in *ibid.*, p. 88.

6 Harvey and McGuinness, *Guide to British Medieval Seals*, pp. 48–9.

7 Chassel, 'L'usage du sceau', pp. 84, 89. For notions of authority conveyed by seals and their validatory functions see *ibid.*, pp. 76–8.

8 D. Crouch, *The Image of Aristocracy, 1000–1300* (London: Routledge, 1992), pp. 226–8, 232–7, 242–6.

9 T. A. Heslop, 'The Virgin Mary's regalia, p. 52. For ecclesiastical seals see also P. Bony, 'An introduction to the study of Cistercian seals: the Virgin as mediatrix, then protectrix, on the seals of Cisterican abbeys', *Studies in Cistercian Art and Art and Architecture*, 3 (1987), 201–40. For sealing practice at a specific religious house see J. Cherry, 'The seal of Haltemprice Priory', in Buckton and Heslop (eds), *Studies in Medieval Art and Architecture*, pp. 14–23.

10   Heslop, 'Towards an iconology of croziers', p. 43; *idem*, 'Seals as evidence for metal-
     working in the England in the later twelfth century', in S. Macready and F. H.
     Thompson (eds), *Art and Patronage in the English Romanesque* (London, Society of
     Antiquaries, Occasional Papers, new ser., 8; 1986), pp. 50–60. For an outdated but
     still useful survey see J. Harvey Bloom, *English Seals* (London: Methuen, 1906). For
     a survey of thirteenth-century personal seals see P. D. A. Harvey, 'Personal seals in
     thirteenth-century England', in I. Wood and G. A. Loud (eds), *Church and Chronicle
     in the Middle Ages* (London: Hambledon Press, 1991), pp. 117–27; the focus is again
     on men's seals.

11   For an excellent article discussing pre-Conquest seals with some analysis of pre-
     Conquest women's seals see T. A. Heslop, 'English seals from the mid-ninth century
     to 1100', *Journal of the British Archaeological Association*, 133 (1980), 1–16; also *idem*,
     'Seals', in G. Zarnecki, J. Holt and T. Holland (eds), *English Romanesque Art, 1066–
     1200 [Exhibition at] Hayward Gallery, London, 5 April–8 July 1984* (London: Weidenfeld
     & Nicolson, in association with the Arts Council of Great Britain, 1984), pp. 298–
     320. Harvey and McGuinness have also begun to locate seals in a framework which
     takes account of socio-cultural perspectives, for example describing seals as 'the most
     striking symbol of feudal power and status'. Although extremely useful, their work is
     nevertheless a synthesis of existing scholarship which draws together commonalities
     in discussions of seals, and makes pertinent comments about the potential of seals
     as sources for the study of, for example, the medieval land market: Harvey and
     McGuinness, *Guide to Medieval British Seals*, pp. 50, 78–9.

12   C. H. Hunter Blair, 'Armorials upon English seals from the twelfth to the sixteenth
     centuries', *Archaeologia*, 89 (1943), 1–26 and plates 1–16. See C. A. H. Franklin, *The
     Bearing of Coat Armour by Ladies: A Guide to the Bearing of Arms by Ladies of all
     Ranks, whether Maid, Wife, or Widow, in England, Scotland, and Ireland* (London:
     J. Murray, 1923; reprinted Baltimore MD: Genealogical Publishing Co., 1973), for a
     discussion of heraldic devices.

13   M. A. F. Borrie, 'A sealed charter of the empress Matilda', *British Museum Quarterly*,
     34–5 (1969–71), 104–7. T. A. Heslop included the seals of Queen Matilda and Isabella
     countess of Gloucester in his 'Seals', in *English Romanesque Art*, with excellent bib-
     liographical details, p. 305 (no. 336) and p. 307 (no. 337) respectively. Harvey and
     McGuinness, *Guide to Medieval British Seals*, p. 78, comment that four-fifths of all
     seal survivals from medieval Britain were personal, non-heraldic seals of traders,
     artisans, clerks, peasants, etc.

14   B. Bedos-Rezak, 'Women, seals and power in medieval France, 1150–1350', in M.
     Erler and M. Kowaleski (eds), *Women and Power in the Middle Ages* (Athens GA and
     London: University of Georgia Press, 1988), pp. 61–82; developed in her 'Medieval
     women in French sigillographic sources', in J. T. Rosenthal (ed.), *Medieval Women
     and the Sources of Medieval History* (Athens GA and London: University of Georgia
     Press, 1990), pp. 1–36; *eadem*, 'Ritual in the royal chancery: text, image and rep-
     resentation of kingship in medieval French diplomas (700–1200)', in H. Duchhardt,
     R. A. Jackson and D. Sturdy (eds), *European Monarchy: Its Evolution and Practice
     from Roman Antiquity to Modern Times* (Stuttgart: Steiner, 1992), pp. 27–40.

15   Bedos-Rezak, 'French sigillographic sources', p. 8.

16   *Ibid.*, pp. 10, 67.

17 Harvey and McGuinness, *Guide to British Medieval Seals*, p. 48.

18 Chassel, 'L'usage du sceau', p. 68. Ailes also suggests such political contexts explain the appearance of a fleur-de-lys motif upon the 1157 seal of Earl Roger de Mowbray, who had tenurial and kindred links with Stephen count of Brittany, whose shield depicted lys imagery: Ailes, 'Heraldry: the evidence', p. 5.

19 D. Bates, 'The Prosopographical study of Anglo-Norman royal charters', in K. S. B. Keats-Rohan (ed.), *Family Trees and the Roots of Politics* (Woodbridge: Boydell, 1977), 89; Stafford, 'Emma', p. 10.

20 I. Short, 'Tam Angli quam Franci: self-definition in Anglo-Norman England', *ANS*, 18 (1996 for 1995), 154.

21 Catalogue, 1.

22 Bedos-Rezak, 'French sigillographic sources', p. 3.

23 As n. 26??; Catalogue, 1.

24 *RRAN*, 2. no. 1108. See Heslop, 'Seals', in *English Romanesque Art*, no. 336; see also Heslop, 'Towards an iconology of croziers', pp. 36–7, for comments on different meanings of the orb and sceptre regalia.

25 Heslop, 'English seals from the mid-ninth century to 1100', p. 4.

26 *RRAN: The Acta of William I, 1066–1087*, no. 289.

27 Catalogue, 2; Heslop, 'Seals', in *English Romanesque Art*, p. 305, no. 336.

28 Catalogue, 3.

29 Catalogue, 20. Queen Joan of Sicily, the daughter of Henry II, used a seal which imaged the specific authority on which her powers were predicated. The obverse has an image of a standing female figure, crowned, wearing a long dress with armorial design. The legend reads: + S. REGINE IOHE. FILIE. QUONDAM. H. REGIS. On the reverse, her full authority as duchess, countess and marchioness is explicitly stressed in the legend: S [reversed]. IOHE. DUCISSE. NARB'. COMITISSE. THO' MARCHISIE PROV., yet, interestingly, in this image she is depicted uncrowned but seated in a magisterial pose. It is clear that this seal was a conscious expression of her queenly status and authority as well as of her royal descent, which was imaged as distinct from that of her position of duchess, countess and marchioness: Catalogue, 5.

30 M. Chibnall, *The Empress Matilda: Queen Consort, Queen Mother and Lady of the English* (Oxford: Blackwell, 1991), pp. 101–5; K. J. Stringer, *The Reign of King Stephen* (London: Routledge, 1993), p. 40; W. L. Warren, *Henry II* (London: Eyre Methuen, 1977), p. 28, stresses the critical nature of 1141 in the Angevin cause.

31 *RRAN*, 3. xxix, nos 115–16, 392, 394, 409, 628, 651, 748; Catalogue, 4.

32 Catalogue, 131. A second extant impression dates from 1150–54.

33 Catalogue, 32. The charter is in favour of Thorney, conjointly granted with her children, Gilbert, Walter, Baldwin and Rohais, confirming the gift of a tenant, Tovi, whose wife (Agnes) claimed the land in dower and consented to her husband's grant. It was also consented to by Tovi's son and daughter-in-law, who are both named. Alice also gave a mill at Tathwell (Lincolnshire) to St Peter's Abbey, Gloucester, which was confirmed by her brother, Ranulf of Chester, in 1153: *Chester Charters*, no. 116.

34 Catalogue, 48.

35 Catalogue, 92.

36 BL, Harl. Ch. 50. F. 32 (Catalogue, 49A).

37 *Ibid.* Ch. 55. E. 13 (Catalogue, 49B).

38 Although of these, six can only be broadly dated to the reign of Henry II, two may date from later in the reign. 1150: no. 142. 1150–53: no. 72. 1150–57: no. 28. 1150–60: no. 64B. 1153–78, no. 94. 1150–82: no. 140. 1154–89: nos 101, 104, 105, 115, 134. Other seals which date from later in the reign are listed in the decade where the earliest date they were used is known. Late Henry II: no. 85.

39 *Circa* 1160: Catalogue, no. 130. 1160–65: no. 109. 1160–70: no. 93, no. 114. Post-1160– 75: no. 20. 1162–72: no. 29. 1163–98: no. 132. 1165: no. 80. 1166–80: no. 119. 1166–98 (probably *temp*. Henry II), no. 23.

40 1170: no. 122. *Circa* 1170: nos. 44, 60, 64A, 95. 1170–74: no. 33. 1170–98: no. 67. 1172: no. 13. 1174–89: no. 21. 1175–1205: no. 61. *Circa* 1176: no. 87.

41 Catalogue, 27, 45. 1183–97: no. 54. 1185–87: no. 59. 1185–98: no. 97. Post-1189: no. 73.

42 1190: no. 123. 1190–98: no. 19. 1192–1214: no. 117. Before 1194: no. 120. 1195: no. 126.

43 *Temp*. Richard I: nos 79, 124.

44 Early twelfth-century: no. 57. Twelfth-century: nos 15, 17, 34, 88, 102, 121. Mid to late twelfth-century: nos 25, 69. Late twelfth-century: nos 37, 46, 50, 51, 52, 63, 68, 75, 90, 96, 103, 106, 107, 111, 116, 127, 141. Late twelfth/early thirteenth-century: nos 11, 36, 39, 47A, 47B, 65, 84. Late twelfth-century to 1220s: nos 136, 137, 138.

45 Nos 9, 12, 16, 118.

46 *Circa* 1200: nos 6, 7, 10, 58, 66, 76, 89.

47 Early thirteenth-century: nos 8, 22, 35, 43, 62, 70, 71, 82, 99. 1200–8: no. 31. 1200–10: no. 30. 1200–25: no. 133. 1210: no. 125. *Circa* 1210: nos 26, 41, 86, 91.

48 1202–3: no. 74. 1204: no. 108. 1206: no. 112.

49 1210–15: no. 110. 1214–17: no. 55. 1215: no. 24. 8 September 1216: no. 38. 1218: no. 56. 1218/19: no: 83. Before 1219: no. 100. *Circa* 1220: nos 18, 113, 139. Post-1220: nos 77, 128. 1220–30: no. 135. 1222: no. 129. 1225: no. 42. *Circa* 1225: no. 98. 1220–30: no. 14. 1226: no. 81. 1226–32: no. 53. 1227–32: no. 78.

50 Chassel, 'L'usage du sceau', pp. 62–3.

51 *Chester Charters*, no. 6. Her seal may thus have represented joint comital legitimacy: see above, Chapter 4. Other examples: the cartulary of Stixwould, BL, MS Add. 46,071, ff. 1–7, clauses relating to possible seals of Matilda countess of Warwick, Margaret de Lacy and others. For other twelfth-century/early thirteenth-century examples of women's charters containing sealing clauses see *Early Charters of Waltham Abbey*, pp. 90, 151, 175, 178, 348, 349, 387, 416; *Chartes au Prieuré de Longueville de l'ordre de Cluny au diocèse de Rouen antérieures à 1204 publiées avec introduction et notes après les origineaux conservés aux Archives de la Seine-Inférieure par Paul Le Cacheux* (Société de l'Histoire de Normandie, Rouen, 1934), pp. 33, 54; Cartulary of Christchurch Twynham, BL, MS Cott. Tib., pt 2, ff. 8–8v, pv 10v (late twelfth to early thirteenth-century); Cartulary of St Evroult, Bibliothèque Nationale, MS Latin 11055, ff. 33v–35v; *The Cartulary of St. Michael's Mount: Hatfield House MS No. 315*, ed. P. L. Hull (Devon and Cornwall Record Society, new ser., 5, 1962), pp. 17, 89; *The Thurgarton Cartulary*, ed. T. Foulds (Stamford: Watkins, 1994), nos 17, 155. Mabel, widow of Otes de Tilly, may have had a seal *c*. 1195–1205: *EYC*, 8. no. 118. M. Clanchy, *From Memory to Written Record: England, 1066–1307* (2nd edn., Oxford: Blackwell, 1993), p. 316, discusses sealing clauses. *Regesta Regum Anglo-Normannorum: The Acta of William I, 1066–1087*, 'Introduction', p. 103.

52 Chassel, 'L'usage du sceau', p. 68.

53 Harvey and McGuinness, *Guide to British Medieval Seals*, pp. 43–4, although they cite three men's seals which were pointed oval. Chassel, 'L'usage du sceau', pp. 61–2, briefly discusses Roman and Mesopotamian antecedents.

54 1150: no. 142. 1170: nos 44, 122. Others: nos 14 (1220–30), 26 (1210), 27 (1180), 37 (late twelfth-century), 46 (late twelfth-century), 58 (*c.* 1200), 68 (late twelfth-century), 70 (early thirteenth-century), 71 (early thirteenth-century), 76 (*c.* 1200), 86 (*c.* 1210), 98 (1225), 121 (twelfth-century? before 1180), 136–38 (late twelfth-century to 1220). Of indeterminate shape: nos 28, 39, 50–2, 67, 94, 116, 134.

55 Heslop, 'Seals', in *English Romanesque Art*, p. 306, no. 338.

56 Blair, 'Armorials upon English seals', p. 258.

57 R. N. Swanson, 'Angels incarnate: clergy and masculinity from Gregorian reform to Reformation' in Hadley (ed.), *Masculinity in Medieval Europe*, p. 174.

58 For the seals of male ecclesiastics see Heslop, 'Seals', in *English Romanesque Art*, nos 338–47.

59 Nos 76 (*c.* 1200), 142 (1150).

60 T. A. Heslop, 'English seals in the thirteenth and fourteenth centuries', in J. Alexander and P. Binsky (eds), *Age of Chivalry* (London: Royal Academy of Arts, in association with Weidenfeld & Nicolson, 1987), p. 116; Harvey and McGuinness, *Guide to British Medieval Seals*, p. 43.

61 BL, Harl. Ch. 50. B. 33: the seals of Geoffrey, Lawrence and John, the sons of Cecilia, daughter of Sabelina, co-seal her charter. The seal of Geoffrey measures 2.7 in. diameter and depicts an equestrian image: a knight with shield on horseback; the seal of ? Lawrence depicts a bird; the fourth seal is indistinct but is possibly a figure with a falcon and a hound. For the seal of Cecilia see Catalogue, 111.

62 Bedos-Rezak, 'Women, seals and power', p. 67.

63 Catalogue, 32.

64 Catalogue, 131.

65 Catalogue, 8–9, 12–13, 15–17, 19–23, 25, 29, 30–5, 38, 42–3, 45, 47–9, 53–7, 61–6, 69, 72–82, 84, 87–8, 90, 93, 99–100, 102, 104–5, 107–12, 115–21, 124–5, 128–30, 131–4, 139–42. Sample of 135 out of 142 women's seals (five royal women's seals were excluded, and nos 94 and 106 are illegible), 63.7 per cent.

66 Ornate, geometric designs: Catalogue, 27, 58, 123. Fleur-de-lys: nos 6–7, 14, 24, 40, 51 (developed from fleur-de-lys), 59, 67, 85–6, 101, 103, 113, 127, 135–8; 68 (hand holding fleur-de-lys). Ornate, floral design: nos 26, 71. Stylised sheaf of corn: nos 83, 95. Ornate knot: nos 46, 89. 'Ornament of five points', no. 52.

67 Catalogue, 11, 18, 28, 37, 50, 97, 114, 122. Nos 10, 39 depict an eagle standing upon a tortoise.

68 Catalogue, 60; no. 74 depicts a tall standing female figure holding a fish in her right hand.

69 Catalogue, 49A, 49B (mid-twelfth-century). No. 92 (1140–60); no. 126 (*c.* 1195); no. 110 (1209–10). *Circa* 1210: no. 41 (quatrefoil); no. 91 (*c.* 1210); no. 43 has an estoile of eight points in the field (early thirteenth-century). No. 42 (1225, obverse standing female figure, reverse armorial); no. 128 (1220s) armorial counterseal.

70 Lady handed hawk: Catalogue, 33 (in the use of standing female figures this is conventional); figure and child: no. 47A; mermaid: no. 70; Roman intaglio: no. 36.

71 Harvey and McGuinness, *Guide to British Medieval Seals*, pp. 48–50.

72 Heslop, 'Seals of lords and ladies', in Alexander and Binsky (eds), *Age of Chivalry*, p. 251.

73 Chassel, 'L'usage du sceau', p. 72: most categories of sealers were established by *c.* 1200.

74 Harvey and McGuinness, *Guide to Medieval Seals*, p. 48.

75 G. Zarnecki, 'General introduction', in Zarnecki *et al.* (eds), *English Romanesque Art*, p. 24.

76 Bedos-Rezak, 'Women, seals and power', p. 75.

77 Catalogue, 15, 19.

78 Catalogue, 23.

79 For example, Catalogue, 34–5, 38, 53, 64, 78, 81–2, 140.

80 For example, Catalogue, 49A, long hair flowing over neck and shoulders; 56, queue of hair; 69, hair unbound; 75, long hair; 84, hair band. R. Bartlett, 'Hair in the Middle Ages', *TRHS*, 6th ser., 4 (1994), 44: hair is part of the symbolic grammar of the Middle Ages, and long hair was equated with high status.

81 Heslop, 'Seals', in *English Romanesque Art*, p. 306.

82 Catalogue, 8.

83 Catalogue, 19, 42, 45, 54–5, 63, 64A, 75, 107, 132ii. Others which hold two objects: nos 20 (orb and fleur-de-lys), 49A (lily and fleur-de-lys). No. 32 (? indistinguishable object), 80, ?88 (both, two objects held, though one indistinguishable), 87 (wavy branch and falcon).

84 Catalogue, 12, 15–17, 22–3, 31, 38, 53, 56, 62, 66, 69, 73, 76, 79, 82 (two fleur-de-lys held), 84, 99, 102, 104–5, 108, 110–12, 115, 118, 125, 131, 134, 139 (armorial), 140, 141 (fleur-de-lys and branch).

85 Catalogue, 9ii, 21, 35, 48 (damaged), 57, 61, 65, 77, 117, 120–1, 133.

86 Catalogue, 13, 81, 129 (one hand on breast, other extended).

87 Heslop, 'Seals', in *English Romanesque Art*, no. 337. Catalogue, 84, 110, 125, 131 (although scholars interpret similar imagery differently – thus a 'flower' to some is a fleur-de-lys to others). Once the image has become conventional by the thirteenth century see the example of Idonia de Herst, Catalogue, 63.

88 There are sixty seals, or nearly 52 per cent, with fleur-de-lys imagery. Forty-seven standing female figures holding fleur-de-lys: Catalogue, 12, 15, 16 (wavy branch – derivative of lys?), 17, 19–20, 22–3, 31, 38, 42, 45, 49A, 53–5, 56, 62–4, 66, 69, 73, 75–6, 79, 82 (two fleur-de-lys held), 84, 99, 102, 104–5, 107–8, 110–12, 115, 118, 125, 131–2, 134, 139 (armorial), 140, 141 (fleur-de-lys and branch). Sole fleur-de-lys devices depicted on nineteen seals: Catalogue, 6–7, 14, 24, 40, 51 (developed from lys), 59, 67, 85–6, 101, 103, 113, 127, 135–38; 68 (hand holding lys) (total, sixty-six). Indistinct: Catalogue, 29–30, 32, 43, 72, 94, 96, 106, 109, 116, 119, 124. 51.6 per cent (i.e. sixty-six of a sample of 128, which comprises 145 seals (three women have two seals, nos 47, 49, 64), of which royal women's seals were excluded, and the above twelve indistinct ones were also excluded. This is a conservative count, since there are six which are damaged but which possibly show ladies holding fleurs-de-lys, and others which are geometrical devices which may have grown from fleur-de-lys imagery: Catalogue, 17, 27, 58, 123. Cf. knot designs: 46, 89.

89 Catalogue, 49, 131.

90 See above, n. 88.

91 J. E. Cirlot, *A Dictionary of Symbols*, trans. from the Spanish by J. Sage (2nd edn, London: Routledge, 1971), p. 109.

92 Bedos-Rezak, 'Women, seals and power', p. 75.

93 R. A. Koch, 'The origin of the fleur-de-lis and the *lillium candidum* in art', in L. D. Roberts (ed.), *Approaches to Nature in the Middle Ages: Papers of the Tenth Annual Conference of the Center for Medieval and Early Renaissance Studies* (Binghamton NY: Center for Medieval and Early Renaissance Studies, 1982), pp. 109–30.

94 Koch, 'Origin of the fleur-de-lis', cites Bernard of Clairvaux, the seventieth sermon on the *Canticum Canticorum*: 'And consider how close is the analogy between the truth of God and the Lily of the Valleys. . . . From the centre of this flower there springs a number of little golden rods . . . which are surrounded by petals of a dazzling white, beautifully and fittingly arranged in the form of a crown. You have symbolised the gold of Christ's divinity,' pp. 110–14.

95 Bedos-Rezak, 'French sigillographic sources', p. 7.

96 See Bloch, *Etymologies and Genealogies*, p. 90.

97 See above, n. 67, and discussion following: references to seals which depict birds, only thirty of 128, 23.4 per cent.

98 Bedos-Rezak, 'French sigillographic sources', p. 7.

99 Shahar, *Fourth Estate*, p. 152; Bedos-Rezak, 'Women, seals and power', p. 76.

100 Cirlot, *Dictionary of Symbols*, p. 140.

101 Ailes, 'Heraldry: the evidence', pp. 5–7.

102 Catalogue, 49A. Ailes, 'Heraldry: the evidence', p. 7.

103 Bedos-Rezak, 'French sigillographic sources', p. 6.

104 Catalogue, 92.

105 BL, Egerton Ch. 430.

106 Ailes, 'Heraldry: the evidence', p. 7.

107 Bloch, *Etymologies and Genealogies*, p. 78.

108 Hudson, 'Anglo-Norman land law and the origins of property', p. 199.

109 Blair, 'Armorials upon English seals', p. 22.

110 Catalogue, 126; date given as 1236–47. For comments see Blair, 'Armorials upon English seals', p. 22, where the seal is assigned a late twelfth-century date.

111 *EYC*, 10. 13–17.

112 Blair, 'Armorials upon English seals', p. 22.

113 Catalogue, 110.

114 Catalogue, 91.

115 The counterseal is a gyronny of fourteen and an escutcheon: Catalogue, 9. Elienor countess of Saint-Quintin and Valois had a counterseal inscribed with a shield of arms, lions rampant and the legend + SECRETUM ELIENOR (Catalogue, 120).

116 Ailes, 'Heraldry: the evidence', p. 7.

117 Catalogue, 55. Her seal and counterseal were the same as those of her father and mother respectively. For further description see Heslop, 'Seals', in Zarnecki *et al.* (eds), *English Romanesque Art*, no. 337 and plate 37.

118 Heslop, 'Seals', in Zarnecki *et al.* (eds), *English Romanesque Art*, p. 306.

119 Catalogue, 43.

120 Catalogue, 33.

121 Catalogue, 25.

122 Catalogue, 10.

123 Catalogue, 28.

124 Catalogue, 70. This extant impression supports Harvey Bloom's assertion that Gunnora, widow of William Banastre, may have used a seal showing a mermaid and a flower, c. 1228: *English Seals*, p. 163.

125 Muriel, the widow of Hugh Pumfol: Catalogue, 103.

126 Emma Mustel: Catalogue, 89. Pavia, daughter Svan Thornet: Catalogue, 123. Alice Foliot: Catalogue, 46.

127 Catalogue, 83, 95.

128 Bedos-Rezak, 'Women, seals and power', pp. 68–71.

129 Catalogue, 9, 30, 33, 49B, 54–5, 72–3, 78, 80, 90, 92–3, 100, 125, 129, 132, 139. No. 81 describes the countess as 'Lady' of Flanders. No. 77 is described as wife of Robert fitz Erneis.

130 Catalogue, 49B, 49A.

131 Catalogue, 72.

132 Catalogue, 54. Other examples: Catalogue, 9, 33, 73, 78, 81, 90, 100, 125, 129, 132, 139.

133 Catalogue, 20.

134 Catalogue, 19.

135 Catalogue, 9. Hawise was married three times, firstly to Geoffrey de Mandeville earl of Essex (d. 14. November 1189); her wedding of 1180 was the 'social event of the year', D. M. Stenton, *The English Woman in History* (London: Allen & Unwin, 1957), p. 36. She was compelled to remarry by Richard I, and thus married in 1190 William de Forz (d. 1195) and subsequently Baldwin de Béthune (d. 13 or 14 October 1212). She was the heiress of her father, William of Aumâle; for the complex genealogy of the Mandevilles see *CP*, 5. 116 ff.

136 Other examples: Constance of Brittany (Catalogue, 19); Isabella de Brus (Catalogue, 22); Cecily de Crevequer (Catalogue, 37); Alice de Gant (Catalogue, 48).

137 Bedos-Rezak, 'French sigillographic sources', p. 4.

138 Catalogue, 13, 15, 27, 41, 50–2, 60, 62, 64B, 65, 69, 74, 82–3, 86, 95, 98–9, 104–5, 107–8, 123, 135–7. Eighteen seal legends illegible/fragmentary, Catalogue, 29, 32, 39–40, 48, 57, 70, 91–3, 106, 111, 115–16, 127–8, 130, 133, 142. Out of a sample of (140–18) extant impressions, 22.1 per cent.

139 Catalogue, 14, 18, 34, 56, 96–7, 103 (*LA FAME*). Other women adopt their husband's name but without the *uxor* designation: Catalogue, 53, 87, 113. Rohais as wife of Gilbert de Gant: Catalogue, 49A; Isabel countess of Pembroke: Catalogue, 100.

140 Bedos-Rezak, 'Women, seals and power', p. 69.

141 Burgesia, the sister of Walter Burre (mid-twelfth-century, Catalogue, 23). Her sister Emma is similarly defined by her connection with her brother in a charter of their immediate lord, William de Roumare: *Danelaw Charters*, no. 513. This charter agrees an exchange of land in Camel, which is similar to the agreement contained in Burgesia's charter, and was probably made at a similar date.

142 Alice Foliot 'de Hakethorn', in the late twelfth century gave land to Bullington Priory *in libere uiduitate mea*: Catalogue, 46.

143 Robert Grimbald died in 1163; Catalogue, 64B, 64A.

144 Catalogue, 47A.

145 Catalogue, 47B.

146 *RD*, p. 32 and n. 3; *Cartulary of Old Wardon*, pp. 318–19; *Early Charters of Waltham Abbey*, p. 61, notes to charter no. 104.

147 *Early Charters of Waltham Abbey*, nos 104–5.

148 Catalogue, 82; the charter was witnessed by, among others, *vidua Petronilla et fuit uxor Rob; le Gag'*. This charter supplies the name of her father, which has been elusive to date. Millo Dunton and Stratton (Bedfordshire) were of her inheritance, and the office of chamberlain passed with them to her husbands; she was co-heiress with her sister Juliana, wife of Hugh Rikespaud: *Cartulary of Old Wardon*, pp. 319–21.

149 *Early Charters of Waltham Abbey*, no. 241.

150 Stafford, 'Emma', p. 12.

151 For example, in 1144–55 Alice de Gant, the wife of Roger de Mowbray, granted lands from her first marriage to Ilbert de Lacy (d. 1141). Roger's charter confirms the grant: *Mowbray Charters*, no. 105. For his equestrian seal see *ibid.*, pp. lxxxii–iii. For Alice's charter see *ibid.*, no. 101, her seal, *ibid.* (Catalogue, 48). Another example: Alice de St Quintin, who granted land of her dower from her marriage to Robert, son of Fulk, during her marriage to Eustace de Merc: *EYC*, 11. no. 96. She was the heiress of Herbert de St Quintin.

152 For example, Cassandra *de Estodlei*, Catalogue, 44. Emma Mustel, Catalogue, 89. Isabella countess of Warenne, Catalogue, 132. Alienor, daughter of William de Monte Alto, Catalogue, 86. Hawise countess of Aumâle, Catalogue, 9. Alice de Rumilly, Catalogue, 110; see *Book of Seals*, no. 465.

153 For example, Marjorie, daughter of Baldwin de Disceford (Catalogue, 41); other examples: Catalogue, 43, 47, 61, 64.

154 Catalogue, 140.

155 Catalogue, 12 i–iv.

156 Both seals are appended via a woven bobbin, although both seals are badly worn. His seal is round and depicts an intaglio of a unicorn; the seal on the right is very defective. Her seal appends her charter granting similar lands in similar terms to the same beneficiaries of the same date, John Rylands University Library, Manchester, Rylands Charters, nos. 1276, 1277 (Catalogue, 27). Mabel was the daughter and heir of William Fleming and married Bertram *c.* 1180; see *Chester Charters*, no. 194 and notes 199–200.

157 Catalogue, 117.

158 Both in favour of Bullington Priory. Basilia: Catalogue, 85. Cecily de Crevequer: Catalogue, 37.

159 When Alice countess of Northampton *c.* 1140 granted and sealed a charter, her husband confirmed her grant by his charter (Catalogue, 92). Juliana Foliot and her husband Robert of Wendover may have co-sealed a charter: her seal is extant, but his may have been lost, since there is a slit for another seal in the parchment, Catalogue, 59.

160 PRO, E 42/226 (*Seals PRO*, 1. P159). For another example where a husband's seal may have authenticated a grant made by a wife see *Chartulary of St John of Pontefract*, 1. no. 309. Chassel, 'L'usage du sceau', p. 78, for examples where women borrowed seals to authenticate documents. The nephew of Emma de Scampton sealed her charter, BL, Harl. Ch. 47. 1. 14 (*Danelaw Charters*, no. 210); the seal is damaged, but

possibly depicts a lion rampant. Robert Croc sealed a charter of his widowed daughter *c.* 1200: H. Laing, *Descriptive Catalogue of Impressions from ancient Scottish Seals, Royal, Baronial, Ecclesiastical and Municipal, embracing a Period from A.D. 1094 to the Commonwealth* (Edinburgh: printed T. Constable, 1850), no. 221.

161 Catalogue, 62.

162 Catalogue, 111. Hyams, 'Warranty and good lordship', pp. 437–503, notes that warranty clauses were akin to 'written contracts of obligation'.

163 Catalogue, 136–8.

164 *Danelaw Charters*, no. 551; *Northants. Charters*, no. 62, for another example of three sisters co-sealing in the late twelfth century, and no. 63 for an identical charter dated by Stenton to *c.* 1220.

165 *The Chartulary of the High Church of Chichester*, ed. W. D. Peckham (Sussex Record Society, 46, 1946 for 1942–43), pp. 126–7, no. 482.

166 Catalogue, 32; see *Northants. Charters*, no. 18 and nn. 53–5.

167 Catalogue, 29.

168 Catalogue, 30. *RD*, pp. 15–16.

169 Catalogue, 20.

170 Catalogue, 19.

171 *Gloucester Charters*, nos 67 (1183–97), 78 (1194–97), 160 (1183–89) (Catalogue, 54).

172 *Ibid.*, no. 140 (general confirmation charter in favour of Margam Abbey).

173 *Ibid.*, nos 142–7.

174 Catalogue, 73. When she granted a charter in favour of Garendon Abbey she held the lands she granted in dower: *Book of Seals*, no. 5, and notes following.

175 In the following calculation (h) designates an heiress; those whose seal legends use the *filie* phrase, which may indicate the woman is an heiress, are symbolised by (h*f*). Catalogue, nos: 9 (h), 12 (h), 16 (h), 18 (h) 19 (h), 20, 22 (h), 27 (h), 35 (h), 37 (h), 39 (h), 48 (dower), 49, 58 (h), 59, 64B (h*f*), 66, 74 (h*f*), 76, 83 (h*f*), 85, 87, 92, 100 (h), 101, 104 (h), 105 (h*f*), 108 (h), 114, 117 (h), 118, 119 (h, dower), 121 (h), 124, 130, 131 (h), 133 (h), 134 (h), 135 (h*f*) (total 39). But the total of 43 also includes those who sealed as both a wife and a widow: see note following.

176 Catalogue, nos: 10–11, 13 (h*f*), 17 (h), 21 (h), 24, 29–32, 36 (h), 38, 41 (h*f*), 43–6, 54, 60–3, 65 (h*f*), 67 (h), 68, 69 (h*f*), 72–3, 78 (h), 79 (h), 86 (h*f*), 89–1, 94, 95 (h*f*), 103, 109 (h), 110 (h), 111, 113, 115–16, 123 (h*f*), 124, 126 (h) (total forty-six). Indeterminate: Catalogue, nos 6–8, 14, 15 (h*f*), 25–6, 28 (h*f*), 33–4, 42, 50–2 (h*f*), 53, 56, 57, 60 (h*f*), 63, 67, 70–1, 75, 77, 80–1, 84 (h), 88, 93–4, 96–7, 98 (h*f*), 99 (h*f*), 102 (h), 106, 107 (h*f*), 108 (h*f*), 112 (h), 125, 127–9, 136–8 (h*f*), 139, 141–2 (total 51).

177 As wife and widow: Catalogue, 47, 55 (h), 64 (h), 132.

178 For Norman women see Bedos-Rezak, 'Women, seals and power', p. 66; for Normandy more generally in the context of a general discussion of French seals, Chassel, 'L'usage du sceau', pp. 68, 70.

179 Catalogue, 130; her seal depicts an eagle, as does that of her husband, *ibid.*, no. 836. Other examples, *ibid.*, nos 482, 832, 1197 (all *c.* 1220 in favour of Melrose Abbey).

180 H. Laing, *Supplemental Descriptive Catalogue of ancient Scottish Seals, Royal, Baronial, Ecclesiastical and Municipal, embracing the Period from A.D. 1150 to the Eighteenth Century* (Edinburgh: Edmonston & Douglas, 1866), no. 134; *Seals BM*, 5.

no. 21,099 (Catalogue, 20). See also the seal of Avicia de Moreville of *c.* 1176: Catalogue, 87.

181 B. R. S. Megaw, 'The ship seals of the kings of Man', *Journal of the Manx Museum*, 6 (1957–65), 78–80, plates 239–41.

182 1135–49: wife and daughter involved in conjoint alienation to religious house, *Cartulaire des Îles Normandes : recueil de documents concernant l'histoire de ces Îles, conservés aux archives du département de la Manche et du Calvados, de la Bibliothèque Nationale, du Bureau des Rôles, du château de Warwick*, ed. N. V. L. Rybot (Jersey: Beresford Library for the Société Jersiaise, 1924), no. 34 (involvement of wife); *ibid.*, nos 35, 117 (consent of wife) and other examples of female participation, nos 118, 166, 206, 287, 303.

183 Catalogue, 100. For noblewomen with lands in Cheshire see Catalogue, 27, 29–30.

8

Women of the lesser nobility

I N 1180 BERTRAM, the chamberlain of Earl Hugh II of Chester, married Mabel, the heiress of William *Flamenc*, and by grant of charter received her inheritance. Little is known of the origins of Bertram, and likewise the descent of Mabel's inheritance, from the time of Robert of Rhuddlan, who held the manor of Great Meols in 1066, is also obscure.[1] What is clear, however, is that Bertram's service in his lord's household as chamberlain was rewarded with marriage to an heiress. Earl Hugh was here evidently exercising his right of marriage of the heiress of a tenant to reward a retainer in a way which facilitated his social mobility; what is made of Mabel's position is less clear. However, these are well worn themes. Bertram received only lands assessed at the value of one-fifth of a knight's fee. It is striking that, despite their relative obscurity, both Bertram and Mabel as landholders issued their own charters. *Circa* 1195–1200 Bertram and Mabel issued a joint charter on the occasion of the marriage of their daughter Alice with William fitz Bernard, granting three bovates of land as her marriage portion.[2] Of even greater significance, however, is the fact that this charter was sealed with two seals. The seal appended on the left of the charter, which is possibly that of Bertram, depicts a unicorn and is considerably smaller than the seal on the right. The other seal is possibly that of Mabel, since it is of similar dimensions to her extant seal, a specimen of which authenticates a charter granted by Mabel, and is similar to that affixed to the joint grant made with Bertram. Further, both charters have the same witness list, so they were probably issued on the same occasion. Mabel's seal is round, of green wax, and depicts an ornate stylised fleur-de-lys.[3] The lands concerned were of Mabel's inheritance, so it was Mabel's position as heiress which gave her the right to alienate them, and she did so to benefit her daughter. It is unlikely that Mabel would go to the effort of commissioning a seal die just for one document, so it is likely that she granted more charters to authenticate other documents, now lost, concerning her patrimonial lands.

A central problem for the study of lesser noblewomen's roles is the fragmentary nature of the evidence. This can partly be resolved where sequential or near-sequential copies of charters by the same grantors or their family exist. This chapter discusses female patronage of St Mary's, Clerkenwell, by the Munteni family in the second half of the twelfth century and shows how land tenure and kin connections could underpin active female patronage over two generations. It also assesses the interactions of the female life cycle and social status upon the participation of wives and widows in land transfers. Finally, the discussion of female lesser nobility will be extended to include examples of noblewomen who exerted power more formally, perhaps as public office holders. In so doing a wider context for discussion of noblewomen and power will be drawn. The evidence, although far from being comprehensive, shows how the roles of lesser noblewomen could resemble those of women of higher status.

Compiled in the first half of the thirteenth century, the cartulary of St Mary Clerkenwell is a rich source because it contains a large number of grants which involved women as witnesses, alienors and consentors. The priory of St Mary was a house of Augustinian canonesses founded *c.* 1145 on the inherited land of Muriel de Muteni, wife of Jordan Brisset, which eventually grew to become the twelfth richest nunnery at the Dissolution.[4] Jordan and Muriel had four daughters, Lecia, Matilda, Emma and Roesia, who were all involved in the patronage of St Mary's. Muriel de Munteni and her daughter Lecia were particularly active in their support for the priory. There are charters of both in favour of Clerkenwell as wives and as widows; they thus acted to exert influence in similar contexts to women of the high nobility.[5]

Muriel de Munteni was married twice, firstly to Jordan de Brisset and secondly to Maurice, son of Robert de Totham. She carried her interest in Clerkenwell through both her marriages. There are twenty-three documents in the cartulary which show the various ways that Muriel directly participated in religious patronage as grantor, co-grantor with her husband, consentor and as a witness.[6] It is worth considering her role in detail, since this will clarify the contexts of her activity and thus the importance of family connections and the impact of the female life cycle upon her participation. In 1152–62 Jordan and Muriel confirmed various gifts of tenants to Clerkenwell for the sake of their souls, their heirs, their friends and parents. The witness list has

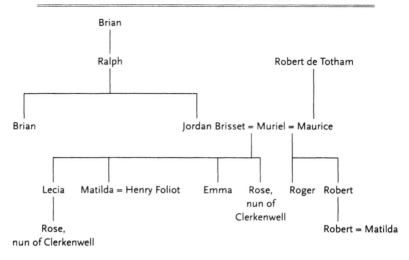

FIGURE 2   The genealogy of Muriel de Munteni

ten witnesses, including Muriel, who is called *domina donationis*.[7] The use of the term suggests that the scribe who compiled/transcribed the charter sought a way to describe her key role as patron and benefactor, and suggests that the nunnery, although founded by Jordan and Muriel conjointly, may have been her initiative.[8] In the same period they also made arrangements with Clerkenwell for their daughter's entry as a nun there. The charter's witness list includes Michael Capra and Roesia, his wife, who is probably Roesia the daughter of Muriel and Jordan, who later became a nun at Clerkenwell.[9]

Muriel de Munteni also used her influence to secure additional gifts to Clerkenwell during her second marriage. In a charter of 1176–79 she and Maurice de Totham (d. before 1196) conjointly granted various rights in the land they held of the bishop of London, a charter which was witnessed by Robert and Michael de Munteni and Roger, son of Maurice.[10] Muriel also witnessed a grant made by Maurice in 1181–86, as did her daughter Lecia, as well as Roger and John, the sons of Maurice, and Michael de Munteni.[11] Maurice also made three other donations to Clerkenwell of land near Tottenham.[12] He also acted as a witness to grants made by family members and undertenants connected with the de Munteni fee.[13] This is important because it indicates that he patronised the foundation of his wife's previous husband, which shows beyond doubt that he was influenced by Muriel in the direction of his religious patronage.

Muriel's concern for the welfare of her daughter was expressed through the careful arrangements she made to ensure that Roesia was properly clothed and fed once she entered the convent. In 1175–79 Muriel gave rents to Clerkenwell from land which was of her marriage portion and stipulated that the money was to be in effect Roesia's clothing allowance.[14] In total there are eight charters in Muriel's name.[15] Lecia, the daughter of Muriel and her husband, Henry Foliot, in 1193 to Michaelmas 1196 confirmed to Clerkenwell the service of Solomon of Stepney, for which they received eight marks from the nuns of Clerkenwell for the quitclaim.[16] By the address clause Henry and Lecia greet 'all of Christ's faithful', and thenceforward all the verbs are in the plural: they *concessisse et dedisse*, and they made their affidavit conjointly. The closing protocol contains the phrase *et sigillorum nostrorum appositione communimus*, which suggests that Henry and Lecia strengthened the charter by their seals: there were separate sealing clauses for Henry and Lecia, and another for Muriel. The sealing clause for Muriel suggests that she gave her consent. Muriel also witnessed a charter of Lecia and her husband before 1182 and one of Emma and her husband, Reginald de Ginges, prior to 1186; further, she witnessed a charter by an undertenant before March 1190.[17] There are seven charters in her name from her second widowhood, the period 1193–96.[18] Muriel was probably acting to secure her gifts in her old age, and was thus seeking to ensure the security of her favourite foundation after her death.

Muriel de Munteni is a truly remarkable example of female influence expressed through two marriages and widowhood. The ways that she was involved in religious benefaction shows how noblewomen could participate in land transfers as witnesses, alienors and confirmers despite changes in the female life cycle. Without doubt Muriel's position as an heiress underpinned her power as a secular landholder, which therefore facilitated her participation in grants to the religious house that she had played a key role in founding. Her commitment was crystallised when she took care to provide for her daughter Roesia, who became a nun there. There is no evidence that Muriel retired to the convent, although it is of course possible.

Lecia's attachment to her sister, the nun Roesia, is evident in the cartulary. Her concern for her sister's welfare is shown *c.* 1178 when, as widow, Lecia granted her sister land held of her by an undertenant to pay for her sister's clothing.[19] The land was to revert to Lecia or her heirs upon the former's death. Her mother Muriel had made a grant of 5s rent for clothing, but in Roesia's grant the rent was to remain with the nuns after Roesia's death.[20] It was thus the female members of the family which maintained close connections with the priory. Indeed, Lecia named her daughter after her sister, showing the close relationship between the two sisters. This close relationship between female kin of the de Munteni family was further emphasised when Lecia, with her husband, Henry Foliot, before Michaelmas 1196 gave land in order that their daughter Roesia could become a nun, and Lecia also at her will – *quando voluero mutare vitam meam ut recipiar ad habitum monialem in domo de Clerek[enwelle]*. Henry Foliot and Lecia conjointly sealed the charter to ensure their gift, the sealing clause neatly summing up their joint responsibility to secure the gift through a warranty clause. They acted *versus omnes homines et feminas* and also announced that *presentis carte attestatione et sigillorum nostrorum appositione communimus.*[21] The conjoint sealing clause stressed equal authority. It is unclear when or whether Lecia entered the priory, but it seems likely that she did, given her support and patronage, the fact that her sister was already there and the arrangements that she made for her daughter. Lecia was involved with donations and gifts to Clerkenwell for over twenty years during the period 1176–98 in various capacities which include co-alienor, grantor and witness.[22] There are eight charters of Lecia and her husband in favour of Clerkenwell, one in 1176–October 1186, three in the 1180s and four in the 1190s.[23] In return for their gift to Clerkenwell in 1181–89 they received twenty-five marks and for their grant of 1182 they received two marks and one mark respectively. Henry, Lecia and Muriel received eight marks for a quitclaim they made between 1193–96.[24] As a wife she granted two charters as sole alienor, one *c.* 1178, which was to the benefit of her sister Rohais, and one in *c.* 1178/79 in favour of Mabel, the wife of Stephen Barre.[25] *Circa* 1197 *in viduitate mea* Lecia confirmed all previous gifts made by her husband, father and mother as well as those by her sisters Emma and Matilda. In return the nuns gave her ten marks.[26] Out of twenty-four charters which involve Lecia as grantor, witness or as lord of the lands in question, Lecia received countergifts on seven occasions worth in total over forty-four marks, 2s, one bezant and a pair of sandals.[27]

Landholders exploited the value of their land when they accepted relief payments such as those received *in gersum* for enfeoffment in return for specific rents or services. In a grant by Lecia of Ravenildescroft in Newington to Emma, daughter of Wimund, the condition of service was that Emma should render two headdresses (*coifas*) per year, saving service to the king for the *defensio* of eight acres. For this concession Emma gave Lecia some sandals.[28] This was a confirmation of her mother's gift to Emma when Muriel had received a *peplum* – a robe, veil or possibly a wimple.[29] Further Lecia stipulated that Emma's sister, another Emma, should be her heir, rendering 2s yearly, saving service to the king.

Circa 1175 Robert de Munteni gave 'his man' Ailward land worth 3s per year which was given for the sake of his soul and that of his wife, Matilda, who witnessed the charter.[30] Matilda also, with her husband, Robert, witnessed a charter of Michael Capra and his wife, Rohais, c. 1156–62.[31] Emma de Munteni, who married Reginald de Ginges, like Lecia and Matilda, her sisters, participated in religious benefaction of Clerkenwell. The cartulary records six *acta* of Reginald and Emma concerning various grants and agreements related to lands held by Clerkenwell.[32] In a notification charter Emma and her husband informed the bishop of London that they had confirmed a grant by Maurice de Totham, Emma's stepfather, of the parochial rights in the bishopric of London belonging to their fee.[33] Like her sister Lecia, Emma participated in the religious patronage of Clerkenwell as a wife, and her position as co-heiress facilitated her participation in religious benefaction when, for example, before 1182 she witnessed a tenant's charter.[34] The founder's daughters thus maintained the family connection with the nunnery. Undertenants of the de Munteni family also donated land: for example, Robert Brito de Aldwych made a series of grants to Clerkenwell.[35] These entailed the procuration of a series of confirmation charters issued by Robert's son Roger, Reginald de Ginges, Emma, his wife, Henry Foliot and Lecia de Munteni.[36] Robert Brito de Alwych was thus an undertenant of the Muntenis, and to secure their gift the nuns pursued every possible avenue of confirmation, recording such from the heir (Roger de Brito) of the tenant, and the co-heiresses/co-lords Lecia and Emma de Munteni and their husbands. The nuns were obviously anxious to secure their grants, and it is interesting that the only individuals who are not recorded as receiving countergifts were Emma and her husband. This suggests that Lecia was the elder co-heiress, with greater right to the land in question and this position enabled her to exploit the revenue which could be generated when confirmation *acta* were granted. This accounts for the confirmation charter issued by Henry Foliot and Lecia in the period 1176– October 1186, when they confirmed a gift of five acres to the nuns by Emma and Reginald de Ginges.[37]

As wives Muriel, Lecia, Emma and Matilda de Munteni participated in actions to further the interests of the nunnery, and their power to do so rested on their position as heiresses. As widows Lecia and Muriel were involved in the patronage of the nunnery. Such family group action is also apparent in the charter evidence relating to the Capra family. Alice Capra, wife of William Capra, and one of her nieces became nuns at Clerkenwell before July 1176.[38] This charter was co-granted by her three daughters, Agnes, Alice and Constance, and their husbands for the soul of William Capra and Alice, who had become a nun there. Agnes, Alice and Constance were co-heiresses of the manor of Langford, Essex, from which the rent of 30*s* was granted.[39] The participation of the women of the Capra family as wives was related to their position as heiresses. Thus as both wives and widows in the specific context of religious patronage women pursued their own policies and initiatives.

The ways that the de Munteni family acted to maintain family links through the conduit of religious patronage are not unusual. The problem with identifying such patterns of behaviour within families from the lower ranks of the nobility lies with the survival rate of documents. There are examples of noblewomen making benefactions for their family and kin. In 1144–59 Beatrice de Chevrecurt with her brother and nephews, Jordan and Richard, conjointly gave the town of Barnsley to Pontefract.[40] In return the monks agreed to appoint a monk for their mother, one for Beatrice and one for Ralph to pray for them. By this agreement, Beatrice's nephew Ralph, the son of Ralph, her brother, received a monk's tunic and boots yearly from the abbey. Beatrice was therefore actively participating in the context of the religious patronage of her natal family and by so doing publicly confirmed her spiritual affiliation to her lineage. Juetta and William de Arches gave six carucates to Nun Monkton, which they founded for their daughter, Matilda, to be a nun there in 1147–53. Matilda became prioress, and her sister Juetta gave the town of Stainton (Co. Durham) and alms to the priory.[41]

The importance of the female life cycle in defining the place of women in society can be tested with an examination of the evidence relating to unmarried women. There are very few examples of young unmarried women granting charters, and thus maidenhood may have disbarred young women from acting as religious patrons in their own right. Nevertheless there is evidence, albeit fragmentary and rare, to show that young noblewomen could participate in religious patronage, in their own right or as witnesses to their parents' gifts. Sibyl lady of *Wilfrechston* gave land by hereditary right, and placed the Gospels on the altar as token of her gift. She did this before her marriage.[42] In 1165 Philippa de Rosel, a patron of Notre-Dame d'Ardennes, near Caen, gave land as a maiden, and she was an important benefactor throughout all three of her subsequent marriages.[43] A member of the urban bourgeoisie, Preciosa, the daughter of Master Benedict granted lands by charter in 1200–15 when she was fourteen years old.[44] All three women were heiresses, again indicating that it was the relationship between landholder and land that affected ways that women could participate in land transfers.

Women's power to grant land in the context of religious patronage gave them a public role which was considerably magnified if the woman was an heiress or a widow. Women generally did not hold formal public office: such roles as chamberlain, mayor, juror, sheriff or other administrative roles, as they developed, were gendered male in twelfth-century England. There is, however, evidence to suggest that at least one noble household, that of Matilda de Percy countess of Warwick, had a female official employed as a chamberlain. The language used within the charter which suggests that a female chamberlainship existed is precise. *Circa* 1184–99 Matilda granted to *Juliane camerarie mee sorori Roberti camerarii mei* various lands in Spofforth (Yorkshire) to be held *in feodo et hereditate libere quiete et solute*.[45] Juliana's brother, described as Countess Matilda's chamberlain, had previously received these lands from Adam, son of Copsi, confirmed by Matilda de Percy in 1175–*c.* 1184.[46] It is possible that the lands which Countess Matilda conveyed by charter to Juliana devolved to her by right of inheritance as her brother's heir. It is unclear whether this position of chamberlain in Matilda de Percy's household was heritable and linked to specific land. However, the charter suggests that she was a household official prior to his death and it is possible that they shared responsibilities.[47] This is indicative that positions of office in a noble household of a powerful dowager countess like Matilda de Percy were perhaps kindred-linked, a familial concern and heritable to the extent that women could perform such roles on occasion. Matilda de Percy also confirmed to the Benedictine nunnery of Stainfield a grant of twenty acres by Juliana, *camerarie mee*.[48] It is significant that Juliana did not witness Matilda's charters in any official capacity as chamberlain, unlike her brother and her husband, Nigel de Plumpton.[49] Her office as chamberlain may have been familial and heritable but it was also personal and linked with the patronage and power of Matilda de Percy. Matilda probably chose to have a female official and this may reflect personal connections between Juliana and Matilda de Percy. The exercise of public duties may well have been a function of the wife of a sheriff, as the discussion of Bertha de Glanville, who received affidations from women, has previously suggested, and indeed the witnessing and sealing of documents by women also suggest recognised roles and duties by wives and widows.

There are other examples of aristocratic and noblewomen retaining female household servants and followers, but few examples of women giving land to female servants/retainers, and these are mostly granted by women of comital or royal status. This suggests that economic resources that underpinned social status were important in enabling women to make secular grants to female servants. Eleanor of Aquitaine granted Amicia Pautos her servant the manor of *Wintreslewe*, which enabled Amicia to retire to a convent as a nun.[50] In the late eleventh century Queen Matilda had given Gundreda de Warenne a *mansio* named Carlton.[51] Hawise countess of Aumâle gave land to her wet nurse as a reward for her service in the early thirteenth century.[52] In the mid-twelfth Amice countess of Leicester gave her lady-in-waiting 4s annually on her marriage to a retainer of the earl.[53] In 1190–1210 Alice Basset, with the consent of her son Hugh and her daughters Iseult and Helen, gave her land at Patrick Pool, York, to Thomas de Langwath to be held by rendering a pound of pepper annually *pro labore suo exhibito circa doctrinam predicte Hugonis filii mee*.[54] In the early thirteenth century Agnes de Condet willed various valuable gold rings to her sons and daughters, sums of money to her maidservants, including a scarlet cloak and linen cloth, as well as gifts to servants, friends and religious houses of various sums of money.[55]

There is evidence that women could hold public office if they had a claim through patrilineal hereditary right. Nichola de la Haye was the eldest daughter and co-heir of Richard de la Haye, hereditary constable of Lincoln Castle and sheriff of Lincolnshire, and his wife, Matilda, the daughter of William of Vernon. She was married twice, firstly to William of Erneis and subsequently, before 1185, to Gerard de Camville, passing the office of constable to each of her husbands.[56] She was actively involved in the process by which her inheritance passed to her husbands; for example, in August 1189 she and Gerard de Camville had crossed to Barfleur to obtain a charter confirming her inheritance from King Richard. The charter confirmed to both Gerard and Nichola her inheritance and lands and the constableship of Lincoln Castle, together with lands at Poupeville and Varreville in the east Cotentin.[57] Nichola was twice besieged at Lincoln Castle, once in 1191 with her second husband, Gerard de Camville, and again in 1217 as a widow after his death.[58] In 1194 she accounted for the sum of 300 marks to marry her daughter, Matilda, according to her will, excepting one of the king's enemies.[59] She continued to account for this debt until 1212.[60] She had renegotiated the amount in 1200, and in 1212 she still owed £20, forty marks and one palfrey.[61] As a widow she held the manor of Swaton in Lincolnshire, which was worth £20 in 1185 and had been held by her mother as dower before her.[62] In 1217, probably during the siege of Lincoln, Nichola, as castellan, and Geoffrey de Celand issued letters of protection to the church of Lincoln, the deans and canons and their households.[63] There is no doubt that Nichola was a significant individual who held the office of castellan in her widowhood in her own right.[64]

This chapter began with a detailed study of de Munteni family grants to the nunnery of St Mary's, Clerkenwell, to show how charter evidence can be used to discuss the ways in which in a specific locality women of the lesser nobility maintained family contacts and networks of association through their religious patronage. This suggested that such women did so in their multiple identities as wives, widows, sisters, aunts, mothers and daughters, participating in land transfers as grantors, co-grantors and witnesses. These patterns of activity are similar to those of women from the higher nobility. As the discussion of, for example, Juliana de Plumpton and Nichola de la Haye showed, women of the lesser nobility occasionally held offices which were normally the preserve of men. Such examples, however, are rare and confirm that in general women did not hold office in formal ways. Yet the distinctions between formal public office holding and public roles are hard to define, and to draw them does little justice to the ways that women exerted power and influence. Powerful countesses and women of the lesser nobility such as those of the de Munteni family were able to enact policies and strategies irrespective of their exclusion from formal positions of office, and this is the key to understanding the power of twelfth-century women. Although the evidence discussed has been inevitably somewhat limited, it suggests that we should expect such patterns of activity to be general among twelfth-century noblewomen, whatever their social status.

Notes

1 *Chester Charters*, no. 194, and see nn. 199–200.
2 John Rylands University Library, Manchester, Rylands Charter, no. 1276.
3 *Ibid.*, no. 1277.
4 *VCH Middlesex*, 1. 170, which states that Clerkenwell was founded by Jordan and his wife, Muriel, based on a confirmation charter of Henry II of *c.* 1176–78. Yet although she was associated with later grants with her husband and gave gifts of her own, it seems that the initial endowment was made by Jordan, possibly at Muriel's instigation. J. H. Round, 'The foundation of the priories of St Mary and St John, Clerkenwell', *Archaeologia*, 56 (1899), 225–6; S. Thompson, *Women Religious: The Founding of English Nunneries after the Norman Conquest* (Oxford: Clarendon Press, 1991), pp. 189–90.

5 Matilda countess of Warwick in the 1180s took action on behalf of her father's foundation: see pp. 70–1. Lucy countess of Chester continued to patronise Stixwould through
her three marriages: see pp. 60–1. So did Philippa de Rosel in the latter half of the
twelfth century: see p. 158.

6 *Clerkenwell Cartulary*, nos 2, 6, 9–10 (royal confirmations by Henry II and Richard
of various grants, including those of the de Munteni family); as co-grantor with her
first husband: nos 43, 74; as co-grantor with second husband: no. 53; as grantor:
nos 64, 73, 81, 84–6, 90, 109, as a witness: no. 48 (grant of second husband), 79
(grant of younger daughter and son-in-law), 98 (elder daughter and son-in-law),
108 (charter of tenant); consent: no. 82, mentioned in text: nos 65, 80, 328, 324 (same
as 328).

7 *Ibid.*, no. 43.

8 Thompson, *Women Religious*, p. 177.

9 *Clerkenwell Cartulary*, no. 74.

10 *Ibid.*, no. 52.

11 *Ibid.*, no. 48.

12 *Ibid.*, nos 49–51.

13 *Ibid.*, nos 92, 97, 113, 139, 149, 289.

14 *Ibid.*, no. 90.

15 *Ibid.*, nos 64, 73, 81, 84–6, 90, 109.

16 *Ibid.*, no. 82.

17 *Ibid.*, nos 48, 79, 98.

18 *Ibid.*, nos 64, 73, 81, 85–6, 90, 109.

19 *Ibid.*, no. 44.

20 *Ibid.*, no. 90.

21 *Ibid.*, no. 72.

22 *Ibid.*, nos 39, 61–2, 72, 80, 82, 87, 98 (co-grantor with husband), 44–5, 63, 65, 83, 328
(grantor), 48, 79, 90, 108 (witness), 73 (recipient), 81 (recipient of countergift),
64 (mentioned in mother's charter, which confirmed her grant, no. 63); 304 (mentioned in tenant's charter), 334 (same as no. 328).

23 *Ibid.*, 1176–86: no. 39; 1180s: nos 80, 87, 98; 1190s: nos 61–2, 72, 82.

24 *Ibid.*, no. 82: *Pro hac autem concessione et donatione et hac quieta clamatia dederunt
predicte nobis predictis Henrico et Lucie et Muriele octo marcas argenti.*

25 *Ibid.*, nos 44 (*c.* 1178); 45 (1178/9).

26 *Ibid.*, no. 83.

27 *Ibid.*, nos 65 (a confirmation of 73), 80–3, 98, 328.

28 *Ibid.*, no. 65.

29 *Ibid.*, no. 73.

31 *Ibid.*, no. 75.

32 *Ibid.*, no. 302.

33 *Ibid.*, nos 54–5, 79, 88, 97, 110.

34 *Ibid.*, no. 54, confirming Maurice's grant (see nn. 11–12 above).

35 *Ibid.*, no. 95.

36 The nuns paid him five marks and his son 20s and, in another charter recording
the same grant, ten marks; for another grant the nuns paid ten silver marks: *ibid.*,
nos 91–3.

37 *Ibid.*, nos 91, 93 (charter witness list includes Aubrey de Vere earl of Oxford and Countess Agnes, his wife), 95–8.

38 *Ibid.*, no. 39.

39 *Ibid.*, no. 34.

40 *HKF*, 3. 17; *Mon. Ang.*, 4. 85; *VCH Middlesex*, 1. 172.

41 *EYC*, 3. no. 1771.

42 *EYC*, 1. no. 535 and nn.

43 *CDF*, no. 579.

44 *CDF*, no. 517; confirmed by Ranulf (III) earl of Chester, *Chester Charters*, no. 319.

45 *EYC*, 1. no. 207.

46 *EYC*, 11. no. 63. H. M. Thomas, 'An upwardly mobile medieval woman: Juliana of Warwick', *Medieval Prosopography*, 18 (1997), 109–21, who discusses the translation of *camerarie* and suggests that it was a female equivalent of male chamberlain *camerarius* (pp. 111–12).

46 *Ibid.*, no. 64.

47 Thomas, 'Upwardly mobile medieval woman', pp. 112–13.

48 *EYC*, 11. no. 59.

49 *Ibid.*, no. 38 (joint gift of Matilda and her husband, William earl of Warwick); Matilda de Percy's charters: nos 40–6, 50–2, 54–67. Juliana and Nigel had a son called John: *EYC*, 11. no. 63 and nn. 63–4. Juliana was the daughter of Richard de Warwick (d. 1205); she married Nigel de Plumpton as his second wife. She had dower in Plumpton, Grassington, Idle and Ribston: *Plumpton Correspondence: A Series of Letters, Chiefly Domestick, Written in the Reigns of Edward IV, Richard III, Henry VII, and Henry VIII*, ed. T. Stapleton (Camden Society, old ser., 4, 1839), p. xvi. Juliana had a sister Sarra who married Gilbert de Beningworth and then Simon de Hauton. *HKF*, 2. 134–5, 180; *Chester Charters*, notes to no. 296.

50 *CDF*, no. 1091.

51 *HKF*, 3. 309. Gundreda d. 27 May 1085: *CP*, 12(1). 494.

52 Humberside County Record Office, Chichester-Constable Deeds, DDCC/135/1 (DBC).

53 D. Crouch, *The Beaumont Twins: The Roots and Branches of Power in the Twelfth Century* (Cambridge: Cambridge University Press, 1986), p. 157 n. Service in a countess's household could be one way in which working women earned a living and found a marriage partner.

54 *EYC*, 1. no. 295.

55 *The Registrum Antiquissimum of the Cathedral Church of Lincoln: Volume I*, ed. C. W. Foster (Lincoln Record Society, 27, 1931), pp. 293–5. This is a fascinating insight into the material culture of a woman at the turn of the twelfth and early thirteenth centuries, and compares with the bequests made by Queen Joan of Sicily, the daughter of King John, in 1199, when she made a similar mixture of gifts to family, friends, servants and religious benefactions in her will: *CDF*, no. 1105.

56 *HKF*, 3. 56.

57 *Ancient Charters*, no. 55.

58 See above, pp. 22–5, for a discussion of the portrayal of Nichola in the context of a discussion of the portrayal of women in chronicles and narratives generally.

59 *P.R. 6 Richard I*, p. 119.

60 She appears in the Pipe Rolls successively: *P.R. 8 Richard I*, p. 237, where she owed
    £94 6s 8d; *P.R. 9 Richard I*, p. 100 (£94 6s 8d); *P.R. 10 Richard I*, pp. 50 (£94 6s 8d),
    63 (fifty marks); *P.R. 1 John*, p. 136 (£20).

61 *P.R. 3 John*, pp. 4, 290; *P.R. 14 John*, p. 103.

62 *RD*, p. 12; *Rotuli Hundredorum*, I, 309.

63 *The Registrum Antiquissimum of the Cathedral Church of Lincoln: Volume II*, ed.
    C. W. Foster (Lincoln Record Society, 28, 1933), pp. 23–4, no. 337.

64 In 1221 she granted various lands to Peter the Woadseller; in return he gave her £20
    and a pound of wax annually: *The Registrum Antiquissimum of the Cathedral Church
    of Lincoln: Volume VIII*, ed. K. Major (Lincoln Record Society, 51, 1958), no. 2297.
    Charter no. 2298 shows that John, son of Peter, sold the land and in the process
    'handed over the charter of lady Nichola'.

9

Royal inquests and the power of noblewomen: the Rotuli de Dominabus et Pueris et Puellis de XII Comitatibus *of 1185*

Introduction and historiography

THE *Rotuli de Dominabus et Pueris et Puellis de XII Comitatibus* of 1185 are a record of a royal inquiry into widows and wards who were in the king's gift.[1] It is an important insight into the position of noblewomen in the later twelfth century, and in particular the way that they were seen by local juries under the direction of the agents of central government – and the way the intervention of that government might affect their lives. The surviving records cover twelve counties in England: Lincolnshire, Northamptonshire, Bedfordshire, Buckinghamshire, Rutland, Huntingdonshire, Norfolk, Suffolk, Hertfordshire, Essex, Cambridgeshire and Middlesex. Women from all ranks of the landholding classes are represented in the rolls relating to the twelve counties surveyed: from the twice widowed Margaret duchess of Brittany and countess of Richmond and sister of the Scottish king, who is listed as holding land worth £55 2s and eight marks per annum, to the two unnamed sisters who hold lands in frankalmoign which would be worth 60s per annum if properly stocked.[2] Of the 128 families represented in the rolls, the greater tenants-in-chief account for only 31.3 per cent; 56.3 per cent were of knightly rank and one-eighth were serjeants.[3] The range of ages of widows represented is broad: from the ten-year-old child widow Matilda de Bidune to the octogenarian Beatrice de Say.[4] Since the primary function of the inquiry was to record royal rights, the document presents the official or royal view of women. The *Rotuli* provide an account of the value of the land associated with widows and wards in the king's gift, such as the current value of the land and whether it was properly stocked, the potential value of the land if additional stock were added and the number of heir(esse)s and their custodian(s). The *Rotuli de Dominabus* are a rich resource for the history of noblewomen in the twelfth century and for the study of social history, since they contain much valuable information on the operation of the institutions of dower, *maritagium*, inheritance and wardship, and also on the economic value of estates and marriage patterns. They offer a unique view of widows in the king's gift, since they list women from all ranks of landholders, that is, from most economic levels, who were all tenants-in-chief.

The inquiry into widows and wards in the king's gift in 1185 falls into a pattern of royal inquiries originating with Domesday. It is likely it was made as part of the proceedings of a judicial eyre, but was a distinct royal inquest within the eyre. As such the information was acquired by the sworn verdicts of jurors for each hundred or wapentake, termed a *veredictum* in the *Rotuli*.[5] Round argued that it is likely that a similar inquiry had been made *c.* 1177, the returns for which have not survived, based on the formulaic phrase *intra hoc annos*, which appears under some entries. However, although there is some sporadic use of this phrase it is possible that a similar inquiry may have been made in some counties and in connection with some individuals but had not been as wide-ranging or comprehensive as the *Rotuli de Dominabus*. Whether or not an earlier, similar inquiry existed, it is more useful to place the *Rotuli de Dominabus* into the context of other royal and judicial inquiries during the reign of Henry II such as the 1166 *Cartae Baronum*, the 1170 Inquest of Sheriffs, the 1176 Assize of Northampton and the Assize of Arms in 1181. It is possible that the *Rotuli de Dominabus* served as a prototype for the later *Testa de Nevill* in the thirteenth century. There are similarities between the *Testa de Nevill* and the *Rotuli de Dominabus* in, for example, the way that widows are listed by age, land tenure and male relations.[6]

As a source they facilitate analysis of the broader contexts of noble-women's lives. Traditional and empirical historians have generally studied the *Rotuli de Dominabus* in the context of debates about the nature of royal lordship in the late twelfth century, examining, for example, the character of Angevin government and reform. This has led to an emphasis on the effectiveness or otherwise of Henry II's government, which has been analysed either narrowly in England or in the wider context of the nature of the Angevin empire. Similarly the roots of Magna Carta have been traced to the reign of Henry II to emphasise the impact of royal government upon families and family strategies, and the treatment of widows by royal government has been seen as a barometer of these.[7] Thus Thomas Keefe, on the basis of a study of the 1166 *Cartae Baronum*, argued that Henry II ruled as a traditional medieval ruler, did not exploit royal rights and dues remorselessly and that the relationship between Henry II and the great magnates was based on mutual dependence.[8] John Gillingham thought Henry II was inefficient,[9] but Warren argued that under Henry II inquiries such as the 1185 *Rotuli de Dominabus* represent a significant restoration of royal authority over the magnates, baronage and knightly classes.[10]

This debate is focused on the development of institutions in a historiography dominated by concerns about government control over a 'feudal' society seen as male-dominated in which women played a passive role; and further this has become unhelpfully centred on the question of whether Henry II's regime was efficient and ruthlessly exploitative or reformist in nature. By its nature this debate is not directly concerned with the power of women. This focus upon the power and impact of the bureaucratisation of Henry II's regime, rather than seeking to question how power was devolved through society, and how individuals were able to exert influence and achieve outcomes, necessarily makes those who were subject to inquiries such as the *Rotuli de Dominabus* victims of royal bureaucratic authority. Sir James Holt certainly thought that the system was designed for the exploitation of widows.[11] Doris Stenton commented that there was 'nothing romantic about a society' which produced the *Rotuli de Dominabus* as a list of marriageable widows and wards.[12] These views assume that all the widows in the *Rotuli de Dominabus* were worth marrying whatever their age, status or economic resources and therefore ignore the yawning gulf in social status between some widows in the rolls. Such approaches assume, albeit unconvincingly, that gender was the key determinant of the nature of the inquiry, since the same factors affected all widows as women equally, and minimise the importance of the widow's fine for freedom from marriage at the royal will.[13] By contrast Janet Senderowitz Loengard and Sue Sheridan Walker have placed the study of the *Rotuli de Dominabus* in the context of the study of dower, the importance and rates of remarriage, and the operation of wardship, and so suggested that the victimisation of women at the hands of a more or less effective government was not the only possible reading of the document.[14]

The following discussion will place the analysis of the *Rotuli de Dominabus* in a framework which takes account of the way that social status, gender, the female life cycle and patterns of land tenure impacted upon the multiple identities of the women who are its subjects. The analysis of widows will be principally concerned with those who have an entry relating specifically to them or their lands, that is, they are the subject of a separate entry whether or not they are entered under their own name or that of their husband, as in the phrase *quondam uxor* [name of husband]. However, where information relating to a widow under the entry of her heir is included in the *Rotuli*, it has been incorporated where possible into the following analysis.[15] Important specific methodological and interpretative problems should be noted. For example, many of the widows who appear in the *Rotuli* do not appear in other sources such as charters or the Pipe Rolls, so it is difficult to place them in a broader social context. The survey was rooted in the knowledge of the local juries and as such provides a view of widows in each shire and hundred conditioned by that locality. Different juries gave different ages, or names, for some women, and often the rolls merely list women without their forename, which makes identification of obscure individuals difficult. Further, some of the high-status widows may have held land in counties or hundreds that are not covered in the *Rotuli de Dominabus*; for example Bertrada countess of Chester held land abroad, and the jurors were unable to evaluate its worth.[16] Taking this approach allows us to see with far greater clarity the power of the twelfth-century noblewoman. This appears in the numbers of their marriages and of their children. The nature, value and patterns of female land tenure will be considered, that is, whether women held land by right of dower, *maritagium* or inheritance, or a combination of these. Other important questions include the difficulties of interpreting rates of widows' remarriage and the importance of social status in affecting the rate of remarriage. The role and significance of social status in determining the economic independence of a widow can be considered through an examination of patterns of land tenure. Also, as well as the evidence to be read, as it were, within the rolls, there is also the evidence of the rolls themselves, as a product of the complex interaction of multiple forces, not simply the power of royal government, among which the influence of the women themselves was highly important.

Naming patterns

The way that women are identified on the rolls indicates the way that the clerks of the royal justices in eyre viewed those in the king's gift. Their principal concern was with royal justice and the legal position and identification of widows and wards. This was not the only factor, however, and the way that widows and wards were identified offers an insight into naming patterns current among the landholding classes. A number of categories of women's identification were visible in the document. All those women who were identified first as 'uxor [name of husband]' count as primarily identified with their husbands; if the same individual was then identified with her father by the use of a 'filia [name of father]' formula, this counts as a secondary designation. If that individual was then further listed as 'soror [name of sister]' this is considered to be a tertiary designation. Those who had a second name recognisably based on their husband's surname, for example Mabel de Tresgoz, also count as identified by their husband's name, but are a separate group from those identified by the simple *uxor* phrase. Further categories include those whose identification is based on a place name, as 'mother of', and title holders, such as countesses.

Widows might also be primarily identified with their fathers through the use of the *filia* [followed by name of father] formula. Cecily Clark concluded that the *filia/filius* phrase in administrative records of the earlier twelfth century represented by-names, not surnames proper.[17] The appearance of such formulas in the *Rotuli de Dominabus* suggests that such names may have served as descriptive phrases in the late twelfth century, but also indicates that the adoption or creation of surnames was not uniform.

A further descriptive category of women in the rolls includes those who are identified as 'mother of [a named heir or heiress]'. Since the twelfth-century shift to primogeniture is also argued to be the point at which patronymics became the norm, this small sample of maternal identities is an important variable which deserves explanation.[18] There are some interesting examples which do not fit easily into any single category and these will be discussed separately.[19] A further significant group are countesses, all of whom were identified by rank and clearly constituted a separate category in the eyes of the royal justices, which is suggestive that countesses were viewed as office holders, and as such were de-gendered in our record.

The most common formula used in the rolls to identify women is that of [forename (although in some cases it is not given)] (*que fuit*) *uxor* followed by [name of husband]: there are fifty-eight entries where the woman is identified in this way, and it is the primary designation in forty-three cases, for fifteen it was the secondary designation, and for three of them it was both, that is, they have more than one entry in the *Rotuli de Dominabus* and were identified differently by the juries in each entry.[20] In addition twenty-four women have a surname as their primary designation which is clearly derived from that of their husband, four of whom also appear elsewhere in the *Rotuli de Dominabus* with a different primary designation.[21] This clearly shows that women's public legal name, which served the purposes of the king's justices in eyre and those who made the sworn returns, was associated with or derived from that of their husband in the first instance. The *filia* formula first identified by Clark as a descriptive phrase was used to record forty-four women in the *Rotuli de Dominabus*; in all but four cases it was a secondary designation.[22] Five women had names derived from a place name.[23] Women's multiple identities as wives and mothers impacted on their identity, depending on specific contexts. Thus five women's secondary designation was described in broader kinship terms through the use of the terms *consanguinea, cognata* or *de parentela*.[24]

The nature of land tenure also defined both men and women. Albreda de Harcourt, for example, as a widow kept her maiden name, which was also a name derived from a place name, because the lands with which she was identified in that context were her inheritance.[25] Eight women have a recognisable surname based on their father's name as their primary designation.[26] Ten women were further identified as sisters of male kin, none as their primary designation. Only two women were identified by a *soror* formula which related to female kin, and these are the 'two sisters of Papworth' who were mutually identified with each other.[27] Matrilineal identification is important in one case. Matilda de Saint Liz is also named as Matilda de *Beaverio*: she was given two surnames in two entries and she held *maritagium* and dower. In the entry in which she was given her mother's name she held dower; where she held *maritagium* she was given a surname based on that of her husband. Her case indicates that women's names were mutable and dependant on context, sometimes interconnected contexts, and that maternal links, as expressed through naming patterns, were not always extinguished by a landholding system increasingly based on primogeniture and patrilineal associations. It further indicates that women of the nobility could derive a surname from a geographical location which could change as their place of residence changed.[28]

Four widows are specifically identified as 'mother of [named heir]'; for two this is the primary designation.[29] However, twelve women are entered in the rolls under the main entry for the heir.[30] They include, for example, the mother of the heir of William de Vesci (d. 1183), who has no *tenementum*, except *dotem*,[31] and the unnamed mother of the son of Robert fitz Odo, who holds one-tenth of a knight's fee and is living in poverty with the heir, her son, on this land.[32] Two others are entered together under the name of the son and heir of Gilbert Bolebec: one is forty, the other seventy, years old, so these are probably the widow of Gilbert Bolebec and his mother.[33] The widow of Walter de Burton is entered under the name of the heiress her daughter.[34] Two other women have their own entries and are the mother of Ralf de Humberston, who holds land worth half a mark and whose son is thirty,[35] and Alexandria, the mother of Gilbert de Coleville, who is sixty and holds 20s.[36] Her son's wife is the subject of the previous entry, so her son predeceased her and thus she is identified through him. Only one woman is called *vidua*, the wife of Geoffrey de Turs and Herbert fitz Gilbert.[37] On the whole, therefore, women in the *Rotuli* are identified by their sons or husbands, but this is inevitable, given the nature of the record, and just as significant are the few examples where other references, usually related to the nature of their land tenure, form the basis of naming.

In the *Rotuli de Dominabus* high-status women, of comital rank, were identified only through the title *comitissa*. They are the countess of Richmond, Margaret de Bohun, the widow of Humphrey de Bohun; Matilda countess of Chester; Bertrada countess of Chester, her daughter-in-law; Eva countess of Leinster, widow of Richard 'Strongbow'; and Juliana countess of Norfolk, widow of Roger Bigod.[38] Margaret duchess of Brittany was known variously as the countess sister of the Scottish king, or countess of Richmond, which differs from her seal legend, which deployed the *ducissa* appellation.[39] This of course was an official identity acquired and kept through marriage, but it also defined their social status. One noblewoman of lower rank was given a title: she must therefore be exceptional, a widow given the title 'Lady of'. This was *domine de Lathburia*: Alice, the wife of John de Mauduit (no. 54). In only a few entries were women described as *domine*, and this is a descriptive, not a naming, phrase.[40] This is in contrast to charters where noblewomen were often called *domine* in address clauses, consent and closing protocols as well as witness lists.

This difference may well be predicated on the differences in the nature of the documents and the way they were created, since donors may have had a greater impact upon the construction of charters. The *Rotuli de Dominabus* were constructed as an administrative document concerned with the identification of individuals and their economic resources for the purposes of royal officials. As such it is indicative of their hierarchical conception of social status, since as well as the *comitissa* appellation there are entries which provide information on the social status of a ward or a widow. For example, the children of Beatrice de Saiton *sunt nati de militibus*; the unnamed wife of Peter de Pelleville was described as *nata de militibus*.[41] Hierarchy is an organising principle throughout the document: countesses always head the list in the individual rotulets – in a similar pattern to the Pipe Rolls and the 1166

Cartae Baronum. It is significant that the conception of hierarchy within the document is not so dominated by gender as the initial findings might imply, but gender itself worked with hierarchy to determine how noblewomen were portrayed.

The above discussion has focused on the development of surnames and by-names and has illustrated the complexities involved in analysing them. The rolls allow us an unusually direct and comprehensive insight into the pattern of forenaming among women in noble families. Historians have attached significance to naming patterns as expressions of both cohesion and shifts in cultural identity.[42] Thus, for example, Holt thought that the adoption of patronymics in the twelfth century was linked with the general shift to primogeniture.[43] Forenaming patterns have been used by historians to illustrate the impact of the Norman Conquest on the English peasantry as well as the Anglo-Norman nobility, with a view to illustrating both change and continuity in the immediate post-Conquest period and during the twelfth century. Cecily Clark looked at women in particular and found that there was a difference in male and female naming patterns, female names 'lagging behind' male names when change occurred owing to fashion. Clark found that women's forenames in twelfth-century England were more insular and men's forenames were more Continental.[44] David Postles, building on these foundations, found that there was a 'virtual revolution' in patterns of forenaming in the mid-twelfth century and that women's names were more archaic than men's. He suggested that women's role as bearers of English cultural influence explains this pattern. Postles agreed with Holt, who saw the development of notions of patrimony in society as the central dynamic which explains the creation of by-names and surnames among the Anglo-Norman aristocracy.[45] Constance Bouchard places the emphasis on family structures and finds that, in particular in royal circles, female naming patterns represented complex changes in kin structures towards a more patrilineal pattern.[46] The significance of naming patterns is beyond dispute, and the *Rotuli de Dominabus* are a source which neither Clark nor Postles considered.

An analysis of the names in the *Rotuli* shows that the most popular name was Matilda.[47] The age profile for this 'Matilda' group shows that the majority of women, as in the whole of the document, were aged over forty; five were younger, including the youngest widow in the document, the ten-year-old Matilda de Bidune. The octogenarian Matilda, daughter of Robert de Riblemunt, would have been given her baptismal name when Edith/Matilda the queen of Henry I was on the throne, and she was the daughter of a Norman. Michel Le Pesant identified a broad range of male and female names in families in Evreux in the eleventh to fourteenth centuries.[48] The *Rotuli de Dominabus* show that there was a similar pool of female names available to Anglo-Norman and Angevin families.[49] Given this, the overwhelming dominance of Matilda as a popular name is even more striking and demonstrates conservatism as well as political allegiance: Henry I's queen Matilda, Stephen's queen and the empress all shared the same forename. This modifies Clark's speculation that women's names were more insular than men's and shows that by the end of the twelfth century in all districts and ranks 'Continental' names became popular.[50] In this particular case the name Matilda is a Norman name and was pre-eminent as the most popular name within the nobility. This is not Anglo-Norman insularity but an expression of Anglo-Norman identity. Further, it differs from the Continental trends, where according to Constance Bouchard the names Gerberge and Matilda migrated through families together.[51] As the twelfth century progressed the nobility began to use the names of Christian saints, as well as traditional familial forenames.[52] The evidence presented by the *Rotuli de Dominabus* demonstrates the variety of women's names in England and suggests that whilst there was considerable variety in women's forenames, a woman's surname, or by-name, was likely to be derived from her husband's kin.[53] Certainly the evidence within the *Rotuli de Dominabus* shows that women were likely to be identified through their male kin, as wives, daughters and mothers, because marriage was the key defining factor in the acquisition of land. Thus the patrilineal association was important, but not predominant.

Social and economic contexts

AGE RANGE

A hundred and eight widows are listed, of whom the ages of twenty-eight (25.9 per cent of the total) are unrecorded.[54] There are a further seven women whose ages are recorded variously by different juries.[55] If these are removed from the calculation the total number of widows whose age is recorded is seventy-three (see Table 1).

Women in their forties, fifties and sixties account for approximately two-thirds of the sample where an age is known: the overwhelming number of widows in the king's gift in 1185 were aged between forty and seventy. It is also notable that the ages of young widows are listed with relative accuracy compared with those of older women. For example, women above fifty are most often entered in rounded figures such as

TABLE 1   Ages of widows in the *Rotuli de Dominabus*

Age band	No.	% of total known
0–10	1[a]	1
11–19	1[b]	1
20–29	8[c]	11
30–39	10[d]	14
40–49	17[e]	23
50–59	15[f]	21
60–69	16[g]	22
70–89	5[h]	7
Total	73	100

Notes
[a]Appendix 2: 63, and see *RD*, p. xxxvii.
[b]Appendix 2: 45 (eighteen years old).
[c]Appendix 2: 31 (20); 7, 23, 83 (24); 44, 94 (25); 78 (27); 19 (29).
[d]Appendix 2: 11, 33, 37, 43, 62, 64, 70 (30); 1, 17, 92 (34, 35, 36).
[e]Appendix 2: 13, 26–7, 32, 38, 40–1, 53, 59, 68, 71, 77, 80, 103 (40); 50 (45); 47, 66 (46).
[f]Appendix 2: 5, 28–30, 34, 54, 56, 61, 67, 76, 102, 107 (50); 15, 18, 22 (50 or more); 14 (57).
[g]Appendix 2: 35, 46, 48–50, 65, 72, 74–5, 79, 91, 100–1 (60); 21, 25, 105
  (60 *et amplius*).
[h]Appendix 2: 20, 52, 104 (70, 70 *et amplius*); 57, 90 (80).

'she is fifty years old and more', whereas the ages of women below fifty are more often precisely given. This is presumably, as Round concluded, an indication that the age (and hence fertility) of a widow was important to the royal justices in deciding her remarriage value.[56] The younger a widow the longer a prospective husband might enjoy any land she brought with her to the marriage.

NUMBER OF CHILDREN[57]
Nearly a quarter of widows listed had no children listed, or an unknown number.[58] These not only illustrate that some family lines would fail but also reflect the age of some of the widows, such as eighty-year-old Beatrice de Say (no. 90), whose children might have reached their majority, and ten-year-old Matilda de Bidune (no. 63), who presumably would not have had any yet. It is also evidence of the concerns of the royal justices, since those who had no claims on the lands listed, such as younger married daughters, would not be entered on the rolls.

This pattern of recording almost certainly also reflects the limited and local knowledge of the jurors.[59] Twenty-seven widows are listed as having only one child, of whom eighteen were male heirs.[60] Of course, the jurors may well have ignored those children who would have had no claim to the lands recorded and therefore took more care when they recorded the eldest son, and certainly Albreda de Harcourt, who is listed as having only four sons, also had three daughters, one of whom was similarly a widow in the king's gift.[61] The jurors naturally ignored deceased children.[62] Certainly in four cases the jurors knew there were more children than they could account for,[63] but for the most part we can assume that the *Rotuli* underrecorded children. To take two examples which show that this is a problem across social status: Alice, the widow of William fitz Chetell, the king's goshawk keeper, is stated to have the custody of her son (singular) in the *Rotuli de Dominabus*.[64] Yet the Pipe Roll for 1184–85 states that she owed four marks that year for the custody of her boys (plural).[65] Bertrada countess of Chester is known to have had one son and four daughters by Earl Hugh, yet these children are not listed in the *Rotuli*.[66] The figures derived from the *Rotuli de Dominabus* must be treated with caution and may be taken as only an approximate guide to the minimum number of children which a widow was likely to have. These are shown in Table 2.

TABLE 2   Widows' children

No. of children	No. of women	% of total women (known)
0	22	20
1	27	25
2	6	6
3	9	8
4	11	10
5	7	6
6	6	6
7	10	9
8	4	4
10	2	2
11	2	2
13	2	2
Total	108	100

The royal justices were concerned to record who had control of wards and their lands. The fines for marriages and for entering into inheritance could be a profitable source of income for the custodians of heirs and heiresses. Widows could fine with the king to retain custody of their children, and thus in cases where widows had fined for their children's custody this was recorded in the returns. At first sight the rolls seem to confirm the view that widows were relatively unsuccessful in getting custody of their children. Out of eighty widows who are listed in the rolls as having children, only sixteen (18.6 per cent) had custody of them.[67] Scott Waugh has argued that, after 1217, widows represented more than a tenth of all those who received wardship, but their grants amounted to 7 per cent of the total.[68] Waugh, however, has also shown that in the thirteenth century widows were charged more often than other grantees for wardships, but were not exploited unduly by the Crown in this respect, and were generally charged small fines slightly below average.[69] So these headline figures, suggesting that over 80 per cent of widows with children in the *Rotuli de Dominabus* had not fined for the custody of their children, represent a minimum and should be treated with care. It is hard to know how many children had been in their mother's custody and had died prematurely, and whether those of age have not been listed. Further, many of the widows had children who, explicitly, were already married, had attained the age of majority or had become nuns. Also, it is worth noting that the widows who had control of their children were geographically clustered: five each in Lincolnshire and Buckinghamshire, four in Essex, three in Norfolk and one in Bedfordshire. This may well reflect different patterns of enforcement of royal lordship within these counties (or even simply of record creation) as much as the influence of individual women within that locality.

PATTERNS OF LAND TENURE: ECONOMIC RESOURCES

The *Rotuli de Dominabus* provide an unusually large sample of information on the value of noblewomen's lands. The value of the land of ninety-one women can be calculated, and the results are summarised in Table 3. All monetary values have been standardised as far as possible. However, there has been no attempt to convert knights' fees or *librates* into exact figures because of the difficulty of estimating their precise value.[70] Those values which are given only as *librates* in the *Rotuli* are marked in the table with an asterisk. Seventeen entries have been excluded from the table, again in the interests of precision, including one widow who may have remarried[71] and sixteen cases where no specific value is attached to their land, or where women are listed as holding land without a specific monetary value attached, such as one-third of a knight's fee.[72]

Considerable wealth is evident in the group of widows represented in the *Rotuli*, but it is striking that the largest group of women in the king's gift, twenty-two in total, were those with lands worth between £1 and £5 (24 per cent). It is less surprising that the smallest group of widows consisted of those who had more than £40 worth of land. Among the remainder, no clear pattern emerges. It is of course possible that high-status women held land in counties and hundreds not covered in the *Rotuli*. There are relatively few poor widows, but this is reflective of sub-infeudation, since few poor freeholders held directly of the king and in the case of escheats they appear in the *Rotuli*. There are few very wealthy widows in the king's gift, those with over £40 worth of lands. The most numerous group of widows consists of those who held under or about the equivalent of one knight's fee. However, more informative for our purposes is to substitute for the value of the land the type of property held. Mapped against the age of the woman holding it, this can tell us a great deal about the nature of female land tenure.

NATURE OF LAND TENURE

Women's land tenure was different in nature from that of men because the way that dower and *maritagium* were acquired rested on the female life cycle. Women could acquire land in three ways: they might inherit as sole heir or, with the development of co-parceny in the late twelfth century, they might acquire land as co-heiresses. Land could also be acquired through the institution of dowry: land which was given by a family to the husband when a daughter married (*maritagium* which could revert to a widow on her husband's death); and through dower (a third share of her husband's land allocated to her either on the day of her marriage by her husband or after his death).

The correlation of type of land and age of widow in Table 4 shows that the institutions of dower and *maritagium* were in operation across all ranks of landholders. However, on closer examination it seems that the custom of endowing daughters with *maritagium* in the form of land was more prevalent among those families who held enough land to endow daughters with land worth £5 and over. There are only two cases where widows hold less than £5 worth of *maritagium*: the widow of Walter Furmage, and Matilda Malherbe.[73] The former is twenty-four and has only 17s worth of land. However, it is likely that she has not yet received dower, since her husband must have died within the im-mediately previous twenty months, so in fact she may have eventually

TABLE 3 Economic resources

Under £1			£1				£5				£10				£15				£20–£40				Over £40			
no.	s	d	no.	£	s	d	no.	£	s	d	no.	£	s	d	no.	£	s	d	no.	£	s	d	no.	£	s	d
23	17		41	4	15	4	37	9	0	0	68	14	0	6 (+?)	29	19	0	0	19	35*	10	0	4	82	12	0
57	16		71	4	8	10	61	8	0	0 (+¼kf)	20	14	0	0	40	18	0	0*	48	27	0	0 (+? kfs[b])	46	60	0	0 (+16*)
101	15		13	4	0	0	8	8	0	0	38	14	0	0	34	18	10	0	42	25	0	0 (+3kf)	36	67	0	0
102	15		75	4	0	0	18	8	0	0[d]	86	14	0	0	54	18	4	0	70	38	16	8	82	44	0	0
43	15		106	4	0	0	59	8	0	0	26	13	13	0	63	17	12	2	14	30	0	0	18	40	0	0
92	14		30	3	5	1	107	8	0	0	93	12	17	0	1	15	0	0	12	29	0	0	85	40	0	0
51	12		25	3	6	8	47	7	10	0	103	12	0	0*	90	15	0	0	105	29	0	0				
21	6	8	94	3	6	8	27	7	6	8	15	12	0	0					60	28	0	0				
			11	3	2	0	39	7	0	0	83	12	0	0					31	27	7	6[c]				
			67	3	0	0	62	7	0	0	95	12	0	0					81	27	0	0				
			79	2	15	6	49	6	3	6[a]	78	4	0	0 (+7*)					5	25	0	0				

	£	s	d			£	s	d			£	s	d			£	s	d
56	2	10	0		**35**	2	0	0		**7**	10	10	0		**58**	24	1	0
							+ 4*											
55	2	0	0		**28**	6	0	0*		**22**	10	0	0		**84**	24	0	0
65	2	0	0		**64**	5	0	0		**104**	10	0	0*		**91**	24	0	0
77	2	0	0		**72**	5	0	0		**24**	10	0	0*		**2**	20	0	0
87	2	0	0		**66**	5	0	0										
100	2	0	0		**96**	5	0	0										
45	1	18	1		**17**	4	13	4										
33	1	10	0															
88	1	6	8															
76	1	2	0															
74	1	0	0															

Notes

The number to the left of each column (in bold) refers to the number of the widow as Appendix 2, allowing individuals to be identified.

*a*Plus four geese and two capons.

*b*Plus three parts of one knight's fee, plus two enfeoffed knights, plus two parts of a knight's fee.

*c*Plus 2 lb of pepper and rent of three sums (*umma*) of oats.

*d*This sum represents the income for approximately one year The *Rotuli* record the sum of £9 3s 8d for the farm of a year and three-quarters; there was additional income of £5 12s for grain sales.

TABLE 4   Age of widows and nature of land tenure ranked according to wealth

< £1	£1 < £5	£5 < £10	£10 < £15	£15 < £20	£20 < £40	> £40
23 24 M	**41** 40 M	**37** 30 M	**16** ? D	**29** 50 D	**19** 29 D M?	**4** 30–40 D
57 60?	**71** 40 I	**61** 50?	**68** 40 D M	**40** 40+ D	**48** 60 D?	**46** 60 D I
101 60?	**13** 40?	**8** ? TiC	**20** 70?	**34** 50 M TiC I	**42** ? D	**36** 60–80 D
102 50?	**76** 60?	**59** 40 D	**38** 40?	**54** 50 D M	**70** 30 D?	**82** 50–60+ D I
43 30 D	**105** ? D	**107** 50 M	**86** ? I D	**63** 10 D	**14** 57 D	**18** 50+ D
92 36 D	**30** 50 D	**47** 46 D	**26** 40 D M	**1** 34 D	**12** 50–60 I M	**85** ? M
51 ? D	**25** 60+?	**27** 40+ D	**93** ?	**90** 80 M	**105** 60+ D,?	
21 60+ D	**94** 25?	**39** ?	**103** 40 M		**60** 40–50 D?	
	11 30 D	**62** 30 D	**15** 50+ D		**31** 20 D	
	67 50 I	**35** 60 D	**83** 24 D		**81** ? D	
	78 60 M	**28** 50 D M	**95** ? D		**5** 50 D M	
	56 50?	**49** 60?	**78** 27 M		**58** 60–80 D M	
	55 ? D	**64** 30 D	**7** 24?		**84** ? I	
	65 60 D	**72** 60 D	**22** 50+ D		**91** 60 D	
	77 40?	**66** 46 D	**104** 70+		**2** 50–60 D M	
	87 ? I	**96** ? I	**24** ? D			
	100 60+?	**17** 35 M				
	45 18 D					
	33 30 D					
	76 50?					
	88 ?					
	74 60?					

Notes

The number on the left (in bold) indicates the widow as listed in Appendix 2, the middle number the age of the widow, the letter on the right the type of land tenure. *D* dower, *M maritagium* (marriage portion), *I* inheritance, *TiC* tenant in chief, *?* information unknown. The same entries are excluded as in Table 2.

held both *maritagium* and dower. The other widow, Matilda Malherbe, is forty years old and has an income of £4 15s 4d. However, it is evident that her land is being under-farmed: if it were properly stocked it would be worth £5 15s 4d. Thus she holds land worth in reality over £5 – or the equivalent of over one knight's fee. It can therefore reasonably be inferred that the practice of endowing a daughter with *maritagium* in the form of land was more common in those families whose economic resources facilitated it, holding considerably more than one knight's fee.[74] However, it is very likely, in fact, that the partial record represented by the *Rotuli* means that women's wealth as it appears there is only a fraction, and possibly a small fraction, of their total wealth. Matilda Malherbe, for example, is stated to hold land worth £5 15s 4d in Bedfordshire which she holds of her brother Robert Malherbe.[75] In the Pipe Roll for the year 1185, however, a Matilda Malherbe, widow of John Malherbe, accounted for £14 6s 8d.[76] Matilda had in fact fined with the king for her inheritance in 1182. She had accounted for the sum of £100 for her inheritance in Appleby (Lincolnshire) and paid £50 as a down payment, then discharged the outstanding amount annually until 1189, when she was quit of the debt.[77] She does not appear in the *Rotuli de Dominabus* holding these lands, and it must be assumed that they were overlooked during the survey. If such is the case, Matilda held *maritagium* and inheritance in different counties, but this is not shown in the *Rotuli*.[78]

Although the figures suggest that it was customary among the landed nobility to give daughters a marriage portion of land worth £5 or over, some caution is necessary. It is quite possible that many gifts of dowry were in fact sums of money or of goods, and as such would not appear in our record.[79] Scott Waugh has suggested that within the nobility by 1300 the custom of endowing daughters with *maritagium* in the form of land had diminished and it was more normal for a daughter to be given a dowry in the form of a sum of money.[80] Waugh considers that *maritagium* in reality functioned as a woman's share of the patrilineal inheritance, citing Bracton's statement that a woman cannot claim both *maritagium* and inheritance should she eventually become an heiress.[81] Milsom argued that it was usual for marriage portions to be given in the form of land in the twelfth century and that *maritagium* could function as part of an heiress's inheritance, but that it did not necessarily exclude women from a greater share of her inheritance.[82] The *Rotuli* show that the custom of endowing daughters with land in the form of *maritagium* was in operation in the late twelfth century. Further, the custom of returning *maritagium* to the inheritance for the purpose of calculating the shares was already in operation. This could perhaps explain the lower incidence in the *Rotuli de Dominabus* of land stated to be held by right of *maritagium* and inheritance, since women may have given up their claim on *maritagium* if they became an heiress to the overall assessment of the land before division among female co-heirs, as Bracton advised in the thirteenth century.[83] Milsom argued that land held by *maritagium* returned to the patrilineal family if there were no heirs within three generations from the daughter's marriage and *maritagium* returned to the 'hotchpot' so that partition of inheritance could be decided in the king's court.[84] As Milsom suggests, *maritagium* was different in nature from inheritance, and this was recognised by contemporaries.[85]

There are just eleven cases where a widow held only *maritagium*. This is significant because it implies that few women had *maritagium* as their only means of support. However, because local juries were not in a position to know how much land and by what right an individual held land in other counties or hundreds, caution is necessary when interpreting these figures from the *Rotuli de Dominabus*. These suggest that a multiplicity of female tenure of lands was likewise not the norm, since the majority of widows in the *Rotuli de Dominabus* hold by one right only.[86] Although families could by legal right endow daughters with *maritagium* in the form of land few widows actually held by this right.[87]

No widows were recorded as holding land by virtue of a combination of all rights by which women could hold land, that is, dower, *maritagium* and inheritance. This suggests that although the principle may have been established, the custom was still in the process of definition in the 1180s and that, as Milsom suggested, *maritagium* may have returned to the inheritance for the calculation of division. By 1215 King John accepted that women could hold land by dower, *maritagium* and *hereditas*.[88]

Dower was the predominant form of land tenure for widows. Three widows had custody of the heirs' lands (nos 42, 45, 51), which may have provided extra resources. Given the age statistics of widows in the *Rotuli*, it is interesting that Table 5 also shows that age was one factor which affected tenurial patterns of widows who held over £10 worth of land. A younger widow was likely to hold land gained through one form of tenure only. It is tempting to conclude from these figures that older widows were richer than younger ones, but it is possible that there were more of them in the king's gift, since at an advanced age they were unlikely to remarry.[89]

TABLE 5 The nature of the widows' lands

Tenure type	No. of women holding in this way	% of whole sample holding in this way	No. of women holding only in this way	% of whole sample holding only in this way	% of those holding in this way who hold only in this way	No. of women holding by this combination	% of whole sample holding by this combination
Dower	57	73.1	47[a]	60.3	82.5		
Maritagium	20	25.6	10[b]	12.8	50.0		
Inheritance	13	16.7	6[c]	7.7	46.1		
Dower and maritagium						10[d]	12.8
Dower and inheritance						4[e]	5.1
Inheritance and maritagium						4[f]	5.1
Total	78[g]						

Notes

For the purposes of the calculations those whose land tenure is not specified are excluded from the percentage calculation: Appendix 2: 3, 7, 8, 13, 20, 25, 38–9, 56–7, 61, 69, 74–80, 88–9, 93–4, 97–9, 101–2, 104; no. 11 has no land.

[a] Appendix 2: 1, 4, 14–16, 18, 21–2, 24, 27, 29, 30–3, 35–6, 40, 42–5, 47–8, 51–5, 59–60, 62–6, 70, 72–3, 81, 83, 91–2, 95, 100, 105, 108.

[b] Appendix 2: 17, 23, 37, 41, 78, 85, 90, 103, 106–7.

[c] Appendix 2: 6, 8, 50, 71, 87, 96.

[d] Dower and maritagium: Appendix 2: 2, 5, 19, 26, 28, 54, 58, 68.

[e] Dower and inheritance: Appendix 2: 46, 82, 84, 86.

[f] Inheritance and maritagium: Appendix 2: 12, 32, 34, 67.

[g] Two have no land, and in another twenty-nine cases it is not specified by which tenure land is held.

TABLE 6   Percentage of sample holding by different forms
of tenure, according to overall value

Value	Maritagium	Dower	Inheritance
< £1	13	50	
£1 < £5	9	32	14
£5 < £10	24	53	6
£10 < £15	25	56	6
£15 < £20	43	71	14
£20 < £40	33	87	13
> £40	17	83	33

MARRIAGE PATTERNS

A significant number of noblewomen who appear in the *Rotuli* had survived more than one marriage. Nine women had outlived two husbands,[90] of whom seven had land worth over £14, and two, Margaret of Brittany and Agnes de Montchesney, were among the richest widows recorded in the *Rotuli*. With the exception of thirty-year-old Eugenia Picot and the widow of Geoffrey of Turs and Herbert fitz Gilbert, most of this group of widows were all over forty, and seven of the nine had dower in 1185. The varied nature of their land is also interesting. Three were heiresses and held both dower and their inheritance, one held both dower and *maritagium*, two held dower only, two more held dower and other land but by which right is unknown. These patterns conform to those already outlined: dower constituted the major form of female land tenure, but the conditions under which women held other land are hard to clarify. Margaret of Brittany, sister of King William I of Scotland, for example, received a marriage portion of 100 librates of land and twenty *infeft* knights as *tocher* when she married her second husband, Humphrey de Bohun earl of Hereford in 1175, yet in the *Rotuli* it can be established only that she held dower.[91]

Few widows survived three husbands: two are listed in the *Rotuli de Dominabus*. Maria, called the wife of her last husband, Guy l'Estrange, held dower in Norfolk worth £14, as well as land in other counties.[92] Similarly Matilda Peche, who was fifty years old, had eleven children and held *maritagium* in Cambridgeshire worth £8, which if properly stocked would be worth £10.[93] No widows are listed who had survived more than three spouses. Although there are known examples of twelfth-century women who had multiple husbands, such a high rate of remarriage, whilst not unknown, must have been unusual.[94]

It is common for historians to assume that the rate of widows' remarriage was high. James Brundage, for example, in his exploration of the position of widows in canon law, assumes that women routinely married twice, but does not cite any evidence.[95] Judith Bennett found that remarriage rates on the manors of Halesowen and Brigstock in the fourteenth century were 1 : 13 and 6 : 10 respectively. Bennett explains the differences in these statistics by focusing on the economic imperatives which may have facilitated/mediated second marriage.[96] There are obvious difficulties in comparing figures from the late twelfth century which are derived from a royal administrative survey with those of early fourteenth-century manorial records, since not only are the records themselves of a different provenance but they relate to women of different social and therefore economic classes. Yet in one sense they are comparable because they were constructed from the lord's point of view. The evidence from the *Rotuli de Dominabus* is decisive: there is a remarriage rate of at least 1 : 6, and a 1 : 53 chance of a noblewoman surviving a third spouse. This should be compared with Scott Waugh's calculation that in the baronage in the thirteenth century women had a 1 : 3 chance of remarrying. His much higher rate of remarriage is culled from an assessment of eighty-one baronial family pedigrees traced throughout the thirteenth century and therefore differs significantly in two main ways. Firstly the *Rotuli de Dominabus* are more time-specific, since they centre upon a particular decade or so, the years *c.* 1176–85, but they have a broader social focus, since they list all those in the king's gift and therefore include those of not only baronial but also knightly and freeholder status. Yet as a comparative figure it is likely that the rate of remarriage derived from the *Rotuli de Dominabus* is not an accurate reflection of the patterns of marriage, since those women who were widowed and quickly remarried would not appear in them except if the heir(esses) were still minors. Since older widows predominate in the *Rotuli*, younger women who found themselves widowed may well have remarried. Thus the real rate of remarriage of noblewomen probably lies between 1 : 6 and 1 : 3. The discrepancy between Waugh's figure and the above reveals the importance of social status in determining remarriage rates: the sample of women from the *Rotuli de Dominabus* includes poorer people than Waugh's. It is therefore possible that lesser noblewomen were less likely to remarry than greater. Further, in reality, although noblewomen could theoretically hold land through different rights, there was not in general landholding by all three methods. In this respect, the reality on the ground lagged a little behind the development of theory and the expectations of the judges.

Conclusion

The *Rotuli de Dominabus* confirm that dower was the principal form of female land tenure of widows in late twelfth-century England. Although women could acquire other land in the form of *maritagium* or as inheritance only a few women held by a combination of these tenures, as evidenced by the *Rotuli*. However, this may be a specific problem of the source and the way it was constructed, county by county, by local juries, rather than a reflection of tenurial realities. There were even fewer unmarried widowed heiresses in late twelfth-century England and this may be accounted for by the rapid remarriage of richer widows who were heiresses.

It remains to be considered how the evidence from the *Rotuli de Dominabus* can throw light on the nature of royal government of England in the 1180s and its impact on women. Whilst the dynamic for inquiries such as the *Rotuli de Dominabus* of 1185 originated in the royal court they are evidence neither solely of an efficient exploitative regime nor of a reformist government attempting to make feudal society work according to its own rules. The *Rotuli de Dominabus* are evidence that Henry II's government, which, through the 1185 inquiry, sought to pin down widows and wards, was thus attempting to enforce royal lordship. This in turn acted to examine the activities of sheriffs who had responsibility for widows and wards in the localities. It may well be that Henry II sought to increase his control over some elements of the landed noble classes: it is clear that in this case, while the focus was ostensibly on widows and wards, the real target may well have been sheriffs and royal servants. There can have been little or no economic gain in discovering septua- and octogenarians, or widows who held by serjeantry tenure. Similarly, it is inconceivable that it came as a surprise to find high-status women such as Margaret of Brittany or Matilda countess of Chester in the king's gift, although the exact value of the land they held may not have been known. In reality this inquiry fell hardest upon the wives and widows of the knightly classes, who predominate numerically in the survey and sheriffs.

The officials who compiled the *Rotuli de Dominabus* defined wives and widows as an homogeneous group who shared similar status based on the impact of the gendered nature of the female life cycle. Thus the wives and widows in the *Rotuli de Dominabus* for the purposes of the inquiry were seen as a separate social category. However, these widows and wives were separated by economic categories and, thus, social status. In reality their marital status as wives or widows, and their position as tenants-in-chief, can be all that was common to the women in the *Rotuli de Dominabus*. To Doris Stenton the *Rotuli de Dominabus* were a list of marriageable ladies. To the individuals who compiled the record the *Rotuli de Dominabus* served to clarify the marital status of noble-women as landholders in the king's gift and also the economic value of their land. This is indicative not of an efficient bureaucratic regime, but of one which used existing administrative structures to clarify the social and economic position of widows and wards. In effect the document, in bringing royal justices to the shire courts, may well have helped to clarify claims of widows and wards on dower and inheritance in a royal context: bypassing the family, kin and local sources of power. Further, if Henry II sought to extend his authority into the shires the survey struck at the heart of the Angevin political system: the nexus of family rela-tions was laid bare for the royal justices to see. All landholders could find themselves subject to the king's scrutiny. The royal justices thus trespassed on shrieval areas of authority, although sheriffs continued to administer wardships, etc., prior to the institution of permanent escheators in the thirteenth century.

It is possible that the survey benefited widows, since the inquiry effectively short-circuited the tortuous legal process to seek redress for land or dower withheld: the *Rotuli de Dominabus* set down indelibly on parchment their rights and position, clarified and publicly sworn. Conversely, it may well have suited women to avoid the jurors if they were occupying land without 'legitimate' reason: this may explain the vagueness of some of the entries. As a royal survey it was inevitably framed and made with the interests of the royal justices at its heart, and thus may appear as nothing more than a roll of those within the grasp of the king and subservient to men. Indeed, the system of identification and naming women through their male kin would seem to confirm this. Yet, given the nature of the *Rotuli de Dominabus* document as a royal survey, it would inevitably portray women in such a way. The document was made in the context of a working relationship between the centre and the localities, since royal government relied on the co-operation of local juries to compile the document. The *Rotuli de Dominabus* as a royal survey portray neither simply the power of royal justice nor the weakness of widows at the mercy of relentless royal interference. Rather they show complexities inherent in patterns of women's land tenure. It is evidence of the way that the varied interactions of the economics of female land tenure, combined with the vagaries of the female life cycle, defined and constructed women's identities, tenurial patterns which underpinned their power as landholders.

Finally, an account of the wives and widows in the *Rotuli de Dominabus* which sees them merely as victims of royal authority is inadequate. The *Rotuli de Dominabus* are more than a list of marriageable ladies. They are a complex document framed with the interests of royal lordship at their heart. This fundamentally affects how the document should be interpreted, since it inevitably portrays women as victims of an efficient bureaucratic regime. Thus the apparent listing of widows by age, number of children and land tenure does seem suggestive of an intrusive royal inquiry. Yet the complexities of women's land tenure defeated the jurors on more than one occasion, since they were unable (or unwilling) to give evidence on women's land tenure in other counties. Dower was the predominant form of female land tenure; there were few rich heiresses in the king's gift; widows do appear likely to remarry. This would seem to confirm truisms of the Middle Ages. Yet a more subtle reading of the document suggests that there were complex patterns of female land tenure, which even in the twelfth century were hard to define; that widows did not necessarily remarry; that the development of by-names and surnames would *prima facie* reflect marital and patrilineal connections, because this was a document which listed widows and wards, but that women's multiple identities were fluid and mutable, dependent on immediate context. Finally, the *Rotuli de Dominabus* suggest that the royal administration viewed widows as a significant group and that they were dealt with as such, and that the relationship between royal government and widows of tenants-in-chief was not necessarily an exploitative one. The *Rotuli de Dominabus* confirm that noblewomen had significant and important roles to play in the two dominant power structures of the twelfth-century, kinship and lordship, and the document shows that royal government recognised this. It shows how their power was structured, and thus, like charters and literary sources, shows the complex ways that women's power can be measured within key social structures to cast new reflections upon the nature of twelfth-century society.

Notes

1 *RD*; for ease of citation throughout this chapter where a number is cited it refers to the number of the widow as listed in Appendix 2, which is organised around the ordering of the women as they appear in the document.

2 For Margaret of Brittany, *RD*, pp. 4–5, 6–7, 62 (Appendix 2: 4); for the two sisters of Papworth (Cambridgeshire), *ibid*., p. 83 (Appendix 2: 101–2).

3 J. S. Moore, 'The Anglo-Norman family: size and structure', *ANS*, 14 (1992 for 1991), 153–96, at p. 166.
4 For Matilda de Bidune, *RD*, pp. 49, 55 (Appendix 2: 63); for Beatrice de Say, *ibid.*, p. 76 (Appendix 2: 90).
5 *RD*, introduction, p. xix.
6 *Ibid.*, pp. xviii–xix.
7 W. L. Warren, *The Governance of Norman and Angevin England, 1086–1272* (London: Edward Arnold, 1987); J. Gillingham, *The Angevin Empire* (London: Edward Arnold, 1984); S. F. C. Milsom, 'Inheritance by women in the twelfth and thirteenth centuries', in M. S. Arnold, T. A. Green, S. A. Scully and S. D. White (eds), *On the Laws and Customs of England: Essays in Honor of Samuel E. Thorne* (Chapel Hill NC: University of North Carolina Press, 1981), pp. 60–89, at pp. 74–8, was more concerned with legal developments; J. C. Holt, 'Feudal society and the family in early medieval England', IV 'The heiress and the alien', *TRHS*, 5th ser., 35 (1985), 1–28, at pp. 21–8. S. L. Waugh, *The Lordship of England: Royal Wardships and Marriages in English Society and Politics, 1217–1327* (Princeton NJ: Princeton University Press, 1988), p. 119.
8 T. Keefe, *Feudal Assessments and the Political Community under Henry II and his Sons* (Berkeley CA: University of California Press, 1983), p. 118. Milsom argued that Henry II merely tried to make feudal society work according to its own rules: Milsom, 'Inheritance by women'; see, for example, the discussion of women inheriting, pp. 64–9.
9 Gillingham, *Angevin Empire*, pp. 55–9.
10 Warren, *Governance of Norman and Angevin England*, chapter 6, esp. pp. 165–6.
11 Holt, 'Heiress and the alien', p. 21.
12 D. M. Stenton, *The English Woman in History* (London: Allen & Unwin, 1957), p. 38; Holt, 'Heiress and the alien', p. 21.
13 For which see S. Sheridan Walker, 'Feudal constraint and free consent in the making of marriages in medieval England: widows in the king's gift', in *Historical Papers: A Selection from the Papers presented at the Annual Meeting* [of the Canadian Historical Association] *held at Saskatoon* (1979), pp. 97–109.
14 The document has mostly been used to study the institution of dower: see Haskins, 'Development of common law dower', pp. 91–116, who sees dower as a threat to a military economy. Senderowitz Loengard, 'Of the gift of her husband', pp. 215–55; Sheridan Walker, 'Feudal constraints and free consent in the making of marriages', pp. 97–109, discusses the *RD* in the context of widows and remarriage, and her 'Free consent and marriage of feudal wards in medieval England' *JMH*, 8 (1982), 123–34, discusses the remarriage of male wards with reference to the *RD*, and stresses that widows and wards tended to remarry as they chose. Holt, however, sees the *RD* as evidence of the exploitation of widows and wards by the Crown: 'Heiress and the alien', pp. 1–28. Scott Waugh also placed the emphasis on the impact of royal lordship on families: 'Marriage, class and royal lordship' in England under Henry III, *Viator*, 16 (1985), 181–207; his *Lordship of England* argues similarly, that widows and wards did not 'flout royal lordship'. J. S. Moore used the *RD* to calculate the size and structure of the Anglo-Norman family: see 'Anglo-Norman family', 153–96.
15 The focus here is upon wives and widows: the information concerning the treatment of wards in the king's gift in the *RD* deserves a far more comprehensive analysis which is beyond the remit of this book. For the political complexities of wardship,

S. Sheridan Walker, 'Widow and ward: the feudal law of child custody in medieval England', in S. Mosher Stuard (ed.), *Women in Medieval Society* (Philadelphia: University of Pennsylvania Press, 1976), pp. 159–72.

16 *RD*, p. 15, Appendix 2: 19.

17 C. Clark, 'English personal names ca. 650–1300: some prosopographical readings', *Medieval Prosopography*, 8 (1987), 43.

18 J. C. Holt, 'Feudal society and the family in early medieval England', II 'Notions of patrimony', *TRHS*, 5th ser., 33 (1983), 193–220; D. A. Postles, 'The baptismal name in thirteenth-century England: processes and naming patterns', *Medieval Prosopography*, 13 (1992), 21.

19 Eight individuals have eluded classification: Appendix 2: 5, 20, 36, 39, 64, 67, 69, 96.

20 In the following discussion italicised numbers indicate that the designation is other than primary, and an asterisk indicates that the entry appears as a primary designation in a different category, Appendix 2: 1, 3, 5–7, *11*, *12*, 13, *14*, 15–16, *17*, *19*, 22, 23, 24, 25–7, 29–30, 31*, *32–3*, *37*, 41, 43–5, 47, 49–50, *54*, 56, 58*, 62, 63*, 66, 68, *70–1*, 75–8, 80, 83–4, *87*, 88–9, 92, 95, 97–8, *100*, *105*, 108.

21 Appendix 2: 8, 12, 24, 17, 24, 28*, 31*, 37, 42, 46, 54*, 55, 58, 60, 63*, 65, 72, 83, 86, 90–1, 93, 103, 105.

22 Appendix 2: *1*, *2*, *5*, *7*, *12–5*, *17–9*, *23*, *26*, *31–3*, *35*, *37*, *43–6*, *49*, *55–6*, *57*, *59–60*, *62–3*, *65*, *71–2*, *78*, *80*, *83*, *84*, *86*, *88*, *93*, *94*, *103–5*, *107*.

23 Appendix 2: 22, 56, 59, 61, 87 (place name based on father's name), 104.

24 Appendix 2: *21*, *38*, *48*, *61*, *84*.

25 Appendix 2: 34.

26 Appendix 2: 34–5, 41, 48 (see *HKF*, 3. 38); 70–1, 82 (see J. H. Round, 'Comyn and Valoignes', *Ancestor*, 11, 1904, 132), 107.

27 Appendix 2: *4*, *15*, *29–30*, *35*, *54*, *75*, *82*, *86*, *103*. Two sisters of Papworth: Appendix 2: 101–2.

28 C. B. Bouchard, 'Patterns of women's names in royal lineages, ninth–eleventh centuries', *Medieval Prosopography*, 9: 2 (1988), 1.

29 Appendix 2: *2*, *15*, 21, 79.

30 Appendix 2: 9–10, 51–3, 40, 62, 69 (unclear why this widow is in the rolls), 70, 80, 99, 108.

31 *RD*, p. 10; Appendix 2: 10.

32 *RD*, p. 82; Appendix 2: 99.

33 *RD*, p. 43; Appendix 2: 52–3.

34 Appendix 2: 51.

35 *RD*, pp. 16–17; Appendix 2: 21.

36 *RD*, pp. 61–2; Appendix 2: 79.

37 Appendix 2: 11.

38 Appendix 2: 4, 18, 19, 81, 85.

39 For her seal see Appendix 1: 20.

40 Appendix 2: 1, 24, 52–3.

41 *RD*, p. 53.

42 R. R. Davies, 'The peoples of Britain and Ireland, 1100–1400', II 'Names, boundaries and regnal solidarities', *TRHS*, 6th ser., 5 (1995), 1–20. For thoughtful comments on the importance of aristocratic naming patterns in twelfth-century aristocracies

see R. Bartlett, 'Colonial aristocracies of the high Middle Ages', in R. Bartlett and A. Mackay (eds), *Medieval Frontier Societies* (Oxford: Clarendon Press, 1989), pp. 23–47. For naming as an indication of *gens* in a wider European perspective see R. Bartlett, *The Making of Europe: Conquest, Colonization and Cultural Change* (London: Allen Lane, 1993), pp. 56–8, 101–5.

43 Holt, 'Notions of patrimony', pp. 193–220; for comments see Postles, 'Baptismal name', p. 21.

44 C. Clark, 'Women's names in post-Conquest England: observations and speculations', *Speculum*, 80 (1978), 223–51.

45 Postles, 'Baptismal name', pp. 1–52.

46 C. B. Bouchard, 'Patterns of women's names in royal lineages, ninth–eleventh centuries', *Medieval Prosopography*, 9: 1 (1988), 1–32, and see *eadem*, 'The migration of women's names in the upper nobility, ninth–twelfth centuries', *Medieval Prosopography*, 9:2 (1988), 1–19.

47 Nineteen in total, Appendix 2: 2, 14, 15, 17–18, 25, 27, 35, 39, 41, 43, 47, 55–7, 63, 77, 78, 83, 103, 107.

48 M. Le Pesant, 'Les noms de personne à Évreux du XIIme au XIVme siècles', *Annales de Normandie*, 6 (1956), 47–74. His tables on pp. 48–50 are invaluable in determining the origins of Germanic and Christian names in Normandy. For comments on male names see Bartlett, 'Colonial aristocracies', p. 26.

49 Ten women were called Alice (Appendix 2: 3, 5, 8, 24, 29, 31, 36, 54, 59, 86), which is the second most popular name and is of Germanic origin. This is followed by Agnes (four Christian: 13, 46, 60, 82), Beatrice (four Christian, Capetian), Margaret (four Christian, Scottish: 4, 28, 91, 105); Avice (3, 87–8); Christiana (three, Christian: 76, 94, 96); Mabel (three: 72, 93, 100). There are two each of Emma (English: 26, 48); Hawise (22, 42); Isabella (16, 108); Juliana (Christian: 85, 106); Maria (38, 68) and Sibilla (30, 104). There is a wide range of sole examples of women's names such as Alda, Alexandria, Amfrid, Ida, Claricia, Cecilia, Eugenia, Eva, Leticia, Lauretta, Maria, Rohais and Ysoude.

50 Clark, 'Women's names in post-Conquest England', p. 235.

51 Bouchard, 'Migration of women's names', pp. 5–6.

52 Postles, 'Baptismal name', pp. 1–2.

53 The significance of female naming patterns could be considerably analysed from both personal and royal charters, and is a subject which would repay further study.

54 Appendix 2: 3, 6, 8–10, 16, 24, 39, 42, 51, 55, 69, 73, 81, 84–9, 93, 95–9, 106, 108.

55 Appendix 2: 2, 4, 12, 36, 58, 60, 82.

56 Appendix 2, 'introduction', p. 239.

57 This is no guide to the total numbers of children that they may have had: for example, some widows had children who had reached majority yet had predeceased them, e.g. Appendix 2: 19, Matilda countess of Chester, whose son, Earl Hugh, had died in 1181; Matilda de Bidune, Appendix 2: 63, was a child herself, being only ten years old. See also Matilda, wife of Reginald de Crevequer, Appendix 2: 25.

58 No children listed: appendix 2: 8, 18–19, 22, 25, 27–8, 44, 52–3, 55, 57, 63, 68–9, 75, 79, 82, 85, 90, 94, 102. Unknown number: 41, 65, 97, 106.

59 Waugh, *Lordship of England*, p. 115, comments on this in the context of thirteenth-century hundred juries.

60 One child: Appendix 2: 2–3, 6, 9–10, 15–16, 23–4, 31, 45, 50–1, 53, 55, 58–9, 72–3, 77, 81, 83, 87, 91, 96, 99, 108. Male heir: Appendix 2: 2–3, 6, 9–10, 16, 24, 31, 50, 53, 55, 59, 72, 77, 81, 87, 91, 99.

61 Albreda de Harcourt, Appendix 2: 34. Her sons all died young, and the three sisters, Roese, Hilary and Agatha, were the eventual co-heirs of William Trussbut: see *EYC*, 10. 9–10. For Albreda's eldest daughter, Roese de Ros, see *RD*, p. 1, Appendix 2: 1. Moore's findings on the size of Anglo-Norman families similarly suggest underrecording of girls: Moore, 'Anglo-Norman family', pp. 159–65, which suggests there were thirty-five families with one boy and no girl, but only ten with one girl and no boys.

62 Agnes de Valognes had six sons predecease her; these are unmentioned on the rolls: *HKF*, 3. 393.

63 Appendix 2: 41, 65, 97, 106.

64 *RD*, p. 9 (Appendix 2: 9).

65 *P.R. 31 Henry II*, p. 85.

66 See above, Chapter 4. The children were all minors in 1185. Bertrada had married Earl Hugh when she was thirteen in 1169; he had died in 1181. For the purposes of the following calaculations she is counted as having had five children. Albreda de Trussbut (Appendix 2: 34) is included in the total of those with seven children and Beatrice de Say (Appendix 2: 90) as having had two children.

67 Eighteen out of ninety; the total ninety excludes those who are not listed as having any children, but includes four who had children but the number was not known: see n. 24 above. Appendix 2: 7, 9, 10, 13, 16, 42–3, 45, 52, 60, 62, 70, 95–7, 99. Cf. Scott Waugh's qualification of his figure of 32.7 per cent of the fines for wardship recorded in the Pipe Rolls being offered by widows, on the grounds that it is based on a tiny sample. Waugh stated that 15.9 per cent of those who obtained wardship in the *RD* were widows: *Lordship of England*, p. 196.

68 Waugh, *Lordship of England*, pp. 196–7.

69 *Ibid.*, p. 197.

70 There are difficulties in assessing how many knights' fees there were in England: P. Coss, *The Knight in Medieval England, 1000–1400* (Stroud: Sutton, 1993), p. 24.

71 Appendix 2: 3.

72 Appendix 2: 3, 6, 9, 10, 32, 44, 50, 52, 53, 69, 73, 80, 89, 97–9, 108.

73 Appendix 2: 23, 41.

74 Milsom, 'Inheritance by women', p. 81.

75 *RD*, p. 33, Appendix 2: 38.

76 *P.R. 31 Henry II*, p. 84. She paid about half this, and had £7 6s 8d of the amount outstanding.

77 *P.R. 28 Henry II*, p. 57; *P.R. 29 Henry II*, p. 67; *P.R. 30 Henry II*, p. 18; *P.R. 31 Henry II*, p. 84; *P.R. 32 Henry II*, p. 73; *P.R. 33 Henry II*, p. 70.

78 Cf. Maria, the widow of Guy l'Estrange, who had married three times; her dower in Norfolk was said to be worth £14, but the value of her dower and *maritagium* in *divers' comitatibus* was unknown by the jurors: *RD*, p. 53, Appendix 2: 68; see also Appendix 2: 19, Bertrada countess of Chester.

79 Thompson, 'Dowry and inheritance patterns', p. 47.

80 Waugh, *Lordship of England*, p. 24.

81 *Ibid.*, p. 24.

82 Milsom, 'Inheritance by women', p. 81.

83 *Ibid.*, p. 81.

84 *Ibid.*, pp. 70–2.

85 *Ibid.*, p. 81.

86 Of the widows who hold less than £10 worth of land only one example is recorded where a widow held both *maritagium* and dower, Margaret Engaine, fifty years old and the subject of two entries in the *RD*: pp. 23–4, 27 and nn., Appendix 2: 28. In neither of the entries is the nature of her land tenure described, yet it can be inferred from other sources that she holds six *librates* as her dower from her first husband. The value of her other lands, her *maritagium*, is unrecorded and is difficult to identify. On the basis of the model suggested above, it is likely that these were worth more than £5. Thus Margaret may well have held over £10 worth of land in total – which is the income level where women generally hold more than one type of land. However, Margaret had married without a licence and was widowed for eight years prior to her marriage to Geoffrey Brito: her case was under consideration by the royal justices and therefore she is an untypical example.

87 For a discussion of restrictive practices as they impact on women and younger sons as landholding developed in Europe see J. Goody, *The Development of the Family and Marriage in Europe* (Cambridge: Cambridge University Press, 1983).

88 Milsom, 'Inheritance by women', p. 63.

89 Some caution is, of course, necessary: for example, two widows who feature in the *RD*, Matilda countess of Chester and her daughter-in-law, Bertrada, were both widowed relatively young and neither remarried. See Chapter 4. Linda Mitchell discusses examples where young widows did not remarry: 'Noble widowhood in the thirteenth-century: three generations of the Mortimer widows', in L. Mirrer (ed.), *Upon my Husband's Death: Widows in the Literature and Histories of Medieval Europe* (Ann Arbor MI: University of Michigan Press, 1992), p. 171.

90 Appendix 2: 4, Margaret of Brittany (aged forty), dower, £82 12s. Appendix 2: 11, widow (aged thirty) of Geoffrey of Turs, Herbert fitz Gilbert, dower + ?£4 6s. Appendix 2: 12, Rohais de Bussei (aged fifty to sixty), inheritance and *maritagium*, £29. Appendix 2: 26, Emma (aged forty), widow of Hugh fitz Gilbert and Robert Saint Paul, dower and *maritagium*, £13 13s. Appendix 2: 46, Agnes de Muntchesney (aged sixty), dower and inheritance, £60 + sixteen *librates*. Appendix 2: 60, Agnes de Mundeville (aged forty to fifty), dower + ?£28. Appendix 2: 61, Cecilia de Bowthorpe (aged fifty), £8(?). Appendix 2: 70, Eugenia Picot (aged thirty), dower, £38 16s 8d. Appendix 2: 86, Alice de Tany (aged ?), dower and inheritance, £14.

91 *Regesta Regum Scottorum*, 2: 554, 476. See Chapter 2 and nn. 70, 72–3.

92 *RD*, p. 53; Appendix 2: 68.

93 *RD*, pp. 85–6; Appendix 2: 107.

94 Isolda, the daughter and heir of Hugh Pantolf, married five times between 1180 and her death in 1241; *CP*, 11. 295–6; 12. 648–9. For a discussion in the context of thirteenth-century developments see Waugh, *Lordship of England*, p. 24.

95 J. Brundage, 'Widows and remarriage: moral conflicts and their resolution in classical canon law', in Walker (ed.), *Wife and Widow in Medieval England*, pp. 17–31.

96 J. Bennett, 'Widows in the medieval English countryside', in Mirrer (ed.), *Upon my Husband's Death*, pp. 69–114.

10

Conclusion

THE PLACE of noblewomen in the twelfth century was not marginalised by the increasing shift to patrilineal primogeniture and the bio-politics of lineage, two of the key broader changes in the way that society was organised. These were seismic shifts in societal organisation, rightly identified by Bloch, Duby, Goody and Holt as fundamental.[1] Within these changes the sources show that, increasingly, the place and roles of noblewomen were articulated with greater clarity through the definition of appropriate gender roles. These wider cultural shifts, far from disempowering noblewomen, confirmed their importance within society: as progenitors of the lineage, for example, as Duby would suggest, and as transmitters of property rights, as Holt would maintain.[2] Yet the avenues for the dispersal of power through society followed demarcated gender lines: for women, power was channelled through property rights linked with changes in status which followed the female life cycle. Within the female roles of wife, widow and mother, social status was pre-eminent in determining the range of power and influence that women could exert. Thus, paradoxically, the position of women within the nobility was secured by their tenurial patterns, despite the cultural shift to primogeniture.

The history of the twelfth century need not be understood only in terms of the dynamics of male tenurial lordship, which was itself in the process of development. As Paul Dalton has shown, even in the first half of the twelfth century there was a gulf between ideal society and the social and tenurial reality.[3] Indeed, this book has shown that although historians such as Duby, Pollock and Maitland and Stenton believed that women could not and did not play any significant roles in tenurial lordship, the social and tenurial reality was that as wives and widows noblewomen were so involved.[4] Further debate on tenurial lordship patterns which does not take account of the importance of gender roles is in danger of becoming sterile, lacking as it is in the tools comprehensively to decode the dispersal of power throughout society. The family as a unit of lordship gave women prominence and in specific contexts – for example, religious patronage – could be a key route for such dispersal.

These themes have been developed in an analysis of private and royal charters as sources for the place of powerful noblewomen as landholders in twelfth-century society. This argued that it is essential to understand the fragmented nature of the discourse on women that charters articulate. In the process of committing land transactions to parchment, élites created a broken narrative which paradoxically both recorded and created custom, practice and procedure. Bloch argued that the twelfth century was one great writing lesson for the nobility, and as a result the process of writing dispersed power yet also concentrated it. He argued that literature 'stands at the crossroads of medieval social practice and culture'.[5] What is significant here is that this collective writing lesson was gendered. If the definition of literature is expanded to include not only poetry, history and romance, the main sources which Bloch uses, but also administrative documents and charters, the ways in which individual noblewomen exerted power become apparent. Charters have a particular usefulness in that they are evidence of women's private initiative and policies. Examination here of charter evidence showed that the public roles, policies and initiatives of noblewomen were defined by their marital status and the female life cycle. The interplay of these factors and the role of social status were vital components in the definition of noblewomen's roles within the family and also society more generally.

The interpretative challenge posed by charters is intrinsically a problem of the nature of the source material, since their purpose was to record land transactions, and this defined their construction. The role of women as witnesses, as givers and receivers of countergifts and in the affidation ceremony showed the complexity of noblewomen's involvement in land transfers. Countergifts were discussed in the social context of patronage, and the ways in which they may be interpreted, in specific contexts, to reveal cultural and economic relations which simultaneously both defined and expressed the place of noblewomen in society, were explained. When women gave affidations they usually did so in the hand of another woman; it is striking that it was women below the rank of tenant-in-chief who gave affidations. Therefore it was possible for hierarchies of lordship to operate within and between groups of women. These roles were deeply gendered, since the female life cycle especially impacted on women's opportunity to exercise power.

These themes were developed in the discussion of women's sealing practice. The practical role of seals as validators of documents and the symbolic meaning of the motifs used on seals show how women's power and authority in reality and symbolically were imaged in their seals. The spread of the use of seals by women of the nobility occurred in both England and France in the twelfth century. Through the process of cultural diffusion this practice filtered down through the ranks of the higher aristocracy to the lesser nobility by the end of the century, and in the process the iconography of women's seals developed to show social status as well as gender symbolism. Women's seals expressed the basis of women's power in specific iconographic representations of lineage, sexual and cultural functions. These symbols could articulate different meanings which might be invisible and varied, a phenomenon inherent in the medieval conceptual framework of the universe in the West. In the words of St Hugh of Victor, 'A symbol is a collecting of visible forms for the demonstration of invisible things'.[6] Meanings could be varied, since the symbols used, such as birds of prey and the fleur-de-lis, were ambiguous and invisible, since women's place in the lineage was imaged but was an invisible link with the past. Further, women's seals were discussed within the social and political context of their use and production, since their purpose was to authenticate documents. The texts of women's seals show the importance of land tenure and the female life cycle in defining the legitimate place of noblewomen as landholders in society.

These themes were discussed with specific reference to countesses. An analysis of the contexts in which countesses appeared in charters, as alienors, co-alienors, witnesses and consentors showed these appearances to be related to female tenurial patterns and predicated on women's roles within the family and the female life cycle. Charter evidence indicates that conceptions of lordship in the twelfth century were deeply gendered. The role of noblewomen was structured into lordship in ways not previously perceived, since their spheres of power and influence were constructed differently from those of noblemen. The subtle interplay of the politics of gender, family and lordship explains the place of noblewomen in society. Opportunities for women to enact policies within this framework were predicated on possible combinations of each, some or only one of these factors. For example, Lucy countess of Chester made alienations in favour of Spalding Priory conjointly with her husbands. Yet it was as a widow that she acted independently when she founded Stixwould Priory. Matilda countess of Chester was active in her husband's military initiatives and likewise made religious benefactions conjointly with Earl Ranulf, yet the charter evidence shows that she too, like Lucy, had more power and authority to act independently as a widow. This pattern is confirmed by other examples of powerful countesses, such as Matilda de Percy and Margaret de Bohun.

Noblewomen's roles changed as they moved through the female life cycle and their status was affected by the transition from wife to widow. Thus, despite the view of the church that widows were *miserabiles personae*, society accorded widows greater autonomy than other categories of women. Married women, who theoretically were 'covered' by their husbands, were nevertheless often involved in the religious benefaction of their families, both natal and marital. The role of wives in land alienations was often to give legitimacy to joint grants, because the involvement of a wife was in some circumstances legally necessary or at the very least advisable.

The ways in which charters may be used to analyse the place and roles of noblewomen from the lesser nobility – the wives of knights in the localities, the lesser barons and sheriffs – were illustrated in the study of the cartulary of St Mary, Clerkenwell. This chapter showed that gender and social status were key constructs which in their interaction defined the place and role of noblewomen in society. The female members of the de Munteni family and others like them, whose connections and status suggest a social rank akin to that of the 'county gentry', exerted power and influence in ways and at stages of the female life cycle comparable with the cases of noblewomen of higher rank. The rarity, but conversely the possibility of, public office holders who were noblewomen was also discussed in this context: social status was a key determinant in defining the amount of influence noblewomen could sometimes extend into a male domain. Countesses occupied an important and often public role in the social hierarchy: lesser noblewomen exerted power and influence in similar ways but in a way which was peculiar to their locality.

The portrayal of noblewomen in the literature of the twelfth century was analysed in Chapters 2 and 3 to show how noblewomen exerted power and influence on the production of texts, as patrons and as objects within them. Noblewomen's spiritual relationships with clerics were an indirect route for female influence in both personal affairs and in wider politics. Such relationships could be close and influential. The portrayal of women in hagiographic sources indicates that women could affect the production and content of saints' lives. This theme was explored in greater detail in a discussion of the role of noblewomen as patrons of the chroniclers and narratives. Such female influence may well have affected the popularity of important texts in the twelfth century such as Geoffrey of Monmouth's *History of the Kings of Britain*. The activity of noblewomen as patrons affected the way that specific genres developed, and they had important roles to play in the process of cultural diffusion.

The development of views of women in chronicles and narratives was discussed in Chapter 2. Chroniclers portrayed noblewomen in a complex and contradictory manner. The portrayal of women was politicised, and increasingly in the twelfth century chroniclers viewed women's agency in gendered terms. The authenticity or historicity of the portrayal of women in chronicles and narratives was discussed in the context of an assessment of the methodological and interpretative problems which are particular to the study of women. In accordance with the analytical framework of the book, it was argued that the complex view of women in chronicles and narratives reflects the socio-political and economic reality of the place of women in society seen in the charter evidence. This varied portrayal offers the key to a complex understanding of the ways that power was disseminated within society. Historians have been ready to accept the marginalisation of women's roles because of their acceptance of the dominant historiographical constructs which have defined men as society and women as passive victims of male violence, as in the Duby model of society or indeed the Stentonesque view of honorial society. Women had, however, as full a role to play in society as men, but the way their power was structured in society was different from that of men because gender roles affected their position and power. Finally, chronicles and narratives acted as a legitimating discourse which reflected deep-seated and fundamental changes in the way that society was organised and conceptualised, and in which gendered categories of women were central.

The complexities of the image of noblewomen in chronicles and narratives as contrasted with the reality of the place of widows as land-holders in society was discussed in specific relation to the 1185 *Rotuli de Dominabus et de Pueris et de Puellis de XII Comitatibus*. This analysis considered whether the increased powers of a widow were anything more than a legal fiction and provided the context for wider discussion on the position of women at that most powerful stage in the female life cycle. The possibility to assess numbers of marriages, children, patterns of land tenure of widows means the *Rotuli* provide important data for the interpretation of the boundaries of noblewomen's lives. The *Rotuli* make it clear that noblewomen's tenure of land underpinned their status, dower was the principle form of land tenure by which widows were supported and the practice of endowing daughters with *maritagium* was restricted.

In Chapter 1 it was shown how 'women' as a separate undifferentiated category were lumped together in the writing of Hugh abbot of Flavigny at the bottom of his hierarchy.[7] The definition of categories of women is fraught with problems, but this book has suggested ways in which it can be addressed in different sources. Countesses were a distinct status group in terms of rank. Social gradations were recognised in all contemporary writings, not only most obviously by late twelfth-century writers such as Andreas Capellanus and Étienne de Fougères, but also in charters through hierarchically organised witness lists, and in the *Rotuli de Dominabus*. Social gradations based on rank mattered. They defined and underpinned the exercise of power.[8] Noblewomen were also defined by their marital status. Such a project must take account of the complexities of gender and lordship in defining social gradations. The debate over lordship, the way that women's land tenure is accommodated within a system based on patrilineal inheritance, problems with defining gradations of social status, and wider theoretical explanations for the dynamics which shape society are all factors which help explain the place and power of noblewomen in society.

Finally this book is intended to contribute to existing debates in three ways. First, as a study of women and gender it has shown that gender was a developing idea that in the twelfth century was articulated through diverse sources. Charters are an important source which can be used to uncover the articulation of gender roles despite the problem of the disjointed nature of the narrative. Second, it has shown that conceptions of lordship were gendered and that the construction of gendered modes of behaviour was ultimately inclusive of noblewomen, since property relations underpinned the exercise of power. Third, the book argues against simplistic explanations of the way that twelfth-century society worked, and urges that the dynamics of society can be full understood only when the role and place of women are fully integrated within the analysis. The status of women is fundamentally linked with land tenure and with socio-economic and political factors as much as marital and family status. Noblewomen saw themselves as members of the élite, as wives, mothers, sisters, daughters, widows and as women. Such complex identities require a complex explanation. When Petronella countess of Leicester ended up in a ditch indignantly throwing her rings away, when Matilda countess of Chester visited Lincoln Castle in February 1141, or when Nichola de la Haye grimly clung on to her castle during a long siege, they were not victims of a patriarchal system that subordinated them, but rather powerful members of the landed nobility who were actively involved in deciding their own fates.

Notes

1 H. Bloch, *Etymologies and Genealogies: A Literary Anthropology of the French Middle Ages* (Chicago: University of Chicago Press, 1983); G. Duby, 'Women and power', in T. N. Bisson (ed.), *Cultures of Power: Lordship, Status, and Process in Twelfth-century Europe* (Philadelphia: University of Pennsylvania Press, 1995), pp. 69–85; *idem, Women of the Twelfth Century*, trans. J. Birrell (2 vols, Oxford: Polity Press, 1997); R. Bartlett, 'Colonial aristocracies of the high Middle Ages', in R. Bartlett and A. Mackay (eds), *Medieval Frontier Societies* (Oxford: Clarendon Press, 1989), pp. 23–47; *idem, The Making of Europe: Conquest, Colonization and Cultural Change* (London: Allen Lane, 1993); J. Goody, *The Development of the Family and Marriage in Europe* (Cambridge: Cambridge University Press, 1983); J. C. Holt, 'Feudal society and the family in early medieval England', II 'Notions of patrimony', *TRHS*, 5th ser., 33 (1983), 193–220; *idem*, 'Feudal society and the family in early medieval England', IV 'The heiress and the alien', *TRHS*, 5th ser., 35 (1985), 1–28.

2 Duby, 'Women and power', pp. 69–85; *idem, Women of the Twelfth Century*; Holt, 'Feudal society and the family in early medieval England', II 'Notions of patrimony', pp. 193–220; *idem*, 'Feudal society and the family in early medieval England', IV 'The heiress and the alien', pp. 1–28.

3 P. Dalton, *Conquest, Anarchy and Lordship: Yorkshire, 1066–1154* (Cambridge: Cambridge University Press, 1994), p. 259.

4 Duby, 'Women and power', pp. 69–85; *idem, Women of the Twelfth Century*; F. Pollock and F. W. Maitland, *A History of English Law before the Time of Edward I* (Cambridge, 1985; 2nd edn, 1898, repr. London: Cambridge University Press, 1968); F. M. Stenton, *The First Century of English Feudalism, 1066–1166* (Oxford: Clarendon Press, 1932; 2nd edn, Oxford: Clarendon Press, 1961).

5 Bloch, *Etymologies and Genealogies*, pp. 13–15.

6 As cited in G. B. Ladner, *Images and Ideas in the Middle Ages: Selected Studies in History and Art* (2 vols, Rome: Edizioni di Storia e Letteratura, 1983), 1. 241.

7 *Hugonis Abbatis Flaviancensis Chronicon*, ed. J. P. Migne, Patrologiae cursus completus . . . series latina. Patrologiae latinae, CLIV (Paris: Garnier, 1881), 384.

8 Andreas Capellanus, *On Love*, ed. P. G. Walsh (London: Duckworth, 1982), pp. 16–18, 44–47; Étienne de Fougères, *Le Livre des Manières*, ed. R. A. Lodge, *Textes Littéraires Français*, 275 (Geneva: Droz, 1979), vv. 244–313, 93–102. He also satirised women's sexual behaviour and alleged tendency to lasciviousness, yet also praised their piety, using the countess of Hereford as a model of appropriate female behaviour.

Appendix 1

Catalogue of seals from the twelfth and early thirteenth centuries

Royal women's seals

1   Queen Matilda, wife of Henry I [1107–18]

Two extant impressions, both 80 mm × 58 mm.

The queen standing crowned, wearing a long robe embroidered down the front and falling in voluminous folds over her feet, above this a sleeveless mantle with embroidered border, draped over her head, fastened at the throat by a brooch and falling in folds over her arms. In her right hand a sceptre surmounted by a dove, in her left an orb surmounted by a cross parry.

+ SIGILLVM MATHILDIS . . . CVN . . . GRACIE REGINAE ANGLIE

C. H. Hunter Blair, 'Durham seals: catalogue of seals at Durham from a manuscript made by the Reverend Greenwell', *Archaeologia Aeliana*, 3rd ser., 13 (1916), no. 3018, plate 45 (*RRAN*, II. no. 1108; cf. no. 1143).

2   Adeliza of Louvain, second wife of Henry I [after 1135]

Oval, 87 mm × 62 mm, brown wax, appended via thick white leather thong.

Standing figure, in long flowing robe with maunches, indistinct object in the right hand, in the left hand an orb. Cf. the description of Matilda, first wife of Henry I (above), since it is possible that Adeliza used the same seal matrix.

BL, Add. Ch. 19,573 (*Seals BM*, 1. no. 789).

Another impression: of similar dimensions, white, indistinct, lower part chipped away.

BL, Add. Ch. 19,574 (*Seals BM*, 1. no. 790).

3   Queen Matilda of Boulogne, wife of King Stephen [1152]

Pointed oval, 94 mm × 51 mm, brown and chipped.

Queen standing crowned in mantle and gown, a fleur-de-lys in the right hand, a bird on her left.

. . . MATILDIS DEI GRATIA

BL, Cott. Ch. xvi 35 (*Book of Seals*, no. 424; *RRAN*, III, no. 503).

4   The empress Matilda [1136–54]

Round, appended via tag.

The empress seated and crowned, in a long robe with long sleeves, holding a sceptre in her right hand, her left hand at her midriff.

S + MATHILDIS DEI GRATI ROMANORUM REGINE

BL, Add. Ch. 75,724.

5   Joan, daughter of Henry II, duchess of Narbonne, countess of Toulouse and marchioness of Provence [before 1199]

Oval, 77 mm × 48 mm, plaster cast from original seal matrix found at the abbey of Grandselve, Toulouse.

Obverse. Standing figure, full-face, with closely fitting robe belted at waist, a jewelled crown of three fleur-de-lys, long plait of hair, robe clasped at the shoulders, the right hand laid on the breast, in the left hand a fleur-de-lys, regal and graceful execution.

+ S. REGINE IOHE. FILIE. QUONDAM. H. REGIS. ANGLORUM

Reverse. Regal – seated and full face, with elegantly folded robe, belted at the waist, the head bare, long mantle diapered with vair, the hair hanging and curled, the right hand laid on the breast and in the left hand the cross of Toulouse, the feet on a rectangular floorboard, ornamented with a diapered pattern set in a frame.

+ S. IOHE. DVCISSE. NARB'. COMITISSE. THOL'. MARCHISIE. PROV'

BL, plaster cast. [cxxv. 59 (obverse), 60 (reverse)] (*Seals BM*, 5. no. 19,870; impression made from a silver matrix found in the ruins of the Cistercian abbey of Grandselve, Toulouse).

Noblewomen's seals

6   Avina, daughter of Athelstan [*c.* 1200]

Oval, 29 mm × 44 mm, appended via tag, mark of handle visible.

Stylised fleur-de-lys.

+ SIGILLV. AVINE . . .

The Registrum Antiquissimum of the Cathedral Church of Lincoln: Facsimiles of Charters in Volumes V and VI (Lincoln Record Society, 42, 1950), plate VII.

7   Richenilda, daughter of Athelstan [*c.* 1200]

Oval, 43 mm × 25 mm, appended via tag.

Stylised fleur-de-lys.

+ SIGILLVM RICHENILD

Registrum Antiquissimum of Lincoln, plate VII.

8   Matilda de Auberville, of Sandwich, Kent [early thirteenth-century]

Pointed oval, mottled green: fine, edge chipped.

Appended by a woven cord of faded bobbin.

To the left, standing, in a long dress, and a maunch at each wrist, on the right wrist a hawk, the field diapered with very elegant scrollwork of foliage and flowers.

+ SIGILLVM. MATILDIS : DE ALBERVILLA'.

The S's reversed. Fine.

BL, Harl. Ch. 45 E. 33 (*Seals BM*, 2. no. 6569).

BL, Sulph. cast. [D.C., D. 217] (*Seals BM*, 2. no. 6570).

9   Hawise of Aumâle countess of Essex [early *temp.* John]

i) Pointed oval, green: fine originally, now very imperfect and injured.

About 72 mm × 49 mm when perfect.

To the right, standing, wearing a long transparent dress closely fitting.

Legend wanting.

R. A small round *counterseal*, imperfect, 34 mm. An early shaped shield of arms: gyronny of fourteen (?) an escutcheon.

+ S'. .AEWIDIS COMIT A [LB]AMA. . . . .

The letters MA in *Albama* conjoined.

BL, Add. Ch. 20,559 (*Seals BM*, 2. no. 6566).

ii) On yellow cord, pointed oval, 52 mm × 34 mm, red.

A lady standing in a long dress, a bird on her left hand;

SIGILLVM HAWIIS DE ALBE [M]ARLA. COMITISEE ESSEXE

Counterseal. Round, 29 mm, red; shield of arms curved at top and sides, a bordure with lines possibly indicating vair.

+ SIGILLVM: . . . .

Description as in *Book of Seals*, no. 444, 311, citing BS facsimile, printed *Mon. Ang.*, V. 334, 'ex autogr, in bibl Hatton'.

BL, sulph. cast. [D.C., D. 212].

10   Cecilia, mother of William de Avranches [*c.* 1200]

Oval, approx. 35 mm × 28 mm, appended via tag, clear, edges lost.

An eagle, with wings extended, standing upon a tortoise and facing to the right.

. . . ILLVM. CE

PRO, E 42/497 (*Seals PRO*, i, p. 28 and plate).

11   Margaret Banastre [late twelfth/early thirteenth-century]

Oval, 38 mm × 26 mm, green wax, appended via tag.

Eagle standing with wings raised and head turned back.

+ SIGILL MARGARET BANSATRE

Durham Cathedral Archives, Durham, DCD 3–4 EBOR 1.

12   Eustachia Basset [*temp.* John]

Pointed oval, greenish-yellow, mottled, fine imperfect, 50 mm × 32 mm. With mark of the handle.

To the left, standing wearing a long dress, in the right hand a fleur-de-lys.

+ SIGILLVM EVSTCHIUS [*sic*] BASSET.

The S's are reversed.
i)   BL, Add. Ch. 10,594 (*Seals BM*, 2. no. 6581).
ii)   BL, Add. Ch. 10,601 (*Seals BM*, 2. no. 6582).
iii) BL, Add. Ch. 10,605 (*Seals BM*, 2. no. 6583).
iv)   BL, Add. Ch. 10,607 (*Seals BM*, 2. no. 6584).

13   Alexandria, daughter of Ralph fitz Bernard [twelfth-century]
Pointed oval, red, chipped, with mark of the handle, 58 mm × 39 mm. Attached via tag.
> Standing with long dress and maunches, lifting up the hands. Her hair long.
> + SIGILLVM . ALEXANDRIE . FILIE. RADVLFI . BERNARDI.
> BL, Egerton Ch. 428 (*Seals BM*, 2. no. 6589).
> Green varnished : chipped. [*c.* 1172]
> SIGILLVM ALEX ... ... .RADULFI BERNARDI
> BL, Egerton Ch. 434 (*Seals BM*, 2. no. 6580); NB. Birch states this was Ralf
fitz Bernard of Hundington or Honington (Lincolnshire), 377.

14   Legarda, daughter of Bernard [1220–30]
Round, damaged, 40 mm, appended via tag.
> Fleur-de-lys.
> ... D [A]. UXORIS A ... RE
> *The Registrum Antiquissimum of the Cathedral Church of Lincoln: Facsimiles
of Charters in Volumes VIII, IX and X* (Lincoln Record Society, 68, 1973), plate IX.

15   Hawise Blund [twelfth-century]
Plaster cast from fine but chipped impression, 45 mm × 30 mm.
> Standing; to the right, in girdled dress with mantle. In the left hand a fleur-de-lys; right hand on the breast.
> S' HELEWISE . FIL' ALBREDE . RODING
> BL, Plaster cast. [lxxviii. 33] (*Seals BM*, 2. no. 6702).

16   Isabella Bolebec [*temp.* John]
Pointed oval, yellowish-brown, varnished, edge chipped, 48 mm × 32 mm.
> Standing, with a long dress, in the right hand a wavy branch.
> + SIGILL' YSABELE . DE. BOLEBE [C]
> BL, Add. Ch. 6026 (*Seals BM*, 2. no. 6593).

17   Petronilla, daughter of Andrew Burnstake [twelfth-century]
Plaster cast from indistinct impression, 50 mm × 32 mm.
> Standing in girded dress, holding in the left hand a long-stemmed fleur-de-lys.
> SIGILLV PETRONILLE.
> BL, Plaster cast. [lxxvii. 49] (*Seals BM*, 2. no. 6697; E. E. Baker, *Talbot Deeds*, Lancashire and Cheshire Record Society, 103, 1953, p. 13).

18   Alice, wife of Richard de Brerton [*c.* 1220]

Vessica, brown wax, approx. 35 mm × 29 mm, appended via tags.

A bird.

S. ALICIE UXOR RICARDI

Vyner Deeds, deposited at Leeds, West Yorkshire Archive Service: Leeds, no. 2027.

19   Constance of Brittany [1190–98]

Pointed oval, pale greenish-white, points broken, edge chipped; originally fine, 90 mm × 58 mm when perfect.

To the right, standing with tightly fitting dress (which emphasises the female figure), long fur-lined cloak, pattern visible on inside, fastened at the throat, belt at the waist which falls to the floor, hair long, falling over the shoulders, in the right hand a lily flower, on the left hand a hawk with long jesses.

. . . C]ONSTANCIA DVCIS . . .

The N's reversed.

BL, Cott. Ch. xi. 45 (*Seals BM*, 2. no. 6594; *EYC*, IV, no. 83, 77).

BL, Sulph. cast. [D.C., D. 214] (*Seals BM*, 2. no. 6595).

20   Margaret duchess of Brittany [post-1160–75]

Pointed oval, standing figure, full face, long dress with maunches, cloak, headdress, in the right hand an orb crowned by a fleur-de-lys, in her left hand a bird of prey.

+ SIGILLVM : MARG. . . . . .NORUM DUCISSE

BL, Plaster cast (detached seal) [xlvii. 963] (*Seals BM*, 4. no. 15,759; Laing, *Supplemental Descriptive Catalogue of Ancient Scottish Seals*, p. 24).

21   Eva de Brock [*c.* 1200 and 1174–89]

Pointed oval, standing figure, to the right, long robe with close-fitting bodice, a cloak turned back on her shoulders, her right hand on her breast, and a hawk in her left hand.

. . . IGILL 'EVE DE BROC . . .

PRO, DL 27/55 (*Seals PRO*, II, P1105).

Pointed oval, cast from fine but chipped impression, 50 mm × 32 mm.

To the right, with girdled dress and mantle; on the left wrist a large falcon (?).

+ SIGILL' . EVE [D]E . BROC

BL, Plaster cast. [lxxviii.48] (*Seals BM*, 2. no. 6596).

22   Isabella de Brus [early thirteenth-century]

Pointed oval, dark green, mottled, fine, 52 mm × 41 mm.

Standing on an elegantly carved corbel, with long dress, cloak and headdress, in the right hand a fleur-de-lys, the left hand on the breast. In the field on each side a wavy sprig of foliage.

+ SIGILLVM : YSABELLE : DE : BRUS :

BL, Add. Ch. 28,479 (*Seals BM*, 2. no. 6597).

23   Burgesia, sister of Walter Burre [mid-twelfth-century]

Pointed oval, approx. 62 mm × 50 mm, green, appended via tags. Good, deep impression, in a linen bag with parchment label.

Standing, wearing long pleated skirt, close-fitting upper garment with high neckline, small round cap, holding in the left hand a rod tipped with a fleur-de-lys, the right hand spread upon the breast.

+ SIGILLVM BVRGESIE . . . RI. BURRE

PRO, DL 27/23 (Seals PRO, II, no. P1130).

Cast from chipped impression, oval, 60 mm × 48 mm.

Standing full face with high neckline or necklace, pleated petticoat, in the left hand a long-stemmed fleur-de-lys. Rather crude.

+ SIG [I]LLVM . BVRIGHTESIE. . . . .I . BVRRE

BL, Plaster cast. [lxxix. 63] (Seals BM, 2. no. 6600).

24   Cecilia Camera, 1215

Oval, 47 mm × 25 mm, appended via tag.

A conventional device crowned by a fleur-de-lys (?).

+ SILLV. CECILIA D'HEW

Durham Cathedral Archives, DCD 2–3 ACR 6; see *Feodarium Prioratus Dunelmensis: A Survey of the Estates of the Prior and Convent of Durham Compiled in the Fifteenth Century. Illustrated by the Original Grants and other Evidences,* ed. William Greenwell (Surtees Society, 58, 1872), p. 162 n.

25   Alice Capra [twelfth-century]

Plaster cast from fine but 'imperfect' impression, pointed oval, 70 mm × 41 mm.

Standing on a small goat, to the right, a tightly fitting dress with long maunches, conical headdress.

+ SIGILLVM : ALICE : CAPRE

BL, Plaster cast. [lxxviii. 61] (Seals BM, 2. no. 6606).

26   Agnes Carew [c. 1210]

Round, 28 mm, uncoloured, appended via tag.

A conventional flower of lyre shape.

+ S'AGNET'CAROU

PRO, DL 27/282 (Seals PRO, II, no. P1158 and plate).

27   Mabel, wife of Bertram the Chamberlain* [c. 1180]

Damaged, green, round, approx. 39 mm, appended via woven bobbin of pink and cream weave.

A geometrical wavy design.

. . . .L MABILIA FIL . . .

Manchester, John Rylands University Library, Rylands Charter 1277.

28   Agnes, daughter of William constable of Chester [1150–57]

Uncertain shape, red, appended via tag.

A bird to the sinister, with a long beak, perched on a wavy branch.
Missing: the description in *EYC*, II, no. 1109 follows *Book of Seals*, no. 515.
PRO, Chancery Miscell. bundle 9, n. 5. m. 9; *Mon. Ang.*, vi. 955, where the
charter is dated 1157–66. A charter of Agnes exists at PRO, C 47/9/5 and an
inspeximus of these is likewise in the same bundle. My thanks to Adrian Ailes at
the PRO for assistance in tracking this charter.

29 Matilda countess of Chester [1162–72]

Pointed oval, creamy white, dark brown wax varnish, 64 mm × 44 mm.
   Standing, tight-fitting dress, long maunches.
   BL, Stowe Charter 159, 158 (*Seals BM*, 2. no. 6608).

30 Bertrada de Montfort countess of Chester [1200–10]

Pointed oval, approx. 69 mm × 43 mm, appended via tag.
   Standing female figure.
   Legend defaced.
   PRO, DL 25/41 (*Chester Charters*, no. 331).
   Plaster cast from indistinct impression, pointed oval, 70 mm × 44 mm.
   Standing, tightly fitting dress with long maunches.
   SIGILL' BERTREE COMITISSE CESTRIE
   BL, Plaster cast. [lxxix. 74] (*Seals BM*, 2. no. 6609).

31 Lucy de Charwelton 'Chokefeld/Cockefeld' [*c.* 1200–8]

Pointed oval, dark-green, fine, 51 mm × 32 mm.
   Standing, to the left, in tightly fitting dress, long headdress, or long plait of
hair, in the right hand a lily or fleur-de-lys. Left hand on waist.
   + SIGILL' .LUCIE DE CHOKEFLED'.
   BL, Harl. Ch. 85. B. 17 (*Seals BM*, 2. no. 6611).
   BL, Sulph. cast. [D.C., D. 215] (*Seals BM*, 2. no. 6612).
   Discoloured, yellow edge chipped.
   BL, Harl. Ch. 85 B. 18 (*Seals BM*, 2. no. 6613).

32 Alice, wife of Gilbert fitz Richard de Clare [1136–38]

Pointed oval, 70 mm × 48 mm, red wax, when perfect, appended via tag.
   Standing, long gown with maunches, in her right hand a fleur-de-lys or
possibly a hawk.
   Legend missing.
   Northants. Charters, no. 48.

33 Matilda countess of Clare [1170–74]

Oval, pale greenish-brown, varnished red : very imperfect 70 mm × 38 mm.
   Standing to the left, an attendant to the right handing the countess a hawk
with jesses on a staff. Both wearing long dress, and cloaks.
   . . . .ILLVM COMI. . . . .

BL, Add. Ch. 21,703 (*Seals BM*, 2. no. 6614).
Northants. Record Office, Andrew Collection A.Z (*Northants. Charters*, no. 49).

34   Cecilia, wife of Radulfi Cofinel [twelfth-century]

Plaster cast from fine impression, pointed oval, chipped at points, 41 mm × 25 mm.
   Standing to the left, on a corbel or pedestal, tightly fitting dress. Hands raised to the left, possible headdress, emphasis on the female form.
   [+] CECIL' UXORI [S R]ADVL' COFINEL.
   BL, Plaster cast. [lxxviii. 71] (*Seals BM*, 2. no. 6616).

35   Joanna de Coruhill' [early thirteenth-century]

Plaster cast from fine impression, pointed oval points chipped, 45 mm × 28 mm.
   To the right, tightly fitting dress, flat headdress, long mantle, a falcon on the left wrist. Standing on a cushion.
   + SIGILLVM IOHANNE : DE CORVHILL'.
   BL, Plaster cast. [lxxviii. 74] (*Seals BM*, 2. no. 6621).

36   Egelina de Corthenai [late twelfth/early thirteenth-century]

In very poor condition, small, green/brown wax, 30 mm × 19 mm, possibly originally a pointed oval, appended via tag.
   Impression of an intaglio – a roman head.
   . .VISINCINS . . . .AS(?)
   BL, Add. Ch. 10,600 (*Seals BM*, 2).

37   Cecily de Crevequer, wife of Walter de Neville [late twelfth-century]

Round, 42 mm × 45 mm, green wax, good sharp impression.
   Hawk.
   + SIGILL : CECILIE : DE : CREVEWER
   Harl. Ch. 54 B 26 (*Danelaw Charters*, no. 99, p. 65).
   Note. This seal is attached to a joint gift with her husband in favour of Bullington. His seal is attached oval impression of an intaglio/gem S WALTERI DE NEVILA, and is smaller than Cecily's, appended on the left.

38   Amicia of Croft [8 September 1216]

Brown, 47 mm × 30 mm. Appended via a strip of parchment, red/burgundy material (silk?) outer covering still enclosing seal.
   Standing, long close-fitting dress, left hand on waist, right hand holding fleur-de-lys on long stem. Possibly plait or headdress.
   SIGILLVM AMICE DE CROFT.
   BL, Add. Ch. 47,615.

39   Alice de Curcy [*c.* 1200]

Almost perfect, an eagle with wings extended, standing upon a tortoise and facing to the right.

CDF, no. 1200 (original in the Archives of the Orne).

40   Matilda, daughter of Reginald the Dean's son [*c.* 1200]

Lys, legend obliterated.

Danelaw Charters, no. 355.

41   Marjorie, daughter of Baldwin de Disceford [*c.* 1210]

Oval, brown/orange wax, 54 mm × 38 mm, armorial quatrefoil.

SI . ILL MARGAR. FIL BALDEWIN

Newby Hall Deeds deposited at Leeds, West Yorkshire Archive Service: Leeds, no. 268.

42   Alice countess of Eu [1225]

Oval, pale-green wax varnished brown, large fragment centre and left side.

Obverse. Standing figure in long dress and mantle, a flower (lily) in her right hand, a hawk on her left wrist. Head broken away.

. . . COM . . . IS . . .

Reverse. Armorial device on triangular shield barry, a label of seven points.

. . . ILLVM HA.

BL, Add. Ch. 46,912 (DBC).

Fragment of oval seal white wax, varnished brown, obverse female gown visible, reverse armorial (Lusignan).

Berkeley Castle Muniments, Select Charter 87 (DBC).

43   Letia de Edisfeld [early thirteenth-century]

Oval, green, mottled, fine, imperfect, chipped at top, 60 mm × 33 mm.

Standing, to the right, in tight-fitting dress, holding object (indistinct) with both hands before her. In the field, on each side, an estoile of eight points. Fine lettering. Beaded borders.

. . . IG . . . M : LECIE : DE : . . . . GES . . .

BL, Harl. Ch. 49. G. 21 (*Seals BM*, 2. no. 6626).

44   Cassandra de Estodlei [*c.* 1170]

Round, orange wax, appended via tag, damaged approx. 44 mm. Mark of handle visible, good clear impression.

Geometric design.

+ SIGILLVM CASSIANDRE

Vyner Deeds, deposited at Leeds, West Yorkshire Archive Service: Leeds, 965; *Abstract of the Charters and other Documents contained in the Chartulary*

of the Cistercian Abbey of Fountains in the West Riding of the County of York,
ed. W. T. Lancaster (2 vols, Leeds: J. Whitehead & Sons, 1915), pp. 850–4.

45   Emma de Etuna [*c.* 1180]

Pointed oval, 60 mm × 40 mm, light brown, tags nearly complete, deep clear impression.

A lady standing, wearing a close-fitting bodice and girdle, small waist, a cloak lined with ermine. Holding a hawk by the jesses in the left hand and a stemmed fleur-de-lys in the right.

PRO, DL 27/53 (*Seals PRO*, II, P1351).

Cast from fine but chipped impression, 64 mm × 43 mm.

Standing, in girdled dress, long mantle gathered on the arm with arm circlet (?), slim waist, well proportioned, centre parting, long hair decoration. In the right hand a fleur-de-lys on a long stem, on the left hand a falcon (bird) by the jesses. Decoration detailed enough to see the bird's feet and her fingers. Fairly large.

[+ S] IGI [L]LVM : EMME : DE ETVN [A].

BL, Plaster cast. [lxxix. 34] (*Seals BM*, 2. no. 6629).

46   Alice Foliot (alias Alice de Hackthorn) [late twelfth-century]

Round, 29 mm × 33 mm, cream wax, appended via tag.

Knot.

SIGILL ALICIE FOLIOT

BL, Harl. Ch. 51. B. 21 (*Danelaw Charters*, no. 35).

47   Matilda de Fressenville [late twelfth/early thirteenth-century]

A   Oval, 41 mm.

A grotesque figure holding, apparently, a child in swaddling clothes.

SIGILL M . . . . DE FRESSENVILLA

Calendar of Charters and Documents relating to Robertsbridge, no. 11.

B   Oval, 44 mm.

Standing, in her left hand a staff, in her right hand a fleur-de-lys.

SIGILL : MTILDIS DE MEINERS

Calendar of Charters and Documents relating to Robertsbridge, no. 117.

48   Alice de Gant [1144 × May 1155]

White wax, legend broken off, appended sideways on tag.

Standing figure, long maunches, holding bird of prey

Vyner Deeds deposited at Leeds, West Yorkshire Archive Service: Leeds, V.R 4818, 4819. (*Mowbray Charters*, no. 104)

49   Rohais, wife of Gilbert de Gant, countess of Lincoln [1149–56]

A   *As uxor Gilbert de Gant*

Pointed oval, red, well preserved, fine, 70 mm × 52 mm.

Standing in long close-fitting dress with ornamental pattern, hair long, close to neck and shoulders, holding in the right hand a lily, in the left a fleur-de-lys. In the field on the right a waved sprig, on the left a quatrefoil.

+ SIGILL . . . .HAIS VXORIS GILLEBER . . . .E GANT.

The letters OR in *uxoris* conjoined.

BL, Harl. Ch. 50 F. 32 (*Seals BM*, 2. no. 6645).

BL, Sulph. cast. [D.C., D. 207] (*Seals BM*, 2. no. 6646).

B   *As Rohais countess of Lincoln*

Oval, 64 mm × 45 mm, light brown, imperfect and indistinct, appended sideways on tag.

Eight chevrons.

. . . . LLVM. ROHS ... ... SSE. LINCOLNIE

BL, Harl. Ch. 55. E. 13 (*Seals BM*, 3. no. 13,408); *The Topographer and Genealogist*, 1 (1846), 318–19.

50   **Pupelina, wife of Arnald Galle [late twelfth-century]**

A bird.

+ SIGILLVM . PVPELINE . F

Danelaw Charters, no. 551.

51   **Alice, daughter of Arnald Galle [late twelfth-century]**

Device developed from lys.

+ SIGILL ALICE F ARNALDI

Danelaw Charters, no. 551.

52   **Geva, daughter of Arnald Galle [late twelfth-century]**

Ornament of five points.

+ SIGILL . GENEVEVE . F. ARNALD

Danelaw Charters, no. 551.

53   **Sibilla Gargate [1226–32]**

Pointed oval, dark-green, mottled, fine, chipped at top, 52 mm × 44 mm.

Standing on carved corbel in long dress, cloak, headdress, in the right hand a lily flower, the left hand on breast.

+ SIGILLVM SIBILLE GARGATE.

BL, Add. Ch. 10,608 (*Seals BM*, 2. no. 6647).

54   **Hawise de Beaumont countess of Gloucester [1183–97]**

One seal: more than one impression.

Pointed oval, green wax, approx. 89 mm × 50 mm, appended via woven bobbin dyed blue.

Standing facing sinister, gowned, girt at the waist, forearms extended, long maunches. Flower or fleur-de-lys in the right hand, bird in the left.

+ SIGILLVM HATHEWIS COMITISSA GLOECESTRIE
Gloucester Charters, p. 24, no. 67, plate XXXIc.
Appended via blue woven bobbin, cream and green wax, this impression is
wanting at the bottom.
IGILLVM . . . . . . .GLOESCES
BL, Add. Ch. 47517 [A] transcr. in Oxford, Bodleian Library, Dugdale MS.
12, fo. 266.

55 Isabella countess of Gloucester and Mortain [1214–17]

One seal and counterseal, more than one impression extant.
Pointed oval, 89 mm × 54 mm, dark green wax.
Full standing female figure to the front, gowned, girt at the waist, forearms
extended with long maunches, flower or fleur-de-lys in the right hand, a bird in
the left hand.
+ SIGILLVM ISABEL' COMITISSE GLOECESTRIE ET MORETVNE
Counterseal. An antique intaglio gem, oval, 29 mm × 25 mm. A helmeted
bust to the dexter between two figures of Nike, each holding a wreath to the
bust, an eagle below, rising regardant between two standards.
+ EGO SV' AQILA CVSTOS D'NE MEE
NLW, Penrice and Margam MS 113; Clark, *Cartae at alia*, II, no. CCCXLII
(Birch, *Catalogue*, 1st ser., 39; *Margam Abbey*, 211–12; *Episcopal Acts*, II. L 280,
690; *Gloucester Charters*, no. 140).
NLW, Penrice and Margam MS 113c; Clark, *Cartae et alia*, II, no. CCCXLIX
(Birch, *Catalogue*, 2nd ser., 99, and *Margam Abbey*, 213–15; *Gloucester Charters*,
no. 144).
NLW, Penrice and Margam MS 2043; B, NLW P & M MS 2092/5 (Birch,
Catalogue, 4th ser, 156–8; *Gloucester Charters*, no. 145).
NLW, Penrice and Margam MS 2042; Clark, *Cartae at alia*, II, no. CCCI
(Birch, *Catalogue*, 4th seright 155; *Margam Abbey*, 212–13; *Episcopal Acts*, II. L
280, 690; *Gloucester Charters*, no. 146. Plate XXXi *d* and *e*).
NLW, Penrice and Margam MS 2041 (Birch, *Catalogue*, 4th ser., 154–5;
Gloucester Charters, no. 148; Clark *Cartae eyt Alia*, II, no. CCCXLIX).
NLW, Penrice and Margam MS 104; Clark, *Cartae et al.ia*, II, no. CCCXXV
(Birch, *Catalogue*, 4th ser, 154–5; *Margam Abbey*, 209–10; *Episcopal Acts*, II, L
279, 689–90; *Gloucester Charters*, no. 149).

56 Alicie, wife of William Grandorge [1218]

Plaster cast from fine impression, pointed oval, 40 mm × 27 mm.
Standing to the right, with long queue of hair falling to the left as pony tail,
long robe belted at the waist, left hand on the waist, in the right hand a fleur-de-lys.
+ SIGILL' ALICIE VXORIS WILLI' GRANDORGE.
The S's and N's reversed. DOR in last word conjoined.
BL, Plaster cast. [lxxix. 25] (*Seals BM*, 2. no. 6652).

57   Hawise Gumin [early twelfth-century]

Plaster cast from chipped and poor impression, 77 mm × 38 mm.

Standing, in tightly fitting long dress with long maunches, on the left wrist a bird of prey (falcon?) drinking from a container (saucer?), the right hand on her waist, dress rucked at the hem.

[V]NDA . . . . . . VS . . . . . W . . EVA (?)

BL, Plaster cast. [lxxix. 31] (*Seals BM*, 2. no. 6655).

58   Alice, daughter of Habraham, *c.* 1200

Round, green varnish over cream wax, the left side damaged and wanting, appended via tag.

Geometrical design.

S. ALI(CIAE)

Cheshire County Record Office, Cholmondeley Collection, DCH/C/12.

59   Juliana Hackthorn [1185–87]

Oval, cream wax, 40 mm × 32 mm, but damaged and chipped away, appended via tag.

Stylised lys.

+ SIGLL GILLIANE . . . OLIOT

BL, Harl. Ch. 51. B. 20 (*Danelaw Charters*, no. 36).

60   Petronella, daughter of Adam Haranc [*c.* 1170]

Pointed oval, 37 mm × 25 mm, plaster cast.

'Herring line waved, three herrings hooked thereon.'

+ S . . . . .LE. .F. . . . ADE HARANC

BL, Plaster cast. [xlvii. 947] (*Seals BM*, 4. no. 17,144; Laing, *Descriptive Catalogue of Impressions from Ancient Scottish Seals*, no. 669, plate vii, fig. 6).

61   Aubrey de Harcourt [1170–1205]

Oval, 37 mm × 25 mm, green wax.

Standing female figure, holding a hawk on her left hand.

+ SIGILLVM . . . AUBERDE H . . . C . . . T

BL, Add. Ch. 47,736 (*EYC*, X, no. 35 and plate II).

62   Avicia Herbert [early thirteenth-century]

Pointed oval, green, fine with mark of handle, 42 mm × 25 mm, and elegant seal, appended via tags (reused).

Standing, to the left, in long dress, waist defined, cloak with hood, in the right hand a fleur-de-lys.

+ SIGILL' .AVICIE . FILIE . HERBERT.

BL, Harl. Ch. 83 D. 30 (*Seals BM*, 2. no. 6633).
BL, Sulph. cast. [D.C., E. 286] (*Seals BM*, 2. no. 6634).

63 Idonia de Herst [late twelfth-century]

A   Pale semi-opaque brown; fine, edge chipped, 70 mm × 44 mm.
Standing in long, tightly fitting dress with long maunches, heart-shaped brooch. In the right hand a lily flower or double fleur-de-lys, on the left a bird of prey (hawk?) with jesses.
+ SIGILLVM IDONIE DE HERST.
BL, L.F.C. xxv. 20 (*Seals BM*, 2. no. 6662).

B   *Another seal*
Oval.
A draped female figure standing holding in her right hand an ornamental cross, in her left hand a bird.
SIGILLVM ID . . . . . HERST
Calendar of Charters and Documents relating to Robertsbridge, p. 17, no. 51 (*c.* 1202).

64 Matilda de Hohtun [*c.* 1170]

A   Off-white, the points broken off, appended by plaited cord of woven bobbin cream and green, 60 mm × 43 mm.
Standing, in tightly fitting dress with long maunches, hair or headdress, on the right hand a bird of prey (hawk?), in the left hand a fleur-de-lys or lily.
SIGILLVM MA . . . . DE HOHTVNE.
BL, Harl. Ch. 86 C. 40 (*Seals BM*, 2. no. 6663).
BL, Sulph. cast. [D.C., D. 218] (*Seals BM*, 2. no. 6664).

B   *Second impression [late Henry II]*
Pale brownish-white with dark brown varnish, approx. 57 mm × 32 mm.
Standing in long dress with cloak.
. . . . .GILL' . . . . . DIS FILIE. . . . .
BL, Add. Ch. 84. D. 1. (*c.* 1150–60) (*Seals BM*, 2. no. 6665).
Seals BM notes that Matilda was the daughter of Pagan de Hohtun and wife of Robert Grimbal of Houghton, Co. Northampton, and also gives reference to BL, Harl. Ch. 86. C. 41.

65 Matilda de Hosdeng [twelfth to thirteenth-century]

Green, imperfect and indistinct, 60 mm × 42 mm; applied by a thick piece of white leather, generally in poor condition.
Standing, to the right in tightly fitting dress, waist defined, in the left hand a bird, right hand on hip.
SIGILL' AMICE . FIL' HVG ; D'HVESD'N.
BL, Harl. Ch. 51 G. 41 (*Seals BM*, 2. no. 6666).

66   Emma, wife of William Hotot [c. 1200]

Pointed oval, approx. 42 mm × 30 mm, uncoloured, appended via tag, deep but indistinct impression.

> Standing female figure, the left hand on hip, the right hand holding flower.
> + SIGILL'. HEMME.D'.HOT . . . T
> PRO, DL 27/54 (Seals PRO, II, P1567).

67   Matilda, daughter of Roger de Huditoft de Stikeney [c. 1170–98]

An incomplete fleur-de-lys.

> . . . DIS DE HUD
> Lincolnshire Archives Office, Stanhope Deed 23; Early Medieval Miscellany, p. 233.

68   Tecent, widow of Maurice of Kelham [late twelfth-century]

Brown varnish over cream wax, round, 34 mm, appended via tag.

> Hand holding a very ornate lys.
> + SIGILLVM TISANDE DE . . . . VM
> BL, Harl. Ch. 83. F. 45; Danelaw Charters, no. 360.

69   Emma, daughter of Roger of Kent [c. 1200]

Pointed oval, green, 37 mm × 27 mm.

> Standing, fleur-de-lys in right hand, left hand on breast, long close-fitting gown, cloak hanging from shoulders, hair unbound.
> + SIGILL EMME'FIL ROGERI
> PRO, DL 27/61 (Seals PRO, II, no. P1953).

70   Hawise, daughter of Philip de Kime [early thirteenth-century]

Round with oval base, brown wax, 46 mm × 40 mm, appended via tag.

> A mermaid holding an object to the left.
> BL, Harl. Ch. 52. G. 44.

71   Alice, daughter of Robert, son of Gilbert of Legbourne
[early thirteenth-century]

Round, 50 mm, good clear impression, appended by tag.

> Ornate geometrical/floral design.
> Registrum Antiquissimum of Lincoln, plate IX.

72   Amice countess of Leicester [1150–53]

Brown wax, appended via tag, oval, 65 mm × 40 mm, chipped.

> Standing figure, long robe, long maunches, in the left hand an indistinct object (bird or fleur-de-lys), feet visible below the hem
> Legend chipped: . . . ISSE. . . .LEICES . . .
> BL, Add. Ch. 47,351; cf. BL, Add. Ch. 47,382.

73   Petronella countess of Leicester [post-1189]

Pointed oval, cream, brown varnish, 61 mm × 47 mm, appended via parchment.

Standing figure, long mantle, long dress holding a lys in the right hand.
SIGILL . . . ONEL . . . . . ISSE LEGERCE
BL, Add. Ch. 47552 (*Danelaw Charters*, No. 322, 242–3).

Evidence of lost seal [1190–1212]
On tag, pointed oval, approx. 89 mm × 54 mm, yellow.
Standing female figure, facing to the dexter, long mantle, in her right hand
a fleur-de-lys.
[SIGIL]LVM . . . . .RCEST.
Book of Seals, no. 5.

74 **Wimarc, wife of Consald the Lombard, daughter of Richard [*c.* 1202–3]**
Pointed oval, 45 mm × 30 mm, bronze-green, appended via tag.
Standing full face, in close-fitting dress with flared skirt, cloak hanging
from the shoulders, a veil on her head, holding a fish in her right hand.
*SIGILL'. WIMARC.FIL'RICARDI
PRO, E 42/146 (*Seals PRO*, i, no. P482 and plate).

75 **Sibilla de London [late twelfth-century]**
Plaster cast from fine impression or from the matrix, edge bevelled, mark of the
handle visible, 54 mm × 34 mm.
Standing, in tight-fitting long dress with maunches at the wrists, short
cloak, long hair, in the right hand a flower, in the left hand a bird of prey
(hawk?).
+ SIGILLV . SIBILLE DE LVNDONIE.
The N's reversed.
BL, Detached seal lxxxvi. 42 (*Seals BM*, 2. no. 6677).

76 **Hawise, wife of Richard de Lyons [*c.* 1200]**
Round, approx. 55 mm, uncoloured, varnished brown, appended via tag, good
impression, edge badly rubbed.
Standing robed figure with nimbus or hood, in her right hand a
fleur-de-lys.
. . . .LERA
PRO E 329/245 (*Seals PRO*, I, no. P498).

77 **Ela countess of Alençon, wife of Robert, son of Erneis Mallet,
sister and heiress of Robert III count of Alençon [1220]**
Plaster cast, pointed oval.
Lady standing in profile, to the right, long dress with waist, light sleeves
and long maunches; in the left hand she holds a falcon by the jesses.
+ SIGILL' :EVE;:UXORIS. ROBERTI.FILII.ERNEWIS:
BL, Plaster cast. [cxxix. 4] (*Seals BM*, 5. no. 19,081).

78   Matilda de Mandevill countess of Essex and Hereford [1227–32]
Oval, 70 mm × 45 mm, appended via tag.
Standing figure on a corbel, her headdress and wimple clear, long robe with ermine spots.
+ S'MATILDIS: DE: MA . .EVIL': COMITISSE ESSEXIE ETHERFORDIE
Berkeley Castle Muniments 227 (*Descriptive Catalogue of the Charters and Muniments in the Possession of the Rt. Hon. Lord Fitz-Hardinge, at Berkeley Castle*, ed. I. H. Jeayes, Bristol: C. T. Jefferies & Sons, 1892, p. 77, DBC).

79   Alice Mauduit [*temp.* Richard I]
Dark-green, damaged, imperfect and cracked, 70 mm × 50 mm.
Standing in tight-fitting dress, girded at the waist, with long maunches, plaited hair, in the right hand a fleur-de-lys, left hand on waist.
SIGILLVM AL . . . . E MAVD. . T.
BL, Harl. Ch. 47 I. 7 (*Seals BM*, 2. no. 6683).

80   Matilda countess of Meulan [*c.* 1165]
Oval, red wax, varnished brown, 55 mm × 38 mm, appended via leather tag.
Standing figure in long gown, both hands raised, each holding an indistinguishable object.
. . . . OM . . . MELLENTI
Archives departmentales de la Seine-Maritime 1814 (Le Valosse Deeds), carton 7 (DBC).

81   Marie lady of Meille, Flanders [1226]
Oval.
Standing form, turned to the right, in profile, close-fitting robe girt at waist, flat-topped head dress, long mantle of vair, her hands before her.
SIGILLVM MA . . . DNE . DE. NIVELLA
BL, Plaster cast. [cxxxii, 12] (*Seals BM*, 5. no. 19,873).

82   Margeret de Merch [early thirteenth-century]
Pointed oval, creamy white, with yellow varnish, 77 mm × 44 mm.
Standing, long tightly fitting dress, headdress, long maunches, fleur-de-lys in each hand. A cross at the neck, hands raised either side of the body, suggestive female form.
+ HOC = SIGILLVM MARGRETE FIL . . . . I .
BL, Harl. Ch. 84. I. 22 (*Seals BM*, 2. no. 6631).
BL, Sulph. cast. [D.C., D. 213] (*Seals BM*, 2. no. 6632).

83   Eva, daughter of Simon, son of Lessing de Merkington, 1218/19
Pointed oval, brown, 43 mm × 33 mm, appended via tag.
Sheaf of corn, stylised geometrically.

SIGILL . EVE. FIL. SIMONIS
Vyner Deeds deposited at Leeds, West Yorkshire Archive Service: Leeds,
nos 2023, 2026.

84 Milysant, daughter of William de *Mitdehorguill*, late twelfth/ early thirteenth-century

Pointed oval, red wax, appended via tags, 48 mm × 33 mm.
Standing figure, hair band, full length robe, girdled at waist, flower in the
left hand.
+ SIGILLVM MILYS . NT
NLW, Penrice and Margam MSS, no. 39.

85 Basilia, wife of Hugh le Moine of Burgh le Marsh [late Henry II]

Oval, brown, cream wax, 45 mm × 40 mm.
A lys.
+ SIGILL BASIL . . . .IE MAGNI
BL, Cott. Ch. xxvii. 121 (*Danelaw Charters*, no. 12).

86 Alienor, daughter of William de Monte Alto and Amicia of Swinton [*c.* 1210]

Round, 40 mm, red wax, appended via parchment.
Very decorative fleur-de-lys.
SI . . . LL : ALIENOR FILIE : AM
Vyner Deeds deposited at Leeds, West Yorkshire Archive Service: Leeds,
nos 4939, 4940 (W. T. Lancaster, *Chartulary of Fountains Abbey*, pp. 694–702).

87 Avicia (Lancaster), wife of Richard of Morville constable of Scotland [*c.* 1176]

Oval.
Standing female figure, tighly fitting dress, long maunches, on the right
hand a wavy branch, on the left a falcon,
SIGILLVM AVICIE DE MORAVILLA
Seals BM, 4. no. 15,753; Laing, *Descriptive Catalogue of Impressions from
ancient Scottish Seals*, no. 482, plate V, fig. 7.

88 Agnes [De Muntpinsun?] [twelfth-century]

Plaster cast from fine but imperfect impression, 64 mm × 44 mm.
Standing, full face, tightly fitting dress. Long maunch attached to each
wrist, in the right hand a branch or sceptre, left hand holding an indistinct
object.
+ SIGILLVM X AGNET . . . . ETE.
BL, Plaster cast. [lxxx. 91] (*Seals BM*, ?. no. 6689).

89   Emma Mustel [*c.* 1200]

Oval, green, appended via tag, 40 mm × 34 mm, in poor condition.
> Symmetrical and ornate knot.
> + SIGILL EMME . DE MALTON
> BL, Cott. Ch. xii. 4 (*Danelaw Charters*, pp. 70–1, no. 108).

90   **Gundred countess of Norfolk [late twelfth-century]

Secondary evidence: pointed oval, green, 89 mm × 50 mm on tag.
> A lady standing in tight gown with false long sleeves, sprigs on either side.
> SIGILLVM GUNDREDE . . . . . . SSE DE NVRFOLC . E.
> *Book of Seals*, no. 345.

91   Matilda, daughter of Norman [*c.* 1210]

Pointed oval.
> A shield of early style, diapré (?): a bend. Indistinct. The bend appears to be charged with some fur or other uncertain marks.
> BL, Harl. Ch. 47. D. 47 (*Seals BM*, 3. no. 7,915; Blair, 'Armorials on English seals', plate XVI e).

92   Alice countess of Northampton [1140–60]

Cream, 80 mm × 50 mm, appended sideways on tag.
> Chevron design, the chevrons of the house of Clare.
> COMITI . . E . . . E . . . . T
> BL, Egerton Ch. 431.
> Large oval, orange-brown, much damaged, approx. 55 mm × 40 mm
> Six chevrons visible.
> Legend defaced.
> BL, Cott. Ch. XVI. 37 (*Danelaw Charters*, no. 205, pp. 142–3).

93   Isabel countess of Northampton [1160–70]

Oval, white wax, 62 mm × 39 mm, appended via tag, in pink silk bag.
> Standing figure, long gown girt at the waist
> Legend defaced: . . . . .MN. .
> BL, Add. Ch. 47,584.

94   Ada countess of Northumbria [1153–78]

? 'A small portion only'.
> *Calendar of the Laing Charters, A.D. 854–1837, belonging to the University of Edinburgh*, ed. J. Anderson (Edinburgh: Thin, by authority of the University of Edinburgh, 1899), no. 2.

95   Alienor, daughter of Robert l'Osseler [*c.* 1170]

Oval, appended via tag, 50 mm × 37 mm.
> A stylised sheaf of corn.

SIGILL: ALINOR: FILIE ROBER
The N reversed.
Vyner Deeds deposited at Leeds, West Yorkshire Archive Service: Leeds, no. 969.

96 Agnes of Orby [late twelfth-century]

Oval, broken and in poor condition, approx. 72 mm × 53 mm, cream wax, appended via tag.

> A fleur-de-lys to top of seal ?, device almost illegible.
> + SIGILLVM A . . . . .OR HERBERTI
> BL, Harl. Ch. 54 E 9 (*Danelaw Charters*, no. 68).

97 Aldith, wife of Osmund the forester [1185–98]

White, oval, 50 mm × 39 mm.

> An eagle displayed.
> SIGILLVM ALDIT VXOR . . . OSM
> *Luffield Priory Charters*, ed. G. R. Elvey (2 vols, Northamptonshire Record

Society, 22, 26, 1968 for 1956–57, 1975 for 1973; jointly published with the Bedfordshire Record Society), II. 399, no. 75, citing Westminster Muniments 2570.

98 Matilda, daughter of Robert de Oxon [*c.* 1225]

Round, white, 25 mm in diameter.

> SIGILL MATIELD FIL.E.RO. . . .
> *Luffield Priory Charters*, ed. Elvey, II. no. 731, p. 375: Westminster Muniments 2375.

99 Petronilla, daughter of Alfred Parva [early thirteenth-century]

Dark-green, fine, 44 mm × 29 mm.

> Standing, in long dress, in the right hand a fleur-de-lys, left hand on hip.
> + SIGILL' . PERNILE. FILIE ALFRE. PARVE.
> The letter N reversed.
> BL, Harl. Ch. 86 B. 5 (*Seals BM*, 2. no. 6693).
> BL, Sulph. cast. [D.C., D. 219] (*Seals BM*, 2. no. 6694).

100 Isabella de Clare countess of Pembroke [*ante* 1219]

Plaster cast from indistinct impression, 50 mm × 28 mm.

> Standing, in tight-fitting dress, pointed headdress, long mantle, the right hand laid on the breast, in the left hand a bird of prey (falcon?) held on the wrist by jesses.
> SIGILL' ISABEL. COMITISSE. PEMBROC . VXORIS. WILL'I . MARESC.
> BL, Detached seal lxxx. 9 (*Seals BM*, 2. no. 6682).

101 Agnes, daughter of Hugh Pincerna [*temp.* Henry II]

Oval, brown wax, app. via tag, 28 mm (probably 34 mm when complete) × 25 mm.

Two impressions extant, both with mark of handle.

(1) Brown, fine impression with ornate lys.

SIGILL AGNETIS PINCVN

BL, Harl. Ch. 50. B. 19 (*Danelaw Charters*, pp. 120–1, no. 177).

BL, Harl. Ch. 50. B. 21 (*Danelaw Charters*, no. 178, pp. 121–2); cf. Harl. Ch. 50. B. 20 (no seal).

102 Sibilla (de Dinant)/de Plugenet [twelfth-century]

Oval.

A lady standing, to the right, holding a fleur-de-lys in the right hand, the left hand on the waist.

SIGILLVM SIBILLE PLUGENET

Seals BM, plate 22, no. 5.

103 Muriel, widow of Hugh Pumfol [late twelfth-century]

Oval, cream, 44 mm × 29 mm, appended via tag.

Fleur-de-lys.

+ LE SEL MVRIEL LA FEME HVE PVMFO

BL, Cott. Ch. xii. 17 (*Danelaw Charters*, no. 86).

104 Lecia, daughter of Ralf of Rouen [*temp*. Henry II]

Pointed oval, dark-green, fine, edge chipped, 64 mm × 43 mm.

Standing, to the right, in tightly fitting dress with ornamental maunches, long riband (or hair?) tied in three tails at the end. In the left hand an ornamental fleur-de-lys. The right hand on the hip, belt at waist, skirt flared at the bottom.

. . GILLVM . LIECE . . . . LIE RADVLFI

BL, Harl. Ch. 50. B. 23 (*Seals BM*, 2. no. 6637; *Book of Seals*, no. 107).

BL, Plaster cast. [lxxxi. 38] (*Seals BM*, 2. no. 6638).

BL, Sulph. cast. [D.C., D. 209] (*Seals BM*, 2. no. 6639).

105 Mary, daughter of Laurence of Rouen [early Henry II]

Pointed oval, 63 mm × 43 mm, green, on tag.

Standing female figure, close-fitting dress with maunch on the left wrist, fibula at neck, necklace, in the left hand an ornamental fleur-de-lys, the right hand on the hip.

. . . .IGILL' MARIE . . . LIE LAVRENCI

BL, Cott. Ch. v. II (*Seals BM*, 2. no. 6635; *Book of Seals*, no. 108).

BL, Sulph. cast. [D.C., D. 210] (*Seals BM*, 2. no. 6636).

106 Alice de Redvers, daughter of Earl Baldwin [late twelfth-century?]

Oval, green wax, 65 mm × ? mm, appended via green and white silken cords.

Almost completely defaced.

Devon Record Office, 312M/TY25 (Hole Park Deeds). (DBC)

107 Cristina, daughter of Roderi de . . . ail (?) [twelfth-century]

Cast from good impression, indistinct in places, pointed oval, 52 mm × 32 mm.

Standing, in tightly fitting dress, girdled at the waist, in the right hand an ornamental fleur-de-lys or lily flower, in the left hand a hawk with long jesses.

SIGILL' CRISTINE FIL' RO [GE]RI D' . . . IL'

The NE in Christine conjoined.

BL, Sulph. cast. [D.C. D. 216] (Seals BM, 2. no. 6640).

BL, Plaster cast. [lxxxi. 21] (Seals BM, 2. no. 6641).

108 Desirea, daughter of Ernaldi Ruffi [1204]

Plaster cast from fine impression, 34 mm × 23 mm.

Standing full face, flat headdress, girdled dress, a fleur-de-lys in the left hand, on straight stem, right hand on waist.

+ S' DESIREE FIL' ERNALDI RVFFI

BL, Plaster cast. [lxxix. 3] (Seals BM, 2. no. 6703).

109 Aelina de Rullos [c. 1160–65]

Pointed oval, 52 mm × 38 mm, appended sideways via tag, uncoloured wax.

Standing in long gown with headdress, with maunches, holding an indistinct object in the right hand, her left hand on hip.

+ SIGILL .. . . A RELL . . . .

Northants. Charters, pp. 82–3 and plate, Drayton Series, XXX (a).

110 Alice de Rumeli [1210–15]

Pointed oval, 55 mm × 35 mm, red, deep impression, but rather crude, appended via tag.

Standing, with unbound hair, her left hand on her hip, her right hand holds a long-stemmed flower. On her breast a six-armed escarbuncle with knobbed ends.

+ SIGLLVM . . . DE RVMELI

PRO, DL 27/132 (Seals PRO, II. no. P1977).

BL, Plaster cast. [lxxxi. 42] (Seals BM, 2. no. 6704).

111 Cecilia, daughter of Sabelina [late twelfth-century]

Oval, 75 mm × 50 mm, green.

Standing figure, to the right, maunches, belted gown, holding a fleur-de-lys in the left hand.

Legend defaced.

BL, Harl. Ch. 50. B. 33.

112 Eufemia de Saquenville [1206]

Plaster cast, pointed oval.

Figure to the left, standing on a corbel, wearing a close-fitting robe with train, flat-topped headdress and mantle, left hand held before the breast, in the right hand a fleur-de-lys on a stalk.

BL, Plaster cast. [cxxxix. 400] (*Seals BM*, 5. no. 19,886).

113 Constance, widow of Henry Screvi [c. 1220]

Vessica, orange wax, 45 mm × 32 mm, appended via tag.

An elegant stylised fleur-de-lys

SIGILL CUSSTANCIE D'SCRE

Vyner Deeds deposited at Leeds, West Yorkshire Archive Service: Leeds, no. 2024.

114 Emma de Selveleia [c. 1160–70]

White, oval 64 mm × 39 mm.

A bird displayed, with head erect.

+ SIGILL' EMME DE SEL . . . .LEIA

Luffield Priory Charters, ed. Elvey, I. 104–5.

115 Matilda de St Liz [*temp.* Henry II]

Light-green, imperfect, indistinct and in poor condition; appended sideways by a finely woven bobbin with damasked pattern of various colours cream and brown (?) once red. Outer covering is brown wax covering inner cream cast.

Standing in tight-fitting dress with long maunches, in the right hand a fleur-de-lys.

Legend indistinct.

BL, Harl. Ch. 55. G .9 (*Seals BM*, 2. no. 6706).

Red, attached via strip of parchment which then goes through a bag which contains the seal: red. Broken, in poor condition. Difficult to determine the image.

BL, Cott. Ch. xi. 25.

116 Matilda de Stafford [late twelfth-century]

Cream wax, light brown varnish: a fragment, in poor condition, approx. 42 mm × 32 mm when perfect.

Standing, to the left, in the right hand an uncertain object, left hand on hip, tight-fitting dress, long maunches.

Legend missing.

BL, Harl. Ch. 56. E. 2. (*Seals BM*, 2. no. 6714); cf. BL, Harl. Ch. 56. G. 23.

117 Milysent de Stafford [1192–1214]

Creamy-white, with yellowish-brown varnish: archaic style (?) imperfect, approx. 47 mm × 41 mm when perfect, not fine, rather damaged.

Standing, to the right, with narrow waistband, tightly fitting dress, with sash, long hair or headdress, on the right wrist a bird of prey (a hawk?). Hands raised to the right, the left hand on the waist.

..... LWM . MIL . .ENTE : DE STA ....
BL, Harl. Ch. 46 E. 54 (*Seals BM*, 2. no. 6715; *Book of Seals*, no. 92).

118 Joanne de Storton [*temp.* John]

Oval, green wax, 45 mm × 32 mm, appended via tag.

Standing female figure, headdress, long robe, belted at the waist, fleur-de-lys in the left hand, right hand on the breast.

Manchester, John Rylands University Library, Rylands Charter 1808.

119 Alice de St Quintin [1166–80]

Oval, white wax, 70 mm × 43 mm, much rubbed.

Standing with open cloak.

SIGILLVM ALI . . .

EYC, XI, 103 (reference to original charter in the collection of H. L. Bradfer Lawrence, esq.; charter printed in *Yorkshire Deeds, Volume VII*, ed. C. T. Clay (Yorkshire Archaeological Society, Record Series, 83), p. 203.)

120 Élienor countess of St Quintin and Valois [before 1194]

Plaster cast, pointed oval.

Standing full face, close-fitting robe, girt at waist, headdress, right hand on hip, left hand falcon and jesses.

BL, Plaster cast. [cxxix, 658] (*Seals BM*, 5. no. 19,884).

121 Petronella, wife of Alan de Tatton [twelfth-century, pre-1180?]

Round, 50 mm, uncoloured, appended via tag, complete but not sharp impression.

Standing, in a long gown with maunches, veiled, holding a hawk on her left wrist.

+ SIGILL'PETVNELE DESTATVN

PRO, 27/292 (*Seals PRO*, II, P2113 and plate 30).

BL, Plaster cast. [lxxx. 94] (*Seals BM*, 2. no. 6717).

122 Leticia, wife of Jordan Tesson [1170]

Round, 48 mm, blob of wax, appended via cream laces.

A bird with wings extended, decorative background.

+ SIGILLV. LETICIE DE S . . . . ATORE +

Paris, Bibliothèque Nationale, Nouvelle Acquisitions, 1649.2

123 Pavia, daughter of Svan Thornet [*c.* 1190]

Oval, green, sides damaged, approx. 49 mm × 31 mm, good clear impression, appended via tags.

Geometrical design.

+ SIGNU' PAVIE FILIE SWANIDETOR

Vyner Deeds deposited at Leeds, West Yorkshire Archive Service: Leeds, no. 447.

124 Agnes de Truleris [*temp.* Richard I]

Tall, thin oval, 64 mm × 32 mm. Dark green, mottled, indistinct, appended by an ornamental cord of bright green and tan diapered taffeta.

Standing, to the left, in long dress, flat headdress and maunches. In the right hand an indistinct object, the left hand on the hip.

SIGILL' . AGNETIS . DE TRVLERIIS.

BL, Add. Ch. 5526 (*Seals BM*, 2. no. 6721).

125 Blanch countess palatine of Troyes [1210]

Pointed oval.

Standing figure, turned to the left, tight-fitting robe and mantle, cap, long hair, left hand on breast, in the right hand a flower.

+ SIGLLVM. BLANCH COMITISSE. TRECENSIVM. PALATI. .

BL, Plaster cast. [cxxxii, 17] (*Seals BM*, 5. no. 19,893).

126 Agatha Trussbut (dAgace Trusbut) [1195]

Round, black wax.

A water bouget.

+ SIGLL' AGACE TRVSBVT.

BL, Harl. Ch. 57. A. 52 (*EYC*, X, no. 42, plate VII, and 17–19; Blair, 'Armorials on English seals', plate VX m).

127 Emma Trussbut [late twelfth-century]

Oval.

Lys.

Legend obliterated.

Danelaw Charters, no. 533.

128 Agnes de Vescy [thirteenth-century, *c.* 1220s?]

Pointed oval, 67 mm × 45 mm. Beaded borders.

Obverse. Standing full face, in girdled dress, fur-lined mantle, flat head-dress, on the right a shield of arms: a cross flory, VESCY, standing on a carved corbel left. On the left in the field, a shield of arms vaire, FERRARS. On each side, in the field, an elegantly designed wavy scroll of foliage and flowers.

. . . . .I * D DE . . . .

Reverse. On a branching tree, a shield of arms hung by a strap VESCY. Below this, another shield of arms, three garbs, two and one, CHESTERIGHT, the branch on the left-hand side destroyed; on that on the right-hand side a similar shield of arms: a lion rampant, contourne, MARESCHAL.

. . . . IBUNT : P . . . . .

BL, Plaster cast. [lxxxi. 16, 17] (*Seals BM*, 2. no. 6726).

129 Eleanor countess of Salisbury [1222]

Pointed oval, approx. 55 mm × 35 mm, uncoloured, appended via tag, good impression.

Standing figure, wearing a flowing gown with a short mantle, the left hand held to the breast and her right hand extended, to the right a quatrefoil.

... LVM ALIENOR'C/MITISSE SALESBIR

PRO, DL 27/92 (*Seals PRO*, II o. no. P1989).

BL, Plaster cast. [lxxviii. 94] (*Seals BM*, 2. no. 6729).

130 Isabella, wife of William Wallace [*c.* 1160]

'A device, not upon a shield, an eagle alighting'.

Laing, *Descriptive Catalogue of Impressions from ancient Scottish Seals*, no. 837; cf. no. 836.

131 Matilda de Wallingford [1122–47]

Oval, 80 mm × 60 mm, brown wax varnished brown.

A standing figure wearing headdress, long robe with maunches, holding in the right hand a flower.

+ SIGILLVM ... O II W A INGEFORDE

King's College Cambridge Library OGB23 (Old deed 17) (DBC).

Another impression: red wax, varnished brown, with deep impression, 72 mm × 48 mm.

Female figure in long gown with robe looped over her arm, flower in her right hand, head draped.

+ SIG. .LV MATILDIS DOMINE WARINGEFORDE

Windsor Dean and Chapter Muniments xi. G. 1 (DBC).

132 Isabella countess of Warenne [1163–98]

i) Pointed oval, pink wax varnished brown: originally fine, very indistinct and imperfect; approx. 82 mm × 62 mm, appended by thick silken cords of cream and green and copper brown

Standing, in tightly fitting headdress, girdle, mantle (?), arms outstretched, in the right hand a fleur-de-lys, in the left some indistinct charges.

Legend destroyed.

BL, Harl. Ch. 43. C. 15 (*Seals BM*, 2. no. 6730).

[c. 1203]

ii) Pink wax, varnished brown, distinct impression, imperfect in places, originally fine. Attached via tag.

Standing female figure holding fleur-de-lys in right hand, a bird (hawk?) with jesses in the right.

...... OMITISS ..... ET. MO

BL, Add. Ch. 24,634 (*Seals BM*, 2. no. 6731; *EYC*, VIII, no. 86 and plate 20).

133 Gundreda de Warenne (of Fakenham, Suffolk) [1200–25]

Rather squat oval, creamy-white, imperfect indistinct, 50 mm × 39 mm. Appended by a woven bobbin of diapered bright green (faded?) brown and cream threads.

Standing, to the right, holding to the left hand a bird of prey (hawk?).

. . . . DE . . . .

BL, Harl. Ch. 57. E. 24 (*Seals BM*, 2. no. 6732).

134 Matilda de Wateville [early *temp.* Henry II]

Red, indistinct, 62 mm × 30 mm.

In tightly fitting dress, mitre-shaped cap, in the left hand a fleur-de-lys on a long stem, the right hand on the hip, standing.

SIGILLVM MA [H]ALT DE WATEVILA.

BL, Add. Ch. 20,394 (*Seals BM*, 2. no. 6736). NB Alice de Watevile's seal, dated post-1228, is listed *Seals BM*, 2. no. 6734.

135 Ingrid, daughter of Roger, son of Walwan, widow of Nicholas, son of Wido [*c.* 1220–30]

Oval, white, varnished, 38 mm × 25 mm.

A fleur-de-lys.

+ SIGILL' HINGRID FIL' ROGERI

Luffield Priory Charters, ed. Elvey, I, no. 270 (Westminster Muniments, no. 2979. Luffield Cartulary, fo. 92r (Whitlebury)); and another reference to an extant impression at no. 273 (Westminster Muniments, no. 2950; Luffield Cartulary, fos 92v–93r), from which the above description is taken.

136 Adelina, daughter of William [late twelfth-century – *c.* 1220]

Circular, 33 mm, light brown wax, appended via tag.

A fleur-de-lys.

+ SIGILL' ADELIN FILE WILLELMI

Northants. Charters, no. 53.

137 Botilde, daughter of William [late twelfth-century – *c.* 1220]

Circular, 37 mm, light brown wax, appended via tag.

A crudely drawn fleur-de-lys.

+ SIGILL BOTILDE FILIE WILLELMI

Northants. Charters, no. 53.

138 Eva, daughter of William [late twelfth-century – *c.* 1220]

Circular, 33 mm, appended via tag.

A geometric design, based on fleur-de-lys.

SIGILL EVE FILIE WILLELEMI

Northants. Charters, no. 53.

139 Margeret countess of Winchester [c. 1220]

Green, originally fine, imperfect, 81 mm × 52 mm.

Standing, to the left, in tightly fitting dress, charged with the following armorial bearings: masculy, QUINCY; fur cloak, flat headdress. In the left hand a fleur-de-lys. Above her head a round-arched doorway, elaborately masoned with cinquefoil in allusion to the paternal arms of BELLOMONT. The doorway is supported, on the right-hand side only, by a masoned jamb or toweright. On the left a wavy tree with trefoiled foliage and spikes of flowers, with two shield arms suspended from it. The upper shield: seven mascles, three, three and one, QUINCY; the lower shield: a fess between two chevrons, FITZ WALTER?. In the field on the right an estoile of six points.

GILL . . . . . OMITISSE : W . . . . .

BL, Harl. Ch. 112. C. 27 (*Seals BM*, 2. no. 6700); cf. BL, Harl. Ch. 55. B. 5.

BL, Sulph. cast. [D.C., E. 281] (*Seals BM*, 2. no. 6701).

140 Hawis de———fort, [c. 1150–82]

Pointed oval, white, varnished, edge imperfect, 54 mm × 37 mm when perfect, appended by plaited threads.

To the left, standing wearing a long dress, belted at the waist, with long maunches at the wrists, in the right hand a fleur-de-lys. Headdress, long hair, left hand on hip.

+ SIGILLVM : HAW . . . .DE. . . . FORT

BL, Harl. Ch. 45. B. 27 (*Seals BM*, 2. no. 6567).

141 Maheut de —— [early twelfth-century]

Green, mottled, fine but imperfect, in poor condition. 50 mm × 39 mm. Cut from charter to which it was appended by woven flat bobbin with damask patterns green and yellow dye in interesting block pattern.

Standing, in long dress belted at the waist, holding a wavy branch in the right hand, in the left hand a seeded fleur-de-lys.

. . . . ILLVM MAHVT. DE . . . .

BL, Detached seal, xxxix. 67 (*Seals BM*, 2. no. 6681).

142 ? of the Pincerna Butler family [1150]

Round, broken at the edges.

A standing female figure with close-fitting dress flaring to the feet, holding a round object in the right hand, the left hand on the waist. In the field two geometrical/floral designs.

S . . . SINE

Seals BM, plate 31, no. 6.

Appendix 2

Noblewomen in the Rotuli de Dominabus

Place names have been put into their modern form where they are identifiable. Personal names have likewise been modernised. Square brackets indicate that the information has been derived from sources other than the *Rotuli de Dominabus*, and an asterisk indicates that the information is entered under another individual's name, usually that of the heir. *w* wife of, *m.* married, *libr.* librates, *KF* knight's fee, *D* dower, *MP* marriage portion (*maritagium*), *I* inheritance, *T* tenant, *TiC* tenant-in-chief. Lower-case abbreviations of the same indicate that although the land is not listed as dower, etc., it is likely to have been land held by that tenure, which can be deduced from the *Rotuli de Dominabus* or other sources.

Lincolnshire

Ref. no.	Page no.	Name	Age	Land	Value 1	Value 2	Husband(s)	Children	Father/mother	Other
1	1	[Roese de] Ros	34	D	£15		Edward de Ros	2 sons (eld. 13)	William Trussbut	Ranulf de Glanville has custody of heir (13)
2	1	Matilda de St Liz,	60	d	£10		William d'Albini	Son	Robert fitz Richard de Clare	
	63	(Suffolk) 'de Beaveria'	50	mp	£10					
3	3–4	w of Peter de Billinghay					Peter of Billinghay	Son (15)		Marital status unknown
4	4–5	Margeret of Brittany countess	40	D	£21	£23	(1) Conan earl of Brittany	1 dau.		Sister of William I of Scotland, her dau. Constance by Earl Conan m. Ranulf of Chester 1189. Her son by Humphrey de Bohun in custody of Margaret de Bohun. *Omitted from the *Rotuli*, *Pipe Roll 31 Henry II*, 206.
	6–7	of Richmond		D	6s 2d					
	62	(Suffolk)	30	D	£28			1 son (10)		
	84	(Cambridgeshire)		D	£27 10s		(2) Humphrey de Bohun	1 dau.*		
5	5	Aeliza of Tateshall	50				Robert fitz Hugh de Tateshall	10 sons	William fitz Walter of Wells Claxby	Niece of Gilbert de Gant
	9			D	£20					
	11			MP	100s					
6	6	w Peter Paynel*		I						
7	7	w Simon de Crevequer	24		100s		Simon de Crevequer	2 sons (eld. 5),	Robert fitz Ernis de Goxhill	Has custody of eldest son (Alexander)
	18				110s	£8 10s		2 daus		
8	7	Alice Basset		TiC	£8					Six bovates (?)
9	9	w William fitz Chetell					William fitz Chetell	1 son (12)		Has custody of son and fined not to marry

No.	Ref	Name	Age	Status	Fine	Value	Children	Husband	Other husband	Notes
10	10	w William de Vesci		none			1 son (14)			King has custody of son
11	10	? widow of Geoffrey de Turs, niece of Geoffrey de Neville, w Herbert fitz Gilbert	30	(land + D)	62s	£4 6s	7 sons (eld. 10)	Geoffrey de Turs Herbert fitz Gilbert		Archb. York has custody of heir, she has no land
12	11 / 45	Rohais de Bussei (Rutland)	50, 60	I, MP	£15, £4, £10		2 daus married	(1) William de Bussei (2) Baldwin Butelot	Baldwin fitz Gilbert (de Clare)	Eldest dau. (Cecily) m. John de Builli, other (Matilda) Hugh Wac. Two bros were dead; see RD, 11 n. 3
13	12	Agnes, w Walter of Haconby	40		£4		2 sons (eld. 18), 4 daus	Walter of Haconby	Colgrim de Welburn	Has custody of son; fined 5m
14	12	Matilda de la Haye	57	D	£30	£30 16s	3 daus	Richard de La Haye	William de Vernun	1 dau. (Nichola) m. Gerard de Camville (as her second husband, her first was William fitz Ernis), 1 dau. (Juliana) m. Richard de Humez, 1 m. William de 'Rolles'
15	13–14	[Matilda] de Caux	50+	D	£12	£14	1 dau. (m.)	Robert de Cauz	Richard Basset	Sister of William Basset, her dau. m. Ralf fitz Stephen, the king's chamberlain

Ref. no.	Page no.	Name	Age	Land	Value 1	Value 2	Husband(s)	Children	Father/mother	Other
16	14	[Isabella] w Albert Gresle m. Guy de Craon (1182)		D	Approx. £8 per year		(1) Albert Gresle (2) Guy de Craon	1 son (11)	Thomas Basset	Gilbert Basset has custody of heir's land, Nigel fitz Alexander has custody of heir; Corn had been sold for 100s 12d. The farm for one and three quarters of the year was £9 3s 8d
17	14–15	Matilda de Dives	35	MP	7m	10m 5s 4d	William de Diva	2 sons (eld. 10) 2 daus	Geoffrey de Wateville	William of Dives has custody of heir
18	15	Matilda countess of Chester	50+	D	£40		[Ranulf earl of Chester]		Robert earl of Gloucester	Farm is worth £22
19	15	Bertrada countess of Chester	29	D MP Other	Abroad Abroad 35 librates 10s	£40	Hugh earl of Chester	[Son and 4 daus]	Simon count d'Evreux	King assigned her 40 librates of land. NB. Her children are not mentioned
20	16	Avice de Crevequer	70		£14			3 daus m.		+ 1 KF, her grandson (22) is her heir
21	16–17	? mother of Ralf of Humberston	60+	D	< m			2 sons (30, 24), 1 dau. (20)		2 bovates of land, cognata Ralf fitz Drogo
22	17	Helewis of Swinhop	50+	d	£10		Simon de Canci			5m p.a. for son, half the fee is of the king, half of the count of Brittany, she is from Flanders

No.	Ref	Widow	Age	Status	Dower	Extra	Husband(s)	Heir / children	Grantee	Notes
23	17–	w Walter Furmage	24		5s	+ mill / 2m	Walter Furmage	Heir (not yet 1)	Thomas de Nevill	Dower not yet assigned?
24	19	Alice de Eincurt	19	MP	12s		John d'Eincurt	Heir (24)		10 librates
25	20	Matilda, w Reginald de Crevequer	60+	D	10 librates / 5m	£15	Reginald de Crevequer			2 sons, deceased: Alexander and Simon de Crevequer

Northamptonshire

No.	Ref	Widow	Age	Status	Dower	Extra	Husband(s)	Heir / children	Grantee	Notes
26	22–3	Emma, w Hugh fitz Robert and Robert de Saint Paul	40	D / MP	50s / 63s	£8	(1) Robert de Saint Paul (2) Hugh fitz Robert	Heir (20), dau. (18 m.), girl (16), 2 nuns, 2 juniors	Henry Tiart	D – Oxfordshire mp Brington + dower of a house Northants.
27	23	Matilda, w Ingelram de Dumard	40+	D	£7 6s 8d		Ingelram de Dumard			Has her third
28	23–4 / 27	Margeret Engaine, has m. Geoffrey Brito	50	? mp / d	6 librates		[(1) Richard Engaine (2) Geoffrey Brito]		Richard fitz Urse	Married without licence 6 librates
29	24	Alice, w Fulco de Lisores	50	D	100s	£14	Fulc de Lisores	4 sons, 9 daus		2 sons knights, she has custody of 3 daus to be married
30	24–5 / 28	Sibilla, w Geoffrey Ridel	50	D / D	65s 1d		Geoffrey Ridel	2 sons, 1 dau		Sister William Mauduit 20 librates
31	25 / 45 / 58	Alice, w Thomas de Beaufour	20	D / (d)	£20 / 8m first year: 36s 10d + 2 lb pepper		Thomas de Beaufour	1 son (2 or 3)	Waleran de Oiri	1 < KF Rutland: + farm of 36s 10d, 2 lb pepper, 3s + 3 sum oats. Nigel fitz Alexander has custody of heir's land

Ref. no.	Page no.	Name	Age	Land	Value 1	Value 2	Husband(s)	Children	Father/mother	Other
32	25 69	Ysoude, w Stephen de Beauchamp	40	MP TiC			Stephen de Beauchamp	1 son (4), 5 daus	Robert earl Ferrers	Plus land in Worcester and Essex
33	26	Beatrice, w Robert Mantel	30	D	30s		Robert Mantel	3 sons (eld. 10), 1 dau.		Robert Sauci' has custody of heir, other boys are with their mother
34	27–8	Albreda de Harcourt [Trussbut]	50	MP 1	£14 £4 10s		[William Trussbut]	4 sons, *1 dau. m. and widowed	Daughter of Roese, a sister and co-heir of William Peverel	Holds by will of the king, her dau. is Roese de Ros (no. 1 above). She has land in Yorkshire, *Pipe Roll* 31 Henry II, 60. Has 2 other daus, EYC, X, 9–10
35	28	Matilda Gulaffre	60	D	40s 4 librates			3 sons, 2 daus	Roger Gulaffre	Sister of Herbert Gulaffre; her son is a knight, she has given him some land. Dower is held of the honor of Peverell
36	29–30 76–7	Alice of Essex	60 80	d D	£27 £40	£30	[Roger fitz Richard (of Warkworth)]	2 sons, 1 dau. m.		Aunt of William de Mandeville, sister Aubrey de Vere earl of Oxford, her sons are knights, her dau. m. John the constable of Chester

Bedfordshire and Buckinghamshire

#		Name	Land							Notes
37	30–1	Alda de Beauchamp m. William Maubanc	30	MP	£9	£12	William Maubanc	4 daus (eld. 16)	Hugh de Beauchamp	Hugh Beauchamp has custody of heir's land
38	31	Maria de Traili	40		£14		Geoffrey de Trailli	2 sons, 2 daus		*Cognata* earl Simon Northampton, Walter her son is her heir. Other son a monk, 1 dau. m., 1 to be married, 1 a nun
39	31	Matilda de Chesney			£7		[Henry fitz Gerold]	2 sons (18, 12)		Fined £200 to have her land and wardship of her son's land; *Pipe Roll 30 Henry 11*, 72, *RD*, 31 n. 3
40	32–3	Beatrice, w Richard Gubion (jurors unsure gift of king?)	40+	D	18 librates		Richard Gubiun	7 sons, 6 daus		Plus land in Northants.
				d				1 son, knight, + x		
41	33	Matilda Malherbe	40	MP	£4 15s 4d	115s 4d		sons and daus		Sister of Robert Malherbe

Buckinghamshire

#		Name	Land							Notes
42	35	Hawise de Windsor	Son's land	d	£20		William de Windsor	1 son (18), 7 daus		Custody of heir + land 9 years + 3 KF = £20 in total; 2 daus are overseas, 2 are nuns, 3 in the king's gift, 6 daus in the king's gift
40			100s + 3 kf	d						
88										p. 88

Ref. no.	Page no.	Name	Age	Land	Value 1	Value 2	Husband(s)	Children	Father/mother	Other
43	37	Matilda, w Angot of Wycumbe	30	D	15s		Angot of Wycumbe	Heir (13) + 3 sons, 4 daus	Robert de 'Hauechford'	28d fixed rent she holds of Robert of Rouen, she has custody of son
44	37	w Roger Pinel	25	D					Jord de Ratdene	Has a third hide + 1 virgate.
45	37	Basilia, w David Pinel (bro. of the above)	18	D / heirs land	30s + 1 virgate + 2s 37d 2s 12d		David Pinel	*1 dau. (3)	Robert Tailard de Merlawe	*From entry of heir she has custody of heir, and lands for Gilbert Basset. Freehold tenure
46	38	Agnes de Montchesney	60	d	£22		[(1) Warin de Montchesney	3 sons (2 knights, 1 cleric), 2 daus m.	Pagan fitz John [by Sibyl, see Ancient Charters, no. 22]	Fee of earl of Sussex
	50	(Norfolk)		i	£11	£13				Fee of bishop of Ely 16 libr. fee of Roger Bigod
	54	(Norfolk – Burgh Apton)			£20					Norfolk
		(Norfolk – Sutton)		i	£16 librates	£9	(2) Hadenald de Bidun HKF, III, 103]			
	58	(Norfolk)			£7					52s 6d to feed family
47	39	Matilda w Hamo Meinfelin	46	d	£7 10s	£10	Hamo Meinfelin	*Heir 20 3 daus m., 1 dau. nun		*From entry of heir who has her MP
48	40–1	Emma de Langetot	60		£14	£15	Geoffrey fitz William	2 daus (30 and 24 m.)		2 daus are her heirs, their ages and names of their husbands given.
	44			D	£10	£11	HKF, III, 38			Fee of Rohais d'Auberville.
	56				60s + 1 KF, 3 parts of 1 KF + 2 KF + 2 parts KF					Has 2 enfoeffed knights in Eynesford hundred

No.	Ref	Widow	Age	Tenure	Dower / payment	Value	Former husband	Heir	New husband	Notes
49	42	Ida w William de 'Schirinton'	60	pars dni shf / l	£6 3s 6d + 2 geese, 4 capons, 1/6 30s, 62s 7d	£10; 40s	William de 'Sherrington'	3 sons (eld. 30), 3 daus	Hugh de Builli	King has her land and rents for 5 years
50	42	Claricia, w Peter Morell	45	l	1 < hide 1 KF		Peter Morell	Heir (15)*		*Fee heir 1 < hide + service 1 KF; Richard de Columbaris has custody of heir
51	43	*w Walter Burton		*D dau.	12s	19s	Walter Burton	*dau. (10)		* Mother holds all but 1 virgate of inheritance. Serjeanty tenure
52	43	Unnamed: grandmother of heir	70	d	2 parts town of Eye shared with her dau.					Heir + son of Gilbert Bolebec land = £10/£11 + 3m, effect of dower William Chp has custody of heir + land
53	43	Unnamed (mother of heir?)	40	d	As above		Gilbert Bolebec?	1 son		
54	43	Alice de Lathbury, w John de		d	£7	8	John de Bidune	4 daus m., 1 to be m.	Baldwin fitz Gilbert	The names of her daughters' husbands are given
	45	Bidune (Mauduit) Alice de Bidune, sister William Mauduit. (Rutland)	50	mp	£10 + 24s aid					
55	43–4	Matilda Vis-de-Lu, dau. John de Bidune		D 2 hides	40s			1 son (22)	John de Bidune	2 hides, son is with the king

Ref. no.	Page no.	Name	Age	Land	Value 1	Value 2	Husband(s)	Children	Father/mother	Other
56	44	Matilda of Cranwell, w Richard Albi	50		50s		Richard 'Albi'	2 sons (eld. 22), 9 daus	Anfrid, son of Ruald	King gave land
57	44	Matilda, dau. Robert de Riblemunt	80		16s					Small serjeantry tenure 40 acres; has no heir 2 field system

Huntingdonshire

Ref. no.	Page no.	Name	Age	Land	Value 1	Value 2	Husband(s)	Children	Father/mother	Other
58	47	Clemencia de St Clare	60	d	£20		Hubert de St Clare	[1 dau. Gunnor]		Her daughter m. William de Lanvalei
	66	(Herts – Westone?) Norfolk	80	d/mp	4s 12d +	100s				
59	47	Alice of Hainford	40	D	£8	£10	Gilbert Blund	Son (20)	Richard de Colechurch	Son Hubert Blund; bishop of Ely has custody of son
60	47	Agnes de Mundeville	50		£18	£20	Theobald Hautein ? Amundeville	3 sons T.H. (eld. 15/14) 2 sons (eld.	Robert Gresley	Holds of Humphrey de Bohun, has custody of sons
	55		40	D	£10			24), 2 daus by Eustace, 3 sons by Hugh		
61	48	Cecilia of Bowthorpe	50		£8; 1/4 KF held of her		(1) Eustace de Leiham (2) Hugh de Scotia			Eldest son has married niece of Earl Wimar
62	48–9 54	? w Richard de La Veile	30	D	£7		Richard de la Veile	2 sons (eld. 6), 5 daus	Amfrid Bute-turte	Custody of son with Thomas Basset, his uncle

No.	Ref	Name	n	Status	Amount	Husband	Children	Other husband	Notes
63	49 55	Matilda de Bidune	10	D	£6 £11 12s 2d £12 15s 8d	John de Bidune junior	1 son (15), 5 daus	Thomas fitz Bernard	Her mother Eugenia Picot (no. 70) has her and her land Holds of son
64	51	Ade de Tony	30	d	100s			Robet de Chaumunt	Holds of son
65	51	Amice de Limesey	60	d	40s	(Gerard de Limesey)	2 sons, ? daus	Hanelath de Bidune	Holds of son John, her sons are knights
66	53	? w Peter de Pelleville	46	D	100s £8	Peter de Pelleville	2 sons (24, x months), 2 daus (14, 5)		Eldest son leper, in the custody of the king in hospital, *nata de militibus*
67	53	Beatrice de Saiton	50	I, < KF	60s		6 sons, 1 dau.		Eldest son 21; her children *sunt nati de militibus*
68	53	Maria, w Guy l'Estrange	40	D D MP	14 – –	3 husbands: Guy l'Estrange			D + MP in 'divers counties'
69	54	*w Richard de Colechurch – re-marriage of widow				*(1) Richard de Colechurch *(2) Geoffrey Peche has m. her			Niece is heir m. to Roger 'de Dinosio', who has the land worth £12
70	55 87	*Eugenia Picot (Cambridgeshire)	30	D	£11 11s 2d 45s 6d £25	(1) William Malet (2) Thomas fitz Bernard	By T.B. 3 sons, 1 dau. m.	Ralph Picot of Kent	Custody of dau., sons (10, 8, 3), dau. (10), amerced £10 11s for forest offence of her husband in Oxfordshire, *Pipe Roll 31 Henry II*, 106
71	56	Lauretta Picot	40	I	£4 8s 10d 100s 12d	Hugh of Burdeleys	6 sons (eld. 26), 2 daus	Eustace Picot	Hugh d. 1181 (*HKF*, iii, 442)

Ref. no.	Page no.	Name	Age	Land	Value 1	Value 2	Husband(s)	Children	Father/mother	Other
Suffolk										
72	59	Mabel of Heliun	60	D	100s		[William of Heliun]	1 son	Roger fitz Richard de Clare	Heir Robert of Heliun
73	60	*? w Ralf de 'Haudebouill'		⅓ d			Ralf de Haudebouill	1 son (x months)		Ranulf de Glanville her uncle has her custody
74	60	Amfrid of Withermarsh	60		20s			7 children (eld. 18)		
75	60	Leticia, w William fitz Mabel	60		£4		William fitz Mabel			Sister of William Kivel, the king's butler
76	60	Cristiana, w Wareng de Hoxne	50		1m 2s		Wareng of Hoxne	1 son (18), 3 daus		Holds 2s of the bishop of Norwich, 5s of Archdeacon Walchelin
77	60–1	Matilda, w Philip de Colombièrs	40		40s rent < m		Philip de Colombièrs	Son (18)		Son has land of the king and is with him
78	61	Matilda, w Gilbert de Coleville	27	MP	7 librates rent £4 of fee of Roger Bigod		Gilbert de Coleville	2 sons (eld. 12), 6 daus	Robert de Boseville	She and her son are in custody of R.G., *maritagium* – fee of Stephen de Montchesney
79	61–2	Alexandria, mother of Gilbert de Coleville	60		20s 20s 11s 4s 6d					
80	62	* w (Herbert fitz Rolland)	40				Herbert fitz Rolland	1 son (13), 5 daus	Walter de 'Heccham'	Her husband was the king's jester

Hertfordshire

No.	Year	Name	Age		Value		Spouse	Children	Holder	Notes
81	66	Eva countess of Ireland (Essex)		D	£15	£20	(Richard Strong-bow earl of Clare)	Son (12)		The king has custody of the heir
	76			D	£12	£20				Sister of Pagan fitz John; her son's dau. m. Durand de Ostilli and Robert fitz Walter
82	67	Agnes de	50	d	£15	£20				
	77	Valoignes (Essex)	60+	i	£14					
	87	(Cambridgeshire))	60+	i(?)	£15					
83	67	Matilda de Louvetot	24	D	£12	£15	William de Louvetot	1 dau. (7)	Walter fitz Robert	(Sister Robert fitz Walter) Ralf Murdac has the heir

Essex

No.	Year	Name	Age		Value		Spouse	Children	Holder	Notes
84	69–70	(Leonia) w Robert de Stuteville		i	£24		Robert de Stuteville	1 son, 2 daus	Edward de Salisbury	Other land not mentioned in the *Rotuli*, see *RD*, 70 n. 1
85	71	Juliana countess of Norfolk		mp	£30 £10		Hugh Bigod earl of Norfolk			Sister earl of Aubrey de Vere, earl of Oxford, m. twice, her second husband was Walchelin Maminot of Kent, see *RD*, 71 n. 1
86	71	Alice de Tany		i	£7		(1) Roger de Reims	5 sons, 2 daus	William fitz Goscelin	Eldest child 20
	72			d	£7		(2) Picot de Tani			
87	72	Avice de Liston		i	40s		Godfrey *Camerarius*	1 son (21)	Robert de Liston	Waferer serjeanty
88	72	Avicia, w Nicholas de Stelbing			2m		Nicholas de Stelbing	2 sons (eld. 12)	John de Mariny	Eldest son in custody of Peter Picot, his land = 4m

Ref. no.	Page no.	Name	Age	Land	Value 1	Value 2	Husband(s)	Children	Father/mother	Other
89	75	w Guy de Rochford						2 sons (16, 12), 1 dau. (14)		? m. without permission
90	76	Beatrice de Say	80	mp	£15	£20	[William de Say, HKF, iii, 225]	[2 sons]		[Sister Geoffrey de Mandeville earl of Essex]
91	77	Margaret de Tany	60	d	£24			(Son)		
92	78	? w Turstin de Waltham	36	d	14s		[Ralf de Toeni]	2 sons (eld. 6 <), 2 daus 1 son		She's in custody of Richard fitz Aucher, she has heir's land
93	78	Mabel de Tresgoz			£12 17s		Geoffrey de Tresgoz	(17), 4 daus	Robert Gresley	Son in custody of Robert de Lucy for 8 years
94	79	Cristiana, dau. William Gerard	25		20s + 2m		William Gerard		William s of Gerard Toci	Niece of Roger de Langeford
95	81	? w Ralf 'de Busseuill'		D – 4 libr	£4 + £8, has son's land		Ralf 'de Busseuill'	2 sons (eld. 7), 2 daus	Osbert fitz Aucher	Has custody of son + land £8; the holding is worth £12, she has her third
96	81	Cristiani de Ruilli		1?	(100s)			Son (12)		Has custody of son and land
97	81	? w William 'Granuel' (?Grenevilles, Stanbourne?)			⅓ kf			x sons (eld. 18)		Has custody of son and land, fined 8m aid
98	82	? w Robert Camerarii			1 kf		Robert Camerarii	3 sons, 4 daus		Son has his land
99	82	*? mother of son of Robert fitz Odo			*¹/₁₀ kf		Robert fitz Odo	Son (6)		Has custody of heir and heir's land; Rotuli note their poverty

Cambridgeshire

100	83	Mabel, niece Ranulf de Glanville, w Albrici Picot	60+	d	40s	50s	Aubrey Picot	2 sons, 3 daus		Eldest son a knight
101	83	Two sisters in Papworth, eld.	60		30s	60s		4 sons, 2 daus	Gumeri de Stanton	Tenancy in frankalmoign
102		'Puella' (i.e. spinster?)	50							
103	84	Matilda de Ros	40	mp	12 librates		William de Ros	3 sons (eld. 20), 4 daus	Richard de Camville	Sister Gerard de Camville
104	85	Sibilla de Harlton	70+		10 librates			Son + 9 *infantes*	Roger de Gigney	Son Roger de Huntingfeld
105	85	Margaret de Montfichet	60+	d	£13	£16	William de Montfichet	Son + 3 *infantes*	Gilbert fitz Richard de Clare	
	86				£16	£20				
106	85	Juliana de Cathenis (de Cahagnes)		mp	£4	100s+	Richard de l'Estre	x boys (no. unknown)	Ralf de Cathenis	Her father held land in Dorset, her husband in Somerset (*RD*, 85 n. 4)
107	85–86	Matilda Peche Has married 3 times	50	mp	£8	£10	(Baldwin of Rochester)	11 children	Hamo Peche	married Baldwin *c.* 1166, her son is Ralf of Rochester
108	86	* [Isabella] w Gilbert Basset (alive), i.e. mother has remarried		D			(1) Walter de Bolebec (2) Gilbert Basset	1 dau.		* (Isabel) Bolebec – she has remarried

Bibliography

Manuscript sources

Aberystwyth, National Library of Wales
Penrice and Margam MSS: 11, 39; 113, 113c.

Chester, Cheshire County Record Office
DCH (Cholmondeley Collection) DCH/C/12.

Durham, Durham Cathedral Archives
DCD 3–4 EBOR 1; DCD 2–3 ACR 6.

Leeds, West Yorkshire Archive Service
Newby Hall Deeds: 268; 269.
Vyner Deeds: 447; 965; 969; 2023–4; 2026–7; 4819; 4939–40.

London, British Library
Additional Charters 5,526; 6,026; 10,594; 10,600; 10,601; 10,605; 10,607; 10,608; 19,574; 20,394; 20,559; 24,634; 28,479; 47,351; 47,517; 47,552; 47,615; 47,584.

Additional Manuscripts MS Add. 46,701 (Cartulary of Stixwould); MS Add. 35,296 (Spalding Register).

Cottonian Collection Cotton Charters: v. ii; xi. 45; xii. 4; xii. 17; xvi. 35; xvi. 37; xxvii. 21; xxvii. 121.

Detached seals Plaster casts: xlvii. 963; lxxvii. 33; lxxvii. 49; lxxvii. 71; lxxviii, 33; lxxviii. 74; lxviii. 48; lxxviii. 94; lxxix. 3; lxxix. 25; lxxix. 31; lxxix. 34; lxxix. 63; lxxviii. 61; lxxx. 9; lxxx. 91; lxxx. 21; lxxx. 94; lxxxi. 16, 17; lxxxi. 38; lxxxi. 42; lxxxvi. 42; cxxix. 658; cxxix. 4; cxxxii. 12; cxxxii. 17; ccxxxv. 59, 60.
Sulphur casts: D.C.E. 286, D.C.D. 218.

Egerton Charters 428; 431; 434.

Harleian Charters 43.C.15; 45.B.27; 45.E.33; 46.E.54; 47.I.14; 47.I.17; 48.F.27; 49.G.21; 49.H.3; 50.B.19; 50.B.21; 50.B.23; 50.B.33; 50.F.32; 51.B.20; 51.B.21; 51.G.41; 52.G.44; 54.B.26; 54.E.9; 55.E.13; 55.G.9; 56.E.2; 57.E.24; 83.D.30; 83.F.45; 84.D.1; 84.I.22; 85.B.17; 85.B.18; 85.G.17; 86.B.5; 86.C.40; 112.C.27.

Stowe Charters 158; 159.

London, Public Record Office
DL 25/41 Duchy of Lancaster: Deeds, Series L.

DL 27/23; /53–5; /61 Duchy of Lancaster: Deeds Series LS.
E 42/497 Exchequer: Treasury of Receipt: Ancient Deeds, Series AS.
E 329 Exchequer: Augmentation Office: Ancient Deeds, Series BS.
E 198/1/2 Exchequer: King's Remembrancer: Records Relating to Feudal Tenure and Distraints of Knighthood. *Rotuli de Dominabus.*

Manchester, John Rylands University Library
Rylands Charters: 1277; 1808; 1809.

Paris, Bibliothèque Nationale
Bourgogne Collection: 78, 121.
Nouvelle Acquisitions: 1649.2.
Cartulary of St Evroult: MS Latin 11,055.

Seen in transcription by courtesy of Professor Crouch's Comital *Acta* Project, University College, Scarborough

Beverley, Humberside County Record Office
Chichester-Constable Deeds: RO DDCC/76/1; RO DDCC/135/1; DDCC135/51 (2).

Cambridge, Cambridge University Library
Cartulary of Thorney: MS Add. 3,021.

Cambridge, King's College Library
OGB/23 (old deed 17); OGB/24 (old deed 18).

Exeter, Devon Record Office
Fortescue Deeds: 1262/M T531.

London, British Library
Cartulary of Woodford of Bretingby: MS Cotton Claudius A xiii.
Cartulary of Newnham: MS Harley 3656.
Cartulary of Missenden: MS Harley 3688.
Cartulary of Twynham: MS Cotton Tiberius D vi, pt 2.

London, Public Record Office
31/8/140B, pt 1 Record Commission transcripts, Series, Cartulaire de la Basse-Normandie.
C 56/16 Chancery: Confirmation Rolls, Confraternity Roll 3 Henry VII.
C 115/KL/6681 Masters' Exhibits, Duchess of Norfolk Deeds, Cartulary of Llanthony.

Northampton, Northamptonshire Record Office
Montagu-Boughton deeds: 'Luffwick Old Deeds' Box X8669 (formerly Box 24, no. 1).
Finch Hatton MS 170 (*Hatton's Book of Seals*).

Paris, Bibliothèque Nationale
Collection du Vexin, xiii.

Rouen, Bibliothèque Municipale
Cartulary of Foucarmont: Y 13, fo. 72r.

San Marino, California, Huntingdon Library
Stowe Grenville evidences: STG Box 5, no. 18.

Printed sources

Abstract of the Charters and other Documents contained in the Chartulary of the Cistercian Abbey of Fountains in the West Riding of the County of York, ed. W. T. Lancaster (2 vols, Leeds: J. Whitehead & Sons, 1915).
'The acts of King Stephen, and the battle of the Standard, by Richard, prior of Hexham, from A.D. 1135 to A.D. 1139', in Joseph Stevenson (ed.), *The Church Historians of England* (5 vols, London: Seeleys, 1853–58), IV (i) (1856), pp. 33–58.
Adam of Eynsham, *Magna Vita Sancti Hugonis: The Life of St Hugh of Lincoln*, ed. D. L. Douie and D. H. Farmer (2 vols, 1961; corrected reprint, Oxford: Clarendon Press, 1985).
Ancient Charters, Royal and Private, Prior to A.D. 1200, ed. J. H. Round (Pipe Roll Society, old ser., 10, 1888).
The Anglo-Norman Voyage of St Brendan, ed. I. Short and B. Merrilees (Manchester: Manchester University Press, 1979).
Annales Cestriensis: or Chronicle of the Abbey of S. Werburg, at Chester, ed. R. C. Christie (Record Society of Lancashire and Cheshire, 14, 1887 for 1886).
Barnes, Patrica M., and C. F. Slade (eds), *A Medieval Miscellany for Doris Mary Stenton* (Pipe Roll Society, new ser., 36, 1962 for 1960).
Birch, W. De G., *Catalogue of Seals in the Department of Manuscripts in the British Museum* (6 vols, London: Trustees of the British Museum, 1887–1900).
Blair, C. H. Hunter, 'Durham seals: catalogue of seals at Durham from a manuscript made by the Reverend Greenwell', *Archaeologia Aeliana*, 3rd ser., 7–9 (1911–13), 11–16 (1914–19).
Calendar of Charters and Documents relating to the Abbey of Robertsbridge co. Sussex, Preserved at Penshurst among the Muniments of Lord de Lisle and Dudley, ed. P. Sidney (London: printed by Spottiswoode & Co., 1873).

Calendar of Documents Preserved in France, 918–1206, ed. J. H. Round (London: HMSO, 1899).

Calendar of the Laing Charters, A.D. 854–1837, belonging to the University of Edinburgh, ed. J. Anderson (Edinburgh: Thin, by authority of the University of Edinburgh, 1899).

Capellanus, Andreas, *On Love*, ed. P. G. Walsh (London: Duckworth, 1982).

Cartulaire des Îles Normandes: Recueil des documents concernant l'histoire de ces Îles, conservés aux archives du département de la Manche et du Calvados, de la Bibliothèque Nationale, du Bureau des Rôles, du château de Warwick, ed. N. V. L. Rybot (Jersey: Beresford Library for the Société Jersiaise, 1924).

Cartularium Prioratus de Colne, ed. John L. Fisher (Essex Archaeological Society, Occasional Publications, I, 1946).

The Cartulary of Holy Trinity Aldgate, ed. G. A. J. Hodgett (London Record Society, 7, 1971).

Cartulary of St Mary Clerkenwell, ed. W. O. Hassall (Camden Society, 3rd ser., 71, 1949).

The Cartulary of St Michael's Mount: Hatfield House MS No. 315, ed. P. L. Hull (Devon and Cornwall Record Society, new ser., 5, 1962).

Cartulary of the Abbey of Old Wardon, ed. G. H. Fowler (Bedfordshire Historical Society, 13, 1930).

Charters and Documents illustrating the History of the Cathedral, City and Diocese of Salisbury, ed. W. Rich Jones and W. Dunn McCray (RS, 97, London: Eyre & Spottiswoode, 1891).

Charters and Records of Hereford Cathedral, ed. W. W. Capes (Hereford: Wilson & Phillips, 1908).

The Charters of Duchess Constance of Brittany and her Family, 1171–1221, ed. Judith Everard and Michael Jones (Woodbridge: Boydell, 1999).

The Charters of the Anglo-Norman Earls of Chester, c. 1071–1237, ed. G. Barraclough (Record Society of Lancashire and Cheshire, 126, 1988).

Charters of the Honour of Mowbray, 1107–91, ed. D. Greenway (London: Oxford University Press, for the British Academy, 1972).

Chartes au Prieuré de Longueville de l'ordre de Cluny au diocèse de Rouen antérieures à 1204 publieés avec introduction et notes après les origineaux conservés aux Archives de la Seine-Inférieure par Paul le Cacheux (Rouen: Société d'Histoire de Normandie, 1934).

The Chartulary of St John of Pontefract, ed. R. Holmes (2 vols, Yorkshire Archaeological Society, Record Series, 25, 30, 1899 for 1898, 1902 for 1901).

The Chartulary of the High Church of Chichester, ed. W. D. Peckham (Sussex Record Society, 46, 1946 for 1942–43).

The Chronicle of John of Worcester, ed. R. R. Darlington and P. McGurk (3 vols, Oxford: Clarendon Press, 1995–).

'The chronicle of John, prior of Hexham, from A.D. 1130 to A.D. 1154', in *The Church Historians of England*, ed. Joseph Stevenson (5 vols, London: Seeleys, 1853–58), IV (i) (1856), pp. 1–32.

Chronicon Hugonis Abbatis Flaviancensis, Monumenta Germaniae Historica, Scriptores, VII (Monumenta Germaniae Historica Scriptorum).

Chronicon Monasterii de Abingdon, ed. J. Stevenson (2 vols, London: Longman, RS, 2, 1858).

The Cistercian World: Monastic Writings of the Twelfth Century, ed. P. Matarasso (London: Penguin, 1993).

Descriptive Catalogue of the Charters and Muniments in the Possession of the Rt Hon. Lord Fitz-Hardinge, at Berkeley Castle, ed. I. H. Jeayes (Bristol: C. T. Jefferies & Sons, 1892).

Documents illustrative of the Social and Economic History of the Danelaw, ed. F. M. Stenton (London: Oxford University Press, for the British Academy, 1920).

Dugdale, William, *Monasticon Anglicanum*, ed. J. Caley, H. Ellis and B. Bandinel (6 vols in 8, London: Longman . . . , Lackington . . . , and Joseph Harding, 1817–30).

Eadmer, *Historia Novorum in Anglia*, ed. M. Rule (RS, 81, London, 1884).

Earldom of Gloucester Charters: The Charters and Scribes of the Earls and Countesses of Gloucester to A.D. 1217, ed. R. B. Patterson (Oxford: Clarendon Press, 1973).

'Charters of the earldom of Hereford, 1095–1201', ed. D. Walker, in *Camden Miscellany*, XXII (Camden Society, 4th ser., 1, 1964), pp. 1–75.

'Early charters of Sibton Abbey, Suffolk', ed. R. Allen Brown, in Patricia M. Barnes and C. F. Slade (eds), *A Medieval Miscellany for Doris Mary Stenton* (Pipe Roll Society, new ser., 36, 1962 for 1960), pp. 65–76.

The Early Charters of Waltham Abbey, 1062–1230, ed. R. Ransford (Woodbridge: Boydell, 1989).

The Early Records of Medieval Coventry, ed. P. R. Coss (British Academy, Records of Social and Economic History, new ser., 11, 1986).

Early Yorkshire Charters: vols I–III, ed. W. Farrer (Edinburgh: Ballantyne Hanson, 1914–16); *Index* (to vols I–III), ed. C. T. Clay and E. M. Clay (Yorkshire Archaeological Society, Record Series, Extra Series, 4, 1942); vols IV–XII, ed. C. T. Clay (Yorkshire Archaeological Society, Record Series, Extra Series, 1–3, 5–10, 1935–65).

Ellis, R. H., *Catalogue of Seals in the Public Record Office: Personal Seals* (2 vols, London: HMSO, 1978, 1981).

English Episcopal Acta, II, *Canterbury, 1162–90*, ed. C. R. Cheney and B. E. A. Jones (London: Oxford University Press, for the British Academy, 1986).

English Episcopal Acta, V, *York, 1070–1154*, ed. J. E. Burton (Oxford: Oxford University Press, for the British Academy, 1988).

English Lawsuits from William I to Richard I, ed. R. C. Van Caenegem (2 vols, Selden Society, 106, 107, 1990–1).

Étienne de Fougères, *Le Livre des manières*, ed. R. A. Lodge, Textes Littéraires Français, 275 (Geneva: Droz, 1979).

Eynsham Cartulary, ed. H. E. Salter (2 vols, Oxford Historical Society, 49, 51, 1907–8).

Facsimiles of Early Charters from Northamptonshire Collections, ed. F. M. Stenton (Northamptonshire Record Society, 4, 1930).

Facsimiles of Early Charters in Oxford Muniment Rooms, ed. H. E. Salter (Oxford: Oxford University Press, 1929).

Feodarium Prioratus Dunelmensis: A Survey of the Estates of the Prior and Convent of Durham compiled in the Fifteenth Century. Illustrated by the Original Grants and other Evidences, ed. William Greenwell (Surtees Society, 58, 1872).

Gaimar, *Lestorie des Engles solum la Translacion Maistre Geffrei Gaimar*, ed. S. Thomas Duffy and C. Trice Martin (2 vols, RS, 91, London, 1888–89).

Gaimar, *L'Estoire des Engleis*, ed. A. Bell (Anglo-Norman Text Society, 14–16, 1960).

Geoffrey of Monmouth, *The History of the Kings of Britain*, trans. L. Thorpe (Harmondsworth: Penguin, 1966).

Gervase of Canterbury, *The Historical Works of Gervase of Canterbury: The Chronicles of the Reigns of Stephen, Henry II, and Richard I, by Gervase, the Monk of Canterbury*, ed. W. Stubbs (2 vols, RS, 73, London, 1879–80).

Gesta Regis Henrici Secundi Benedicti Abbatis: The Chronicle of the Reigns of Henry II, and Richard I, A.D. 1169–92, Known Commonly under the Name of Bendict of Peterborough, ed. W. Stubbs (2 vols, RS, 49, London, 1867).

Herbert de Losinga, bishop of Norwich, *The Life, Letters, and Sermons of Bishop Herbert de Losinga (b. c. A.D. 1050, d. 1119): The Letters (as Translated by the Editors) being Incorporated with the Life, and the Sermons being now first Edited from a MS in the Possession of the University of Cambridge, and Accompanied with an English Translation and Notes*, ed. E. Meyrick Goulburn and H. Symonds (2 vols, Oxford and London: James Parker & Co., 1878).

Histoire de la Guillaime le Maréchal, ed. and trans. P. Meyer, in *English Historical Documents*, III, 1189–1327, ed. H. Rothwell (London: Eyre & Spottiswoode, 1975), pp. 81–103.

Historia Regum Brittanie of Geoffrey of Monmouth, I: Bern, Bürgerbibliothek MS. 568, ed. N. Wright (Cambridge: Brewer, 1985).

Hugh of Fleury, *Ex Historia Ecclesiastica editio prima libris IIII digesta*, ed. G. Waitz (Monumenta Germaniae Historica Scriptorum, IX, 1851), 349–53.

Jordan Fantosme's Chronicle, ed. R. C. Johnstone (Oxford: Clarendon Press, 1981).

Laing, H., *Descriptive Catalogue of Impressions from ancient Scottish Seals, Royal, Baronial, Ecclesiastical and Municipal, embracing a Period from A.D. 1094 to the Commonwealth* (Edinburgh: printed T. Constable, 1850).

Laing, H., *Supplemental Descriptive Catalogue of Ancient Scottish Seals, Royal, Baronial, Ecclesiastical and Municipal, embracing the Period from A.D. 1150 to the Eighteenth Century* (Edinburgh: Edmonston & Douglas, 1866).

The Letters and Charters of Gilbert Foliot, Abbot of Gloucester (1139–48), Bishop of Hereford (1148–63) and London (1163–87), ed. A. Morey and C. N. L. Brooke (London: Cambridge University Press, 1967).

The Letters of John of Salisbury, ed. W. J. Millor, H. E. Butler and C. N. L. Brooke (2 vols, vol. 1, London: Nelson, 1955; vol. 2, Oxford: Clarendon Press, 1979).

The Letters of Lanfranc, Archbishop of Canterbury, ed. H. Clover and M. Gibson (Oxford: Clarendon Press, 1979).

The Life of Christina of Markyate: A Twelfth-century Recluse, ed. and trans. C. H. Talbot (Oxford: Clarendon Press, 1959).

Luffield Priory Charters, ed. G. R. Elvey (2 vols, Northamptonshire Record Society, 22, 26, 1968 for 1956–57, 1975 for 1973; jointly published with the Bedfordshire Record Society).

Magnum Rotulum Scaccarii vel magnum rotulum pipae, de anno tricesmo primo regni Henrici Primi, ed. J. Hunter ([London]: Record Commission, 1833).

Map, Walter, *De Nugis Curialium: Courtiers' Trifles*, ed. M. R. James, revised by C. N. L. Brooke and R. A. B. Mynors (Oxford: Clarendon Press, 1983).

Memoriale Fratris Walteri de Coventria, ed. W. Stubbs (2 vols, RS, 58, London, 1872, 1873).

Les Oeuvres poétiques de Baudri de Bourgeuil (1046–1130), ed. P. Abrahams (Paris: Champion, 1926).

'The original charters of Herbert and Gervase abbots of Westminster (1121–57)', ed. P. Chaplais, in Patricia M. Barnes and C. F. Slade (eds), *A Medieval Miscellany for Doris Mary Stenton* (Pipe Roll Society, new ser., 36, 1962 for 1960), pp. 89–110.

Paris, Matthew, *Historia Anglorum*, ed. F. Madden (3 vols, RS, 44, London, 1866–69).

Paris, Matthew, *Chronica Majora*, ed. H. R. Luard (7 vols, RS, 57, London, 1872–83).

Patrologiae cursus completus, series Latina, ed. J. P. Migne (221 vols, Paris, 1852–1904).

Petri Blesensis Bathoniensis Archidiaconi Opera Omnia, ed. J. A. Giles (4 vols, Oxford: I. H. Parker, 1846–47), repr. Migne, *Patrologiae cursus completus, Patrologia Latina*, 207 (1904).

Plumpton Correspondence: A Series of Letters, Chiefly Domestick, Written in the Reigns of Edward IV, Richard III, Henry VII, and Henry VIII, ed. T. Stapleton (Camden Society, old ser., 4, 1839).

Reading Abbey Cartularies, ed. B. R. Kemp (2 vols, Camden Society, 4th ser., 31, 33, 1986, 1987).

Records of the Borough of Leicester: Being a Series of Extracts from the Archives of the Corporation of Leicester, 1509–1603, ed. Mary Bateson, Helen Stocks, G. A. Chinnery and A. N. Newman (7 vols, London: C. J. Clay, under the authority of the Corporation of Leicester, 1899–1974).

Recueil des Actes des ducs de Normandie de 911 à 1066, ed. M. Fauroux (Mémoires de la Société des antiquaires de Normandie, 36, Caen, 1961).

Regesta Regum Anglo-Normannorum, ed. H. W. C. Davis, C. Johnson, H. A. Cronne and R. H. C. Davis (4 vols, Oxford: Clarendon Press, 1913–69).

Regesta Regum Anglo-Normannorum: The Acta of William I, 1066–87, ed. D. Bates (Oxford and New York: Clarendon Press, 1998).

Regesta Regum Scottorum, II: The Acts of William I, King of Scots, 1165–1214, ed. G. W. S. Barrow (Edinburgh: Edinburgh University Press, 1971).

The Registrum Antiquissimum of the Cathedral Church of Lincoln: Volume I, ed. C. W. Foster (Lincoln Record Society, 27, 1931).

The Registrum Antiquissimum of the Cathedral Church of Lincoln: Volume II, ed. C. W. Foster (Lincoln Record Society, 28, 1933).

The Registrum Antiquissimum of the Cathedral Church of Lincoln: Facsimiles of Charters in Volumes V and VI (Lincoln Record Society, 42, 1950).

The Registrum Antiquissimum of the Cathedral Church of Lincoln: Volume VIII, ed. K. Major (Lincoln Record Society, 51, 1958).

Richard of Devizes, *The Chronicle of Richard of Devizes of the Time of King Richard the First*, ed. J. T. Appleby (London and New York: Nelson, 1963).

Roger of Howden, *Chronica Rogeri de Hoveden*, ed. W. Stubbs (4 vols, RS, 51, London, 1868–71).

Rotuli de dominabus et pueris et puellis de XII comitatibus [1185], ed. J. H. Round (Pipe Roll Society, 35, 1913).

Rotuli Hundredorum temp. Hen. III. & Edw. I. in Turr' Lond. et in Curia Receptae Scaccarii Westm. asservati, ed. W. Illingworth (2 vols, London: Record Commission, 1812–18).

Sir Christopher Hatton's Book of Seals: To which is Appended a Select List of the Works of Frank Merry Stenton, ed. L. C. Loyd and D. M. Stenton (Northamptonshire Record Society, 15, 1950).

'Some charters relating to the honour of Bacton', ed. B. Dodwell, in Patricia M. Barnes and C. F. Slade (eds), *A Medieval Miscellany for Doris Mary Stenton* (Pipe Roll Society, new ser., 36, 1962 for 1960), pp. 147–65.

'Some Revesby charters of the soke of Bolingbroke', ed. Dorothy M. Owen, in Patricia M. Barnes and C. F. Slade (eds), *A Medieval Miscellany for Doris Mary Stenton* (Pipe Roll Society, new ser., 36, 1962 for 1960), pp. 221–34.

The Thurgarton Cartulary, ed. T. Foulds (Stamford: Watkins, 1994).

The Topographer and Genealogist, 1 (1846).

Tractatus de legibus et consuetudinibus regni Anglie qui Glanvilla vocatur, ed. G. D. G. Hall (London: Nelson, 1965, repr. 1993).

Transcripts of Charters relating to the Gilbertine Houses of Sixle, Ormsby, Catley, Bullington and Alvingham, ed. F. M. Stenton (Lincoln Record Society, 18, 1922).

Vitalis, Ordericus, *The Ecclesiastical History of Orderic Vitalis*, ed. M. Chibnall (6 vols, Oxford: Clarendon Press, 1969–80).

William of Malmesbury, *Historia Novella*, ed. K. R. Potter (London and New York: Nelson, 1955).

William of Newburgh, 'Historia rerum anglicarum', ed. R. Howlett, in *Chronicles of the Reigns of Stephen, Henry II and Richard I* (4 vols, RS, 82, London, 1884–85), vols I–II.

Williams, D. H., *Catalogue of Seals in the National Museum of Wales* (Cardiff: National Museum of Wales, 1993–), I.

Wulfric of Haselbury, by John, Abbot of Ford, ed. M. Bell (Somerset Record Society, 47, 1933).

Yorkshire Deeds, Volume VII, ed. C. T. Clay (Yorkshire Archaeological Society Record Series, 83).

Secondary literature

Abercrombie, N., S. Hill and B. S. Turner, *The Dominant Ideology Thesis* (London: Allen Unwin, 1980).

Ailes, A., 'Heraldry in twelfth-century England: the evidence', in D. Williams (ed.), *England in the Twelfth Century: Proceedings of the 1988 Harlaxton Symposium* (Woodbridge: Boydell, 1990), pp. 1–16.

Alexander, J. W., *Ranulf of Chester: A Relic of the Conquest* (Athens GA: University of Georgia Press, 1983).

Baker, D. (ed.), *Medieval Women* (Studies in Church History, Subsidia I, Oxford, 1978).

Barlow, F., 'The effects of the Norman Conquest', in C. T. Chevallier (ed.), *The Norman Conquest: Its Setting and Impact* (London: Eyre & Spottiswoode, 1966), pp. 125–61.

Barthélemy, D., *La Société dans le comté de Vendôme: de l'an mil au XIV siècle* (Paris: Fayard, 1993).

Bartlett, R., 'Colonial aristocracies of the high Middle Ages', in R. Bartlett and A. Mackay (eds), *Medieval Frontier Societies* (Oxford: Clarendon Press, 1989), pp. 23–47.

Bartlett, R., *The Making of Europe: Conquest, Colonization and Cultural Change* (London: Allen Lane, 1993).

Bartlett, R., 'Hair in the Middle Ages', *TRHS*, 6th ser., 4 (1994), 43–60.

Bates, D., 'The prosopographical study of Anglo-Norman royal charters', in K. S. B. Keats-Rohan (ed.), *Family Trees and the Roots of Politics* (Woodbridge: Boydell, 1997), pp. 89–102.

Beer, F., *Women and Mystical Experience in the Middle Ages* (Woodbridge: Boydell, 1992).

Bell, S. Groag, 'Medieval women book owners: arbiters of lay piety and ambassadors of culture', *Signs: Journal of Women in Culture and Society*, 7: 4 (1982), 742–68, repr. in M. Erler and M. Kowaleski (eds), *Women and Power in the Middle Ages* (Athens GA and London: University of Georgia Press, 1988), pp. 149–87.

Bennett, J., 'Widows in the medieval English countryside', in L. Mirrer (ed.), *Upon my Husband's Death: Widows in the Literature and Histories of Medieval Europe* (Ann Arbor MI: University of Michigan Press, 1992), pp. 69–114.

Bennet, M., 'Military masculinity in England and northern France, *c.* 1050–*c.* 1225', in D. M. Hadley (ed.), *Masculinity in Medieval Europe* (London and New York: Addison Wesley Longman, 1998), pp. 71–88.

Biancalana, J., 'Widows at common law: the development of common law dower', *Irish Jurist*, 23 (1988), 255–329.

Biancalana, J., 'The writs of dower and chapter 49 of Westminster' I, *Cambridge Law Journal*, 49 (1990), 91–116.

Blair, C. H. Hunter, 'Armorials on English seals from the twelfth century to the sixteenth', *Archaeologia*, 89 (1943), 1–26.

Bloch, H., *Etymologies and Genealogies: A Literary Anthropology of the French Middle Ages* (Chicago: University of Chicago Press, 1983).

Bloom, J. Harvey, *English Seals* (London: Methuen, 1906).

Bolgar, R. R., *The Classical Heritage and its Beneficiaries* (Cambridge: Cambridge University Press, 1954).

Bony, P., 'An introduction to the study of Cistercian seals: the Virgin as mediatrix, then protectrix, on the seals of Cistercian abbeys', *Studies in Cistercian Art and Art and Architecture*, 3 (1987), 201–40.

Borrie, M. A. F., 'A sealed charter of the empress Matilda', *British Museum Quarterly*, 34–5 (1969–71), 104–7.

Bouchard, C. B., 'Patterns of women's names in royal lineages, ninth–eleventh centuries', *Medieval Prosopography*, 9: 1 (1988), 1–32.

Bouchard, C. B., 'The migration of women's names in the upper nobility, ninth–twelfth centuries', *Medieval Prosopography*, 9: 2 (1988), 1–19.

Brown, S. A., and M. W. Herren, 'The *Adelae Comitissae* of Baudri of Bourgeuil and the Bayeux Tapestry', *ANS*, 16 (1994 for 1993), 55–73.

Browne, J. Wogan-, ' "Clerc u lai, muïne u dame": women and Anglo-Norman hagiography in the twelfth and thirteenth centuries', in C. M. Meale (ed.), *Women and Literature in Britain, 1150–1500* (Cambridge: Cambridge University Press, 1993), pp. 61–85.

Brundage, J. A., 'Widows as disadvantaged persons in medieval canon law', in L. Mirrer (ed.), *Upon my Husband's Death: Widows in the Literature and Histories of Medieval Europe* (Ann Arbor MI: University of Michigan Press, 1992), pp. 193–206.

Brundage, J., 'Widows and remarriage: moral conflicts and their resolution in classical canon law', in S. Sheridan Walker (ed.), *Wife and Widow in Medieval England* (Ann Arbor MI: University of Michigan Press, 1993), pp. 17–31.

Buckstaff, F. L., 'Married women's property in Anglo-Saxon and Anglo-Norman law and the origins of the common law of dower', *Annals of the American Academy of Political and Social Science*, 4 (1894), 233–64.

Bynum, C. Walker, *Holy Feast and Holy Fast: The Religious Significance of Food to Medieval Women* (Berkeley CA and London: University of California Press, 1987).

Bynum, C. Walker, *Fragmentation and Redemption: Essays on Gender and the Human Body in Medieval Religion* (New York: Zone, 1991).

Chassel, J. L., 'L'usage du sceau au XII^c siècle', in Françoise Gasparri (ed.), *Le XII^c siècle: mutations et renouveau en France dans le première moitié du XII^c siècle* (Paris: Léopard d'or, 1994).

Cherry, J., 'The seal of Haltemprice priory', in D. Buckton and T. A. Heslop (eds), *Studies in Medieval Art and Architecture presented to Peter Lasko* (Stroud: Sutton, 1994), pp. 14–23.

Chibnall, M., 'Women in Orderic Vitalis', *Haskins Society Journal*, 2 (1990), 105–21.

Chibnall, M., *The Empress Matilda: Queen Consort, Queen Mother and Lady of the English* (Oxford: Blackwell, 1991).

Chibnall, M., 'The charters of the empress Matilda', in G. S. Garnett and J. G. H. Hudson (eds), *Law and Government in Medieval England and Normandy: Essays in Honour of Sir James Holt* (Cambridge: Cambridge University Press, 1994), pp. 276–98.

Cirlot, J. E., *A Dictionary of Symbols*, trans. from the Spanish by J. Sage (2nd edn, London: Routledge, 1971).

Clanchy, M., *From Memory to Written Record: England, 1066–1307* (London: Edward Arnold, 1979; 2nd edn, Oxford: Blackwell, 1993).

Clark, C., 'Women's names in post-Conquest England: observations and speculations', *Speculum*, 80 (1978), 223–51.

Clark, C., 'English personal names ca. 650–1300: some prosopographical readings', *Medieval Prosopography*, 8 (1987), 31–60.

Cornog, W. H., 'The poems of Robert Partes', *Speculum*, 12 (1937), 215–50.

Coss, P., *The Knight in Medieval England, 1000–1400* (Stroud: Sutton, 1993).

Coss, Peter, 'Knights, esquires and the origins of social gradation in England', *TRHS*, 6th ser., 5 (1995), 155–78.

Crick, J. C., *The Historia Regum Britannie of Geoffrey of Monmouth, IV: Dissemination and Reception in the later Middle Ages* (Cambridge: Brewer, 1991).

Crouch, D., *The Beaumont Twins: The Roots and Branches of Power in the Twelfth Century* (Cambridge: Cambridge University Press, 1986).

Crouch, D., *The Image of Aristocracy, 1000–1300* (London: Routledge, 1992).

Crouch, D., 'From Stenton to McFarlane: models of societies of the twelfth and thirteenth centuries', *TRHS*, 6th ser., 5 (1995), 179–200.

Crouch, D., 'The local influence of the earls of Warwick, 1088–1242: a study in decline and resourcefulness', *Midland History*, 21 (1996), 1–22.

Dalton, P., 'Aiming at the impossible: Ranulf II earl of Chester and Lincolnshire in the reign of King Stephen', *JCAS*, 71 (1991), 109–34.

Dalton, P., '*In Neutro Latere*: the armed neutrality of Ranulf II earl of Chester in King Stephen's reign', *ANS*, 14 (1992 for 1991), 39–59.

Dalton, P., *Conquest, Anarchy and Lordship: Yorkshire, 1066–1154* (Cambridge: Cambridge University Press, 1994).

Davies, R. R., *Domination and Conquest: The Experience of Ireland, Scotland and Wales, 1100–1300* (Cambridge and New York: Cambridge University Press, 1990).

Davies, R. R., 'The peoples of Britain and Ireland, 1100–1400', II 'Names, boundaries and regnal solidarities', *TRHS*, 6th ser., 5 (1995), 1–20.

DeAragon, R. C., 'In pursuit of aristocratic women: a key to success in Norman England', *Albion*, 14 (1982), 258–67.

DeAragon, R. C., 'Dowager countesses, 1069–1230', *ANS*, 17 (1995 for 1994), 87–100.

Dixon, S., 'Conclusion – the enduring theme: domineering dowagers and scheming concubines', in B. Garlick and others (eds), *Stereotypes of Women in Power: Historical Perspectives and Revisionist Views* (New York and London: Greenwood Press, 1992), pp. 209–25.

Dronke, P., *Women Writers of the Middle Ages: A Critical Study of Texts from Perpetua (203) to Marguerite Porete (1310)* (Cambridge: Cambridge University Press, 1984).

Duby, G., 'Lignage, noblesse et chevalerie au XIIe siècle dans la region mâconnaise', *Annales: Économies, Sociétés, Civilisations*, 27 (1972), 803–23.

Duby, G., *Medieval Marriage: Two Models from Twelfth-century France* (Baltimore MD and London: Johns Hopkins University Press, 1978).

Duby, G., *Le Chevalier, la femme, et le prêtre* (Paris, 1981), trans. B. Bray, *The Knight, the Lady and the Priest: The Making of Modern Marriage in Medieval France* (New York: Pantheon, 1983).

Duby, G., 'The matron and the mis-married woman: perceptions of marriage in northern France *circa* 1100', in T. H. Aston, P. R. Coss, C. Dyer and J. Thirsk (eds), *Social Relations and Ideas: Essays in Honour of R. H. Hilton* (Cambridge: Cambridge University Press, 1983), pp. 89–108.

Duby, G., 'Women and power', in T. N. Bisson (ed.), *Cultures of Power: Lordship, Status, and Process in Twelfth-century Europe* (Philadelphia: University of Pennsylvania Press, 1995), pp. 69–85.

Duby, G., *Women of the Twelfth Century*, trans. J. Birrell (2 vols, Oxford: Polity Press, 1997).

Elkins, S. K., *Holy Women of Twelfth-century England* (Chapel Hill NC and London: University of North Carolina Press, 1988).

Erler, M., and M. Kowaleski (eds), *Women and Power in the Middle Ages* (Athens GA and London: University of Georgia Press, 1988).

Farmer, D. H., 'The canonization of St Hugh of Lincoln', *The Architectural and Archaeological Society of the County of Lincoln Report and Papers*, new ser., 6, pt 2 (1956), 86–117.

Farmer, D. H., 'The cult and canonization of St Hugh', in H. Mayr-Harting (ed.), *St Hugh of Lincoln: Lectures delivered at Oxford and Lincoln to celebrate the Eighth Centenary of St Hugh's Consecration as Bishop of Lincoln* (Oxford: Clarendon Press, 1987), pp. 75–87.

Farrer, W., *Honors and Knights' Fees* (3 vols, Manchester: Manchester University Press, 1923–59).

Finucane, R. C., *Miracles and Pilgrims: Popular Beliefs in Medieval England* (London: Dent, 1977).

Flanagan, M. T., *Irish Society, Anglo-Norman Settlers, Angevin Kingship: Interactions in Ireland in the late Twelfth Century* (Oxford: Clarendon Press, 1989).

Fleming, D. F., '*Milites* as attestors to charters in England, 1101–1300', *Albion*, 22 (1990), 185–98.

Folz, R., *Les Saintes reines de Moyen-âge en Occident (VIe–XIIIe siècles)* (Brussels: Société des Bollandistes, 1992).

Fradenburg, L. O. (ed.), *Women and Sovereignty* (Edinburgh: Edinburgh University Press, 1992).

Fradenburg, L. O., 'Introduction: rethinking queenship', in Fradenburg (ed.), *Women and Sovereignty*, pp. 1–13.

Franklin, C. A. H., *The Bearing of Coat-armour by Ladies: A Guide to the Bearing of Arms by Ladies of all Ranks, whether Maid, Wife, or Widow, in England, Scotland, and Ireland* (London: John Murray, 1923, repr. Baltimore MD: Genealogical Publishing Co., 1973).

Garnett, G. S., and J. G. H. Hudson (eds), *Law and Government in Medieval England and Normandy: Essays in Honour of Sir James Holt* (Cambridge: Cambridge University Press, 1994).

Gibbs, V., and others (eds), *The Complete Peerage of England, Scotland, Ireland, Great Britain, and the United Kingdom* (rev. edn, 13 vols in 14, London: St Catherine Press, 1910–59).

Gillingham, J., *The Angevin Empire* (London: Edward Arnold, 1984).

Gillingham, J., 'Love, marriage and politics in the twelfth century', *Forum for Modern Language Studies*, 25: 4 (1989), 292–303.

Gillingham, John, 'Thegns and knights in eleventh-century England: who was then the gentleman?' *TRHS*, 6th ser., 5 (1995), 129–54.

Gillingham, J., 'Kingship, chivalry and love: political and cultural values in the earliest history written in French: Geoffrey Gaimar's *Estoire des Engleis*', in C. Warren Hollister (ed.), *Anglo-Norman Political Culture and the Twelfth-century Renaissance: Proceedings of the Borchard Conference on Anglo-Norman History, 1995* (Woodbridge: Boydell, 1997), pp. 33–58.

Gold, P. Schine, *The Lady and the Virgin* (Chicago and London: University of Chicago Press, 1985).

Goodall, J. A., 'The earliest impresse: a study of some medieval seals and devices', *Antiquaries' Journal*, 73 (1993), 152–7.

Goody, J., *The Development of the Family and Marriage in Europe* (Cambridge: Cambridge University Press, 1983).

Gransden, A., *Historical Writing in England, c. 550 to c. 1307* (London: Routledge, 1974).

Gransden, A., 'Prologues in the historiography of twelfth-century England', in D. Williams (ed.), *England in the Twelfth Century: Proceedings of the 1988 Harlaxton Symposium* (Woodbridge: Boydell, 1990), pp. 55–81, repr. A. Gransden, *Legends, Traditions and History in Medieval England* (London: Hambledon, 1992), pp. 125–51.

Green, J. A., 'Aristocratic women in early twelfth-century England', in C. Warren Hollister (ed.), *Anglo-Norman Political Culture and the Twelfth-century Renaissance: Proceedings of the Borchard Conference on Anglo-Norman History, 1995* (Woodbridge: Boydell Press, 1997), pp. 59–82.

Green, J. A., *The Aristocracy of Norman England* (Cambridge: Cambridge University Press, 1997).

Guyotjeannin, O., '"*Penuria Scriptorum*": le myth de l'anarchie documentaire dans la France du nord (X^e–première moitié du XIe siècle), *Bibliothèque de l'École des chartes*, 155 (1997), 11–44.

Hadley, D. M. (ed.), *Masculinity in Medieval Europe* (London and New York: Addison Wesley Longman, 1999).

Harrsen, M., 'The countess Judith of Flanders and the library of Weingarten Abbey', *Papers of the Bibliographic Society of America*, 24 (1930), 1–13.

Harvey, P. D. A., 'Personal seals in thirteenth-century England', in I. Wood and G. A. Loud (eds), *Church and Chronicle in the Middle Ages* (London: Hambledon Press, 1991), pp. 117–27.

Harvey, P. D. A., and A. McGuinness, *A Guide to British Medieval Seals* (London: British Library and Public Record Office, 1996).

Haskins, G. L., 'The development of common law dower', *Harvard Law Review*, 62 (1948), 42–55.

Hasledine, J., 'Understanding the language of *amicitia*: the friendship circle of Peter of Celle (*c.* 1115–83)', *JMH*, 20 (1994), 237–60.

Head, T., 'The marriages of Christina of Markyate', *Viator*, 21 (1990), 75–101.

Heslop, T. A., 'English seals from the mid ninth century to 1100', *British Archaeological Association Journal*, 133 (1980), 1–16.

Heslop, T. A., 'The Virgin Mary's regalia and twelfth-century English seals', in A. Borg and A. Martindale (eds), *The Vanishing Past: Studies of Medieval Art, Liturgy and Metrology presented to Christopher Hohler* (Oxford: BAR, 1981), pp. 53–62.

Heslop, T. A., 'Seals', in G. Zarnecki, J. Holt and T. Holland (eds), *English Romanesque Art, 1066–1200 [Exhibition at] Hayward Gallery, London, 5 April–8 July 1984* (London: Weidenfeld & Nicolson, in association with the Arts Council of Great Britain, 1984), pp. 298–320.

Heslop, T. A., 'Seals as evidence for metalworking in the England in the later twelfth century', in Sarah Macready and F. H. Thompson (eds), *Art and Patronage in the English Romanesque* (London: Society of Antiquaries, Occasional Paper, new ser., 8; 1986), pp. 50–60.

Heslop, T. A., 'English seals in the thirteenth and fourteenth centuries', in J. Alexander and P. Binsky (eds), *Age of Chivalry* (London: Royal Academy of Arts, in association with Weidenfeld & Nicolson, 1987), pp. 114–17.

Heslop, T. A., 'Seals of lords and ladies', in J. Alexander and P. Binsky (eds), *Age of Chivalry* (London: Royal Academy of Arts, in association with Weidenfeld & Nicolson, 1987), pp. 251–2.

Heslop, T. A., 'Towards an iconology of croziers', in D. Buckton and T. A. Heslop (eds), *Studies in Medieval Art and Architecture presented to Peter Lasko* (Stroud: Sutton, 1994), pp. 36–45.

Hill, C., *Medieval Lincoln* (Cambridge: Cambridge University Press, 1948).

Hillion, Y., 'La Bretagne at la rivalité Capétiens–Plantagenets. Un exemple: la duchesse Constance (1186–1202)', *Annales de Bretagne et des pays de l'Ouest*, 92 (1985), 111–44.

Hoff, Joan, 'Gender as a postmodern category of paralysis', *Women's History Review*, 3 (1994), 149–68.

Holdsworth, C., 'Christina of Markyate', in D. Baker (ed.), *Medieval Women* (Studies in Church History, Subsidia I, Oxford, 1978), pp. 185–204.

Holt, J. C., 'Feudal society and the family in early medieval England', II 'Notions of patrimony', *TRHS*, 5th ser., 33 (1983), 193–220.

Holt, J. C., 'Feudal society and the family in early medieval England' IV, 'The heiress and the alien', *TRHS*, 5th ser., 35 (1985), 1–28.

Hudson, J. G. H., *Land, Law and Lordship in Anglo-Norman England* (Oxford: Clarendon Press, 1994).

Hudson, J., 'Anglo-Norman land law and the origins of property', in G. S. Garnett and J. G. H. Hudson (eds), *Law and Government in Medieval England and Normandy: Essays in Honour of Sir James Holt* (Cambridge: Cambridge University Press, 1994), pp. 198–222.

Hudson, J., *The Formation of the English Common Law: Law and Society in England from the Norman Conquest to Magna Carta* (London: Longman, 1996).

Huneycutt, L., 'Images of queenship in the high Middle Ages', *Haskins Society Journal*, 1 (1989), 61–71.

Huneycutt, L., 'The idea of a perfect princess: the *Life of Saint Margaret* in the reign of Matilda II (1100–18)', *ANS*, 12 (1990 for 1989), 81–97.

Huneycutt, L., 'Female succession and the language of power in the writings of twelfth-century churchmen', in J. Carmi Parsons (ed.), *Medieval Queenship* (Stroud: Sutton, 1994), pp. 189–201.

Huneycutt, L. L., '"Proclaiming her dignity abroad": the literary and artistic network of Matilda of Scotland, Queen of England, 1100–18', in J. H. McCash (ed.), *The Cultural Patronage of Medieval Women* (Athens GA: University of Georgia Press, 1996), pp. 155–74.

Hyams, P. R., 'Warranty and good lordship in twelfth-century England', *Law and History Review*, 5 (1987), 437–503.

Hyams, P. R., 'The charter as a source for the early common law', *Journal of Legal History*, 12 (1991), 173–89.

Innes, M., 'Memory, orality and literacy in an early medieval society', *Past and Present*, 158 (1998), 1–36.

Jaeger, C. S., *The Origins of Courtliness: Civilizing Trends and the Formation of Courtly Ideals, 939–1210* (Philadelphia: University of Pennsylvania Press, 1985).

Jones, M., 'La vie familiale de la duchesse Constance: le témoignage des chartes', in G. Le Menn with J. Y. Le Moing (eds), *Bretagne et pays celtiques: langues, histoire, civilisation. Mélanges offerts à la mémoire de Léon Flemscot 1923–1987* (Saint-Brieuc-Rennes: SKOL, 1992), pp. 349–60.

Keefe, T., *Feudal Assessments and the Political Community under Henry II and his Sons* (Berkeley CA: University of California Press, 1983).

Keefe, T. K., 'Counting those who count: a computer-assisted analysis of charter witness lists and the itinerant court in the first year of the reign of King Richard I', *Haskins Society Journal*, 1 (1989), 135–45.

Kibler, W. W. (ed.), *Eleanor of Aquitaine: Patron and Politician* (Austin TX and London: University of Texas Press, 1976).

Koch, R. A., 'The origin of the fleur-de-lis and the *lillium candidum* in art', in L. D. Roberts (ed.), *Approaches to Nature in the Middle Ages: Papers of the Tenth Annual Conference of the Center for Medieval and Early Renaissance Studies* (Binghampton NY: Center for Medieval and Early Renaissance Studies, 1982), pp. 109–30.

Ladner, G. B., *Images and Ideas in the Middle Ages: Selected Studies in History and Art* (2 vols, Rome: Edizioni di Storia e Letteratura, 1983).

Lagario, V. M., 'The medieval Continental women mystics: an introduction', in P. E. Szarmach (ed.), *An Introduction to the Medieval Mystics of Europe: Fourteen Original Essays* (Albany NY: State University of New York Press, 1984), pp. 161–89.

Lauer, P., 'Le poème de Baudri de Bourgeuil adressé a Adèle, fille de Guillaume le Conquérant, et la date de la tapisserie de Bayeux', in *Mélanges d'Histoire offerts a M. Charles Bémont par ses amis et ses élèves a l'occasion de la vingt-cinquième année de son enseignement a l'École pratique des hautes études* (Paris: Alcan, 1913), pp. 43–58.

Legge, M. D., *Anglo-Norman Literature and its Background* (Oxford: Clarendon Press, 1963).

Lejeune, R., 'La femme dans les littératures françaises et occitanes du XIe au XIIIe siècle', *Cahiers de la Civilisation Médiévale*, 20 (1977), 201–17.

Lewis, C. P., 'The formation of the honor of Chester, 1066–1100', *JCAS*, 71 (1991), 37–68.

Leyser, H., *Medieval Women: A Social History of Women in England, 450–1500* (London: Weidenfeld & Nicolson, 1995).

Loengard, J. Senderowitz, 'Of the gift of her husband: English dower and its consequences in the year 1200', in J. Kirshner and S. F. Wemple (eds),

Women of the Medieval World: Essays in Honor of John H. Mundy (Oxford: Blackwell, 1985), pp. 215–55.

Loengard, J. Senderowitz, '*Rationabilis dos:* Magna Carta and the widow's "fair share" in the earlier thirteenth century', in S. Sheridan Walker (ed.), *Wife and Widow in Medieval England* (Ann Arbor MI: University of Michigan Press, 1993), pp. 59–80.

LoPrete, K., 'The Anglo-Norman card of Adela of Blois', *Albion*, 22 (1990), 569–89.

Martindale, J., 'Succession and politics in the Romance-speaking world, c. 1000–40', in M. Jones and M. Vale (eds), *England and her Neighbours, 1066–1453: Essays in Honour of Pierre Chaplais* (London and Ronceverte: Hambledon Press, 1989), pp. 19–41.

Mayr-Harting, H., 'Functions of a twelfth-century shrine: the miracles of St Frideswide', in H. Mayr-Harting and R. I. Moore (eds), *Studies in Medieval History presented to R. H. C. Davis* (London and Ronceverte: Hambledon, 1985), pp. 193–206.

McCash, J. H. (ed.), *The Cultural Patronage of Medieval Women* (Athens GA: University of Georgia Press, 1996).

McCash, J., 'The cultural patronage of medieval women: an overview', in McCash (ed.), *Cultural Patronage of Medieval Women*, pp. 1–49.

McGuire, P., *Friendship and the Community: The Monastic Experience, 350–1250* (Cistercian Studies, 95, Kalamazoo MI, 1988).

Megaw, B. R. S., 'The ship seals of the kings of Man', *Journal of the Manx Museum*, 6 (1957–65), 78–80, plates 239–41.

Millett, Bella, 'Women in no man's land: English recluses and the development of vernacular literature in the twelfth and thirteenth centuries', in C. M. Meale (ed.), *Women and Literature in Britain, 1150–1500* (Cambridge: Cambridge University Press, 1993), pp. 87–103.

Millett, Bella, and Jocelyn Wogan-Browne, *Medieval English Prose for Women: Selections from the Katherine Group and* Ancrene Wisse (Oxford: Clarendon Press, 1990).

Milsom, S. F. C., *The Legal Framework of English Feudalism* (Cambridge: Cambridge University Press, 1976).

Milsom, S. F. C., 'Inheritance by women in the twelfth and thirteenth centuries', in M. S. Arnold, T. A. Green, S. A. Scully and S. D. White (eds), *On the Laws and Customs of England: Essays in Honor of Samuel E. Thorne* (Chapel Hill NC: University of North Carolina Press, 1981), pp. 60–89.

Milsom, S. F. C., 'The origin of prerogative wardship', in G. S. Garnett and J. G. H. Hudson (eds), *Law and Government in Medieval England and Normandy: Essays in Honour of Sir James Holt* (Cambridge: Cambridge University Press, 1994), pp. 223–44.

Mirrer, L. (ed.), *Upon my Husband's Death: Widows in the Literature and Histories of Medieval Europe* (Ann Arbor MI: University of Michigan Press, 1992).

Mitchell, L. E., 'Noble widowhood in the thirteenth century: three generations of the Mortimer widows, 1246–1334', in L. Mirrer (ed.), *Upon my Husband's Death: Widows in the Literature and Histories of Medieval Europe* (Ann Arbor MI: University of Michigan Press, 1992), pp. 169–90.

Moore, J. S., 'The Anglo-Norman family: size and structure', *ANS*, 14 (1992 for 1991), 153–96.

Nelson, J. L., 'Literacy in Carolingian government', in R. McKitterick (ed.), *The Uses of Literacy in early Mediaeval Europe* (Cambridge: Cambridge University Press, 1990), pp. 258–96.

Nelson, J. L., 'Women and the word in the earlier Middle Ages', in W. J. Sheils and D. Wood (eds), *Women in the Church* (Studies in Church History, 27, Oxford, 1990), pp. 53–78.

Nelson, J. L., 'The problematic in the private', *Social History*, 15 (1990), 355–64.

Nelson, J. L., 'Gender and genre in women historians of the early Middle Ages', in *L'Historiographie médiévale en Europe* (Paris, 1991), 150–63.

Nelson, J. L., 'Women at the court of Charlemagne: a case of monstrous regiment?' in J. Carmi Parsons (ed.), *Medieval Queenship* (Stroud: Sutton, 1994), pp. 43–61.

Nelson, J. L., 'Monks, secular men and masculinity, *c.* 900', in D. M. Hadley (ed.), *Masculinity in Medieval Europe* (London and New York: Addison Wesley Longman, 1999), pp. 121–42.

Noble, P. S., 'Romance in England and Normandy in the twelfth century', in D. Bates and A. Curry (eds), *England and Normandy in the Middle Ages* (London and Rio Grande OH: Hambledon Press, 1994), pp. 69–79.

Ortner, S. B., and H. Whitehead, 'Introduction: accounting for sexual meanings', in S. Ortner and H. Whitehead (eds), *Sexual Meanings: The Cultural Construction of Gender and Sexuality* (Cambridge: Cambridge University Press, 1981), pp. 1–27.

Painter, S., 'The family and the feudal system in twelfth-century England', *Speculum*, 35 (1960), 1–16.

Parsons, J. Carmi, 'Ritual and symbol in the English medieval queenship to 1500', in L. O. Fradenburg (ed.), *Women and Sovereignty* (Edinburgh: Edinburgh University Press, 1992), pp. 60–77.

Parsons, J. Carmi (ed.), *Medieval Queenship* (Stroud: Sutton, 1994).

Parsons, J. Carmi, 'Introduction – family, sex and power: the rhythms of medieval queenship', in Parsons (ed.), *Medieval Queenship*, pp. 1–11.

Pesant, M. Le, 'Les noms de personne à Évreux du XIIme au XIVme siècles', *Annales de Normandie*, 6 (1956), 47–74.

Petroff, E. A., *Body and Soul: Essays on Medieval Women and Mysticism* (Oxford and New York: Oxford University Press, 1994).

Pollock, F., and F. W. Maitland, *A History of English Law before the Time of Edward I* (Cambridge, 1895; 2nd edn, 1898, repr. London: Cambridge University Press, 1968).

Postles, D. A., 'Choosing a witness in twelfth-century England', *Irish Jurist*, 23 (1988), 330–46.

Postles, D. A., 'The baptismal name in thirteenth-century England: processes and patterns', *Medieval Prosopography*, 13: 2 (1992), 1–52.

Power, E., *Medieval Women*, ed. M. Postan (Cambridge: Cambridge University Press, 1975).

Power, E., 'The position of women', in C. G. Crump and E. F. Jacob (eds), *The Legacy of the Middle Ages* (Oxford: Clarendon Press, 1926), pp. 410–33.

Prell, J. H., 'Les souscriptions des chartes des comtes de Poitiers, ducs d'Aquitaine (1030–1137)', *Bibliothèque de l'École des Chartes*, 155 (1997), 207–19.

Reuter, T., 'Property transactions and social relations between rulers, bishops and nobles in early eleventh-century Saxony: the evidence of the *vita Meinwerci*', in W. Davies and P. Fouracre (eds), *Property and Power in the early Middle Ages* (Cambridge: Cambridge University Press, 1995), pp. 165–99.

Reynolds, S., *Fiefs and Vassals: The Medieval Evidence Reinterpreted* (Oxford: Oxford University Press, 1994).

Rezak, B. Bedos-, 'Women, seals and power in medieval France, 1150–1350', in M. Erler and M. Kowaleski (eds), *Women and Power in the Middle Ages* (Athens GA and London: University of Georgia Press, 1988), pp. 61–82.

Rezak, B. Bedos-, 'Medieval women in French sigillographic sources', in J. T. Rosenthal (ed.), *Medieval Women and the Sources of Medieval History* (Athens GA and London: University of Georgia Press, 1990), pp. 1–36.

Rezak, B. Bedos-, 'Ritual in the royal chancery: text, image and representation of kingship in medieval French diplomas (700–1200)', in H. Duchhardt, R. A. Jackson and D. Sturdy (eds), *European Monarchy: Its Evolution and Practice from Roman Antiquity to Modern Times* (Stuttgart: Steiner, 1992), pp. 27–40.

Richardson, F. G., 'The letters and charters of Eleanor of Aquitaine', *EHR*, 74 (1959), 193–213.

Rigby, S., *English Society in the later Middle Ages: Class, Status and Gender* (Basingstoke: Macmillan, 1995).

Rosenthal, J. T. (ed.), *Medieval Women and the Sources of Medieval History* (Athens GA: University of Georgia Press, 1990).

Rosenwein, B., *To be the Neighbor of Saint Peter: The Social Meaning of Cluny's Property, 909–1049* (Ithaca NY and London: Cornell University Press, 1989).

Round, J. H., *Geoffrey de Mandeville: A Study of the Anarchy* (London: Longman, 1892).

Round, J. H., 'King Stephen and the earl of Chester', *EHR*, 10 (1895), 87–91.

Round, J. H., 'The foundation of the priories of St Mary and St John, Clerkenwell', *Archaeologia*, 56 (1899), 223–8.

Round, J. H., 'Comyn and Valoignes', *Ancestor*, 11 (1904), 129–35.

Scott, J. Wallach, *Gender and the Politics of History* (New York: Columbia University Press, 1988).

Searle, E., 'Women and the legitimisation of succession at the Norman Conquest', *ANS*, 3 (1981 for 1980), 159–70.

Shahar, Shulamith, *The Fourth Estate: A History of Women in the Middle Ages* (London: Methuen, 1983; repr. London: Routledge, 1991).

Short, I., '*Tam Angli quam Franci*: self-definition in Anglo-Norman England', *ANS*, 18 (1996 for 1995), 153–75.

Southern, R. W., *Saint Anselm and his Biographer: A Study of Monastic Life and Thought, 1059–c. 1130* (Cambridge: Cambridge University Press, 1963).

Southern, R. W., *Saint Anselm: A Portrait in a Landscape* (Cambridge: Cambridge University Press, 1990).

Stafford, P., *Queens, Concubines and Dowagers: The King's Wife in the early Middle Ages* (London: Batsford, 1983; London: Leicester University Press, 1998).

Stafford, P., 'Women in Domesday', in Keith Bate and others (eds), *Medieval Women in Southern England* (Reading Medieval Studies, 15, 1989), pp. 75–94.

Stafford, P., 'Women and the Norman Conquest', *TRHS*, 6th ser., 4 (1994), 221–49.

Stafford, P., 'The portrayal of royal women in England, mid-tenth to mid-twelfth centuries', in J. Carmi Parsons (ed.), *Medieval Queenship* (Stroud: Sutton, 1994), pp. 143–67.

Stafford, P., *Queen Emma and Queen Edith: Queenship and Women's Power in Eleventh-century England* (Oxford: Blackwell, 1997).

Stafford, P., 'Emma: the powers of the queen in the eleventh century', in A. Duggan (ed.), *Queens and Queenship in Medieval Europe: Proceedings of a Conference held at King's College London, April 1995* (Woodbridge and Rochester NY: Boydell, 1997), pp. 3–26.

Stenton, D. M., *The English Woman in History* (London: Allen & Unwin, 1957).

Stenton, F. M., *The First Century of English Feudalism, 1066–1166* (Oxford: Clarendon Press, 1932; 2nd edn Oxford: Clarendon Press, 1961).

Stringer, K. J., *The Reign of King Stephen: Kingship, Warfare and Government in Twelfth-century England* (London: Routledge, 1993).

Stuard, S. Mosher (ed.), *Women in Medieval Society* (Philadelphia: University of Pennsylvania Press, 1976).

Stuard, S. Mosher (ed.), *Women in Medieval History and Historiography* (Philadelphia: University of Pennsylvania Press, 1987).

Stuard, S. Mosher, 'Fashion's captives: medieval women in French historiography', in S. Mosher Stuard (ed.), *Women in Medieval History and Historiography* (Philadelphia: University of Pennsylvania Press, 1987), pp. 59–80.

Stuard, S. Mosher, 'The chase after theory: considering medieval women', *Gender and History*, 4 (1992), 135–46.

Swanson, R. N. 'Angels incarnate: clergy and masculinity from Gregorian reform to Reformation', in D. M. Hadley (ed.), *Masculinity in Medieval Europe* (London and New York: Addison Wesley Longman, 1999), pp. 160–77.

Tabuteau, E. Z., *Transfers of Property in Eleventh-century Norman Law* (Chapel Hill NC: University of North Carolina Press, 1988).

Tatlock, J. S. P., 'Muriel: the earliest English poetess', *Publications of the Modern Language Association of America*, 48 (1933), 317–21.

Teunis, H. B., 'The countergift *in caritate* according to the cartulary of Noyers', *Haskins Society Journal*, 7 (1997 for 1995), 83–8.

Thacker, A. T., 'Introduction: the earls and their earldom', *JCAS*, 71 (1991), 15–21.

Thomas, H. M., 'An upwardly mobile medieval woman: Juliana of Warwick', *Medieval Prosopography*, 18 (1997), 109–21.

Thompson, J. Westfall, *The Literacy of the Laity in the Middle Ages* (Berkeley CA, 1939; repr. New York: Franklin, 1960).

Thompson, K. H., 'Orderic Vitalis and Robert of Bellême', *JMH*, 20 (1994), 133–41.

Thompson, K. H., 'Dowry and inheritance patterns: some examples from the descendants of King Henry I of England', *Medieval Prosopography*, 19 (1996), 45–61.

Thompson, R. M., 'England and the twelfth-century renaissance', *Past and Present*, 101 (1983), 3–21.

Thompson, S., *Women Religious: The Founding of English Nunneries after the Norman Conquest* (Oxford: Clarendon Press, 1991).

van Houts, E. M. C., 'Latin poetry and the Anglo-Norman court, 1066–1135: the *Carmen de Hastingae Proelio*', *JMH*, 15 (1989), 39–62.

van Houts, E. M. C., *Local and Regional Chronicles* (Typologie des Sources du Moyen-âge Occidental, fasc. 74, Turnhout, Belgium, 1995).

van Houts, E. M. C., *Memory and Gender in Medieval Europe, 900–1200* (Basingstoke: Macmillan, 1999).

Vaughn, S. N., *The Abbey of Bec and the Anglo-Norman State, 1034–1136* (Woodbridge: Boydell, 1981).

Vaughn, S., 'Anselm in Italy, 1097–1100', *ANS*, 16 (1994 for 1993), 245–70.

Verdun, J., 'Les sources de l'histoire de la femme en Occident au X–XIII siècles', *Cahiers de la Civilisation Médiévale*, 20 (1977), 219–50.

Vincent, N., 'Review of *Family Trees and the Roots of Politics*', *EHR*, 114 (1999), 408–9.

Walker, S. Sheridan, 'Widow and ward: the feudal law of child custody in medieval England', in S. Mosher Stuard (ed.), *Women in Medieval Society* (Philadelphia: University of Pennsylvania Press, 1976), pp. 159–72, also published in *Feminist Studies*, 3 (1976), 104–16.

Walker, S. Sheridan, 'Feudal constraint and free consent in the making of marriages in medieval England: widows in the king's gift', in *Historical Papers: A Selection from the Papers presented at the Annual Meeting* [of the Canadian Historical Association] *Held at Saskatoon* (1979), 97–109.

Walker, S. Sheridan, 'Free consent and marriage of feudal wards in medieval England', *JMH*, 8 (1982), 123–34.

Walker, S. Sheridan (ed.), *Wife and Widow in Medieval England* (Ann Arbor MI: University of Michigan Press, 1993).

Ward, J. C., *English Noblewomen in the later Middle Ages* (London: Longman, 1992).

Warren, A. K., 'The nun as anchoress: England, 1100–1500', in J. A. Nichols and L. Thomas Shank (eds), *Medieval Religious Women*, I, *Distant Echoes* (Kalamazoo MI: Cistercian Publications, 1984), pp. 197–212.

Warren, W. L., *Henry II* (London: Eyre Methuen, 1977).

Warren, W. L., *The Governance of Norman and Angevin England, 1086–1272* (London: Edward Arnold, 1987).

Waugh, S. L., 'Marriage, class and royal lordship in England under Henry III', *Viator*, 16 (1985), 181–207.

Waugh, S. L., *The Lordship of England: Royal Wardships and Marriages in English Society and Politics, 1217–1327* (Princeton NJ: Princeton University Press, 1988).

Waugh, S. L., 'Women's inheritance and the growth of bureaucratic monarchy in twelfth- and thirteenth-century England', *Nottingham Medieval Studies*, 34 (1990), 71–92.

Webber, T., 'The scribes and the handwriting of the original charters', *JCAS*, 71 (1991), 137–51.

Weber, M., *Economy and Society: An Outline of Interpretive Sociology*, ed. Guenther Roth and Claus Wittich (3 vols, New York: Bedminster Press, 1968).

Weinstein, D., and R. M. Bell, *Saints and Society: The Two Worlds of Western Christendom, 1000–1700* (Chicago and London: University of Chicago Press, 1982).

Weiss, J., 'The power and weakness of women in Anglo-Norman romance', in C. M. Meale (ed.), *Women and Literature in Britain, 1150–1500* (Cambridge: Cambridge University Press, 1993), pp. 7–23.

Whalen, G., 'Patronage engendered: how Goscelin allayed the concerns of nuns' discriminatory publics', in L. Smith and J. H. M. Taylor (eds), *Women, the Book and the Godly: Selected Proceedings of the St Hilda's Conference, 1993* (Woodbridge: Brewer, 1995), pp. 123–35.

White, S. D., *Custom, Kinship and Gifts to Saints: The Laudatio Parentum in Western France, 1050–1150* (Chapel Hill NC: University of North Carolina Press, 1988).

Williams, D. (ed.), *England in the Twelfth Century: Proceedings of the 1988 Harlaxton Symposium* (Woodbridge: Boydell, 1990).

Wilmart, A., *Auteurs spirituels et textes dévots du Moyen-âge latin: études d'histoire littéraire* (Paris: Bloud & Gay, 1932).

Zarnecki, G., 'General introduction', in G. Zarnecki, J. Holt and T. Holland (eds), *English Romanesque Art, 1066–1200 [Exhibition at] Hayward Gallery, London, 5 April–8 July 1984* (London: Weidenfeld & Nicolson, in association with the Arts Council of Great Britain, 1984), pp. 15–26.

Index

Note: 'n.' after a page reference indicates a note number on that page.

Milton Keynes UK
Ingram Content Group UK Ltd.
UKHW021443021123
431821UK00034B/387